The publisher and the University of California Press Foundation gratefully acknowledge the generous support of the Robert and Meryl Selig Endowment Fund in Film Studies, established in memory of Robert W. Selig.

Also, the publisher gratefully acknowledges the generous support of Boston College.

Cold War Cosmopolitanism

Cold War Cosmopolitanism

Period Style in 1950s Korean Cinema

Christina Klein

UNIVERSITY OF CALIFORNIA PRESS

University of California Press
Oakland, California

Suggested citation: Klein, C. *Cold War Cosmopolitanism: Period Style in 1950s Korean Cinema*. Oakland: University of California Press, 2020.
DOI: https://doi.org/10.1525/luminos.85

Cataloging-in-Publication Data is on file at the Library of Congress.

Names: Klein, Christina, 1963- author.
Title: Cold War cosmopolitanism : period style in 1950s Korean cinema / Christina Klein.
Description: Oakland, California : University of California Press, [2020] | Includes bibliographical references and index.
Identifiers: LCCN 2019036822 (print) | LCCN 2019036823 (ebook) | ISBN 9780520296503 (paperback) | ISBN 9780520968981 (epub)
Subjects: LCSH: Han, Hyŏng-mo, 1917-1999—Criticism and interpretation. | Motion picture producers and directors—Korea (South) | Motion pictures—Korea—History—20th century. | Motion pictures—Social aspects—Korea.
Classification: LCC PN1998.3.H348 K55 2020 (print) | LCC PN1998.3.H348 (ebook) | DDC 791.4302/33092—dc23
LC record available at https://lccn.loc.gov/2019036822
LC ebook record available at https://lccn.loc.gov/2019036823

A version of chapter 4 was originally published in Sangjoon Lee, ed., *Rediscovering Korean Cinema* (Ann Arbor: University of Michigan Press, 2019) as "*Madame Freedom* (1956): Spectatorship and the Modern Woman."

Portions of chapters 1 and 7 were originally published in *The Journal of Korean Studies*, Vol. 22:2, as "Cold War Cosmopolitanism: The Asia Foundation and 1950s Korean Cinema."

29   28   27   26   25   24   23   22   21   20
10   9   8   7   6   5   4   3   2   1

For Carlo,

Ling-li,

and

Yuan

CONTENTS

ILLUSTRATIONS

FIGURES

MAPS

VIDEO CLIPS

ACKNOWLEDGMENTS

I would not have dared undertake this project but for my fortuitous encounter in 2009–2011 with three remarkable people: Heonik Kwan, who invited me to join his Academy of Korean Studies–funded research project "Beyond the Korean War" (AKS-2010-DZZ-3104), which provided crucial financial support and introduced me to a lively community of Koreanists; Han Sang Kim, then a Harvard-Yenching fellow and former Korean Film Archive researcher, who offered encouragement and aid at the earliest stages; and Eun Kyung DuBois, a Boston College undergraduate and aspiring translator, who translated hundreds of pages of oral histories and other Korean-language material.

It has been my pleasure to enter into the community of Korean studies scholars and to benefit from their intellectual generosity and friendship. Many people have shared information about primary sources, guided me through the scholarship, and commented on early versions of these chapters, including Jinsoo An, Charles Armstrong, Hye Seung Chung, Steven Chung, Bruce Cumings, Gwon Gwi-sook, Seung-hee Jeon, Rachel Joo, Charles Kim, Kim Seong-nae, Sangjoon Lee, Soonjin Lee, Steven Hugh Lee, Roald Maliangkay, Dima Mironenko, and Yoon Jeong-ran. Carter Eckert, Sun Joo Kim, and Susan Lawrence have made Harvard's Korea Institute a welcoming intellectual home-across-the-river. Haden Guest at the Harvard Film Archive has kindly invited me to numerous events with contemporary Korean film directors. Franziska Seraphim, Ian Condry, and Gaspar Gonzalez offered help at key moments. My understanding of the Asia Foundation has been deepened through many conversations with Laura Harrington. The members of the New Haven Women's Research Collective—Kathy Newman, Debby Applegate, Liza McAlister, and Pam Haag—have kept the communal spirit of graduate school alive.

I am grateful to all those who invited me to present my ideas as they were gestating and to the thoughtful audiences they generated: Claire Gullander and Suzanne Enzerink (Brown), Mi-Ryong Shim (Harvard), Karen Fang and Hosam Aboul-Ela (Houston), Denise Cruz, Scott Herring, and Theresa Kang (Indiana), Donald Bellomy and Jae H. Roe (Sogang), Miseong Woo (Yonsei), Jung-Bong Choi and Henry Em (NYU), Holly Allen (Middlebury), Charles Armstrong and Theodore Hughes (Columbia), Mitch Lerner (Ohio State), Steven Chung and Hyun Seon Park (Princeton), Kathy Newman (Carnegie Mellon), Todd Henry (UCSD), Jinsoo An (Berkeley), Erika Doss (Notre Dame), and Josephine Lee (Minnesota).

Librarians make scholarship possible. Warm thanks to Anne Kenny and the entire ILL staff, as well as Stephen Sturgeon, at Boston College's O'Neill Library, and to Mikyung Kang at Harvard-Yenching Library. Assistance with illustrations and video clips was kindly provided by Eric YJ Choi at the Korean Film Archive and Scott Kinder and Katie Anderson at BC.

I could not have accessed the Korean-, Japanese-, and Chinese-language material without a crack team of research assistants and translators working across the United States and in South Korea, Japan, and Hong Kong, many of them students who took time away from their own work to help with mine. My gratitude goes out to Masato Dogase, Takuya Tsunoda, Soojung Chae, Jamie Yoo, Jean Park, Sarah Jung, and especially Donna Ong, who discovered the script for *Because I Love You*. Extra-special thanks to Boram Seo, who worked cheerfully and with amazing speed over many years, and to Seung Hwan Kim, who worked nights and weekends in the final stages to wrap this project up.

Anonymous readers at the *Journal of Korean Studies* and the University of California Press helped clarify my ideas, and editor Toby Lester improved their organization immeasurably. Raina Polivka, Madison Wetzell, Ben Alexander, and Emilia Thiuri at the University of California Press have been patient and extremely helpful in the final delivery. Mary Francis, now at the University of Michigan Press, kept the faith as I let go of one book project and reached out for another.

Boston College is a wonderful place to teach and do research, and I'm grateful for the many people who have made it possible for me to do both there. Thanks to Jack Neuhauser, Joe Quinn, Paul Lewis, and the entire English department for hiring me, and to Greg Kalscheur, Billy Soo, and Gene McMahon for years of research and publication support.

My family has provided both comfort and distraction. Carlo Rotella has been a model of intellectual inquiry and a steadying presence for a good long time, and Ling-li and Yuan have grown up alongside this book. They've all been very patient, for which I am grateful. Now let's do something else.

Note on romanization: I have used McCune-Reischauer for citations of works originally published in Korean, according to the Library of Congress standard. I have generally followed the orthography used by KMDb (the Korean Movie Database) for the names of people involved in the film industry. For other personal names, places, and well-known words, I have employed the form currently in most common use. For authors of English-language publications and names that appear in archival documents, I have retained the original spelling.

Introduction

I will never forget the first time I saw *Madame Freedom* (1956). I was supposed to be working on a book about contemporary Asian cinema and its relationship to Hollywood and was in the midst of what I expected to be a brief detour into postwar South Korean cinema. I had come across references to *Madame Freedom* as the most famous Korean film of the 1950s and had decided it was time to see it for myself. That was how I found myself sitting in front of an old TV in a small, cold, and dusty room deep in the stacks of the Harvard-Yenching Library. I felt a bit out of place. As an American studies scholar, I was unfamiliar with the layout and protocols of this library, which houses the university's Asian studies collection, and I couldn't decipher the titles of the books on the shelves as I walked by. My feelings of out-of-placeness dissipated as I watched the film, however, transformed into what can only be described as joy.

Madame Freedom is a fabulous film. A contemporary melodrama, it tells the story of a middle-class housewife who, after taking a job in a luxury Western goods shop, abandons her domestic duties and begins spending her time in public places of leisure, ultimately entering into an affair with a married man. As I watched, I was captivated by an overwhelming sense of familiarity combined with a curiosity-piquing sense of difference. The film was generically recognizable as a women's picture, and its discontented heroine was kin to the unhappy wives and mothers in Hollywood films such as *Beyond the Forest* (1949) and *The Reckless Moment* (1949). It was the film's style, however, that stood out to me. I was struck by director Han Hyung-mo's mastery of classical Hollywood conventions: the confidence of his analytical editing, the boldness of his moving camera, the density of the film's mise-en-scène, and the abundance of its music. At the same time, I recognized that a full understanding of the film depended upon a deep familiarity with post-war South Korean life that I did not fully possess. There were nuances of meaning attached to the husband's job as a scholar of the Korean language and to a subplot about smuggling that eluded me. Questions immediately arose in my mind. How was it possible to make such a technically polished film only three years after the end of the Korean War, when the country was still rebuilding? What did it mean to present such an audaciously modern female character in a conservative Confucian society? These questions nagged at me for months. I began watching Han Hyung-mo's other films, which also featured modern women navigating contemporary South Korean society. Each of them presented me with a similar combination of familiar and unfamiliar elements, and with each film my fascination grew. Who were these liberated women? And who was the director presenting them in such a sophisticated style? In the end I succumbed to the allure of Han's work and allowed myself to be fully curious about these films. This book is the result of that curiosity.

This book has its origins in a second moment, as well, that occurred while I was reading up on *In the Mood for Love* (2000), Wong Kar-wai's self-consciously retro melodrama that pays homage to the same postwar period in which *Madame Freedom* is set. Wong's film, too, features a spectacular style—including glamorous East-West fashions, a restlessly moving camera, and melancholic Nat King Cole songs—that produced in me a similar sensation of insiderness and outsiderness. I came across a quotation from Wong in which he hinted at the historical origins of the film's art design. Referring to Japanese novelist Haruki Murakami, he said, "He and I are about the same age, and we had very similar formative experiences: we were both marked by what I call 'Seventh Fleet Culture' in those years between the Korean War and Vietnam. We both bought the music, the cigarettes, the lifestyle; seeing big foreigners on the streets made a strong impression on us."[1] The Seventh Fleet was a Japan-based US naval unit of some twenty thousand personnel that participated in the Korean War and made thousands of port calls throughout the Pacific region in the 1950s and 1960s. Wong's words captured my attention because they suggested that the military presence of the United States in Hong Kong, Japan, and Korea during the 1950s and 1960s had served as a privileged conduit for an American lifestyle that had a profoundly shaping effect on local tastes in music, fashion, film, and narrative. "Seventh Fleet Culture" gave a name to something I had felt, but couldn't quite identify, as I watched *Madame Freedom*: the presence in Korea of tens of thousands of American GIs and millions of dollars in US aid, which seemed to be hovering just outside the film's frame and exerting some kind of pressure on what I was seeing inside the frame.

Wong's notion of "Seventh Fleet Culture" joined my fascination with *Madame Freedom*'s style to generate this book's central research questions: Broadly, what is the nature of the relationship between Han's films and the historical moment in which they were produced? More specifically, how are the transnational political, economic, and military forces that we call the Cold War readable in the *style* of his films?

HAN HYUNG-MO

Han Hyung-mo (1917–99) launched the Golden Age of South Korean cinema, a sustained period of cinematic creativity extending from the mid-1950s to the early 1970s in which filmmakers explored their country's experience of modernization from multiple perspectives, as it was happening. Han was the most commercially successful filmmaker of the 1950s, a brilliant innovator who was seen as having his finger on the pulse of South Korean society. As a director, cinematographer, and editor, he was celebrated by his contemporaries as the most modern filmmaker of the day and lauded for introducing new characters, genres, and technologies into Korean cinema. Beginning in 1949, he directed eighteen films, reaching his creative peak between 1954, one year after the Korean War halted, and 1961, when Park Chung-hee seized power in a military coup. Han was deeply interested in women's relationship to modernity, and he foregrounded their experiences and perspectives. He specialized in the making of women's pictures, a genre identi-fied by Steven Chung as "one of the most important and influential of the period's mass cultural products" for their forthright engagement with a rapidly changing society.[2] Han brought the modern Korean woman to life on screen just as she was emerging as a widespread social reality. *The Hand of Destiny* (1954) is a noir thriller about a female North Korean spy. *Hyperbolae of Youth* (1956) is a romantic comedy that contrasts a modern, affluent young woman with a more traditional, less affluent one. *The Pure Love* (1957) features an airline stewardess, and *Men vs. Women* (1959) a female obstetrician. *Because I Love You* (1958) charts the journey of a dancer who embarks on a cultural goodwill mission to Malaya. *A Female Boss* (1959) is a romantic comedy about the publisher of a women's magazine. *My Sister Is a Hussy* (1961) charts the comedic drama of a woman bent on avoiding marriage. Han stood out among his peers as a master stylist. At a time when most filmmak-ers modestly aspired to tell a story via clear images and sounds, Han used film form ostentatiously. His films are masterpieces of commercial art, technically pol-ished and displaying a glamorous aesthetic. For all his commercial success, how-ever, Han has been largely omitted from the canon of major Korean directors, a consequence, perhaps, of both his Hollywood-inflected style and his sympathetic focus on women.[3]

PERIOD STYLE

Han's style is my object of inquiry: it is what I seek to explain. I approach my quarry from two perspectives. The first is as a "directorial style," which entails identifying its distinctive features and charting how Han deployed them across his oeuvre. A version of auteurism, this approach recognizes that Han possessed a dis-tinctive artistic vision that he was able to sustain for much of his career. My second perspective is to read Han's aesthetic as a "period style," which entails recognizing the ways in which it is exemplary rather than exceptional. The concept of period style comes from art history and material culture studies, where it is used to refer to a set of formal conventions that are broadly shared at a given historical moment and that express a more or less coherent set of beliefs.[4] Han was, in fact, a highly skilled presenter of ideas and creative impulses that were very much alive in the broader South Korean culture. The notion of period style, while not often rigorously applied within film studies, enables one to read film form historically and in relation to other forms of culture. It recognizes that cultural producers are in conversation with each other within and across media, and it invites one to see the extent to which style depends upon the period-specific availability of certain ideas and resources. Reading Han's film through a period style lens requires both a deep historical curiosity and a commitment to formal analysis, which is expressed in the book's organization. Part I consists of three chapters that map the period via political, social, and cultural history; Part II contains four chapters that plumb the intricacies of Han's style via close readings of his films. A brief conclusion marks the end of the period with Park Chung-hee's military coup in 1961 and traces some of its legacies into the New Korean Cinema of the twenty-first century.

This book is a cultural history of Han's style, and as such it asks two questions. First, how is any given element of Han's style used expressively within a film in ways that enhance, complicate, or subvert the meanings produced by the narrative? Taking style seriously means treating it as an independent variable that is not always lashed to the demands of the narrative. This is particularly important with Han's films, which often exhibit a tension between these two registers. Second, how can we read specific elements of style as a form of historical evidence? As Jules Prown has written, "style is inescapably culturally expressive" and the "formal data" embodied in cultural artifacts can be useful for historians willing to tap into nonwritten archives.[5] When read with a historian's eye, style can provide clues to postwar Korean life that more traditional forms of historical evidence might miss. By reading style in relation to history, I hope to deepen our understanding of both.

Part of this book's mission as a work of cultural history is to call attention to the 1950s as a distinct phase in Korea's experience of modernization. Prior to the publication of Charles R. Kim's *Youth for Nation: Culture and Protest in Cold War South Korea* (2017), many social and cultural histories of twentieth-century Korea skipped over the 1950s, jumping straight from the collapse of the Japanese empire in 1945 to Park Chung-hee's coup in 1961.[6] As John Lie has written, "the 1950s are something of a forgotten decade in South Korea." I am interested in these years as a dynamic period in which postcolonial aspirations, the upheavals of the Korean War, and the waging of the Cold War transformed virtually every aspect of South Korean life. As a phase of modernization, it differs from early-twentieth-century colonial modernity, when Korea's needs were subordinated to those of the imperial center in Japan, and from Park's developmental modernity of the 1960s and 1970s, when much of social and cultural life was subsumed under the demands of export-driven economic growth. Treating Han's style as historical evidence deepens our ability to see the post–Korean War, pre-Park years as what Lie has called an "emancipatory moment" that was "expunged by military rule."[7]

COLD WAR COSMOPOLITANISM

This book argues that Han's style is an exemplary instance of a period style that I am calling "Cold War cosmopolitanism." Cosmopolitanism is a diffuse term that has been employed in diverse ways by scholars across a range of disciplines. I find it to be a more nuanced and historically grounded term to describe what was happening in the 1950s than the commonly invoked "fetishization" of America, a psychoanalytic term that implies a kind of collective cognitive error.[8] A cosmopolitan framework invites us to think beyond Americanization and recognize the ongoing legacies of Japanese colonialism and the newly forming relationships with Western Europe, Latin America, and Southeast Asia. I join scholars such as Sheldon Pollock and others who are moving beyond the traditional definition of cosmopolitanism as a universalist political philosophy or ethical commitment and are instead investigating the "range of cosmopolitan practices that have actually existed in history."[9] I am indebted to Mica Nava's articulation of "cosmopolitan modernity," which emphasizes the feminist dimension latent in the revolt against forms of "nationalist traditionalism" that are imbued with restrictive gender ideals.[10] I owe the term "Cold War cosmopolitanism" to Antoinette Burton, who, in her book on Indian writer Santha Rama Rau, explores how a postcolonial literary sensibility emerged within, and was decisively shaped by, the new US-centered Cold War geopolitical order.[11]

At first glance, Cold War cosmopolitanism seems to be an oxymoron, given that the Cold War entailed dividing the globe into opposing blocs, separating them with iron and bamboo curtains, and pressuring nations to choose exclusive affiliation with one side or the other. The Cold War radically delimited people's engagement with whole regions of the world and constrained their engagement with ideas deemed to be unacceptably Other. In South Korea, violations of this boundary—in the form of expressions of fellow-feeling for communists in North Korea, China, or the Soviet Union—could be punished with imprisonment and death. The Cold War, however, was a force of integration as well as division, and the binding together of the Free World required of its members a new degree of openness towards noncommunist Others. It encouraged South Koreans to look beyond their national borders and understand themselves as connected to other people in Asia and the West. To see the Cold War in terms of integration is to grasp the truth of Foucault's insight that power is productive: it generated new institutions, new relationships, and whole new geographies, such as Free Asia. (I capitalize the ideological phrases Free Asia and Free World, rather than embed them in scare quotes, to distinguish them from actual quotations.) What emerged in South

Korea in the 1950s, then, was a historically specific form of cosmopolitanism that was contingent upon the Cold War and dependent upon the transnational circuits that it opened up.

Cold War cosmopolitanism is best understood as a cultural formation that emerged alongside the expansion of US power into Asia after World War II. We can define it as a style (a set of textual and aesthetic properties) whose production was stimulated by a body of institutions and practices (a set of material properties) that were launched in accordance with a set of political and social ideas (a set of intellectual properties). It was produced by South Koreans and Americans, working together and apart, who were embarked on a shared project of modernizing a country that had its own culture and history, which included the prior experience of Japanese colonialism. As a cultural formation, Cold War cosmopolitanism had four dimensions. First, it was a *political discourse* about South Korea's membership in the Free World. It was rooted in the United States–led push, largely supported by Republic of Korea president Syngman Rhee, to secure South Korea's integration into the community of noncommunist, capitalist nations and especially into the emerging entity known as Free Asia. It encouraged the forging of diverse networks of economic, political, and institutional ties with other nations in Asia and the West. Some of these networks were new and others were layered over older, colonial-era ties. As a political discourse, Cold War cosmopolitanism offered a vision of an international community in which South Korea would be a full and equal participant—in contrast to its prior status as a subordinate member of the Japanese empire—and the promise of protection from its hostile neighbor to the north.

Second, Cold War cosmopolitanism was an *attitude towards modernity*. It embraced the project of Western-style modernization optimistically and projected a vision of South Korea moving boldly into the future. It emphasized the opening up of new possibilities and opportunities, and valued exchanges with the world beyond Korea's borders. While it acknowledged the risks modernization posed, it embraced the prospect of wide-ranging social change. It suggested the need to shed the oppressive aspects of Korea's patriarchal Confucianism and replace them with liberal Western values, especially individualism and freedom, which applied to women as well as men. As such, Cold War cosmopolitanism had a feminist dimension. Third, Cold War cosmopolitanism was a *material practice of cultural production and dissemination* that was linked to Cold War institutions. The enmeshment of South Korea within the Free World created pathways through which resources—capital, technology, advisors, consumer goods, cultural artifacts, ideas, and techniques of cultural production—flowed into Korea. Some of these flows, such as those encouraged by the Asia Foundation, were intentional; others, such as those that originated on US military bases, often were not. Other networks, such as those created by the Asian People's Anti-Communist League and the Asian Film Festival, facilitated the (much smaller) outflow of South Korean people and cultural production into the Free World. As a material practice, then,

Cold War cosmopolitanism entailed the use of these resources and networks by South Koreans to produce and disseminate their own works of culture.

Finally, Cold War cosmopolitanism was a *cultural style*, a textual feature manifest in South Korean films, magazines, fashion, performance, advertising, and home design. Aesthetically, this style entailed the appropriation and indigenization of a range of stylistic elements derived from Western models. These elements included material objects such as consumer goods, conventions of representation such as genres, and depictions of social practices such as commercial leisure activities. Cold War cosmopolitan style made a claim for Korea's coevalness with the modern West: by demonstrating familiarity with Western cultural trends, it signaled a rejection of Korea's colonial-era status as "traditional" and "backward" and asserted that Korea occupied the same cultural time as other modern noncommunist countries. Ideologically, it was a distinctly Free Asian aesthetic, showcasing the lifestyles that capitalist democracy promised to make possible.

Cold War cosmopolitanism should be understood as the Asian counterpart to America's Cold War Orientalism, both of which functioned as cultural expressions of the ideal of US-Asian integration. Koreans' embrace of certain elements of Western culture mirrored Americans' simultaneous fascination with Asia. Washington, as part of its push for Free World integration, encouraged Asians and Americans alike to turn their attention to the noncommunist world beyond their borders and to engage with each other. In the United States, this led to the proliferation of middlebrow narratives about Americans forging sympathetic bonds with Asian people through narratives of travel, adoption, medical missionary work, and dance. *Cold War Cosmopolitanism* explores how this encouragement of Free World engagement affected the content and style of South Korean culture as well, and it is thus something of a sequel to my previous book, *Cold War Orientalism*. Both are examinations of Cold War liberalism as it found expression in the cultural realm. Sometimes the same institution was intervening in Asian and American culture industries simultaneously, as when the Asia Foundation urged Hollywood producers to make less racist films about Asia at the same time that it was helping anticommunist Asian filmmakers make better-quality films. As Washington encouraged American middlebrow intellectuals to generate sympathetic understandings of Asian peoples, it provided resources for their Korean counterparts to produce works of culture that encouraged sympathetic understandings of American values. At a historical moment when the negative dialectic of anticommunism was omnipresent, both Cold War Orientalism and Cold War cosmopolitanism offered something positive to Americans and Koreans: a way for them to understand themselves as active members in a larger world defined by its "freedom" and as participants in pressing debates about modernity. What we see, then, is that Washington's foreign policies of Free World integration exerted pressures that shaped the cultural fields of both the United States and South Korea in the 1950s, albeit in very different ways.[12]

The 1950s–60s saw the blossoming of diverse cosmopolitan aesthetics across the globe, as cultural producers began imagining into existence new communities and identities. What I am calling Cold War cosmopolitanism was not unique to South Korea or to film, but rather a diversely manifesting style crafted by a broad array of cultural producers, from "free Mandarin" filmmakers in Hong Kong who embraced Americanized visions of capitalist modernity, to editors of highbrow literary journals published around the world and secretly funded by the US government. Its antitheses could be found in the "socialist cosmopolitanism" promulgated within mainland China's literary culture, which encouraged the circulation of texts and authors within communist countries, and in the conventions of a socially critical neorealism, generated in Italy and embraced by filmmakers around the world (including some in South Korea). Cosmopolitan modes of production and consumption likewise flourished among those trying to find a Third Way between capitalism and socialism—from a Buddhist leader-turned-screenwriter in Ceylon to writers, dancers, and filmmakers in Indonesia—as well as those seeking to bypass Cold War frameworks altogether, such as black South African musicians who looked to Hollywood and Harlem to assert a modern urban identity against apartheid's tribalizing logic. Around the world, cosmopolitanism was embraced as a defining feature of modernity and an essential dimension of postcolonial nationhood, one that conveyed an attitude of promise and possibility towards the future. Throughout, cultural production was characterized by what Jennifer Lindsay calls a "magpie-like" process of "taking and shaping" from diverse places and times.[13]

METHODOLOGY

In keeping with my American studies training, I am employing an interdisciplinary methodology that brings together the microanalysis of individual films with the macrohistory of the Cold War in Northeast Asia. One can think of these as two endpoints of an analytical continuum that ranges from the symbolic at one end to the material on the other. In between are numerous points of connections that bridge the gap between them. My analysis is built upon a wide range of English-, Korean-, and Chinese-language sources (the latter two accessed via translators), archival as well as textual. My core texts are the films directed by Han Hyung-mo, with secondary attention devoted to select films by Ozu Yasujiro of Japan, Shin Sang-ok, and other Golden Age directors. I use the biographies of cultural producers to root these artifacts in their historical moment. I open up to the broader field of public culture by reading Han's cinematic style in relation to the popular women's magazine *Yŏwŏn* and the best-selling novel on which *Madame Freedom* was based, as well as to the lives and works of several female public intellectuals, including Korea's first female university president, first female lawyer, and first female fashion designer. Institutions matter in this analysis, and I explore how US military bases and the Asia Foundation functioned as "ports of entry" that funneled resources into the hands of individual artists and into culture industries such as publishing and film production. Korean initiatives figure here as well, including Rhee's efforts to define Free Asia on his own terms and to make Korean culture better known within it. Broadening out still further, I delve into economic history to understand the flow of consumer goods and foreign films into Korea, through legal trading relationships and the illegal black market. The chapters that follow move back and forth along this continuum, illuminating connections among individuals, texts, institutions, economic practices, and foreign policy initiatives.

SCHOLARLY CONVERSATIONS

These chapters participate in several scholarly conversations, in addition to the one on global cosmopolitanisms. This first is among English-language scholars of Korea's Golden Age cinema. While this conversation has not engaged Han's work beyond *Madame Freedom* in much depth[14] and has devoted more attention to male-centered melodramas than to women's pictures,[15] it is rich in transnational analyses[16] and has begun plumbing the work of individual directors in depth.[17] A second conversation is taking place among scholars of the cultural Cold War in Asia. They are revealing the nature and extent of Washington's and Beijing's interventions in Asia's cultural life,[18] piecing together institutional histories of transnational phenomena such as the Asian Film Festival,[19] and illuminating the impact on women of Cold War ideologies and practices.[20] A third conversation is among scholars of transnational American and other national/area studies who are exploring the creative bursts that took place in popular cultures around the world after World War II, as increased flows of American people, ideas, and cultural forms intersected with local traditions.[21] Extending the insights that Arjun Appadurai developed in *Modernity at Large*, they are exploring how the global flows of Americana contributed resources for self- and nation making rather than serving exclusively as instruments of US hegemony.[22] Limited resources make it impossible for me to engage fully with the scholarly conversations taking place in Korean and other languages.

Cold War Cosmopolitanism explores what happened when transnational flows of resources, people, and ideas intersected with a local culture at a specific historical moment. It charts the pathways through which these flows were channeled, and identifies the institutions that enabled cultural producers to tap into them productively. It interprets the works of cinematic art that ambitious, creative individuals produced as they took advantage of these resources and used them to interrogate the modernity that was taking shape around them. To read Cold War cosmopolitanism as a cultural formation is to understand how deeply style is intertwined with the larger forces of history. It is to grapple with Robert Palmer's rhetorical query about the blues: "How much history can be transmitted by pressure on a guitar string?" My hope is that when readers watch Han's films and admire his sweeping camera movements, rich mise-en-scène, and globally sourced soundtracks, they will be able to discern what Carlo Rotella has called "the shaping flows of history" at work beneath the surface of his polished style.[23]

PART I

Period

1

Postcolonial, Postwar, Cold War

On July 16, 1950, a few weeks after the outbreak of the Korean War, a flight of fifty American B-29 bombers dropped five hundred tons of bombs on Seoul's Yongsan neighborhood. The primary target was the Yongsan train station. Built by the Japanese in 1900, it was a major transit hub connecting Seoul to cities in the south and had facilities for manufacturing and maintaining trains; like the rest of the capital, it was in the hands of the North Korean People's Army. US general Douglas MacArthur ordered the attack in an effort to halt the southward advance of the North Koreans. According to an Air Force communiqué issued after the attack, a "large number of bombs fell diagonally across the entire yard," completely severing the tracks and leaving the "yards in flames." "Fire and explosions heavily damaged repair and assembly shops," and many buildings were partially destroyed (figure 1). The Americans considered the bombing a success. The damage was not restricted to the railroad yards, however. The bombs also "demolished and set fire to many buildings surrounding the area" and, according to a North Korean communiqué, "a large number of homes, schools, hospitals, and social facilities were destroyed." The North Koreans noted that "not a small number of inhabitants were killed or wounded." Recent South Korean estimates place the toll of the Yongsan bombing at over fifteen hundred civilian casualties.[1]

Six years later, Han Hyung-mo transformed the shattered Railway Transportation Office into an ad hoc studio and South Korea's first designated film production space. Han's art team repurposed the damaged building, whose walls were still standing, into something culturally productive. They patched together a roof out of planks and tarpaulins, and hung lights from a makeshift ceiling. They used the space to shoot the spectacular dance hall scene in *Madame Freedom* (1956). Han's

FIGURE 1. Yongsan train station, Seoul, after being hit by American B-29 bombers on July 16, 1950. (Courtesy NARA).

art team built an elaborately arched and tiered stage with soaring columns and a central staircase, flanked by walls decorated with large white circles and basket-weave sculptural formations. In this cavernous space, men and women dressed in Korean, Chinese, and Western clothes danced to a Latin jazz band amidst a dozen tables and booths, a palm tree, and a Christmas tree (figure 2). Amidst the postwar rubble, the filmmakers created a place that had no real-world counterpart in South Korea: it was a fantasy of aspiration and desire modeled on images seen in Hollywood movies and American magazines.[2]

The Korean War cleared a space, literally and figuratively, for the production of a distinctive postwar film culture. It shattered what remained of the colonial era's film production system and created an opening for the influx of foreign material and expressive culture that Korean filmmakers appropriated for their own ends. Within a landscape that the war had transformed culturally as well as physically, filmmakers began to produce culturally hybrid—and uniquely Korean—works of film art. Like the studio space constructed out of a Japanese train station shattered by American bombs, these films are redolent of the historical continuities and ruptures across the colonial divide that mark the postwar period.

To read Han's films through the lens of period style requires a thorough understanding of the period in which they were conceived. This chapter charts the historical development of Cold War cosmopolitanism within postwar South Korean political life, focusing on its emergence as a body of material practices and

FIGURE 2. The dance hall set in *Madame Freedom*, which was built in a studio constructed amidst the ruins of the Yongsan train station in 1956. (Courtesy KOFA).

institutional ties aimed at integrating the newly independent nation into the Free World alliance. It introduces the 1950s as a distinct phase in South Korea's modernization. In the wake of liberation and the Korean War, South Koreans confronted the dual tasks of nation building and bloc building.[3] They needed to define a new postcolonial national identity, reconstruct a war-ravaged country, and establish ties with other Free World nations. Modernity in the 1950s was, in part, a consequence of the presence within South Korean's borders of other countries (primarily Japan and the United States) and of the creation of diverse networks that bound South Korea to peoples in Free Asia and the democratic West.

LAYERED MODERNITY: POSTCOLONIAL, POSTWAR, COLD WAR

The 1950s was a period of flux and openness that differed in important ways from the colonial modernity that preceded it (1910–45) and the developmental modernity that followed (1961–88). Modernity in the 1950s had a distinctly cosmopolitan dimension. While Korea had relationships with China and Japan stretching back centuries and had encountered the West through the filter of imperial Japan, it now found itself engaging in new ways with a broader range of countries. Modernity in the 1950s was shaped first and foremost by the unprecedented, large-scale presence of the United States inside the borders of the country.[4] Yet Korea's engagement with the world was more complex than simply "Americanization." Korea in the 1950s was a simultaneously postcolonial, postwar, and Cold War society. Together, these designations point to the layering of multiple foreign presences, and modernities, within Korea's national boundaries.[5]

The Republic of Korea came into being during the first wave of decolonization that swept across Asia in the wake of World War II. Korea had been a Japanese colony from 1910 until 1945, when it was liberated by US and Soviet forces as part of Japan's surrender. The Americans divided the Korean peninsula at the 38th parallel into two zones of Allied occupation, and from 1945 to 1948 the South was governed by the United States Army Military Government in Korea (USAMGIK) and the North, from 1946, by the Soviet-backed Provisional People's Committee for North Korea. In 1948 this temporary division hardened and two separate states were formed, although neither recognized the legitimacy of the other. Kim Il-sung, who had been an anticolonial guerilla fighter in Manchuria, led the Democratic People's Republic of Korea in the North with the backing of Communist China and the Soviet Union. Syngman Rhee, a leader of the Korean government-in-exile who had lived in the United States for decades, was elected president of the Republic of Korea (ROK) in the South, which was supported by the United States and the newly formed United Nations. Rhee led South Korea until he was ousted by the student-led April Revolution of 1960.

Rhee governed South Korea during a period of burgeoning nationalism. During the colonial era Koreans had been economically, socially, and culturally integrated into the Japanese empire, albeit as second-class subjects. Tokyo's cultural assimilation policies, increasingly stringent during the late 1930s and 1940s, mandated the use of Japanese language in schools, restricted the use of the Korean language in public, and recast Korean traditional culture as a mere precursor to that of the more glorious Japanese.[6] After liberation, South Koreans took up the task of postcolonial nation building with enthusiasm, relishing those expressions of Koreanness that had been quashed under colonial rule. Syngman Rhee espoused a potent form of nationalism rooted in anticolonialism and anticommunism, which he developed into something akin to a civil religion. He gave voice to the great bitterness that many Koreans felt towards Japan, and warned that Japan would soon seek to reassert dominion over its neighbors. Rhee urged Koreans to hold on to their memories of colonial "atrocities" even as they eradicated "Japanese things and ways" (*wae-saek*), such as food and clothing, from their lives, and he refused to establish diplomatic relations with Japan.[7] Rhee likewise viewed communist North Korea and its protector, China, as existential threats to the nation. The draconian National Security Law of 1948 outlawed all organizations and activities that could be construed as endangering national security and criminalized expressions of sympathy towards North Korea, as well as criticism of Rhee's government. Rhee used the law to restrict democratic liberties and imprison tens of thousands of political opponents.[8] Rhee's nationalism thus severed South Korea from its two closest neighbors, North Korea and Japan, with which it had extensive historical and cultural ties.

Liberation from Japan did not create an absolute historical break, however, and continuities persisted across the 1945 divide. Elements of colonial modernity, most visibly the broad avenues and multistory buildings that comprised Seoul's downtown, continued into the postwar era. Likewise, the web of connections to Japan did not dissolve overnight. For all Rhee's anti-Japanese rhetoric, he staffed his government with people whose expertise and skills had been developed under the Japanese. Colonial police officers, widely despised as collaborators, morphed into a national constabulary; professionals who had risen through the ranks of colonial bureaucracies continued their ascent in the postcolonial era; and businesses that had partnered with the Japanese expanded after the war. Many Koreans continued to regard Japan, whose economy developed rapidly over the course of the 1950s, as a culturally proximate model of modernity that they might emulate. The "ambivalences of postcoloniality," as Steven Chung has described them, meant that a web of shadowy connections and sub-rosa affinities to Japan coexisted alongside the more public denunciations.[9]

If the bonds of colonialism lingered beneath the surface of the postliberation era, evidence of the recently concluded Korean War (1950–53) was everywhere to be seen. To many observers, poverty defined the 1950s. The economy—already weakened by the global depression of the 1930s, the Pacific War, the withdrawal of Japanese capital and skilled labor, and the loss of access to the industrial capacity in North Korea—was further crippled by the war, which raged up and down the peninsula. According to historian Gregg Brazinsky,

> Total property damage from the war in the ROK was estimated at more than $3 billion. Three years of fighting had annihilated 900 industrial plants, reduced the textile industry by one-third, and wiped out more than half of the country's freight cars, trucks, and locomotives. Its sawmills, papermills, metal plants, and small industries had almost disappeared. The war had destroyed 600,000 homes and rendered thousands of others uninhabitable. In all, five million South Koreans—roughly a quarter of the country's population—had been forced to leave their homes. Finally, the country's weakened industrial base and shattered agricultural economy produced severe shortages of both jobs and food for an expanding population.[10]

With a per capita income of $60 in 1953, South Koreans were desperately poor, their national income smaller than that of San Francisco's population. Koreans suffered from widespread unemployment that sidelined one of every eight workers and from "wild, flamboyant" inflation that eroded the real wages of those who did have jobs to less than half of what they had been in the late colonial era. The social landscape was equally transformed. Out of a population of 21 million, the war had left 1.3 million dead and 5 million destitute, 500,000 widows, and 100,000 orphans. Over 1 million families were separated by the 38th parallel. Seoul, already full of returnees from the far reaches of the Japanese empire and refugees from the communist north, saw its population swell even further as rural migrants flooded in, to nearly 2.5 million by 1960.[11] Living conditions were often rudimentary, as people took up residence in bombed-out buildings, sprawling slums, and even caves. "Houses made out of cardboard boxes and cans from the US army bases were built overnight," recalled one inhabitant, "and began to climb the mountains higher and higher reaching the sky."[12] Crime—including petty theft, juvenile delinquency, prostitution, gangsterism, and black marketing—exploded. Suicides became common. As Bruce Cumings has noted, "South Korea in the 1950s was a terribly depressing place, where extreme privation and degradation touched everyone."[13] An air of desperation and nihilism suffused the country, and public commentators noted with anxiety the rising pursuit of naked self-interest amidst the erosion of collective social values.

As elsewhere in Asia, however, war proved a modernizing force, wiping out old infrastructure and social relations and creating a partially cleared slab on which to build a new society. Reconstruction gradually restored a semblance of urban order, layering new buildings and infrastructure over the colonial remains. War-damaged buildings were patched up, orphanages and schools built from scratch, and electricity slowly restored. Used streetcars imported from Nashville carried residents through the streets of Seoul, past department stores, now stocked with American rather than Japanese goods, and Western-style houses built for those who could afford them.[14] Expanding universities created educational opportunities for middle-class youth, and a reviving textile industry created factory jobs for members of the working class.

This reconstruction was financed through an influx of foreign aid, the overwhelming majority of it coming from the United States. After the war, South Korea emerged as America's largest economic mission in the world: between 1953 and 1961, it received $2.5 billion in economic aid and $1.5 billion in military aid from the United States.[15] As Bruce Cumings puts it, there were "inconceivable amounts of American cash that flowed into the country, down from the presidential mansion, through the bureaucracies civil and military, coursing through the PXs and onto the black market, into the pockets of a horde of people who serviced the foreign presence: drivers, guards, runners, valets, maids, houseboys, black-market operators, money changers, prostitutes, and beggars."[16] This sluicing-in of American cash was accompanied by a similar flood of American food, clothing, medicine, and other goods (much of which was only accessible through the black market: see chapter 6). In an effort to partially privatize its foreign aid program, the Eisenhower administration appealed to ordinary Americans to assist needy South Koreans. American school children "adopted" Korean schools and sent them pencils, paper, and books. Religious congregations sent shiploads of sweaters, dresses, pants, and coats. The Ford, Rockefeller, Carnegie, and American Korean foundations dispensed millions of dollars in grants to hospitals, welfare agencies, and other civil society organizations.[17] By 1958, one umbrella group representing sixty-seven private organizations had donated 12,900 tons of food, worth an estimated $57 million. Diverse American products seeped into everyday Korean life, especially in the cities. Koreans ate bread and noodles made from American wheat, dressed in outfits refashioned from American military uniforms and parachutes, and rode in taxis that had begun their lives as US Army jeeps.[18] This influx of aid stimulated South Korea's struggling capitalist economy and gave rise to small middle and nouveau riche classes. The people who prospered in the 1950s were often those who had access to American resources: bureaucrats who distributed import licenses; businessmen who imported and processed aid commodities such as sugar, wheat, and cotton; and small merchants who sold relief goods in shops.[19] Savvy entrepreneurs, they found ways to make the aid economy work for them.

This torrent of aid formed the foundation of South Korea's economy. Rhee devoted his energies to extracting as much of it as he could from Washington and inflating its buying power by maintaining an overvalued currency, the hwan. For all its abundance, however, it did not jumpstart an industrial economy. Most aid came in the form of commodities, such as fertilizer and fuel, designed to ensure Koreans' survival in the present, and most American officials believed South Korea's economy would remain primarily agricultural for the foreseeable future. Rhee showed limited interest in industrialization and as a result, according to Gregg Brazinsky, "failed miserably at the task of economic development." Instead he used American aid to stay in power and to reward his political allies, many of whom enjoyed an "opulent lifestyle."[20] Corruption existed on a "fabulous scale."[21]

The influx of American money and goods into this desperately poor country imbued daily life with a doubleness that echoed the ambivalent postcoloniality of Korea's relationship with Japan. "Perhaps the most descriptive word for the current Korean scene," wrote one American observer in 1955, "is 'tension.'"[22] The combination of poverty, reconstruction, and foreign goods created the sense of a society in transition, caught between what it had been and what it might become. Alongside the hardships there was often a sense of optimism about the future. Among the younger generation and those whose lives were a bit less straitened, the armistice raised hopes for positive social change. Liberal ideas arrived with the troops from the United States and the fifteen other UN countries that fought the Korean War. Changing social mores opened up possibilities for new ways of being in the world. The 1950s was thus a time of contradictions for Koreans. This sense of multiple realities coexisting with one another was manifest in the physical form of Seoul itself, which appeared to US cultural attaché Gregory Henderson as "half city, with mounting buildings, streetcars, electricity, [and] taxis, and half macrocephalic monster, growing cancerously in hillside shacks and caves, noisome alleys and settlements without water and electricity."[23]

Postcolonial, postwar South Korea in the 1950s was also a Cold War society. As Secretary of State Dulles bluntly noted in 1956, "American economic aid was not accorded on the basis of friendship but as a contribution to winning the cold war."[24] The outbreak of the Korean War in June 1950, coming as it did on the heels of Mao's proclamation of the People's Republic of China in October 1949, shifted the center of the Cold War from Europe to Asia and granted South Korea an importance in Washington's eyes that it had not previously enjoyed. Between 1949 and 1951 the National Security Council issued a series of policy papers, collectively known as NSC 48, that reevaluated Washington's foreign policy towards Asia. NSC 48 acknowledged the "intense nationalism" of new nations emerging out from under Japanese and European colonialism, and it established nation building as one of the foundational principles of US foreign policy, declaring that Washington's primary objective in Asia was to "assist in the development of truly independent, friendly, stable and self-sustaining states."[25] US interests required that the countries of Asia be able to withstand communist attack and subversion, ally themselves securely with the United States, be governed by leaders regarded as legitimate by their people, and have capitalist economies strong enough to support daily life. In this new political landscape, South Korea became a frontline state with an outsize role in the regional balance of power.

South Korea became a crucial site for the military containment of communism. This, in turn, led to a large American presence within the country's borders. After pouring in 1.8 million soldiers during the Korean War, Washington agreed to maintain two US Army divisions and several Air Force units—a fluctuating force of 50,000–80,000—on a network of about seventy military bases that spanned the country from near the demilitarized zone (DMZ) in its northern region to Jeju Island in the southern, with major posts located in Paju, Seoul, Uijeongbu, Dongducheon, Daegu, and Busan (map 1). (Washington also agreed to maintain an ROK army of up to 720,000 troops.)[26] As the Eighth US Army (EUSA) settled in to stay, it moved into buildings that had been constructed by the colonial Japanese military, a symbolism not lost on Koreans. The sprawling Yongsan garrison in Seoul, located adjacent to the bombed-out train station where Han built his studio, became home to EUSA headquarters and was gradually transformed into an outpost of America, complete with suburban-style houses, big-finned cars, and tow-headed children in swimming pools.[27] Across the country, American GIs dressed in fatigues and driving jeeps became a common sight on the streets surrounding the US military bases. Select Koreans had access to these bases as soldiers, employees, guests, dance partners, and sexual partners.

The Republic of Korea was an independent country, but it was also a client state of the vastly more powerful United States. Rhee was no American puppet. He often pursued interests at cross-purposes with those of Washington, as in his

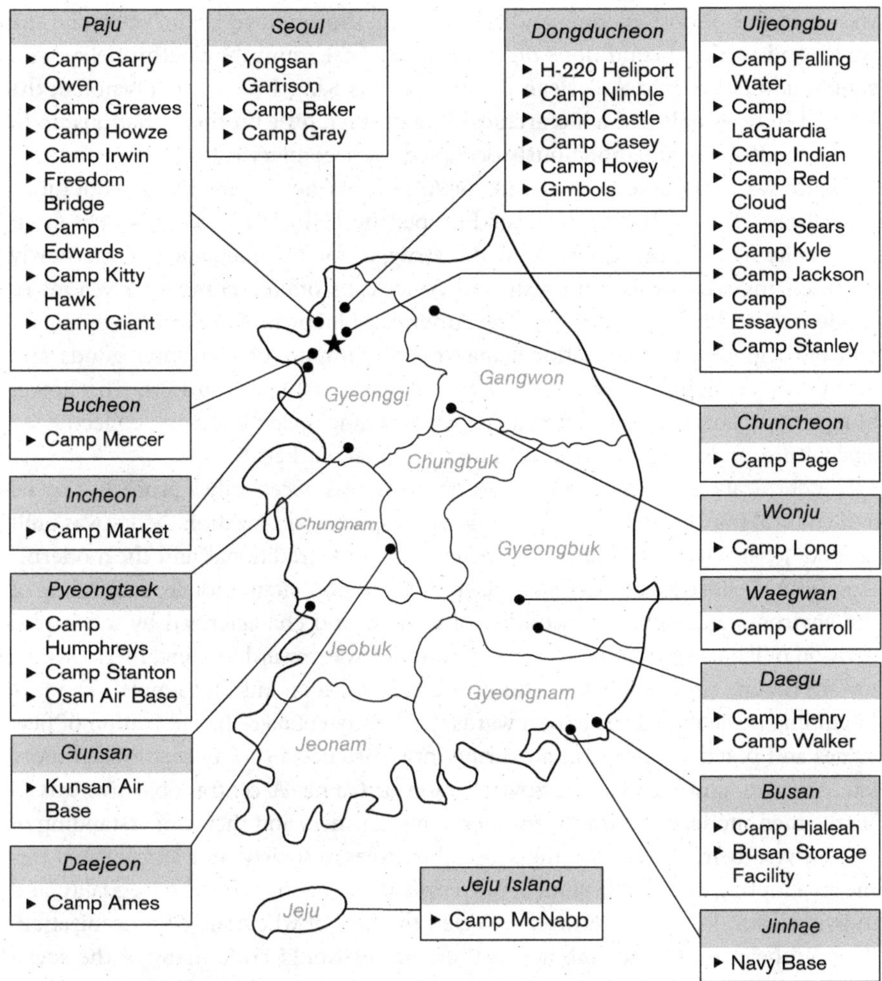

MAP 1. Major US military posts in South Korea, 1950–1960. (Source: Kwang Sub Kwak, "The U.S.-ROK Alliance, 1953–2004," PhD diss., Southern Illinois University Carbondale, 2006).

refusal to restore political and economic relations with Japan and his staunch commitment to an overvalued hwan, and his authoritarian violations of political liberties often frustrated his American patrons. Yet US hegemony over the country was unmistakable. The ROK armed forces, for instance, remained under the UN Command's operational control and thus constrained Rhee's ability to pursue an independent foreign policy, which would likely have included an attack against North Korea. The inequality between the United States and South Korea could be felt across many sectors of society: among the sex workers for whom Americans were a source of both income and exploitation, the employees who protested the wages and working conditions on US military bases, and the youthful elite who sought admission into American universities. As Sang-Dawn Lee has noted, the US and ROK established a hierarchical "big brother, little brother" relationship in which the Koreans unambiguously occupied the secondary role.[28]

South Korea became a crucial site for Americans' developing ideas about modernization. Outside the confines of Europe, the Cold War was as much about modernity as political ideology. In the struggle for the allegiance of the newly decolonizing nations, communists and Americans offered competing visions of modernity and how to get there. The American blueprint emphasized capitalism and participation in international markets, the import of consumer goods and advanced technologies, and the growth of democratic institutions. The Soviet blueprint, in contrast, emphasized central planning, heavy industry, collectivized agriculture, and independence from international markets.[29]

Modernization, as understood by Americans, was necessarily a process of social and cultural transformation. As Nils Gilman writes, modernization theory was built around "a particular rendition of the dichotomy of 'the traditional' and 'the modern.'" Americans believed that "modern society was cosmopolitan, mobile, controlling of the environment, secular, welcoming of change, and characterized by a complex division of labor. Traditional society, by contrast, was inward looking, inert, passive toward nature, superstitious, fearful of change, and economically simple." The task of guiding postcolonial societies towards modernity entailed the cultivation of new values and practices, aimed at nurturing into existence a society that looked more like America, and less like the Soviet Union or China. A central objective was to "make men modern": to transform their consciousness and their understanding of their selves, their relations to others, and their roles in society. To a large extent, this meant adopting the liberal values of universalism, democracy, freedom, equality, and individualism. While modernizers rejected the idea of wholesale Americanization, they did believe that the embrace of these values would erase many of the social limitations that traditional society imposed: according to Gilman, "differences about things like the desirability of social mobility, free speech, or the inclusion of women in the public sphere would necessarily disappear in the course of becoming modern." Cultural differences would still be valued, but as a self-conscious heritage that would be manifest in limited ways, rather than as guidelines for everyday life.[30]

In South Korea, a small army of Americans and their Korean partners sought to implement modernization's blueprint in the fields of government, education, public information, social welfare, the military, and the law. Western standards, adapted to the realities of South Korean conditions, defined the modernity to be achieved. The legacies of Japanese colonialism and the social strictures of Confucianism, in turn, constituted the outmoded ways of life whose constraints would be eased. Both were regarded as antiliberal modes of social organization that fettered the individual, inhibited the development of democratic freedoms, and slowed the growth of an egalitarian ethos. "Liberation" from these hierarchical, collectivist systems constituted modernizers' core mission. With some exceptions, Korean political and cultural elites largely embraced this process and regarded Confucianism as one cause of Korea's "backwardness."[31]

South Korean modernity in the 1950s was thus a complex condition, layered and incomplete and in a state of transition. The development of colonial modernity—which included factories, communications networks, and a vibrant mass culture—had ground to a halt with liberation.[32] As a result, the desire to be modern was widespread in the 1950s and modernization was regarded as integral to the project of postcolonial nation building. According to historian Charles Kim, there was a "widely shared assumption that Koreans, for the benefit of self and nation, had to 'modernize' all spheres of life according to Euro-American models." Korean modernizers, like their American counterparts, believed that "the option of returning to an 'old Korea' is long since gone."[33] Yet the association of modernity with America intersected with Koreans' robust nationalism in complicated ways. How should postcolonial people become modern while simultaneously restoring their sense of Koreanness that the Japanese had tried to crush? While the vast majority of Koreans viewed the United States favorably, these feelings of admiration and gratitude were often shot through with shame, resentment, and anger.[34] Debates over modernization thus centered not on whether to change, but on how quickly and extensively. At the same time, modernity in the 1950s possessed something of an unreal quality in that the epiphenomena of modernity abounded in the absence of a solid foundation.[35] The lack of an industrial economy (which would not develop until the 1960s) meant that Korea did not have the material infrastructure of a genuinely modern society: urbanization was driven by the flood of refugees rather than by any need for factory workers, and the emergent consumer culture was stocked not with Korean-made goods but with items imported, donated, or smuggled in from abroad. Korean modernity in the 1950s was thus largely a social phenomenon rather than a deeply rooted economic one, and a layered experience of both continuities and breaks with the colonial modernity of the prewar era.

INTEGRATION INTO FREE ASIA

If nation building constituted one guiding principle of Cold War US foreign policy, bloc building constituted the other. For US policy makers, it wasn't enough for South Korea to ally itself with the United States; it needed to ally itself with other nations as well. The Cold War, after all, was a conflict between blocs and systems, not just nations. The National Security Council, for all its understanding of nationalism's powerful appeal, wanted to encourage an outward turn among the newly independent nations of Asia. The drafters of NSC 48, troubled by the "antipathies" and "lack of affinity among Asian nations," sought to encourage a "consciousness of common interests" and facilitate "regional collaboration" in all its varied forms.[36] The region's security, and ultimately America's, depended on the forging of substantive ties among Asian countries. Washington was keenly aware of the need to nurture Free Asia into existence as something more than an archipelago of noncommunist states. Free Asia would not come into being automatically; it would have to be created. This insistence on bloc building in Asia went hand in hand with modernization theory, which defined modern societies as "cosmopolitan," in contrast to "inward looking" traditional ones. Modernity was constituted, in part, through an openness to new ideas, a willingness to learn from others, and a capacity for exchange. The outward turn that the NSC promoted as a security measure was thus also an essential part of the development process. From this perspective, it wasn't enough that South Koreans welcomed US and UN troops and advisors into their country. To become truly modern, and truly secure, they also had to reach beyond their nation's borders to engage with other noncommunist people. South Korea's integration into the emerging military, political, and economic networks of the Free World produced a more fully cosmopolitan dimension to 1950s modernity. It also marks the emergence of Cold War cosmopolitanism as a body of material practices and institutional ties.

The phrase *free Asia* became ubiquitous in postwar American and Asian political discourse, its meaning shifting over the course of the 1940s and 1950s. While it had anticolonial connotations during World War II, with the outbreak of the Korean War it came into wide usage to characterize the part of the world seen as threatened by communist aggression and subversion. Eisenhower introduced the more evocative "arc of free Asia" in 1955 to identify the recipients of his new foreign aid initiative, which specifically targeted regional integration (map 2). The phrase became American shorthand to indicate Asia's value to the West, from its large population whose political allegiance hung in the balance to the abundance of vital natural resources to which it was home.[37] Within Asian political discourse, it became a way to affirm affiliation with the West.

Over the course of the 1950s, Washington worked to incorporate South Korea into a series of Free Asia networks. The Mutual Defense Treaty of 1953 incorporated South Korea into Washington's regional military network, a "hub-and-spokes" system that knit the US together with Japan, Taiwan, the Philippines, Pakistan, Thailand, Australia, and New Zealand.[38] Large as it was, the US military presence in Korea was thus merely one node with a much larger network, ultimately global in scope, that stationed one million troops on over eight hundred military bases around the world.[39] Korea's political integration was also seen as essential and from 1948 onward, according to State Department historian Donald Macdonald, the "United States constantly encouraged the South Koreans to broaden their international contacts by campaigning for broader recognition, by establishing diplomatic relations, and by joining international organizations." Washington pushed especially hard for a rapprochement with Japan which, as the region's largest and

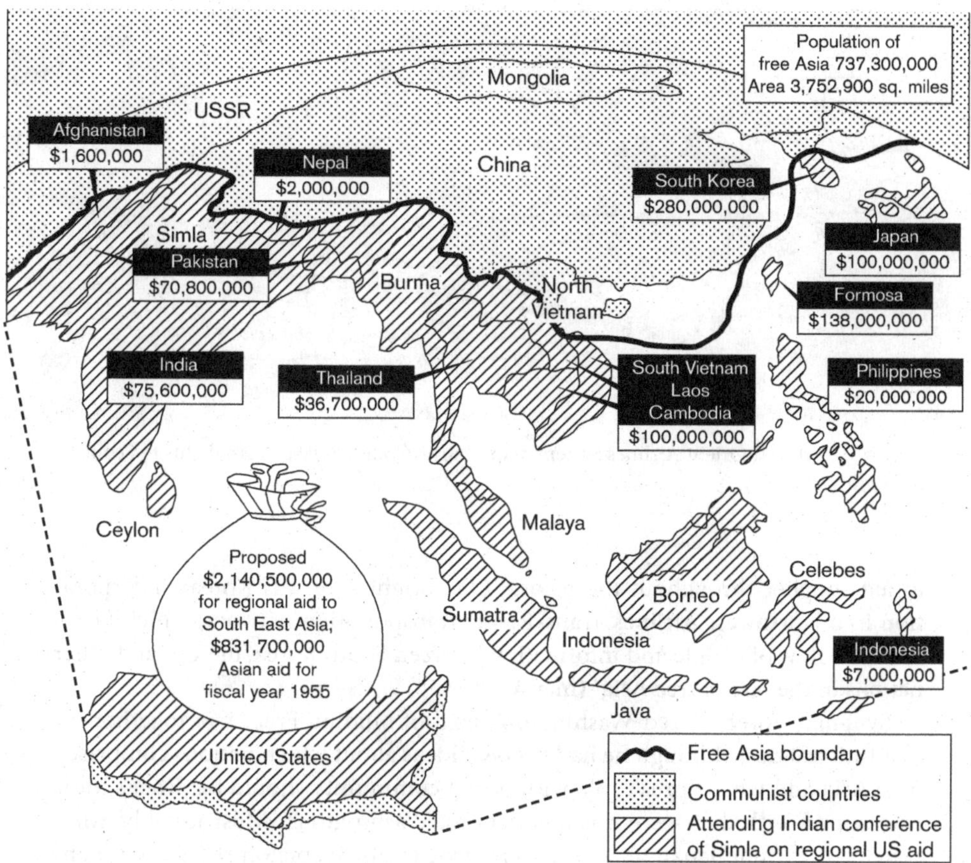

MAP 2. US foreign aid for "the arc of Free Asia" in 1955.

only industrialized economy, was at the center of Washington's conceptualization of Free Asia. The NSC urged the fostering of a "community of interest" between Korea and its neighbors, as well as the creation of concrete opportunities for "joint cooperation" and "multilateral activities."[40] While Rhee did forge close relationships with Taiwan, South Vietnam, and the Philippines, his implacable hostility to Japan precluded any restoration of political ties, and his virulent anticommunism led some other nations to keep their distance. Washington had less success with Korea's economic incorporation. While American officials routinely encouraged Rhee to establish normal commercial relations with other noncommunist countries, particularly Japan, South Korea's exports remained miniscule compared to its imports, and the US remained the country's primary trading partner as well

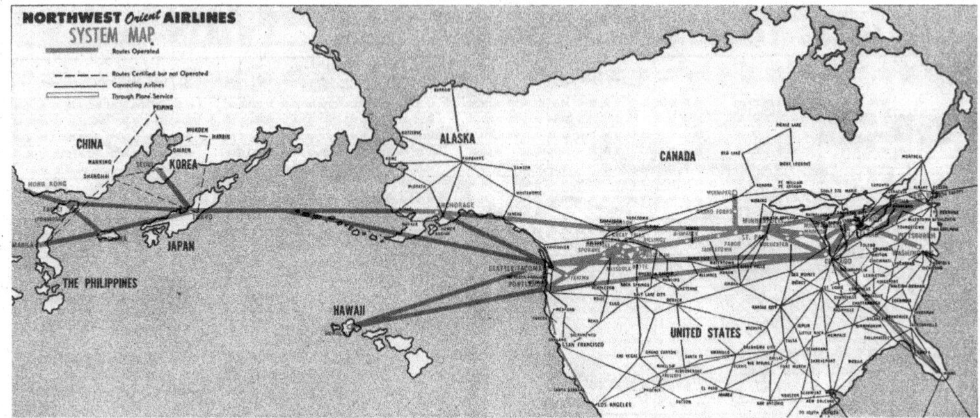

MAP 3. Northwest Orient Airlines System Map, c. 1956. Commercial civilian flights to Seoul began in 1947.

as aid supplier throughout the 1950s.[41] One bright spot was Korea's incorporation into Northwest Airlines' trans-Pacific transportation network, which facilitated the flow of people and information between South Korea, the US, and other nations in the "arc of free Asia" (map 3).[42]

Syngman Rhee shared Washington's goal of binding Free Asia together via institutional ties, although he had his own ideas about which nations comprised Free Asia and what Korea's role within that community should be. Rhee's ideas overlapped with, but were not identical to, Washington's. Most notably, Rhee sought to exclude Japan and he also regarded with suspicion the merely noncommunist nations of India, Burma, Laos, Cambodia, Indonesia, Sri Lanka, and Pakistan. Rhee's notion of Free Asia privileged avowedly *anti*communist nations, and he identified Korea, along with Taiwan and South Vietnam, as its keystones.[43]

Rhee sought to institutionalize his Japan-free vision of Free Asia through formal regional alliances. Beginning in 1949, Rhee worked with Chiang Kai-shek of Taiwan and Elpidio Quirino of the Philippines to form the Pacific Pact security alliance. Despite years of effort, the Pact never got off the ground and it was finally abandoned after Korea signed the Mutual Defense Agreement with the United States in 1953. Rhee had better luck with the Asian People's Anti-Communist League (APACL), which he viewed as the Pact's successor. The League was Rhee's idea and he launched the blazingly ideological and vehemently antineutralist APACL in 1954 at an international conference in Jinhae, South Korea.[44] An international, quasi-governmental organization, it sought to strengthen the political, economic, and cultural ties among the anticommunist nations of Asia. Although the APACL was explicitly aligned with the West, Rhee saw is an opportunity for "the free people of Asia" to "do something for themselves." Its growing membership roster reflected its cosmopolitan mission. The initial meeting in 1954 included seven delegates, from South Korea, Taiwan, Hong Kong and Macao, the Philippines, Okinawa, Thailand, and South Vietnam. Three years later its conference was attended by representatives from fifteen localities that spanned Asia, the Middle East, and Europe, as well as emissaries from groups such as the Anti-Bolshevik Bloc of Nations and the Alliance of Russian Solidarists, who represented the interests of groups in eastern Europe and western and central Asia. Less formally, Rhee in 1954–57 sent General Choi Duk Shin on a series of goodwill missions aimed at forging closer bonds with the nations of Southeast Asia. In scores of meetings and cocktail receptions in the region's capitals, Choi told South Korea's story and listened as local leaders told theirs.[45]

THE CULTURAL COLD WAR IN ASIA

The work of bringing Free Asia into existence and fostering South Korea's integration into it was taken up the agencies of the cultural Cold War as much as by the departments of State and Defense. By the "cultural Cold War," I mean the efforts by the US and other national governments to achieve political ends through social and cultural means. America's instruments for waging the cultural Cold War had their roots in the propaganda machinery of World War II and began developing from the late 1940s onward as a result of Truman's, and especially Eisenhower's, calls for information and psychological warfare campaigns.[46] NSC 48 laid the foundation for the cultural Cold War in Asia when it called for an information campaign that would generate "maximum support both at home and abroad" for US objectives in the region.[47] The cultural Cold War in Asia took off in 1954–56. In the wake of Stalin's death and the Korean War armistice in 1953, Cold War conflicts shifted onto a more ideological plane. At the Geneva conference in 1954 and Bandung in 1955, China launched a "peaceful coexistence" campaign designed to recast its revolutionary image into that of a responsible world power that posed no threat to its neighbors. Turning to strategies of diplomacy and persuasion, it set out to win the allegiance of Asia's neutral populations, assert its leadership of the emerging nonaligned movement, and divide the US from its allies. By 1955, Washington regarded China's cultural initiatives as a serious threat and began to ramp up its own efforts across the region, where Americans often felt themselves to be playing catch-up to communists' more sophisticated techniques. What followed, according to Gregg Brazinsky, was "all-out cultural warfare" in which the United States and China promoted their own "ideologically determined visions of global community with clearly defined adversaries that needed to be excluded."[48] The 1950s was thus a remarkably dynamic period in which competing, outside interventions in Asia's social and cultural spheres became widespread, often with long-term, transformative effects.

The cultural Cold War aimed to shape the consciousness of Asian populations, winning the hearts and minds of elites and masses alike. Washington waged it both overtly and covertly. The USIA, created in 1953 (and known as USIS overseas), became America's central instrument of the cultural Cold War, producing information and propaganda materials that were distributed globally and often identified as products of the American government.[49] The cultural Cold War was also waged in a less forthright manner. Kenneth Osgood has documented Eisenhower's "camouflaged" approach to propaganda, which entailed enlisting the services of a vast array of private individuals and groups to act as surrogates promoting American objectives. This strategy created a "private façade" that masked the involvement of American officials and obscured the propagandistic nature of the work being done. These seemingly private entities generally engaged in long-term information operations that sought to permanently shape the beliefs of artists, intellectuals, and other elites in the developing world. These "slow media" operations, as Osgood calls them, promoted an "ideology of freedom" that sought to inculcate the liberal ideals of democracy, individual rights, and personal responsibility. They also promoted internationalist values, such as universalism and religious faith, that encouraged a sense of engagement with other Free World peoples. These values were disseminated through a broad array of channels, including books, literary and political journals, educational and leadership exchange programs, and diverse people-to-people programs.[50]

The Asia Foundation was Washington's primary "camouflaged" entity waging the cultural Cold War in Asia, and one of the most important instruments working to bring Free Asia into existence. An ostensibly private philanthropic organization, the Asia Foundation (TAF) was a CIA front organization, one of the most expansive created during the early years of the Cold War. The CIA financed covert operations around the world in part by funneling large amounts of money through private foundations, such as Ford, Rockefeller, and Carnegie.[51] With TAF, it created its own foundation. TAF played a singular role in the cultural Cold War in Asia: alone among US agencies, it had as one of its core objectives the fostering of bonds between Free Asian nations by stimulating exchange and cooperation across national borders.[52] The Asia Foundation started life at the height of the Korean War in 1951 as the Committee for a Free Asia (CFA), a name that helped solidify the Cold War meanings of that phrase. Created and fully funded by the CIA, its secret mission was to engage in "psychological warfare in the informational field." It was designed to "have the freedom and flexibility to do things the government would like to see done but which it chose not to do or could not do directly."[53] As with many other front organizations created in the late 1940s and 1950s, the inspiration for the CFA was derived, in part, from the Soviet Union's Popular Front strategy of the 1930s: the CIA admired the Left's ability to mobilize large groups of ordinary people on behalf of an internationalist agenda by tapping into their particular interests.[54] The CFA soon attracted criticism for its stridently anticommunist tone, however, and in 1953–54 the CIA relaunched it as the Asia Foundation under the more sophisticated leadership of Robert Blum, a seasoned intelligence officer with close ties to agency director Allen Dulles.[55]

The Asia Foundation was headquartered in San Francisco, where a staff led by Blum and James L. Stewart, the director of operations, oversaw a network of branch offices across Free Asia, each of which was headed by an American "representative" and supported by local employees. The representatives, many of whom had missionary backgrounds or prior careers in journalism or with government agencies such as USIS, had a good deal of autonomy in how they allocated funds, although the San Francisco office and CIA headquarters kept close tabs on all activities. By 1956, the Asia Foundation had offices in thirteen localities, stretching along the "arc of free Asia" from Afghanistan in the West to Japan in the East.[56]

TAF focused on nurturing Asian initiatives. Blum and the local representatives provided resources for individuals and organizations that were working towards suitably noncommunist goals. The Foundation made direct grants of money, provided equipment and supplies, encouraged private American organizations to assist their Asian counterparts, and offered advice and moral support.[57] While TAF provided most of this support openly, it sought to keep its Asian beneficiaries, rather than itself, in the foreground. TAF had a relatively modest budget: $150,000 in 1951, $1.4 million in 1952, $3.9 million in 1953, $3.1 million in 1954, $5.1 million in 1955, $5.6 million in 1956, $6.5 in 1957, and $6.8 million in 1958.[58] It typically made small grants—anywhere from a few hundred to fifty thousand dollars—directly to Asian organizations, and it generally provided seed money to get a project launched or interim funds to tide over a rough patch, rather than ongoing funding. In keeping with its commitment to capitalist democracy, it aimed to stimulate enterprises that could go on to become self-sustaining. As a result, it gave grants to thousands of recipients across Asia. Unlike USIS, TAF did not produce or dictate content. It sought to stimulate politically sympathetic local practices rather than use local instruments to disseminate American-produced content. Once it decided an organization or individual was worth supporting, it generally maintained a hands-off approach; its ideological work was in the choice of whom to support, not in micromanaging what they did. The foundation typically made grants in response to direct application from Asian individuals and organizations, although it sometimes fostered the creation of a group if it found a compelling program area that did not have adequate institutional support.

The ultimate objective of TAF's philanthropy, according to the CIA, was to "insure political developments in host countries favorable to the United States." To this end, TAF also functioned as an intelligence-gathering operation: through its extensive contacts with Asia's social, cultural, and political leaders, it collected information "not otherwise available to the Agency" and passed it on to the CIA through a steady flow of reports. The CIA relished the "depth of access" the foundation enjoyed and in 1964 gloated that no communist government had among its assets "an independently-chartered organization with capital and personnel capable of making such wide and varied impact throughout Asia." The Asia Foundation's "image, flexibility and effectiveness," exulted the agency, "appear to be unique."[59]

The Asia Foundation made its first foray into Korea in 1951 when it delivered a thousand tons of newsprint for textbook publishing. It established a Seoul office in 1954, and was soon disbursing about $200,000 a year to support a wide range of projects, directing its resources towards intellectuals and the fields of education, culture, and communication.[60] The office was run by a series of representatives who served relatively short terms: Philip Rowe, who died suddenly in office from polio (1954–55); Mary Walker, who stepped in as acting representative (1955–56); Lawrence G. Thompson (1957–58); and John E. (Jack) James (1958–60). They were assisted by six full-time Korean staff members, including program advisor Cho Tong-jae and program consultant Cho Pung-youn.[61]

TAF's Seoul representatives worked to inculcate a Cold War cosmopolitan worldview among postcolonial Koreans, in part by facilitating their entry into transnational networks. The foundation was deeply concerned that Japanese colonialism had left Korea a provincial and isolated nation, and so it devoted a great deal of energy to fostering ties between Korea and other Free World countries. TAF pledged to support projects that promoted "Korean understanding of the modern world, its goals, and its ideologies," that encouraged "Korean ties with the Free World," and that facilitated the "exchange of Korean and other Free World experience."[62] The Seoul office targeted many of its grants in order to bring this worldview into existence. While the Korean government closely controlled overseas travel by its citizens in an effort to limit the outflow of hard currency, TAF representatives enthusiastically supported overseas travel within Free Asia and the Free World. TAF regarded such travel as essential for ending Korea's historical isolation, for enabling Koreans to learn about other cultures, and for making Korea known to the larger world. Travel to international conferences received abundant support. In the 1950s TAF sent South Koreans to intellectual and professional gatherings across Asia, Western Europe, and the United States. These conferences helped knit South Korea into the Free World—and bind the Free World together— via institutional and personal networks, as members of its educated elite joined international civic and professional organizations. A broad spectrum of people were drawn into these networks, including scholars, teachers, writers, scientists, lawyers, Buddhists, Christians, Girl Scouts, musicians, and farmers. In facilitating the travels of South Koreans across the Free World, the Asia Foundation helped fulfill the NSC's recommendation to cultivate political and moral support for Korea among other nations and to develop Korea's own sense of belonging to a "community of interest" among noncommunist peoples.[63]

The political goal of binding South Korea to the Free World intersected with the social goals of modernization, and led Washington to invest heavily in inculcating among prominent Koreans a strong sense of connection to America. Washington cultivated emerging leaders by immersing them directly in American life. The State Department Leadership Grants program, the International Cooperation Administration, the Defense Department, and numerous private foundations sent thousands of Koreans to the United States to experience democratic capitalism and American-style modernity firsthand. Rising politicians observed Congress and state legislatures in action, newly minted officers received advanced military training, and over forty-seven hundred Korean students enrolled in American universities. Hundreds of professionals from the worlds of media, education, engineering, agriculture, and medicine traveled to the US for instruction and observation, staying anywhere from a few weeks to several months.[64] These programs cultivated an educated elite that identified with the United States and embraced many of its liberal values, on the premise that these leaders would influence the views of the majority population.

The waging of the cultural Cold War in Korea, like its political and military counterparts, had as one of its core objectives the enmeshment of South Korea into an array of Free Asian and Free World networks. While the vast majority of Koreans were rural peasants with little substantive contact with the world beyond their country's borders, thousands of educated Koreans participated in transnational activities that spanned oceans and continents. Through the efforts of Koreans and Americans alike, Cold War cosmopolitanism emerged as a vitally important dimension of elite postwar society.

2

———

Cold War Cosmopolitan Feminism

When Han Hyung-mo's film *A Jealousy* opened in May of 1960, it was the rare Korean film to focus on a female same-sex romantic relationship. The film explores the bond between Jaesoon (Moon Jung-suk), who lives with her brother and his family, and Kum (Jeon Gye-hyeon), a college student who has lived with them since losing her parents in the Korean War. Jaesoon and Kum are "S-sisters," which was the term used in Korea (and Japan) for an intimate, although not necessarily sexual, relationship between women. (The *S* reportedly derived from either *shojyo*, the Japanese word for girl, or from sex.) Historically, these relationships began developing in Korea in the 1910s and 1920s in the new, modern spaces of missionary-run women's schools and colleges.[1] These passionate relationships, which typically involved pairings of older and younger students or teachers and students, remained common in the postwar era and were understood to be distinct from those between best friends and adopted or sworn sisters.[2] *A Jealousy* suggests a desire for, if not the fact of, physical intimacy when Jaesoon (*S unni*, or S-older sister) invites Kum (*S tongsaeng*, or S-younger sister) to spend the night in her bed, and Jaesoon's brother explicitly raises the issue of lesbianism. The film's dramatic conflict revolves around Jaesoon's increasing jealousy as a man begins to court Kum: the intensity of her feelings prompts both passionate declarations of love ("I'll love you until I die, Kum. . . . We're one body, a body that can't ever be separated") and acts of physical violence (she tries to strangle Kum in order to prevent her marriage) (figure 3). Narratively, *A Jealousy* delegitimizes Jaesoon's desire, presenting it as a form of mental illness caused by her experience of being raped during the Korean War and bookending the film with scenes in a hospital where Jaesoon has been committed and ultimately cured.

32

FIGURE 3. Moon Jung-suk and Jeon Gye-hyeon in Han Hyung-mo's lesbian drama *A Jealousy*. (Courtesy KOFA)

More important, perhaps, than the film's dismissal of lesbian desire is its forthright expression of feminist ideas. In her dialogue, Jaesoon critiques the patriarchal family as an institution of "slavery" for women and suggests that talented women should pursue careers instead of marriage—ideas that Korean feminists first raised in the 1920s and 1930s and were now expressing with increased authority. In one scene Jaesoon debates Kum's future with her brother, the head of the family, and proposes that Kum continue her musical training and become "a wonderful musician." When her brother suggests that Kum become a "wonderful housewife" instead, Jaesoon explodes: "That's all you can come up with? After all I've gone through to raise my darling Kum into a brilliant artist, do you really think it's right for her to become a slave of a family?" Jaesoon extends her critique of heterosexual marriage in subsequent scenes, when she sneers, "I just can't think it would make a woman happy to become a slave of a man and live only to serve him all day long," and later, "I can't give Kum to men who treat women like slaves and look down on them." Seeking to break with the Confucian past, Jaesoon aspires to save her beloved S-sister from the exploitation that has defined Korean women for generations: "I just can't have

Kum suffer the same treatment our mothers and grandmothers received from men until now."[3] Her proposed solution is to set up a separate household in which she and Kum live together, alone. It doesn't happen. While Jaesoon can envision new possibilities for women, she can't quite bring them into existence.[4]

In articulating these possibilities, *A Jealousy* gestures towards the tremendous changes taking place among women during the 1950s, as the postcolonial, postwar, and Cold War forces remaking Korean society reached deep into their daily lives. This chapter takes up social history, and traces how the ideals and practices of Cold War cosmopolitanism intersected with Korean women's lives. Women across the social spectrum, mostly urban, engaged with the Free World as it was manifest both within and beyond Korea's borders, and some of them absorbed its professed liberal values of democracy, equality, and freedom. One result was the articulation of a "Cold War cosmopolitan feminism," which sought to emancipate women from the patriarchal constraints of Korea's Confucian heritage by claiming for them the liberal ideal of individual freedom. The period also saw the articulation of a counter-discourse of patriarchal cultural nationalism, which identified some of those same traditions as the essence of a Koreanness that must be preserved against foreign encroachments. The tensions between cultural nationalism and cosmopolitanism, like those between nation building and bloc building, helped define the period out of which Han's style emerged.

WOMEN AND SOCIAL MODERNITY

In the postwar 1950s, American and Korean modernizers alike encouraged Korean women to craft broader lives for themselves. Modernity "understood as the birth of the individual," as Cho Haejoang writes, was promoted to women as well as men. In Korea as elsewhere in the developing world, the "emancipation of women" was often regarded as an essential step into modernity, a feminine corollary to the drive to "make men modern," and self-declared "modern" women pushed against what they regarded as the "feudal" patriarchal constraints embedded in Confucianism.[5] This push was often couched in the language of individualism, that core tenet of liberal thought and "one of the most difficult things to recognize, either ideologically or institutionally, in the Confucian tradition."[6] "Individualism," according to Stevi Jackson, Jieyu Liu, and Juhyun Woo, has long been "problematic in East Asia. It is not universally embraced as the inalienable right of the sovereign individual, as in Western philosophy, but as something more troubling and full of contradictions" that threatens to disrupt a widely desired social harmony.[7] Claims of female individuality were, as a result, often contested by self-proclaimed guardians of Korea's cultural identity. The "female individual" thus became an ambivalent incarnation of Korean modernity: she embodied ideals that were desired by some as a pathway into a better future, and feared by others as a threat to an essential Koreanness that was in the process of being restored in the wake of colonialism.

Korea was home to the strictest form of Confucianism in East Asia, and while orthodox neo-Confucianism had been under attack in Korea since the late nineteenth century as an obstacle to modernization and the development of a national consciousness, its ideals still carried weight as the foundation for everyday life.[8] This was nowhere more apparent than in the realm of gender and family relations. "The Confucian ethic," write Jackson et al.,

> privileges order and hierarchy, the needs of the collective over those of the individual, filial piety and women's obedience to men. It thus leaves little scope for women's autonomy or for expressions of sexuality that are not harnessed to the needs of men and of procreation—especially the production of male children who will perpetuate the family. It has been described as "the most patriarchal of all the major normative systems of the world."[9]

The principle of absolute sexual difference (*namnyŏ-yubyŏl*), for instance, historically consigned women to the inner quarters of the home and to the roles of wife and mother, while allotting to men the exterior rooms and the ability to enter the public sphere of business, education, and the law at will. The principle of "honored men, debased women" (*namjon-yŏbi*), in turn, dictated women's inferiority to men in all areas of life, while the principle of the "three obediences" (*samjong*) called for the submission of daughter to father, wife to husband, and widow to son. Self-denial lay at the heart of the feminine virtues of submissiveness, chastity, modesty, and self-sacrifice. Together they rendered female suffering noble. After a woman's marriage, the interests of her husband's family became paramount. A wife was valued for her ability to produce male heirs to continue her husband's lineage and as a source of cheap household labor. Her most important relationship was with her mother-in-law, whom she was expected to serve unquestioningly; an emotionally close relationship with her husband was neither encouraged nor valued. Marriages were understood, however, to endure beyond the death of the husband, and widow remarriage was taboo. A woman who committed one of the "seven disobediences" (*ch'ilgŏ*)—which included disrespect to parents-in-law, failure to bear a son, and adultery—left herself vulnerable to divorce, which entailed losing all rights to her children. The ideal of "wise mother, good wife" (*hyŏnmo yangch'ŏ*) was a modern variation of these patriarchal ideals that incorporated elements of Christian missionary and Japanese colonial ideologies and focused on a woman's role within a nuclear family.[10]

Taken together, these Confucian principles restricted every dimension of a woman's life. Lacking even an individual name until the early twentieth century, a woman possessed no social identity outside of her family relationships and roles. Her space for autonomous action was severely constrained, both physically and socially. No respectable woman could live an independent existence, or establish an independent household, outside of a relationship to father, husband, or son. "According to Confucian ideology," writes Hyun Jeong Min, "a woman seeking to fulfill her aspirations could destroy the peace and harmony of the social world."[11] Female submission served as the foundation for a smoothly functioning social order. The existence of a "female individual"—a woman in charge of her own life and in possession of a social identity separate from her family—was structurally impossible.

This ideal of womanhood was challenged by Christian missionaries beginning in the late nineteenth century and began to fray in the 1920s and 1930s. The Korean *modeon geol* was a local incarnation of the global "modern girl" who emerged in the United States, Europe, Asia, and Africa after World War I and who represented that era's aspirations and anxieties about modernity. Dressed in Western fashion and embracing liberal Western ideas, she was a largely discursive figure who existed primarily in the pages of newspapers and magazines, where she raised the possibility of an autonomous female self and was lambasted as an irresponsible consumer. The New Woman was more firmly rooted in social reality. A small group of educated, urban, and often Christian young women, New Women were Korea's first-generation feminists who challenged Korea's patriarchal social order head-on. They articulated visions of female liberation that they sought to put into practice by creating women's social organizations, publishing women's magazines, and taking up professional careers.[12]

Confucian gender roles were further challenged by the enormous scale of death and injury during the Korean War, which hastened the evolution of women's roles and led to the emergence (mostly in Seoul) of what I am calling the "woman-in-public" as a postwar social type. The social dislocations of the war propelled women in unprecedented numbers into the public sphere and into domains of life that had previously been the preserve of men. This process began when women were mobilized to replace the labor of the millions of men who were fighting. Women enlisted in the army, where they worked in administrative and support positions, and performed sexual labor in government-sanctioned "comfort houses" and dance halls. In the civilian labor force they worked as clerks, policewomen, factory laborers, and office ladies; nearly half a million women became small vendors, selling food and other necessities on the streets.[13] In 1951–52 about 60 percent of the female working-age population was engaged in labor, primarily in agriculture and fisheries, which marked a major increase over the 28.4 percent employment rate in 1949.[14]

While many of these women returned to their homes at the war's conclusion, in 1958 35 percent of the adult female population participated in the labor force, and women comprised 46 percent of the total economically active population.[15] A greater variety of women worked than during the colonial era, including widows, older women, and some married women, alongside single young women.[16] While most of these women had working-class and agricultural jobs, they also occupied a wider range of white-collar positions than in previous decades: the 1955 census counted 10,026 professional, managerial, and clerical workers in Seoul alone; five years later journalist Chung Choong-ryang reported a national tally of 777 female doctors, 1,407 pharmacists, 3,602 nurses, 3 members of the House of Representatives, 3 current and former cabinet ministers, 3 presidents of women's universities, and 1 attorney.[17] Most women worked out of necessity, often taking on the role of breadwinner to support their parents, in-laws, and children following a male relative's wartime injury or death. Others, however, worked out of choice, seizing the opportunity to pursue a dream or achieve an unprecedented measure of personal autonomy. As Sujin Han has written, "the conspicuous presence of women in the public arena of work" was one of the defining features of the postwar period, and the working woman became a vigorous topic of debate, as intellectuals, officials, and workers themselves explored the implications of women's movement into public economic life. Women's work was often tinged with nationalist overtones in public discourse, especially during the war years, and numerous commentators presented women's entry into the work force as a sign of the country's modernization and democratization. Working women themselves often regarded paid employment as a recognition of their individuality and full humanity.[18]

The woman-in-public was also a product of the Cold War, which is to say that her emergence was deeply affected by the presence of tens of thousands of American soldiers inside the country. The work of sustaining this large population made the US military a major employer of Korean women. The US armed forces hired women to work on virtually every major post as maids, cooks, waitresses, dishwashers, receptionists, typists, secretaries, clerks, and cashiers. Many more women found work in the eighteen camptowns that ringed major military bases. Enabled and regulated by US military officials, camptowns were liminal contact zones composed of businesses that catered to GIs, such as bars, nightclubs, pool halls, and souvenir shops. Camptowns were important sites of economic activity that generated essential foreign exchange for use in other areas of the economy, and were thus tolerated and even encouraged by the ROK government. They were also what Seungsook Moon has called "virtually colonized spaces" in which US military authority superseded South Korean sovereignty.[19] As numerous scholars have explored, camptowns generated a dark version of cosmopolitan modernity characterized by militarized prostitution.[20] Driven by poverty, many Korean women found work in the booming sex trade, and in 1958, an estimated 180,000 sex workers—or more than half of Korea's estimated total of 300,000—catered to American soldiers. These women, often comparatively affluent, were among the first to embrace American fashions, learn English, and master Western social practices such as social dancing, and they served as vanguard agents who carried bits of Americanized modernity into Korean society at large.[21] They also became potent symbols of the vast imbalance of power between the United States and Korea and of the pervasiveness of American hegemony. Frequent targets of American violence and Korean hostility, they contributed to the ambivalence many Koreans felt about the American presence inside their country.[22]

Women in South Korea and across the Free World were targeted by American agencies waging the cultural Cold War as a key demographic whose allegiance needed to be won (along with students, workers, intellectuals, and educated elites). The USIS, according to Kenneth Osgood, "drafted elaborate policy guidance papers" that focused on women and the theme of gender across media:

> Women in positions to act as "channels for political information," including leaders, members of organizations, wives of important officials, and university students, were especially targeted. USIS posts devised a number of tactics to reach women directly. They presented books and magazines to women leaders and organizations, hosted special films for women, produced radio programs for female audiences, taught English classes for women, organized seminars and discussions with "outstanding American women," and prepared exhibits and events at USIS libraries and information centers designed to appeal to women. Information officers placed articles of interest to female readers in local newspapers and magazines. Special USIS mailing lists sent information material to women leaders of civic, political, and charitable organizations. Such efforts sought to "assure [foreign] women that American women have interests and goals in common with their own" and "to encourage on a basic human level an identification of the local woman with American women."

Through these efforts the USIS aimed to win the sympathies of women so that they, in turn, could exert pressure on their husbands and their governments "to act in ways commensurate with U.S. interests."[23] The agency disseminated representations of modern American women across the Free World, projecting them as feminized—and thus nonthreatening—symbols of the United States and as objects of identification. In response to socialist promises of gender equality in a revolutionary society, it promoted a vision of women as both domestic denizens and active participants in public life. While the USIS emphasized that American women "lived full, happy lives as mothers and homemakers," it also depicted American women as playing "an increasingly important part in political, economic, and community life." USIS materials portrayed women as community activists involved in clubs and civic organizations and highlighted their status as professionals, noting women's advancement in fields formerly reserved for men. It singled out "outstanding women" who served as congresswomen, senators, state legislators, governors, and presidential cabinet members.[24] Such representations were widely distributed in Korea where, in 1961, USIS films screened in three-quarters of all Korean theaters and reached an annual audience of 76.5 million viewers—in a country with a total population of about 25 million.[25]

Several civilian American agencies actively facilitated the movement of Korean women into public life and encouraged the forging of cosmopolitan bonds with other women in the Free World. The State Department, for one, considered Korean women's assumption of "increasingly important positions outside the home" to be "a most healthy development."[26] While the ranks of publicly prominent South Korean women were limited, the State Department sent a number of them to the

United States for extended tours, including a group of high school principals in 1955, the writer Kim Mal-bong (known as the Pearl S. Buck of Korea) in 1955, and the journalist Chung Choong-ryang in 1960. As part of their grants, recipients wrote and spoke extensively about their experiences in America, educating other Korean women and suggesting ways that Korea could modernize along American lines. The State Department reported that Kim Mal-bong obtained materials for five novels during her four-month tour and published multiple articles about "the equality of women with men in American life."[27]

The Asia Foundation also targeted women and early on began funding women's associations, conferences, and leadership training programs. TAF president Robert Blum was particularly eager to develop a cosmopolitan perspective among Asian women. In 1954 he hired an American women's organization expert whose mission was "to arouse greater women's participation in civic affairs in one country and then encourage them to have links with activities of women's groups in several countries." Blum hoped this expert would stimulate "greater intra-Asian civic consciousness as well as generating greater mutual cooperation, respect and understanding among Asians themselves and Asians and Westerners."[28] The Seoul office increased its attention to women under the leadership of Mary Walker, who in 1955 stepped in as acting representative after the sudden death of Philip Rowe and became the first woman to head a TAF office. Arriving from TAF's Tokyo office with the title of administrative assistant, Walker carried a double load of both programming and administrative duties. In 1956 she hired a local female consultant to produce "a good, objective survey of Korean women's activities and problems," and used her report to encourage "a substantial program of private activity in women's civic and community service groups."[29]

TAF's efforts were complemented by the Committee of Correspondence—another "camouflaged" CIA-funded organization—whose mission was "to seek out and train women leaders" across the Free World and to help them "take their rightful places in the world." The Committee, which was launched in 1952 and run by a dozen women in New York, established a global network of letter-writing correspondents and hosted international women's workshops that facilitated engagement with the Free World. The first two workshops, held in 1956 and 1957, involved professional women and leaders from across Asia, many of whom went on to host additional workshops in their home countries. The Committee solicited the participation of educated Korean women and enabled them to forge connections to their counterparts in Asia, Africa, the Middle East, Latin America, Europe, and the United States. These initiatives increased Korean women's sense of themselves as members of a global community and fostered a cosmopolitan structure of feeling, one that Korean journalist Chung Choong-ryang described as a sentiment of "true friendship surpassing the national and racial boundaries."[30]

None of these agencies was promoting a feminist agenda per se, and the furthering of US interests was always their ultimate objective. Yet their representations and activities intersected with a society in transition, at a moment when South Korean women were reimagining their social roles.

COLD WAR COSMOPOLITAN FEMINISM

The waging of the cultural Cold War and the promotion of modernization in South Korea were enabling conditions for the development of what I am calling "Cold War cosmopolitan feminism." Feminism is a capacious term that has meant different things at different historical moments. I am using it here to refer to a body of ideas and practices that critique women's systemic oppression under patriarchy, call for women's liberation, advocate for social and legal reforms, and identify and model alternative forms of womanhood. The idea of Cold War cosmopolitan feminism is a variation on Mire Koikari's "Cold War imperial feminism." Koikari, writing about postwar Japan, has explored how Washington's democratization efforts led to the expansion of Japanese women's legal rights in the 1947 constitution and beyond. For Koikari, the push for liberation from what Japanese feminists regarded as "feudal" constraints was inseparable from the assertion of US hegemony in East Asia and was thus continuous with older colonial discourses.[31] While US occupation officials did not intervene so extensively in Korea's legal regulation of women, Korean feminists were likewise enabled by Cold War initiatives. These initiatives—which, as in Japan, were instrumental towards the achievement of US political objectives in Asia—legitimated local feminists' challenges to Confucian values and social structures. The notion of Cold War cosmopolitan feminism expands on Koikari's formulation by foregrounding the embrace by Korean feminists of internationalist discourses of universal rights and democratic freedoms; it also highlights how the Cold War facilitated Korean feminists' entrance into international networks of women.

At the core of Cold War cosmopolitan feminism is women's claim to the status of individual, and the conceptual linkage of that status to the noncommunist world beyond Korea's borders. Cold War liberalism validated the idea of women as autonomous human beings with identities distinct from their familial roles—a concept that is foundational to feminism, and deeply problematic within orthodox Confucianism. Like previous generations of reformers in Korea and across East Asia, postwar feminists looked outside the nation for ideals they needed to make changes within the nation. Feminism was thus closely intertwined with cosmopolitanism in the 1950s, and existed in some tension with a patriarchal cultural nationalism that was rooted in masculinist ideas of Korean essence.

Feminism and nationalism had developed interdependently in Korea, both fueled in part by Christian missionaries. Early nationalists in the 1890s–1910s had advocated for the reform of Confucian gender norms as an essential step in the creation of a modern nation-state, and early feminists had supported the nationalist movement as a move towards their emancipation. Yet as Hyaeweol Choi has shown, male intellectuals ultimately regarded women's concerns as secondary to national ones, and they ended up supporting a vision of modernity in which women remained subordinate to men and served the nation by tending to sons and husbands from within the domestic sphere. In the 1920s, this tension erupted into "head-on confrontations between vocal feminist women and male intellectuals," as educated New Women used their access to the public sphere to advocate for women's individuality and male intellectuals dismissed them "as selfish, bourgeois, and unpatriotic." According to Choi, colonial feminists' "emphasis on 'self' was discursively denigrated by androcentric and nationalistic discourses that privileged nation, family, and men."[32] The challenge feminists posed to a male-centered social order was too profound to be easily accommodated. This tension erupted again in the 1950s, as postcolonial nationalists sought to restore what Chungmoo Choi has called Korea's "national masculinity."[33]

HELEN KIM AND LEE TAI-YOUNG

We can see articulations of Cold War cosmopolitan feminism in the lives of two of Korea's most prominent women-in-public: Helen Kim (Kim Hwallan), president of Ewha Womans University, and Lee Tai-young, Korea's first female lawyer. Kim and Lee were native modernizers who greatly expanded the possibilities for Korean womanhood. Both were mature New Women who came to consciousness of women's oppression in the 1920s and 1930s, survived the upheavals of the Korean War, and assumed positions of public authority in the late 1940s and 1950s. While these two middle-aged women often conformed visually to traditional gender norms by wearing *hanbok* and chignon hairstyles, they had achieved the goals of personal and professional autonomy that they had fought for as youth. More importantly, they used their unprecedented professional accomplishments to bring their long-standing calls for women's liberation into the mainstream.[34] Claiming liberal ideals for Korean women, and finding support in Cold War institutions, they challenged the patriarchal Confucian family structure and the "traditional" values that undergirded it to claim new freedoms for Korean women.

Helen Kim (1899–1970) was one of the most influential Korean women of the twentieth century (figure 4). She shaped Korean society for decades as an educator, civic leader, and political actor. One of Korea's first feminists and a committed cosmopolitan, she saw herself as bound to other women both within and beyond the borders of Korea. Born in 1899 and raised as a Christian, Kim experienced a vision as a young woman in which God revealed "a big dug-out moat where a mass of Korean women were crying out for help with their hands outstretched from the haze and confusions that covered them." In the wake of this vision, she dedicated herself to "the emancipation of the women of the world."[35] Kim was an early advocate of Korea's modernization, and like other feminists around the world she used the language of slavery to call attention to women's subjugation.[36] She graduated in

FIGURE 4. Helen Kim, president of Ewha Womans University, in the series "12 Modern Korean Women," *Yŏwŏn*, August 1956.

1918 from the missionary-run Ewha Womans College, Korea's only institution of higher education for women, which Hyaeweol Choi has characterized as the "symbolic center for new womanhood." Kim notes in her autobiography that she was briefly active in the anticolonial nationalist movement of the 1910s, but she soon decided to focus her energies on women's education.[37] She bobbed her hair, helped found *Geunuhoe*, one of Korea's first feminist organizations, and became a career woman when she took a teaching position at Ewha. Encouraged to study in the United States by her American female missionary teachers, she earned a bachelor's degree at Ohio Wesleyan University in 1924, a master's degree in philosophy at Boston University in 1925, and became the first Korean woman to earn a PhD, from Columbia University's Teacher's College, in 1931.[38]

Kim became a builder of women's institutions, nurturing organizations that put her emancipatory ideals into practice and gave them a solid foundation in society. She was a founder of Korea's first feminist magazine, *Sin yoja* (The modern woman), in 1920; organizer of the Korean branch of the YWCA in 1922; and the first Korean president of Ewha College in 1939, after Japanese colonial officials expelled American missionaries. After liberation in 1945, she served as advisor to the US military occupation government on women's education, ran for election to the Constitutional Assembly in 1948 to encourage women to exercise their new right to vote, and engineered the transition of Ewha from a college into Korea's first university. As president of Ewha Womans University, she significantly expanded women's access to higher education, physically enlarging the campus and increasing enrollment from just nine hundred students in 1945 to more than eight thousand in 1961, making it the largest women's university in Asia. Active in many arenas of public life, Kim served as a leader of numerous religious, political, and educational organizations, including the YWCA, the Red Cross, the Korean Association of University Women, and the Korean Christian Teachers' Association. Through these institutions, she enabled the higher education of thousands of women and facilitated their participation in public life.[39]

Helen Kim publicly promoted the radical idea of woman's selfhood. In the past, she said, "a young woman was considered a slave, a wife and a mother, but never an individual." Kim's goal at Ewha was "not only to educate so that women can take their rightful place in social, political and national life, but to establish their individuality." She took as her goal the "humanization of women," which meant helping them achieve their full potential as human beings unfettered by patriarchal constraints. Personally and professionally, Kim challenged the Confucian principles of female inferiority and submission. Defying her own father's authority, she rejected marriage and motherhood and chose a life of professional work and activism instead.[40] Believing that marriage was incompatible with a career, she taught her students to choose one or the other and was known to express disapproval (as Jaesoon would do in Han's *A Jealousy*) whenever a particularly talented young woman chose to marry.[41]

Kim also apparently achieved what Jaesoon so fervently desired: a life partnership with another woman. After returning from the United States with her PhD, Kim entered into what was known in America as a "Boston marriage": a long-term, committed relationship with a woman who shared her home and her life. Such "passionate friendships" among educated women were, like S-sisters in Korea and Japan, socially acceptable in late-nineteenth- and early-twentieth-century America, and they were particularly common in elite women's colleges.[42] Kim and her partner, Lee Jong Ai, had been students together at Ewha, although their relationship did not begin until Kim, a few years older, became a teacher there. Lee divorced her husband after an arranged marriage in which she suffered, according to Kim, "the typical unhappiness of Korean women," and with Kim's help got a scholarship to study nursing in Hawaii. (She would later attend Columbia University, also with Kim's help, to study nursing administration.) After her return in 1931 Lee moved into Kim's home. Lee took care of Kim's personal affairs even as she pursued her own career, enabling Kim to focus on her work, and her personal warmth reportedly offset Kim's often curt demeanor. They maintained a loving and devoted partnership—what Kim called "a world of 'us'"—for thirty years, until Lee's death in 1954.[43]

Helen Kim participated in multiple distinct border-crossing networks. Her decision to accept the presidency of Ewha in 1939 enmeshed her in Japan's imperial network. Kim's feminism sometimes superseded her nationalism: she spoke out publicly in support of colonial rule and encouraged Korean women to seize the opportunities that the Japanese war effort presented, actions that in recent years have caused her to be branded as a collaborator and traitor. Like many colonial elites, however, Kim occupied a gray area in which the distinction between collaboration and nationalism was not always clear-cut, and as a feminist she often prioritized women's needs over a nationalism defined in patriarchal terms. According to Hyaeweol Choi, "collaborating with the (colonial) state was understood as a way to broaden the scope of women's work and influence."[44] Kim's vision of female autonomy drew strength from her sustained engagement with the world beyond Korea's borders. She was the product of a missionary Christianity that transcended the colonial divide and that enmeshed women in global networks of faith and education. She traveled widely in Europe, Asia, Africa, and Latin America, experiences that gave her a sense of deep connection to "the whole world—past, present and future" and led her to believe in the existence of a "Woman's World" composed of capable women leaders from across the globe.[45]

In the 1950s, Kim put her cosmopolitanism in the service of the postcolonial nation. During Rhee's presidency, she became a regular facilitator of Korea's dialogue with the West, serving on numerous delegations to the United Nations beginning in 1949, working as director of the Office of Public Information during the Korean War, and in 1950 founding *The Korea Times*, an English-language daily newspaper aimed at US forces in Korea. As she had during the Pacific War, she hailed the Korean War as a modernizing force for women, one that would enable them to "abandon old customs and ideas" and become, in her word, "cosmopolitans."[46]

Helen Kim was likewise enmeshed in transnational Cold War networks, both US- and Korea-centered. Americans regarded her as an ally in the dual projects of nation building and bloc building, and several US institutions underwrote her work. Kim had a close relationship with the Asia Foundation. Blum, who appreciated "the very energetic way" in which she cooperated with TAF's mission, dined at Kim's home when he visited South Korea in 1956, and Kim, in turn, awarded an honorary Ewha doctorate to TAF representative Mary Walker.[47] TAF supported numerous organizations under Kim's leadership. It financed a program to train female "professional leaders" to run rural branches of the YWCA and provided funds for women associated with Kim's organizations to travel across the Free World; she, in turn, served on the board of the Social Science Research Library, a major TAF initiative.[48] The USIA featured Kim in *Free World* magazine, its highest-circulating publication in Asia, lauding her as a "feminist" who has "guided and inspired" Korean women for more than half a century.[49] The Voice of America featured her in a 1954 radio program, giving her a bullhorn to proclaim that the Korean woman, who had traditionally held power only "within the four walls of her home," was now "proud to take [her] place alongside the men of Korea in rebuilding their country."[50] The Committee of Correspondence enlisted her as well, and Kim wrote numerous letters keeping women around the Free World abreast of developments at Ewha.[51] Helen Kim put her feminism in the service of Syngman Rhee's transnational networks as well, working with the Asian People's Anti-Communist League (APACL), which pledged to "mobilize all freedom-loving women against communism."[52] Kim served as vice-chair of the Korean branch of the regional organization, attended the planning meeting for the second annual conference in Manila in 1956, and that same year served as vice-chair of the APACL-sponsored Asian Youth and Students' Anti-Communist Conference in Seoul.[53] This latter conference required 40 percent of the delegates to be women and hosted a women's committee that called attention to women's lack of equality across Korean society.[54] In all these capacities, Kim's cosmopolitanism combined with her nationalism: she made South Korea visible to other members of the Free World, even as she worked to transform South Korea in keeping with Western standards of social modernization.

Lee Tai-young (1914–98), South Korea's first female lawyer and a close friend of Kim's, spearheaded the public conversation about Korean women's legal equality. She recognized that, to be truly accepted, women's claim to the status of individual needed to be secured in the domain of the law. Lee was an outspoken advocate for women's rights, and like Kim she was a colonial-era New Woman who reached a position of public authority in the 1950s. Born in 1914, Lee attended Ewha Womans College in the 1930s, where she studied under Kim and majored in home economics because, she said, she "wanted to liberate women from kimchee jars, beanpaste jars."[55] When her husband was jailed for anticolonial activities in the 1940s, Lee became her family's breadwinner, teaching at a girls' high school and selling handmade quilts on the street to keep her children and mother-in-law alive.[56] After liberation she enrolled in the law school at Seoul National University, which had just opened its doors to women. As a law student, she challenged norms about a married woman's exclusive service to her family: a thirty-two-year-old wife, mother, and daughter-in-law, she gave birth to her fourth child during her second year

FIGURE 5. Lee Tai-young, Korea's first female lawyer, in the series "12 Modern Korean Women," *Yŏwŏn*, July 1956.

of study and breastfed the baby between classes. In 1952, after sequestering herself away from her family to study, she became the first woman in Korean history to pass the bar exam and become a lawyer, a feat which landed her on the front page of the newspapers and prompted public celebrations at Ewha and elsewhere (figure 5).[57] (No other Korean woman would pass the bar exam for nearly twenty years.) Like Helen Kim, Lee was an institution builder. When she submitted her application for a judgeship, Syngman Rhee summarily rejected it, asserting that "It is neither the time nor the place yet for a woman on the bench." (Lee's status as the wife of opposition politician Jeong Il-hyeong was also an issue.) Unbowed, Lee in 1956 established the Korea Legal Aid Center for Family Relations, Korea's first-ever legal aid clinic, in which she dispensed advice to what her biographer and coworker described as "an endless queue of Korean women waiting 5,000 years to find a woman lawyer who would listen to their stories and give them help." And like Kim, Lee participated prominently in public life: throughout the 1950s she gave lectures, taught at and served as dean of Ewha's College of Law and Political Science, and wrote newspaper and magazine articles and books on women's legal rights. Her activities were widely covered by the press, which alternately celebrated her achievements and mocked her vision of modern womanhood.[58]

Lee Tai-young launched a sustained critique of the patriarchal family as the source of women's oppression and devoted her career to liberating Korean women from a system that rendered her a "slave" in her own home. Lee, like feminists around the world, embraced Norwegian playwright Henrik Ibsen's *A Doll's House* (1879) as a primer on modern womanhood. Ibsen's play became a touchstone in Korean debates about "the woman question" after being serialized in a daily Korean newspaper in 1921 (at the urging of the staff of *Sin yoja*, the feminist magazine of which Helen Kim was a founder) and staged for a public audience in Seoul in 1934.[59] Nora, the play's heroine, is a bourgeois woman who comes to consciousness of her domestic entrapment and leaves her husband, children, and home for an uncertain future. The play charts the birth of an individual female self that is not defined by familial ties. A key exchange takes place at the end of the play, when her husband Helmer reminds Nora of her "sacred duties" to himself and her children. Nora, in perhaps the play's most famous line, responds that she has a duty "to myself" that is just as sacred: "I believe that before all else, I am a human being, just as you are."[60] She then exits the house, closing the door behind her. This decision to prioritize her own needs over those of her family was a shocking—and for some, exhilarating—challenge to Confucian norms. Lee saw a universal truth in Ibsen's play. In a 1935 prize-winning speech delivered when she was a student at Ewha, Lee proclaimed that all Korean women were Noras:

> If the first-generation doll is Ibsen's Nora, then the second-generation doll is the Korean woman. Korean women must break free of the halter of patient submission. To this day Korean women have not been treated as human. They have been slaves, nothing more than property, of husbands. Why should Korean women content themselves with this fate? This has been because they have long been soaked in traditions and customs. Women of Korea must break free of this halter immediately. Before they are wives and mothers, they must be human beings, and they must receive equal treatment as men. Others will not give this to you—each Korean woman must search for it.

Lee urged Korean women to liberate themselves from their role as "slaves," to throw off centuries of oppressive custom and claim their status as full human beings who are equal to men. She pushed Ibsen's feminist icon in a perhaps more radical direction when she went on to suggest that women, rather than leaving home, should remake it to satisfy their own needs: a Korean Nora should make herself "master of the home" by "chasing Helmer, her disrespectful husband, out of the house."[61]

In later years Lee, who claimed that "the real movement for the emancipation of women began only after the Liberation in 1945," celebrated the mass entrance of women into the workforce during the Korean War as "a great female revolution," because it awakened women to their economic power and stimulated their interest in attendant legal protections, and she praised working wives and mothers as "warriors doing battle in society."[62] Similar to Helen Kim in her "Boston marriage," Lee modeled an alternative form of womanhood to the Confucian norm by maintaining a companionate marriage with a man who encouraged her professional ambitions. She became a working wife and mother who challenged the boundary between public and private spheres by occupying both of them. Lee recognized that real reform of the family required a shift in consciousness among men as well as changes in the law, and she gave a pair of aprons, one trimmed in pink and the other in blue, as wedding gifts to her law students to remind them that a happy marriage was created when husbands and wives worked together, even washing dishes.[63]

In her focus on the legal regulation of the family, Lee carried the core concerns of the New Woman into the postwar era. Colonial-era New Women, arguing that arranged marriage was the lynchpin to the suppression of women's individuality in favor of familial interests, had advocated for a woman's right to choose her marriage partners ("free love") and her right of divorce.[64] Lee's early activism focused on changing the adultery laws, which by holding only married women criminally accountable made possible the concubinage system, whereby married men could have multiple mistresses; the law was successfully revised in 1953 to hold married men and women equally culpable.[65] Lee next brought the issue of divorce into public visibility, making it the subject of her first book, *The Divorce System in Korea* (1957). Similar to Helen Kim, Lee expanded the ranks of the modern woman when she educated thousands of women about their legal rights—and lack thereof— within the patriarchal family structure.

Like Helen Kim, Lee Tai-young entered into Cold War transnational networks and received support from various US agencies. She sought and received the Asia Foundation's assistance in challenging the patriarchal family structure. The foundation deemed Lee's Legal Aid Center to be "a very active and promising" organization, one of only two that were "effectively working in the field of law," and in 1957–58 gave it a grant of several thousand dollars. The Foundation also made possible the publication of Lee's book on divorce through a grant of paper.[66] The State Department, in turn, encouraged Lee's cosmopolitan consciousness by means of a leader grant, and in 1957–58 she spent six months in the United States as part of a delegation of lawyers from around the Free World who were studying and observing American legal work. While at Southern Methodist University in Dallas, Lee spent time with local feminist lawyers and legal activists; twenty years later she established a legal clinic in Killeen, Texas, for Korean women married to servicemen stationed at Fort Hood. Lee made an effort to turn the instruments of US propaganda towards her own ends, as when she arranged an interview with the Voice of America while she was in the United States in order to exhort Korean lawmakers to support her feminist legal reforms.[67] She also belonged to the Committee of Correspondence and encouraged her graduate students studying law and international relations at Ewha to become correspondents as well.[68] Engagement with these American institutions enhanced Lee Tai-young's and Helen Kim's status within Korean society, allowing their voices to be more widely heard and their organizations to function more effectively.

Lee's most ambitious legal campaign centered on the revision of the Family Law, the part of the civil code that applied to domestic matters. The head-of-family system (*hojuje*) was at the heart of the Family Law; imported from Japan during the colonial period and embodying five hundred years of Confucian principles, it cemented women's inequality and dependency by limiting their legal rights regarding marriage, divorce, inheritance, property, and legal status. Lee led the drive to revise the Family Law. Drawing on the cosmopolitan language of universal human rights and modern constitutional law, she argued that the head-of-family system deprived women of their full humanity as well as the equality guaranteed them by the 1948 constitution. Between 1954 and 1957 Lee organized a Federation of Korean Women's Groups (the members of which were closely tied to international women's organizations and included two groups headed by Helen Kim) that submitted a draft law to the National Assembly proposing the abolition of the head-of-family system and lobbied tirelessly for its passage.[69]

Their proposed reform of the family law triggered a heated debate about the nature of Koreanness and the best route towards postcolonial nation building. Lee and her compatriots argued that the recognition of women's legal rights as individuals constituted an essential step towards Korean democracy and modernity. They saw the head-of-family system as key to an antiquated Confucian tradition that must be shed in order for the nation to move successfully into the future. Lee railed against patriarchy as an "old, evil custom" and lambasted the "feudal family" as an "anachronistic" institution that perpetuated female suffering by inscribing "deep pain" in the "bones" of half the nation's population.[70] Helen Kim's and Lee Tai-young's notion of Koreanness was forward- and outward-looking, grounded in a vision of a modern Korea that broadly embraced liberal Western norms, and they argued the case for legal reform from an internationalist perspective: if Korea was to join the world community as an equal member, it needed to uphold the principle of sexual equality throughout its legal system. As feminists, Kim, Lee, and the other members of the federation had something to gain from Cold War cosmopolitanism, which allowed them to assert a US-sanctioned ideal of Koreanness that was rooted in the ideals of democracy, modernity, and progress.

Conservatives pushed back strongly against Lee's efforts by mobilizing a cultural nationalist discourse that privileged the very patriarchal values that the federation sought to eradicate. According to legal scholar Ki-young Shin, defenders of the existing law, which included orthodox Confucianists at the Institute of Confucianism and members of their national organization, Yudohoe, frequently couched their arguments within a discourse of "timeless tradition." Seeking to restore and purify the core values of authentic Koreanness that had been devalued by the Japanese during the colonial era and were now being eroded by the incursion of American values, they saw the preservation of the patriarchal family and the "fine, beautiful customs" (*mip'ung yangsok*) that upheld it as an essential part of the postcolonial nation-building project. They argued that the family, as the foundation of Korean society and culture, had to be protected from the encroachment of foreign ideas. According to Sangui Nam, the Confucianists saw the traditional family as a cultural asset that had to be preserved at all costs, and they campaigned vigorously against Lee's proposed reforms, organizing protests, threatening opponents, and warning that any change to the system of gender hierarchy would lead to the erosion of essential values. They also claimed that the proposed legal changes would open the door to same-sex marriage, stoking anxieties about lesbianism that would erupt in Han's *A Jealousy*. For these cultural nationalists, the patriarchal head-of-family system was an essential component of postcolonial national identity. Kim Byeong-ro, chief justice of the Supreme Court agreed and argued that the preservation of the Confucian family was the best way to restore the Koreanness that had been so tarnished under colonialism.[71]

While orthodox Confucianists were a distinct minority, the attachment to patriarchal ideals understood as essential national tradition was widespread. Historian Charles Kim has characterized the dominant attitude toward social change in the 1950s as one of "postcolonial traditionalism." Produced by male intellectuals and aimed at young women, this vision of what Kim dubs "wholesome modernization" advocated the selective embrace of Euro-American practices in combination with the preservation of indigenous lifeways. It sought to eliminate Confucianism's worst abuses while preserving its "fine, beautiful customs" as the foundation of Korean identity. At the heart of those customs lay a conservative vision of Korean women as virtuous exemplars who should maintain the "wise mother, good wife" domestic ideal of generations past and thereby create the foundation for a wholesome society. While the discourse of wholesome modernization distanced itself from "hidebound" orthodox Confucianism, it did extend into the future a fundamentally patriarchal vision of women and the family as the cultural heart of the nation.[72]

Postcolonial traditionalism can be seen as an expression of what Partha Chatterjee has called anticolonial nationalism: the effort by colonized and formerly colonized people to define a nation that is modern yet culturally distinct from the

West. According to Chatterjee, anticolonial nationalism divides the world into material and spiritual domains. The material domain is the world of economics and politics; it is populated by men who embrace Western practices in the name of modernization. The spiritual domain preserves the nation's distinct cultural identity. It is populated by women and the family, who serve as embodiments of national essence and bearers of a self-conscious tradition that defines a resolute difference from an external hegemonic power. Through this gendered separation of spheres, anticolonial nationalism creates what Chatterjee calls a "new patriarchy" that is distinct from both the traditional order and the Western family structure. The new woman of anticolonial nationalism "was to be modern, but she would also have to display the signs of national tradition and therefore would be essentially different from the 'Western' woman." For Chatterjee, the formation of an anticolonial "'national culture' was *necessarily* built upon the privileging of an 'essential tradition'" borne by women and the family. In 1950s Korea, that essential tradition was frequently identified with the patriarchal family.[73]

The struggle between feminists and patriarchal cultural nationalists over the Family Law came to something of a draw by the end of the decade. The revision that was passed in 1958 and came into force in 1960 legally secured women's status as individuals who could own property, take legal action, and in other ways act independently of men; at the same time, it maintained the patriarchal head-of-family system and maintained sexual inequality across various dimensions of family life.[74] Lee Tai-young praised the new law as "a revolutionary change."[75] She also spent the rest of her life fighting for further revisions. (The head-of-family system was not abolished until 2002, four years after her death.) While some gender norms eased over the course of the 1950s—widow remarriage gradually became thinkable, for example, and freely chosen "love" marriages more common—many of the foundational assumptions about female inferiority, self-denial, submissiveness, and chastity continued to carry considerable weight. Women continued to occupy inferior positions in their families even as they moved into the public sphere as students, workers, and consumers.[76] The foundational Confucian principles regulating gender remained strong. Female suffering persisted. "Being a daughter-in-law," recalled one war widow bitterly, still entailed "being a servant who cooks and gives birth."[77]

The tension between Cold War cosmopolitan feminism and postcolonial traditionalism helped mark the 1950s as a distinct historical period within Korea's modernization.[78] During these years, the ideal of the Nora-like female individual who asserted her autonomy and claimed an identity that superseded her familial roles was promoted and contested with equal vigor. This tension suffused Korea's visual culture and contributed to the production of such richly ambivalent texts as Han Hyung-mo's *A Jealousy*. Han's film delivered to a mass audience the feminist critique of patriarchal marriage as a form of slavery for women and a roadblock to their professional ambitions. It also voiced the possibility of a committed, loving relationship between two women, a version of the Boston marriage that Helen Kim enjoyed with Lee Jong Ai. At the same time, the film contained these new possibilities by casting them as expressions of mental illness. In a masterful trick of mass-market filmmaking, Han's film gave voice to both feminist and patriarchal visions of postwar womanhood.

3

Public Culture

Han Hyung-mo had a reputation among his colleagues as "Korea's coolest guy." This exalted status derived in large part from his enthusiastic embrace of modernity and his cosmopolitan worldliness. Like Helen Kim in the field of education and Lee Tai-young in law, Han was a native modernizer of South Korea's film industry and its cinema (figure 6).[1]

Han's ostentatious modernity formed the core of his professional identity. In interviews years later, his colleagues recalled the manner in which he lived and worked as expressions of his open-mindedness and individualist ethos, qualities that set him apart from the era's more typically conservative directors and that made him appear uniquely "ahead of his time." At a moment when many directors were just getting by, Han flaunted his sophisticated lifestyle, living in a Western-style house filled with foreign décor and driving himself around Seoul in a private car.[2] Han was as open to new ideas about filmmaking as he was to new ideas about life. He traveled to Tokyo to buy equipment, to Hong Kong and Manila to attend international film festivals, and even to California to get inspiration on film studio design. He borrowed freely from foreign films and filmmaking practices, and introduced technical and aesthetic changes that reverberated across the industry. Han used his skills to capture Korea's dynamic new culture and society as it was taking shape. Critics singled out his films for their attention to "modern society," "modern lifestyle," "modern environment," "modern theme," "modern sense," "modern emotion," and "modern morals."[3] Han devoted his energies, above all, to the representation of the modern woman, and his career reached its apogee in a cycle of women's pictures he directed between 1954 and 1961. Because Han's films appealed to both popular and critical tastes, he was one of the few directors able to

FIGURE 6. Han Hyung-mo (right) on the set of *The Hand of Destiny*.

maintain a steady flow of production. He was the postwar era's commercial film-maker *par excellence*, and in this he was extraordinary.

In other ways, however, Han was a common postwar figure: the creative, entre-preneurial, market-savvy cultural producer who understood Koreans' desire for something new. Seen in this light, Han can be understood as kin to Heo Gi-suk, a resourceful woman credited with the invention of *budae jjigae*, or army base stew. While *jjigae*, or stew, has long been a staple of Korean cuisine, local lore holds that Heo created this particular version in Uijeongbu during the years of desperate poverty after the Korean War. Like Han, Heo was open to new ideas. She worked as a cook in one of the numerous American army bases (*budae*) and smuggled out processed meats such as Spam, hot dogs, sausage, and ham, for which she was frequently arrested. *Budae jjigae* was born when she put this American meat into a traditional *kimchi*-laden broth and began selling it on the streets of the camptown that surrounded the bases. Over the years, other industrially processed ingredients were added, most notably *ramyŏn*, a version of the instant ramen noodles that were invented in Japan in 1958 and made in Korea with imported American wheat.[4] Mongrel as it was, *budae jjigae* appealed to Korean tastes and soon became part of the national cuisine.

I want to take *budae jjigae* as a metaphor for Han's films and postwar cultural production more generally. Heo's creativity was widely shared among South Koreans: for all its social and economic dislocations, South Korea in the 1950s also experienced a robust cultural boom. As in many postcolonial and postwar societies, there was an unleashing of pent-up creative energy as artists and intellectuals took advantage of greater freedoms and a gradually improving economic situation. The film industry occupied the apex of this cultural rebirth. It experienced tremendous growth beginning in 1955–56, and by the end of the decade was both the most technologically advanced culture industry and the producer of the most popular forms of cultural expression. At the pinnacle of that industry was Han Hyung-mo.

The notion of "*budae jjigae* cinema" invites us to think about this cultural boom within the framework of the Cold War. Not only did the film industry's products convey anticommunist, capitalist, and democratic ideologies; they were also produced with the aid of materials made available by the waging of the Cold War. Washington's efforts to integrate South Korea into the Free World produced pools of resources that inventive South Koreans drew upon during these lean years. Some of these resources were material in nature; others were textual. Many of them ended up in the hands of South Koreans, who used them to create new forms of culture—movies as well as food. From this perspective, the scope of the cultural Cold War extends beyond state-directed cultural projects and into the efflorescence of indigenous cultural production. The idea of *budae jjigae* cinema also invites us to recognize the cosmopolitan intermingling of Korean and foreign elements —the cultural equivalents of *kimchi*, Spam, and *ramyŏn*, as it were— within this efflorescence. Korea's relationships with the United States, Japan, and other Free World countries shaped postwar cultural production in overt and subtle ways. "*Budae jjigae* cinema" invites us to see the suppressed presence of Japan in postwar cultural production, alongside the more manifest influences of America.

"*Budae jjigae* cinema" also calls attention to two modes in which Koreans became cultural producers: as poachers and as cultural entrepreneurs. By poaching, I mean the act of taking without asking within profoundly unequal relations of power, and the incorporation of that material into new cultural production. Heo Gi-suk, for example, poached the meat that she used to create *budae jjigae*. Drawing on the ideas of Michel de Certeau, Miriam Hansen, and Henry Jenkins, I am using the term both literally, to suggest the theft of material goods, and metaphorically, to refer to the textual appropriation of expressive resources.[5] Poaching implies an insurgent claim to power by the weak against the strong; it is a gesture of challenge as much as one of affiliation, and as an assertion of independence it has an implicit political dimension. Poaching was a vital mode of cultural production in the postwar period, as later chapters will explore. South Koreans also acted as Cold War cultural entrepreneurs, which is to say that they seized the opportunities for creative and professional advancement that the Cold War was opening up.[6] Heo, for instance, took advantage of the opportunity to work in a US military kitchen and in the market that the military bases created. (Syngman Rhee was undoubtedly Korea's most outstanding Cold War entrepreneur, brilliantly working his relationship with the Americans to keep the aid spigot open.) To think of Korean cultural producers such as Han Hyung-mo as poachers and entrepreneurs is to highlight their diverse forms of agency and creativity amidst difficult conditions and drastically unequal relations with the United States.

"*Budae jjigae* cinema" captures the particular experience of cultural modernity in South Korea in the 1950s. What's interesting here is not the simple achievement of modernity, but rather how that modernity was defined, created, and debated locally. Arjun Appadurai and Carol Breckenridge coined the term *public culture* to characterize the arena in which this happens and to call attention to the diversity of players, which include mass media industries, the state, and individual cultural producers. Their concept of public culture makes room for a critical engagement with consumption as a powerful imaginative act, one that can expand the horizons of possibility with sometimes emancipatory effects. It also makes room for foreign actors, who often exert an outsize influence in postcolonial societies. Public cultures outside the West thus frequently become incubators of what Appadurai and Breckenridge call a "new cosmopolitanism," as national, transnational, mass, and folk cultures interact with and cannibalize each other.[7]

South Korea's postwar public culture was just such an incubator. Home to a growing number of producers and consumers, it was deeply penetrated by transnational forces. The US military, the Asia Foundation, Hollywood, the Japanese film industry, European intellectual trends, and global popular music trends all contributed to *budae jjigae* cinema. As a result, public culture served as a site in which postwar modernity was produced as well as consumed.[8] As discussed in chapter 1, Korea in the 1950s lacked the solid economic foundation of industrial modernity. Postwar modernity was thus in many ways a cultural phenomenon, a matter of ideas and attitudes, practices and representations.

This chapter parallels chapters 1 and 2 in its attention to the historical development of Cold War cosmopolitanism, focusing here on its emergence within public culture. It charts TAF's interventions in this arena, paying particular attention to its efforts to nurture a cosmopolitan consciousness among South Koreans and to cultivate their personal, institutional, and commercial ties within Free Asia. The chapter explores the country's cultural rebirth in the wake of the Korean War, and shows how TAF fostered the growth of cultural institutions and encouraged the production of high-quality magazines and movies. Two developments take center stage: the emergence of the woman-in-public as a visual icon of modernity, and the rise of the film industry to the apex of public culture. These developments come together in the career of Han Hyung-mo, who was both a modernizer of Korean cinema and one of the most important producers of the figure of the modern Korean woman.

CULTURAL REBIRTH: THE ROLE OF THE ASIA FOUNDATION

South Korea's cultural rebirth took place across many dimensions of public culture. Institutions such as museums and libraries were rebuilt. Select traditional arts were resurrected, including poetry, archery, and some performing arts. Popular music—live, broadcast, and recorded—became increasingly accessible. Commercial venues of leisure and entertainment—dance halls, pool halls, restaurants, teahouses, coffee shops—flourished and became the foundation for a new *enjoi* lifestyle. Fashion appeared, as younger women embraced Western styles of dress and older women modernized their traditional *hanbok* with new fabrics. The rapid expansion of the education system—there were nearly eighty thousand college students by 1961—contributed to this cultural growth, expanding the pool of cultural consumers and fostering the emergence of a liberal intelligentsia. As Charles Kim has shown, this flourishing public culture became the site of robust debates, as artists and intellectuals vigorously interrogated the terms of Korea's much-desired modernization. [9]

The Asia Foundation intervened very intentionally in Korea's public culture, actively seeking to shape the discussions about—and production of—modernity taking place there. The foundation understood with a sophistication unmatched by any other US agency that indigenous cultural production was a central arena for waging the Cold War. It recognized that local mass media were vitally important tools for disseminating democratic and anticommunist ideas, and it established numerous programs to ensure a steady supply of newspapers, magazines, and books sympathetic to US aims. More significantly, TAF had a highly developed understanding of the social and political roles of music, literature, and the arts. In an internal 1962 report summarizing the foundation's arts philosophy and providing guidance for future programming, research fellow George Lerski urged all TAF representatives to recognize the "cultural scene" as a barometer that could give them "an indication of the direction in which society [was] heading" and to develop the skill to read these cultural signals. Support for the arts could also promote healthy nationalism, healing social divisions between urban and rural populations and bridging the gap between old and new ways of thinking. [10]

More ideologically, TAF regarded creativity as a distinctly Free World value intrinsically bound up with individualism. In contrast to communists, who purportedly valued art as a tool of indoctrination, Lerski claimed that "the unrestrictive artistic expression with its creative right of doubt and even error is one of the main attractions possessed by the pluralistic societies of the Free World in the struggle for human minds." The foundation also valued culture as an economic realm, which meant that promoting media and the arts could do double duty as economic development. It was also politically wise, since artists, writers, and intellectuals were potentially volatile social actors whose "frustration" at a lack of opportunity might lead them to "radical solutions." For TAF president Robert Blum, public culture was a crucial realm in which the United States must exercise its power—it was "one of the elements we have to influence in order to make our policies effective."[11]

Korea was at the forefront of TAF's commitment to culture, receiving more support for the arts than did any other office. Even before the establishment of the Seoul office in mid-1954, the Tokyo office in 1952–53 developed a program for Korea that promised to "encourage the artist, build up his ranks, unite the people under a developing indigenous culture, and link cultural progress to freedom under democracy."[12] This cultural vision was greatly expanded in October 1955, when the Seoul office produced its "Plan for Korea," a master blueprint that articulated the foundation's objectives and laid out a roadmap for programming. The report's unnamed author, almost certainly Mary Walker, was greatly encouraged by signs of creative "ferment" and reported that the "Korean talent for music, art, and literature is slowly emerging with . . . amazing vitality." The Plan proposed to encourage this vitality, setting as its objective nothing less than the "renaissance of Korean culture." Such a rebirth was deemed critically important after the "cultural disaster" of Japanese colonialism, which fractured Korea's existing culture and tried to remake its people as "secondary" Japanese, who were "not quite as good as the real thing but who had no other cultural alternatives." The new nation's spiritual and political existence was at stake: "The Republic must re-create a Korean culture in order to maintain its identity," an identity defined in opposition to that of North Korea.[13] As Tokyo representative Delmer Brown had noted a few months earlier, the partition of the peninsula in 1945 had created a "laboratory situation" in which free and communist ways of life were being tried out side by side, and the world was watching.[14] In keeping with this ambition to nurture a new and distinctly South Korean culture and identity, TAF representatives in Seoul funded numerous projects that had a national scope. They donated equipment to enable the National Museum to catalogue its collection, gave funds for the creation of a *hangul* dictionary that would help rationalize the national language, and encouraged the revival of the mask dance, a folk cultural form that had been banned by the Japanese. As George Lerski proclaimed, "cultural heritage is an ally."[15]

The 1955 "Plan for Korea" balanced this sensitivity to nationalism and cultural heritage with a forceful articulation of Cold War cosmopolitan ideals. It made clear that worldliness must be an essential component of Korea's postcolonial culture. The desired "renaissance" could not consist exclusively of the revival of Korean traditions: the few remnants of "archaic" culture that had survived colonialism were "hardly" able to "serve a modern society." Instead, a distinctly modern culture should be cultivated through sustained engagement with "Western models." The national and the cosmopolitan were thus partners in a dual project of nation building and bloc building: a distinctly South Korean national culture would be enmeshed within a network of Free World ties even as it was being born. To this end, the Plan identified as one of its core objectives the "Korean adaptation of Free World cultural experiences to Korean use." TAF sought to midwife into existence a culture rooted in indigenous traditions yet open to Western ideas and engaged with cultural developments across the democratic world. Adaptation was a core feature of what was, in effect, a plan for cultural modernization: Western patterns would "not serve Korea without tailoring to size," and the Plan pledged to identify those Koreans who would be "capable of managing the adaptation." The Plan's cosmopolitan vision also entailed making Korean culture more visible abroad. TAF regarded Korea not simply as a recipient of foreign ideas, but also as an active contributor to world culture. The export and exhibition of Korean culture across the Free World was thus another of the Seoul office's core objectives. The Plan called for programming that would develop "in Asia and other democratic countries . . . an understanding of Korean culture and respect for the developing expression of this culture."[16] This objective had clear political underpinnings. TAF was adamant that the Republic of Korea become globally visible as a newly independent nation whose postwar reconstruction had been financed largely by the United States. Korea's modernity—a product of its alignment with the West—must be displayed alongside its cultural heritage for all the world to see.

As the Seoul representatives made grants designed to bring this new national-cosmopolitan Korean culture into existence, they explicitly encouraged the activities of cultural entrepreneurs. To think of Korean artists, intellectuals, and civic leaders as entrepreneurs is to recognize the extent to which the waging of the cultural Cold War entailed opening up new creative and professional opportunities for select individuals. As part of its efforts to win "hearts and minds," the Asia Foundation willingly made resources available and invited Koreans to take advantage of them for their individual creative and professional advancement, as well as for the social impact that such advancement would deliver. Cold War entrepreneurs were Koreans who took advantage of these opportunities and resources. Sometimes they did so out of a shared commitment to the foundation's values and goals, such as anticommunism or artistic freedom; for others, more opportunistic motives may have been at work. Unlike poachers, who took without asking and often in secrecy, entrepreneurs availed themselves in broad daylight of what the Asia Foundation freely offered.

The writer Oh Young-jin was a classic Cold War entrepreneur who translated his personal experiences with communism into professionally advantageous relationships with Americans. A North Korean refugee, Oh began his South Korean career writing and publishing anticommunist books and magazines. He developed relationships with USIS personnel, helped TAF's Tokyo office forge contacts with Korean cultural organizations during the Korean War, and in 1953–54 toured the United States on a State Department Leaders Grant. The Seoul representatives supported his magazine *Literature and the Arts*, awarded its Freedom Literature Award to a book he published, and tried to find an American publisher for his own memoir about life under communism. They fostered his intellectual engagement with the Free World by providing subscriptions to Western magazines, and in 1959 financed his participation in Henry Kissinger's Harvard International Seminar, which brought together leaders from across the Free World and immersed them in American life. Oh was a cosmopolitan intellectual who possessed the interpersonal and linguistic skills to work easily with Americans, and he developed close personal relationships with Asia Foundation staff. Representative Jack E. James said of Oh, "I do not think we could find anyone who represents so well the intellectual, creative Koreans or who can speak of their problems so well." Oh was just the type of worldly intellectual TAF was looking for: he is "one of the few Korean intellectuals," wrote James, "who is attempting to understand where Korea stands in relation to the cultural community of the world and what are the best contributions she can make to that community."[17] Building on this assistance from TAF and other US agencies in his early years, Oh went on to become a prominent postwar screenwriter, playwright, and critic.

WOMEN AS ICONS OF MODERNITY: *YŎWŎN*

Print culture received steady support from TAF's Seoul office. Immediately after the Korean War, program advisor Cho Tong-jae reported that the publishing industry was on the verge of collapse. Magazine publishers in particular were in "desperate need of help," reported TAF representative Lawrence Thompson: "Unless we give prompt first-aid, the patient may die waiting for the doctor." The issue was a shortage of newsprint. Korea's paper factories had been heavily damaged during the war, and those that remained lacked the resources and skilled labor to make full use of their capacity. Imported paper was very expensive, black-market paper even more so, and corrupt publishers were diverting aid dollars to illegal money traders. In response, the representatives began making direct grants of paper intended to keep a magazine in print for six months, during which time the publisher could hopefully accumulate sufficient capital to restore economic self-sufficiency. Once a grant was made, TAF claimed to exercise "absolutely no editorial control." By the mid-1950s the newsprint program was one of the foundation's most important initiatives, receiving over ten thousand dollars each year. Through these "transfusions" of paper the Seoul office "saved the life of practically every one of the better-quality periodicals in Korea at one time or another."[18] Partially as a result of this aid, Korea developed what Gregg Brazinsky has characterized as an "astonishingly rich and diverse print culture."[19] Serial publication flourished, and by 1960 there were 536 weekly and monthly periodicals authorized to publish. These periodicals, in turn, supported the publication of over one thousand books annually.[20]

TAF's support for print culture intersected with its interest in Korean women. The Seoul office gave substantial support to *Yŏwŏn* (Woman's garden), Korea's premier women's magazine. Publisher Kim Ik-dal launched *Yowon* in October 1955 and Mary Walker made the first paper grant in October 1956, noting that the Seoul office had observed its first year of publication with "keen interest." "It is our feeling," she wrote, "that this magazine can do much to raise the status of women in your country." This initial grant was followed by an additional one in 1957, when it received more paper than any other magazine, and another in 1959. TAF regarded *Yŏwŏn* as a high-priority project, praising its twenty-six-year-old female editor Kim Kwi-hyun as "brilliant" and arranging an internship for her at *Better Homes and Gardens* after she completed graduate training in journalism at the State University of Iowa.[21] (She became further enmeshed in Cold War transnational networks when one of her Ewha professors recommended her to the Committee of Correspondence for a 1957 international workshop.)[22] *Yŏwŏn*, in turn, helped further TAF's mission by occasionally publishing articles written by its employees.

Yŏwŏn became a key site for the visual production of modernity, which emerged within its pages as a combined social, political, and cultural project. *Yŏwŏn* was a substantial publication, in terms of its physical size (issues ran between two hundred fifty and four hundred pages), its audience (educated women, housewives, intellectuals, college students), and its monthly readership (forty thousand by 1958 and sixty thousand by 1963).[23] It offered diverse perspectives on a wide variety of social and political topics, published fiction and poetry, and covered the film industry carefully through articles, reviews, and advertisements. It was an image-rich publication, full of photographs, drawings, paintings, diagrams, advertisements, cartoons, maps, sheet music, and clothing patterns. It presented itself as a manual to modern life, offering visual instruction in modernizing women's everyday activities, from the use of labor-saving appliances like the electric iron to the new social practice of dating. Western fashions appeared prominently, as did photographs and floor plans for Western-style houses. Overall, it communicated an optimistic attitude: modernity wasn't something women should fear, but something they could master and transform into a source of new pleasures and efficiencies.

Yŏwŏn undertook the cosmopolitanizing cultural work of mapping the capitalist-democratic world and imaginatively integrating South Korea into it. In the process it constructed a visually rich Cold War global imaginary. Between 1957 and 1959 it published scores of maps and photographs that brought the Free World into existence as an imagined community. It depicted the cultures of European countries (England, France, West Germany, Spain, Denmark, the Netherlands), explained the contested parts of the globe (Hungary, Suez, Algeria, Tibet, Cuba), and introduced fellow members of Free Asia (Taiwan, Philippines, South Vietnam, Pakistan). It even illuminated the global military network in which South Korea was enmeshed, publishing several maps depicting US and Soviet military bases across the globe. Less overtly, the magazine carried Japan's ghostly presence into public culture: its layout was very similar to the leading Japanese women's magazine, *Shufu no Tomo* (The housewife's friend), indicating both the legacy of colonial ties and the extent to which Korean cultural producers looked to Japan as a culturally proximate model of modernity that they could emulate.[24]

Gender emerged in *Yŏwŏn's* pages, as elsewhere in public culture, as the key symbolic language through which the costs and benefits of modernity were weighed. Women's bodies, their activities, and the spaces they inhabited became the grounds on which public intellectuals mapped the profound social changes taking place around them.[25] Due to the pace and scope of changes taking place in actual women's lives, representations of women became barometers of South Korea's transformation, particularly of the impact of Western ideas and practices. Korea was hardly unique in this respect. Given women's association with childbearing and the private realm of the family, they have long served, in Asia and the West alike, as instruments for measuring the impact of modernity on existing social norms.[26]

Yŏwŏn played a crucial role in constructing the modern Korean woman, and the woman-in-public, as a specifically visual icon. The opening pages of each issue were devoted to her representation. The cover featured a color painting or photograph of a young woman, almost always dressed in Western attire and with bobbed hair (figure 7). This was followed by ten to thirty-five pages of black-and-white photographs, most of which focused on contemporary women in a variety of contexts and situations. A second, similar photo spread appeared later in the magazine. In the pages of *Yŏwŏn*, women appear comfortable in public space: they walk freely in the streets and spend leisure time in coffee shops and at the beach. Occasionally they are represented in sexually suggestive ways that echo American pinups; other times they display their bodies as skilled athletes. Women who border on social respectability, including café waitresses and prostitutes, are depicted thoughtfully. The Asia Foundation supported this visual production directly and intentionally: its first grant was for a supply of special offset paper that enabled the magazine to publish more photographs.

The magazine ran a number of photo series that highlighted different aspects of the modern woman and the routes through which she was entering public life. "Blooming Girls" extended a colonial-era New Woman trope and featured photographs of students at elite high schools and women's colleges, sometimes accompanied by captions identifying their professional aspirations.[27] The magazine devoted substantial visual attention to the working woman, making her the subject of several photo series. "Happy Today: Working Women" launched in the inaugural issue of 1955, followed three years later by "Young People's Lives," about working

FIGURE 7. The first issue of *Yŏwŏn* magazine, October 1955.

women such as a textile factory worker and a nurse.[28] The most innovative series was "Cutting-Edge Jobs," which ran through most of 1958. It showed women working in occupations that fell far outside their traditional domain, including the first female chief editor of a magazine, a script girl at a film company, and a shorthand transcriber at the National Assembly.[29] One entry in this series showed a woman behind the wheel of a large American car, that evergreen symbol of modernity and autonomy (figure 8). The accompanying caption, which identified her as a taxi driver, noted that she had received good-driving awards from her current employer, the UN's Office of the Economic Coordinator (the main distributor of US aid), thereby reinforcing the association of women's progress with the West.

FIGURE 8. Female taxi driver in the series "Cutting-Edge Jobs,"
Yŏwŏn, March 1958.

These photo series supported the editors' pronouncement, published in the third
issue, that "there has never been a time when the position of working women in
society has been as conspicuous and important as the present."[30]

"Twelve Modern Korean Women" ran throughout 1956 and gave its subjects
pride of place at the end of the opening pictorial section. It featured older women
dressed in *hanbok* who visually evoked traditional gender roles, but were in fact

formidable professionals and artists who held positions of authority in the public sphere. Among them were Im Yeong-sin, former minister of commerce and industry and member of the National Assembly; Im Suk-jae, president of Sookmyoung Women's University; and Mo Yun-suk, poet. These are portraits of individuals, rather than images of representative types. Each photograph occupies a full page, and the women's upright poses and forthright gazes convey a sense of self-possession. Their modernity was marked through their accomplishments and, often, their association with the United States: many of these women had ties to the United States, and more than half of them had received State Department leadership grants. Several of them sit behind large, imposing desks that serve as the white-collar equivalent of the taxi driver's car: visual emblems of authority in the public sphere. Lee Tai-young and Helen Kim, the era's most prominent women-in-public, appeared in the July and August installments (figures 4 and 5 in the preceding chapter). Kim and Lee also appeared regularly in *Yŏwŏn*'s pages as authors and subjects of numerous articles, many of which linked women's liberation to democracy. Lee even wrote a regular legal advice column under the assertive headline "Female Lawyer Tae-young Lee in Charge."[31]

While *Yŏwŏn* did not speak with a single voice and often published articles espousing a postcolonial traditionalist position,[32] it did serve as a prominent venue for the expression of Cold War cosmopolitan feminism. As Lee and Kim's presence suggests, it amplified the voices of female modernizers and Cold War cultural entrepreneurs. The magazine served as a forum for women who had traveled to the United States via State Department leadership grants and agreed to publicize their experiences upon their return home. Between 1955 and 1961, it published at least thirty-seven pieces about America by twenty-three highly accomplished Korean women, including a serialized novel by Kim Mal-bong set in Washington, DC. Overwhelmingly positive, these writings extended the work of the cultural Cold War by disseminating, via local voices, carefully curated visions of the United States. They also attested to the creative and professional benefits that accrued to those women who were able to access American resources, both financial and institutional. In *Yŏwŏn*'s pages, professional women were often framed in relation to the United States and depicted as inhabitants of a public sphere that extended far beyond Korea.

The magazine's linkage of the modern woman with the world beyond Korea's borders found perhaps its fullest expression in "Miss Earring's World Adventure" of 1961. In this eleven-part series of articles and photographs, an unseen and unnamed female traveler brings the reader on a tour through the Free World.[33] She begins in the Free Asia (Japan, Hong Kong, the Philippines, Laos, India), moves on to the US-allied Middle East (Israel, Turkey), and ends up in Western Europe (France, West Germany, England). This series is comparable to contemporary around-the-(free)-world travel articles that appeared in American magazines such as the *Saturday Review*, and it served a similar pedagogical function.[34]

"Miss Earring" brings the Free World into existence as an entity that is intellectually accessible to South Koreans, mapping it as an interconnected series of distinct locales whose differences are charming rather than threatening. Her travels around the globe bring the abstract ideal of freedom to life: the transnationally mobile female subject works as a dual metaphor for the expanding sphere of action open to the modern South Korean woman and the liberties that the noncommunist world offers.[35]

HAN HYUNG-MO AND THE REBIRTH
OF THE FILM INDUSTRY

The film industry, like magazine publishing, also flourished in the 1950s. Han Hyung-mo was the leading commercial filmmaker of the 1950s, working across and excelling at virtually all aspects of film production. Between 1949 and 1967 he directed nineteen films, edited sixteen, and served as cinematographer on fifteen; he worked as a producer and an art director, and was known as a superb lighting designer. His films attracted large audiences, participated in international film festivals, won domestic and international awards, were singled out for praise by President Rhee, and earned the admiration of his peers.[36] They were among the first Korean films to be commercially exported.[37]

Han's career developed in parallel with Korean political history from the 1940s through the early 1960s, as he took advantage of the opportunities that each new political situation made available. Han was one of the few filmmakers who spanned the 1945 divide. Han's early life and career took shape within the colonial system. He was born in 1917 into an affluent Christian family in Uiju, North Pyeongan province, where his father was a public official. An artistic youth, Han attended the Singyeong Arts School in Japanese-occupied Manchuria and worked as a sign painter at a department store. Han moved to Seoul and began his film career in 1941, as the colonial government was consolidating the film industry and orienting it more directly towards wartime propaganda. His first job was as the art director on Choi In-gyu's *Street Angels* (1941). Choi, one of the colonial era's leading directors, recognized Han's promise and took him on as a protégé.[38] The Korean film industry during these years was largely adjunct to that of Japan, and personnel moved easily between them.[39] Choi helped Han get professional training in cinematography at Japan's Toho studio from 1941 to 1943, where he apprenticed under Miyajima Yoshio and assisted on the wartime propaganda film *A Story of Leadership* (1941). After passing the cinematography exam, Han returned to Korea to work as Choi's cinematographer on two pro-Japanese films, *Children of the Sun* (1944) and *Promise of Love* (1945).[40]

Although the political turmoil and poverty of the liberation years inhibited the development of the industry as a whole, the emerging Cold War created opportunities that Han was able to seize. During the US occupation period, Han shot

Choi's anti-Japanese liberation film *Hurrah! for Freedom* (1946), which was made with the support of USIS.[41] Han made his directorial debut soon after the formation of the ROK with *Breaking the Wall* (1949), a feature film that dramatized the bloody Yeosu-Suncheon rebellion of October 1948. This was a violent leftist revolt against Rhee's newly formed government that began in the army's own barracks when soldiers refused to participate in the repression of an insurgency on nearby Jeju Island; it quickly spread to the civilian population and culminated in the declaration of a "Korean people's republic" in South Jeolla province. Korean military forces brutally suppressed the insurgency with US assistance, leaving the streets lined with corpses and an unknown number—estimates range from hundreds to thousands—dead. The revolt prompted a political crackdown: in its wake, Rhee pushed through passage of the loosely worded National Security Law, which enabled the suppression of virtually all dissent, purged suspected communists from the military and government, and led to the jailing of tens of thousands of civilians.[42] Han's *Breaking the Wall* presented the rebellion via a family drama in which an ROK officer confronts, and is killed by, his communist brother-in-law. Han made the film with the support of the Korean Ministry of Defense and presented the Army's actions in a favorable light.[43] In doing so, he established a relationship with the Ministry of Defense that allowed him access to its filmmaking equipment and other resources for many years. This early film suggests Han's eagerness to engage with the crises of contemporary life, as well as his sympathy with Rhee's government and its politics of anticommunism.

The outbreak of the Korean War created new opportunities. After the box office success of *Breaking the Wall*, the Navy asked Han to make a film that would present that branch of the military in a similarly positive way. Han agreed and began developing *A Man's Way*, about the maritime pursuit of a smuggling gang bringing in goods from Macao. Han began filming in the southern city of Mokpo, with a script by Cold War cultural entrepreneur Oh Young-jin and one of the country's three naval ships as a set. The North Korean attack in June 1950 brought production to a halt. Han and his crew rushed their equipment and film stock to the frontlines at Daejeon, where they began shooting footage of the war. This ad hoc group went on to become the Ministry of Defense Film Unit, thereby deepening Han's relationship with the military. Han took the footage to Tokyo for editing, recorded a narration written by Oh Young-jin, and screened the completed documentary *An Assault on Justice, Part 1* (1951) for international journalists at the UN foreign correspondents' club. The film created a sensation in both countries and with its sequel, *An Assault on Justice, Part 2* (1952), which was completed with the assistance of USIS, conveyed both the immediacy of war and the government's position on North Korean villainy. It was a highly effective piece of wartime propaganda. It also propelled Han into a new job as a war correspondent for the US-based International News Service, which had better resources than the Ministry of Defense.[44]

The war decimated South Korea's fragile commercial film industry. In its sweep south, the North Korean army confiscated almost all of the existing film equipment and killed, kidnapped, or lured north many of the most talented filmmakers, including Han's mentor Choi In-gyu. After the armistice in 1953, Han resumed work as a cinematographer, shooting documentary "enlightenment" films for the ROK Office for Public Information, including *A Woman Soldier* (1954), about the Korean Women's Army Corps, and *The Hill of the Immortal Bird* (1955), a war film that emphasized friendship between Korean and American soldiers.[45]

The film industry's fortunes began to improve in 1955–56, as the cultural Cold War in Asia was gaining steam. The Asia Foundation captured this turning point in a pair of reports, which to this day remain the most comprehensive surveys of the Korean film industry at this crucial moment. Both reports were written by John W. Miller, the foundation's Tokyo-based motion picture officer. Miller wrote the first report after a two-week tour of Korea in January 1955, during which he consulted with key figures involved in film, government, and foreign aid. Miller described a "disorganized industry" that was in such a state of "chaos" that it barely qualified as an industry at all. There were no major producers, no stable production companies, no organizations that owned their own equipment, and no sound or shooting stages. Camera and lighting equipment was extremely limited; film stock was rare and either outdated or expensively acquired on the black market; processing chemicals were old and often unstable. The available technical and material resources did "not meet minimum needs for the production of high quality pictures." Miller described the mode of production as a "handicraft operation," with a few "shoestring operators" engaged in "spasmodic activity" and limited to producing only a single film at a time. Competent screenwriters were rare, technicians' skills were low, and exposed film was processed by hand. The result was a small output of generally poor-quality films, of which only two or three had been able to recoup their producers' investment. The exhibition sector was equally hobbled, with only fifty-nine theaters in the entire country and these mostly filled with Hollywood and European films.[46]

Two years later, the situation had changed dramatically. In his second, lengthier report written in December 1956, Miller described a very different situation. "Film production is booming in Korea," he wrote, and "the film industry is now entering a crucial period of its growth and development." While the industry was still disorganized and many technical aspects of production still "primitive," it was displaying "an amazing new vitality" and entering into a "colorful period of development." Production capital was flowing "abundantly" into producers' hands, and the industry was in the midst of a "production boom," with an increase from twelve feature films in 1955 to about forty in 1956. These were "'gold rush' days for both talent and technicians." Producers, directors, and production staff had begun following "internationally accepted production practices" while finding creative solutions to problems created by ongoing shortages (such as using bread dough to create bas-relief set decoration). Budgets were rising, and with them production values. The days of "chasing the sun" and building sets in "bombed out buildings"—as Han had done—were numbered. The exhibition sector was likewise strengthening and now contained ninety-four theaters devoted exclusively to motion picture exhibition (although most of them were "crowded, uncomfortable, and often unsanitary"), and more than one thousand mobile or semipermanent 16 mm projectors were in use. Enthusiasm for domestically made films was rising: Miller reported seeing "people in rags and near rags push their hard earned Hwan through the ticket sellers' window. College students who scarcely have enough to pay tuitions or buy their lunch, women apple sellers, and people working on construction road gangs, *all* attend the cinema." Even members of the intelligentsia, who had formerly scorned domestic films, were now being attracted into the theaters to see them. Among audiences a growing "star consciousness" was beginning to emerge, fed in part by two film fan magazines. While the industry still suffered from many material shortages and deficiencies in skill, Miller believed the corner had been turned.[47] While researching his report, Miller published an article in *Yŏwŏn* that singled out Han's *Madame Freedom* (1956) for its attention to contemporary life and praised filmmakers' visual presentation of modern women, noting that they are "almost identical to the women you would meet on the street."[48]

Miller's prediction proved correct, and over the next few years the film industry took off. From 18 films in 1954, filmmakers produced over 111 films in 1959, and the total audience for domestic films surpassed that for imported films.[49] Rhee proudly proclaimed that films made by "our own hands are good enough to match foreign movies," and T. S. Kim boasted in *The Korean Republic* newspaper that "only the most popular foreign films can compete with the domestic ones in the number of cinema-goers."[50] Korean films entered international film festivals, where they began winning awards, and were commercially exported to select freeworld markets in Asia and the West.[51] All sectors of the industry grew: by the end of the decade, South Korea had an estimated 242 theater screens, 118 actors, 74 production companies, 51 directors, 8 private processing labs, 4 commercial film studios, and 1 university film department. Han's career expanded alongside the film industry as a whole. He returned to directing with *The Hand of Destiny* (1954) and two years later released *Hyperbolae of Youth* (1956) and *Madame Freedom*, both of which attracted huge audiences. Han led the industry's production boom, releasing multiple films almost every year through 1961. Over the course of the 1950s a truly national film industry took shape, and by the late 1960s South Korea was producing more than two hundred movies per year.[52]

What enabled the film industry to explode in such a short period of time? The 1955–56 years saw a convergence of factors, which can be summarized as the encounter of creative and ambitious Korean filmmakers with newly available resources.

Like other cultural producers, filmmakers entered the postwar period with a backlog of pent-up creative energy and a burning desire to tell Korean stories.

John Miller, like other Asia Foundation employees in Seoul, was struck by the creative juices he saw flowing among Koreans. He praised the "industriousness, ingenuity, and creative ability of Korean film makers," admired the "charming sets" they built on "improvised stages," and applauded the "great promise" and "frequent flashes of brilliance" he saw in their films.[53] While filmmakers enjoyed relative creative freedom, they operated within political constraints. The National Security Law crimped the expression of political ideas, censorship laws limited representations of sexuality, and nationalist regulations forbade most representations of Japan. Some filmmakers ran afoul of these constraints, such as Lee Kang-cheon, whose *Piagol* (1955) became the first film banned under the National Security Law. According to Miller, however, the "majority of Korean producers" were "reasonably happy with the application of the present system," and "most differences of opinion"—although certainly not all—were "settled without resort to scissors."[54] Filmmakers enjoyed greater opportunities to craft stories and characters than they had had for many years.

This creativity and ambition came into contact with a variety of resources, arising from within and without the country. The influx of Hollywood films generated financial resources for some sectors of the industry. American and other foreign films had begun pouring into Korea in 1945, which Washington encouraged for both economic and ideological reasons. Always eager to penetrate foreign markets, Washington during the Cold War particularly valued the ability of films to convey the values of democracy, freedom, individualism, and capitalism. Hollywood films proved popular—according to Lee Sang-geun, head of publicity at Danseongsa Film Company, Koreans "love foreign films as if it's life-and-death"—and soon dominated the market.[55] This influx initially impeded the production of Korean films as theater owners, who were a major source of production capital, shunned locally made films in favor of more lucrative foreign pictures. The cash generated by foreign films stimulated other sectors of the industry, however. Film import, distribution, and exhibition were all highly profitable endeavors in the 1950s, offering a better return on investment than most other business opportunities, and some of the revenue they generated was used to acquire projectors and screens, rebuild war-damaged theaters, and open new ones. (Oh Young imported Hollywood films to fund his anticommunist publishing enterprise.) Perhaps most importantly, foreign films expanded the market for all films by luring audiences away from traditional live theater.[56]

State support helped increase the flow of resources to Korean film producers. Rhee was eager to have a national film industry, and in an effort to bolster the industry's reputation he urged Koreans to recognize movie production as a worthwhile social activity that employed people who deserved the respect of their fellow citizens. He was also sensitive to producers' calls for protection from foreign competition and responded with targeted measures. In 1954 his government eliminated the 40 percent admissions tax on domestic films, allowing theater owners to return a larger share of box office returns to film producers. (The tax was restored in 1960, but at a lower rate).[57] The administration also began granting producers of what it deemed the year's most "excellent" films a special license to import and distribute one foreign film, the profits from which could be used to fund a local production. Together, these regulations put substantial capital into the hands of producers, who used it to finance higher-quality films. The producers of Han Hyung-mo's films benefited from both these initiatives: *The Hand of Destiny* was released soon after the 1954 admissions tax repeal, and at least four of his films earned the special import license.[58]

This increased access to capital intersected with filmmakers' creativity to produce Korea's first two blockbusters: Lee Gyu-hwan's *Chunhyang Story* (1955) and Han Hyung-mo's *Madame Freedom*, both of which handily outperformed their Hollywood competitors. *Madame Freedom* attracted about one hundred fifty thousand admissions, at a time when the average foreign film attracted thirty thousand viewers and when fifty thousand constituted a big hit.[59] The film delivered a thirty-eight-fold return on its producers' investment and earned them a special import license; it was, in the words of one of Han's colleagues, a "big cash cow." Together with Han's *Hyperbolae of Youth*, which also sold more than one hundred thousand tickets in 1956, these hits demonstrated that domestic films could attract large audiences and generate substantial profits.[60] Additional capital quickly became available to producers as, in John Miller's words, everyone from "wealthy fish merchants, importers, land owners, money lenders and gray marketers" began investing in the now-glamorous movie business.[61] These blockbusters established a new production cycle: more investment capital meant higher budgets, which led to better-quality films, which attracted bigger audiences and generated greater profits, which were used to produce new films or invested elsewhere in the industry.

Some of the most successful producers and exhibitors used their profits to build Korea's first commercial production studios. The Samsung Film Company, producers of *Madame Freedom*, opened the Samsung studio in 1957, which was built to Han's specifications after he traveled to the United States to study the design of a studio at a California art school.[62] Samsung's Western-style complex consisted of one large studio big enough to house the set of a small village, a second studio equipped with a soundstage, a temporary "set operating station," a dormitory, and a cafeteria. While spacious, it lacked its own equipment, so filmmakers had to bring in rented cameras and lights. A reporter for the *Han'guk ilbo* found Han's studio design to be a satisfactory version of the American ideal: "Although it is not as luxurious as the interior of the studio of Cecil B. DeMille in *Sunset Boulevard*," he observed, it has "an atmosphere suitable to a studio where film, a somewhat exotic art, is created."[63] Hong Chan, one of Korea's richest men and owner of Seoul's premier Sudo Theater, which hosted *Madame Freedom*'s forty-five-day run, opened the Anyang Studio on the distant outskirts of Seoul later the same year. Drawing on his close ties to Rhee, Chan spent an estimated $250,000 on construction and imported over $200,000 worth of the most up-to-date American film equipment, making Anyang the largest film studio in Asia at the time. Unfortunately, Korean technicians did not have the skills to use the equipment effectively, which caused several of the early films to fail at the box office, and by 1959 the studio was bankrupt.[64] Han Hyung-mo, more so than Hong Chan, served as one of the Asia Foundation's "tailors," successfully adapting a modern American institution to fit the more modest Korean size.

The waging of the Cold War also contributed to the industry's growth, enabling Korean filmmakers to gain access to an array of material and immaterial resources. These included advanced technical training. Washington considered motion pictures to be the most effective medium of public communication in Korea, and since 1945 the USIS and its occupation-era predecessor, the US Army 502nd Unit, had produced a steady flow of newsreels, documentaries, educational films, and propaganda. The Americans hired Koreans to work as directors, cinematographers, sound recording engineers, lab technicians, and editors.[65] These hiring decisions were both practical (it was cheaper to employ Koreans than to bring over Americans) and political (Washington wanted Koreans to be able to produce their own high-quality films). These employees worked with up-to-date equipment, learned American production techniques, absorbed the conventions of classical Hollywood storytelling, and made personal connections that facilitated access to equipment and other resources for years to come. Many of them went on to work in commercial cinema, where their superior skills made them the backbone of the expanding industry. (Kim Ki-young, director of *The Housemaid* [1960], one of the highest achievements of Golden Age cinema, began his directing career with the USIS-produced film *Boxes of Death* [1955] and other works of Cold War propaganda.)[66] The film unit of the United Nations Korean Reconstruction Agency (UNKRA), although a much smaller operation, provided Korean filmmakers with similar opportunities for training and experience, as well as valuable personal connections.[67] Korea's Ministry of Defense, whose Film Unit Han Hyung-mo had helped establish, likewise provided valuable experience to young filmmakers and became an important training institution for those who later entered the commercial industry.[68]

The waging of the Cold War also led to an influx of modern filmmaking equipment, which filmmakers accessed via US, UN, and ROK agencies. John Miller estimated that between 1955 and 1959, South Korean government agencies received about $2 million dollars from the US and the UN to build studios and purchase modern film technology. The ROK Office of Public Information (OPI), Rhee's domestic counterpart to the USIS, received about $1 million from UNKRA and the International Cooperation Administration (ICA) to construct a fully stocked, up-to-date film production studio and processing laboratory. The film units of other government agencies—most notably the Defense Ministry, but also the Ministries of Reconstruction and Education—also received major grants.[69] While these facilities were intended for the production of information and propaganda films, commercial filmmakers had access to this equipment. Lee Hyung-pyo, head of the OPI film division, remarked in 1956 that its studio was in operation twenty-four hours a day and openly used by "20 or so independent film companies." John Miller noted the same year that "the film staffs of all government agencies" engaged in "semi-officially sanctioned but informally run equipment rental and film processing activities" for commercial producers, the proceeds of which often lined their own pockets. Virtually all commercial filmmakers in 1956, including Han Hyung-mo, used OPI or Ministry of Defense recording studios to post-record their dialogue, music, and sound effects.[70] The USIS and UNKRA film units also occasionally made their own equipment available to commercial filmmakers.[71] While the opening of commercial studios lessened filmmakers' reliance on government equipment, it did not completely eliminate it. Some theater owners, in turn, acquired surplus projection equipment from the US Military Far East Motion Picture Service, which upgraded its theaters in 1956 and discarded its World War II–era 35 mm projectors, or purchased projectors on the black market.[72]

THE KOREAN MOTION PICTURE CULTURE ASSOCIATION (KMPCA)

Of all the US and UN agencies pouring resources into Korea, only the Asia Foundation set out intentionally to nurture the commercial film industry and encourage the production of high-quality entertainment films. It did so largely through the person of John Miller. Miller began his career in California's commercial radio in the 1940s before serving as an information officer in the Pacific theater during World War II and in Korea during the US occupation period. In the early 1950s he moved into film production, working at Palmer Pictures, a small San Francisco company that made films for the Asia Foundation. TAF hired Miller in 1952 to serve as production supervisor on radio in Tokyo; when Radio Free Asia shut down, he became the radio and motion picture coordinator and TAF's primary film consultant. Throughout the 1950s Miller surveyed commercial film industries and advised on film projects across Asia, and he became a passionate and eloquent advocate for commercial Asian cinema.[73] Miller's work was directed from TAF's San Francisco headquarters by James L. Stewart, director of operations, and Charles M. Tanner, liaison to Hollywood, both of whom had close ties to Korea: Stewart had been director of USIS in Seoul before the Korean War,[74] and Tanner had worked as a USIS film editor there.[75] Miller also worked closely with TAF's local representatives, including Tokyo's Noel F. Busch, a former journalist with *Time* and *Life* magazines,[76] and Hong Kong's James T. Ivy, a former foreign aid officer with the Economic Cooperation Administration.[77]

Why was the CIA, through the offices of the Asia Foundation, using American tax dollars to support the production of popular Korean films? The answer is that in the 1950s, commercial cinema in Asia was becoming a highly contested terrain in the cultural Cold War. Over the course of the decade, actors across the political spectrum in Asia treated entertainment films as a space in which their competing visions of modernity could be displayed before mass audiences, their ideologies simultaneously conveyed and masked by engaging stories and attractive styles.

Leftist films began finding wide audiences across Free Asia in the 1950s, which immediately caught the attention of the Asia Foundation and other cultural Cold Warriors in Washington. The People's Republic of China began exporting revolutionary films soon after coming to power in 1949. In 1954–55, its leaders shifted gears, launching a cultural diplomacy initiative that emphasized the production of films that would attract viewers with compelling content rather than hammering them with ideology.[78] The result was a steady flow of well-made pictures, many of them opera films based on folktales and rich with evocations of regional and classical culture. These films, which launched a "golden age" of Chinese opera films, projected a benevolent image of China as it was claiming leadership of the nonaligned movement, and their nostalgic evocations of the motherland proved extremely popular among the millions of overseas Chinese in Southeast Asia—a population that was being wooed by both Beijing and Washington. In Hong Kong, Beijing provided subsidies to three leftist production companies—Great Wall, Phoenix, and New Union—whose socially conscious films played to full houses in communist-owned theaters and were exported to Southeast Asian markets.[79] In Japan, independent producers freed from occupation censorship rules were finding success with films that the Asia Foundation regarded as communist in ideology and anti-American in subject matter—films like Sekigawa Hideo's *Mixed Blood Children* (1952), which focused on orphans abandoned by their GI fathers, and *Hiroshima* (1953), which recreated the horrors of the atomic bombing. Imai Tadashi's *The Tower of Lilies* (1953) told a story, in John Miller's words, about "the American slaughter of Okinawan school girls" during the war; it became the biggest moneymaker in Japanese history.[80] Similar to China's opera films, these often well-made leftist pictures marked the onset of the "golden age" of postwar Japanese cinema.[81]

The Asia Foundation, which had taken an interest in movies from its inception, sought ways to counter the market success of leftist films. In his 1956 report on the Korean film industry, John Miller voiced the foundation's belief in film's unparalleled ability to shape popular consciousness in Asia. Movies were a "powerful social, cultural, and political force" and the "most effective instrument for selling ideas," with a profound ability to "shape the lives" and attitudes of viewers, especially in areas where literacy rates were low and other forms of entertainment limited. TAF was adamant about not ceding this cultural ground to communists. In keeping with its initial orientation towards propaganda, it began by financing the production of individual documentaries (and at least one feature film, *The People Win Through* [1954], about the suppression of a communist insurrection in Burma) that were produced by Americans and aimed at Asians.[82] These films, however, had a hard time reaching audiences. They were seen by too few viewers, failed to engage them emotionally, and were often regarded with indifference and suspicion. "The Asians," wrote Hong Kong representative James Ivy in 1952, "have been bombarded with propaganda from all sides and they can smell it a mile away." Commercial films, in contrast, were becoming the most important form of entertainment across postwar Asia, with low ticket prices and broad distribution networks that enabled them to reach more people than any other form of mass media. Foundation executives realized that "the peoples of Asia paid heed solely to films which reached them through their regular theaters and which were designed chiefly for entertainment." A new approach was clearly necessary. "To be effective," said Ivy, "we must find ways and means of getting the people themselves to do the job—with assistance from us behind the scenes." TAF president Robert Blum agreed, and in 1953 he redirected TAF's film program away from propaganda and towards entertainment—precisely the shift that China would soon make as well.[83] The objective was simple yet audacious: to help anticommunist filmmakers attract larger audiences by making better and more entertaining movies.

TAF launched several commercial film projects in response to leftist initiatives, with uneven success. Its first and most ambitious project was in Hong Kong. Between 1953 and 1959 the foundation poured more than $500,000 into Asia Pictures, Ltd., a TAF-owned studio headed up by Cold War cultural entrepreneur Chang Kuo-sin, who aimed to make high-quality Mandarin films conveying a subtle "ideological message." After seven years, San Francisco concluded that the studio's political impact had been "minor, if not negligible": its films simply did not sell enough tickets in the target markets of Southeast Asia.[84] TAF's Tokyo office, in turn, was receptive to a proposal from Cold War cultural entrepreneur Masaichi Nagata, the anticommunist head of Daiei studio. Eager to improve his films' quality and exportability, Nagata sought TAF's assistance in arranging coproductions with Hollywood studios. In 1954 TAF arranged for Hollywood screenwriter Winston Miller to spend five weeks consulting at Daiei and working on a screenplay that would attract a Hollywood partner. TAF regarded this project as a modest success. While it did not culminate in any coproductions, Tokyo representative Noel Busch claimed (perhaps optimistically) that Miller had achieved the "thorough indoctrination of the active, working writers and directors of Japan's most energetic film company in U.S. methods of production, story construction, editing, cutting, etc., with consequent absorption by these influential persons of the outlook of the western point of view generally."[85]

The foundation had better success with the Asian Film Festival (AFF), which became its main vehicle for supporting commercial cinema across the region. The festival was the brainchild of Daiei's Nagata, who sought to increase regional film exports in the wake of the global success of *Rashomon* (1950) and to forge ties among Asia's noncommunist film industries. He created the Federation of Motion

Picture Producers Association of Asia (FPA), a regional professional organization that sponsored the festival. Launched in 1954, the AFF was the first major international film festival held in Asia and, like the Berlin Film Festival, it was a Cold War institution, open only to noncommunist countries. It was also an exemplary instance of TAF's modus operandi of supporting indigenous initiatives that aligned with Washington's interests. The festival harmonized with TAF's goals of strengthening noncommunist media production and binding Free Asia nations together through institutional, commercial, and personal ties. In addition to raising professional standards across the region by fostering cooperation and competition, TAF valued the festival as a site of cultural exchange: as filmmakers from across Asia watched each other's films, they would hopefully develop the international understanding that Washington saw as vital for the sustenance of Free Asia. The Asia Foundation supported the festival overtly and covertly throughout the 1950s, contributing financial and material resources, providing professional expertise and celebrities from Hollywood, and helping to police its ideological boundaries.[86]

The festival spurred TAF's interest in smaller film industries across the region, including South Korea's. While the festival was dominated in its early years by the more developed industries in Japan and Hong Kong, John Miller was convinced that the prestige of the event would "stimulate the comparatively backward film producers of Asia to higher quality production" as they focused their energies on making films good enough to enter and win prizes. The idea of aiding the Korean film industry seems to have originated in the Tokyo office in 1953, emerging out of early conversations with Nagata. Charles Tanner in San Francisco developed several preliminary proposals in 1953–54, drawing on the advice of his friend Oh Young-jin, who was touring the United States on a State Department grant. Seoul representative Philip Rowe set the project in motion in December 1954 after consulting with Korean officials on their most pressing cultural needs. One month later, in January 1955, John Miller arrived to perform his initial survey of the industry.[87]

Miller made clear in his February 1955 report that the fundamental issue in Korea was not competition from communist films, as was the case in Japan, Hong Kong, and Southeast Asia, but rather the lack of a material foundation on which an industry could be built. This lack of resources left filmmakers vulnerable to defection to the North, where a well-endowed state-run industry was taking shape. Rhee's government, paradoxically, also posed a danger. Miller warned that its monopoly on what little equipment did exist could easily turn into control over film content, stifling creativity and reducing cinema to mere propaganda, with its inevitable loss of popularity and thus ideological effectiveness. The Korean people, suffering as they were from social and economic dislocation, were in danger of becoming disillusioned with their fragile democracy. What they needed, according to Miller, was "information and entertainment which explains democratic ideals."[88]

Miller proposed, as had Oh Young-jin in his 1953 conversation with Charles Tanner, that TAF create an equipment rental company and film processing laboratory that would be available to all commercial producers. His proposal followed TAF's revised media guidelines, developed in the wake of the disappointing Asia Pictures and Daiei studio projects: it did not involve TAF in film production; it provided support for the industry as a whole, rather than a single studio; and it was structured as a single large infusion of aid rather than an ongoing subsidy. Budgeted at $58,000, this was not intended as an elaborate studio. Miller characterized the equipment and facilities as "emergency measures designed to supply such needs only until private enterprise can, without subsidy, do the same job." The objective was to "stimulate" rather than underwrite a commercial industry: "Let us only give them a working chance."[89] Miller had faith that Korea's filmmakers would seize the opportunity.

San Francisco approved the proposal and Miller implemented it between June and December of 1956. When in October of that year Syngman Rhee asked TAF president Robert Blum for assistance for the film industry, he was pleased to hear that a project was already underway. Miller began by shepherding into existence a professional organization, the Korean Motion Picture Cultural Association (KMPCA), whose board of directors was composed of Cold War cultural entrepreneurs from across the film and media industries, including Oh Young-jin.[90] This was one of the instances in which TAF had to create a local organization in order to fund it. Miller purchased modern equipment in Hollywood, including a 35 mm Mitchell synchronized sound camera and Korea's first automatic film-developing machine, and he curated a small library of Japanese and American technical books and two hundred recordings of music and sound effects. The KMPCA studio, as it was initially known, began operations in October 1956, a few months before the privately financed Samsung and Anyang studios. It immediately came into heavy use and within a few months was financially self-supporting. In August 1957 it moved to a new location northwest of Seoul, with a new soundstage built by a Korean investor, and became known as the Jeongneung studio. The automatic developing machine, which was operated by a USIS-trained technician and dramatically improved picture quality, proved particularly attractive to filmmakers and by 1958 was in operation twenty-four hours a day. Cho Tong-jae, program advisor in TAF's Seoul office, estimated that in the first half of 1958 over 80 percent of commercial producers used the lab to process their film.[91] In 1959, the KMPCA claimed that its equipment was being "used in producing nearly all the feature films produced in Korea."[92]

In addition to supplying it with material resources, the Seoul office nudged Korea's blossoming industry in a cosmopolitan direction by underwriting its participation in the Asian Film Festival throughout the 1950s. Rhee's Ministry of Education also supported participation in the festival by working with producers to select the entries. TAF advanced these efforts in diverse ways. The Seoul representatives encouraged the KMPCA to apply for membership in the Federation of Motion Picture Producers Association of Asia (FPA), smoothed the way for the application's quick approval, and made dollars available to pay the association's membership dues. They enabled Korea to send large delegations to the festival by paying the expenses for select members, and provided staffer Cho Tong-jae to act as translator and guide. They paid to send three observers to the 1955 festival in Singapore and for KMPCA board member Oh Young-jin to attend the 1958 festival in Manila as a judge. They even worked with TAF representatives in host cities across Asia to ensure that Korean delegations were accorded a positive reception.[93] As Miller predicted, Korean filmmakers were eager to improve the quality of their films in order to have them accepted into the festival and win prizes. As a result of these combined efforts, at least eight Korean films screened in competition at the Asian Film Festival between 1957 and 1960.[94] Several of these films won prizes, beginning in 1957 with *The Wedding Day* (1956), which was directed by KMPCA board member Lee Byung-il and written by fellow board member Oh Young-jin. Through TAF's efforts, the festival became an important venue for forging professional ties between Korean filmmakers and their counterparts overseas. Participation in the Asian Film Festival stimulated the exhibition of Korean films at other festivals across the Free World, including Berlin, Venice, and San Francisco. This festival exposure, in turn, stimulated the commercial export of Korean films (fourteen in 1958), including to the ideologically contested markets of Southeast Asia.[95] All of this served to make South Korea visible to other Free World nations— a core TAF objective—as an independent country with its own unique cultural traditions, and as a modernizing one capable of producing technologically competent films within a capitalist mode of production.

Han's professional ambitions and the Asia Foundation's cosmopolitan agenda intersected at the Asian Film Festival. Han participated in every festival between 1956 and 1961, save one. He was a member of the delegations to Hong Kong in 1956, Tokyo in 1957, and Manila in 1961, and his films screened in competition in Manila in 1958 (*Hyperbolae of Youth*) and won an award in Kuala Lumpur in 1959 (*Because I Love You* [1958]). Han shared Miller's view on the importance of the festival as a spur to the improvement of Korean films and the modernization of its industry. After returning from Hong Kong in 1956, he wrote an article for the *Chosŏn ilbo* newspaper lamenting the underdeveloped state of Korea's "newborn" film industry. He praised the festival as an "impetus" to improving the technical quality of Korean films so that they would become acceptable from an "international point of view" and thus able to compete at international festivals.[96]

By 1962 TAF considered the Korea project to be its most successful film program in Asia. The foundation's objectives had been achieved and a flourishing private commercial film industry had come into existence: there were now eight commercial film processing labs in Seoul, and individual production companies had become profitable enough to purchase their own equipment. More importantly, both the number and quality of films had improved significantly, and they were having "an increasing influence . . . as an important cultural medium." The program had in fact exceeded foundation expectations. "The KMPCA has had a far broader influence than any of us hoped for in the beginning," wrote former Seoul representative Jack E. James, creating new jobs and outlets for creative energies and stimulating exhibitors to build new theaters. In light of this success, the foundation in 1962 closed out its stake in the studio and transferred the ownership of all the equipment to the KMPCA. Four years later, Cho Tong-jae summarized the effects of the project after meeting with the KMPCA membership: TAF's intervention in the industry had yielded "immediate and swift" results and had "virtually revolutionized motion picture production processes" by reducing costs and enhancing quality. "The Foundation support of the KMPCA has been, as is widely recognized in Korea," he reported, "directly contributory to the growth of the Korean motion picture industry into what it is today."[97] No longer necessary in Korea's thriving commercial film industry and with its equipment worn out, the KMPCA dissolved itself in 1965, its mission complete.[98]

HAN HYUNG-MO AS MODERNIZER

Han Hyung-mo was, in many ways, exactly the type of filmmaker that TAF hoped to cultivate: a native modernizer of Korea's film industry and its cinema. He was, in the words of film scholar Chung Chong-hwa, the "pioneer of the well-made commercial film" and thus the father of the modern Korean cinema that blossomed in the 1950s. Han's commercial success meant that he did not need to apply directly to TAF for assistance, in contrast to colleagues like Oh Young-jin and Lee Byung-il. He did, however, take advantage of TAF's interventions in postwar public culture and sometimes used the facilities at the KMPCA studio.[99] More importantly, Han's ambitions for the development of the industry meshed closely with those of the Asia Foundation. Both TAF and Han shared a vision of a Korean film industry modernized along capitalist lines and producing popular films that expressed an optimistic attitude towards Western-style modernization.

Han's innovations were felt across all areas of filmmaking, including technology. Filmmakers and critics admired Han as a brilliant technician who understood, and was thus able to improve, the mechanical dimensions of filmmaking. Han introduced complex sound editing in *Breaking the Wall*. He built Korea's first camera crane for *Madame Freedom* and engineered a playback system capable of synchronizing music and image. He helped develop Korea's own anamorphic widescreen process—"Buksamscope"—which was first used in *Poor Lovers* (1959). And he was among the earliest directors to use synchronized sound effectively, in *Because I Love You*.[100]

Han saw the potential for Korea's "handicraft" operations to develop into an industrial mode of production, one that was rooted in secure companies that would make serial production possible. He possessed an astute commercial sensibility and aimed for the box office every time, understanding that each successful film provided the capital to produce the next one. In order to create an institutional foundation for his work, he founded Han Hyung-mo Productions in 1954 and two years later affiliated it with the Samsung Film Company. While the two companies shared personnel and resources, they divided responsibilities, with Han's company focused on production and Samsung on distribution. This type of business relationship was new and proved very successful. The two companies had a reputation, rare at the time, for completing their productions, for being honest with investors' money, and for using that money to make high-quality and profitable pictures. Generous with his production crews, Han was able to hire the most skilled people, who in turn gave him their best work. As a result, Han and Samsung had no problems raising investment capital from urban and provincial theater owners, who had confidence that they would get an audience-attracting picture in return. The phenomenal financial success of *Madame Freedom* secured the companies' standing and allowed them to enhance it by building their own production space, the Samsung Studio. Han's entrepreneurial sensibility enabled him to establish himself securely as an independent producer. He owned his own camera and editing equipment that he rented out to other filmmakers, had a stake in a production studio, and had valuable ties to the Ministry of Defense with its US-supplied equipment.[101]

Han Hyung-mo was also a modernizer of Korean cinema—of the films that this developing industry produced. Han used his technical skills to produce visual splendor. At a time when many of his colleagues struggled to convey a story clearly, Han understood how to use film form expressively. In doing so he earned the admiration of his peers. Director Lee Hyung-pyo recalled that Han's masterful cinematography on *Hometown in the Heart* (1949)—a lyrical film set in a mist-shrouded Buddhist temple—made it the single most memorable film of the liberation era. Critics praised *Breaking the Wall* for its dramatic synthesis of ideological and personal conflict, holding it up as the standard to which other filmmakers should aim. Director Kim Kee-duk recalled the influence that Han's noirish spy melodrama *The Hand of Destiny* had on fellow filmmakers, with its expressive deployment of shadows, its surprising use of close-ups, and its sense of rhythm created by camera movement in combination with editing. Lighting directors, in turn, were in awe of Han's "fastidious" attention to lighting in all his films.[102]

Han also modernized the social function of film, abandoning the didactic role that had held sway since the colonial era in favor of mass entertainment in the tradition of Hollywood. With excitement rather than moral uplift as his goal, Han presented characters and scenes more scandalous than exemplary.[103] He pursued originality. He engineered Korea's first on-screen kiss in *The Hand of Destiny*, sparked an uproar with his depiction of a professor's wife engaging in extramarital affairs in *Madame Freedom*, and presented Korea's first lesbian character in

A Jealousy (1960). He introduced new genres into Korean cinema and combined them in innovative ways. *Breaking the Wall* created the anticommunist film as a distinct genre. *Hyperbolae of Youth* combined elements of the musical with those of the romantic comedy, a genre which Han developed further in *A Female Boss* (1959) and *My Sister Is a Hussy* (1961). *Madame Freedom* launched the modern melodrama. *The Devil* (1957) initiated the detective film. Many of his films incorporated elements of film noir.

What stood out most to Han's contemporaries was his ability to tap into Korea's emerging modern life. Han's films were deeply embedded within the larger public culture of which they were a vital part, and like *budae jjigae* they combined disparate elements into something new and delicious. Popular novels became scripts, fashionable restaurants appeared as sets, and hit songs permeated soundtracks. Han filled his productions with all that was fresh and dynamic, treating his films as portals into a cosmopolitan, metropolitan way of life. His characters go to night-clubs and listen to jazz, play miniature golf and watch bicycle races, read *Reader's Digest* and drink Coca Cola, dress in the latest Western fashions and flirt openly with each other. Han incorporated the latest trends into his films and repaid the loan by generating catchphrases and character types that lived well beyond the theater. The currents running through public culture ran through his films as well. His films made visible the ideas and forces that were eroding established traditions and ushering in something new: individualism, sexual liberation, capitalism. More profoundly, Han's films expressed an optimism about modernity. It was this attitude that set him apart from his peers, who, according to one contemporary critic, believed that a film "should show a monster called modernity chasing humans, what that monster is, and what is gained after fighting the monster." Han challenged that view, as well as the "culture of despair" manifested in neorealist films like Yu Hyun-mok's *Aimless Bullet* (1961) that appealed so powerfully to Korea's intellectuals. He was not naïve, however, and the corruptions of modern life—from tax evasion to the abuse of power—found frequent expression in his films. He presented modern urban life, in the words of Cho Junhyoung, "as both attractive and dangerous."[104]

Han's visual vocabulary of modern life overlapped significantly with that of *Yŏwŏn*, with images of glamour, consumption, and leisure figuring prominently in both. Most importantly, they shared a vision of women as active agents in public life. Han's films, like *Yŏwŏn*'s pages, were full of working women from across the class spectrum, including shop girls, office workers, nurses, hairdressers, and media professionals. More strikingly, Han and *Yŏwŏn* depicted women as powerful, and they surrounded them with traditionally masculine markers of authority: stacks of money, towering modern buildings, guns. In Han's films as in *Yŏwŏn*'s pages, one could see women working behind large desks and maneuvering through the city in big American cars. Several of Han's films even nodded towards *Yŏwŏn* in their storylines. *A Female Boss* revolves around a female publisher of a women's

FIGURE 9. Fashionable magazine publisher (Jo Mi-ryeong) in *A Female Boss* (1958) with a cover of *The Modern Woman* and a world map. (Courtesy KOFA)

magazine, the cover of which cover strongly resembles *Yŏwŏn's* (figure 9), and *Men vs. Women* (1959) features an obstetrician heroine who is profiled in an admiring magazine spread acclaiming her as a successful professional woman. Actresses from Han's films, in turn, appeared regularly in *Yŏwŏn's* pages demonstrating the latest fashion trends.

Perhaps most powerfully, Han's films voiced the aspirations of the young postwar generation, portraying the possibilities—for work, love, and pleasure—that modernity was opening up. His films were not accurate depictions of typical Korean lives, which were often unspeakably difficult during these years. They are perhaps best understood, instead, as works of quasi–science fiction, proffering visions of a lifestyle that would not become widespread for another forty years.

Style

4

The Après Girl

Character and Plot

Madame Freedom (1956) opens with a depiction of contemporary Korea in a state of flux. The first several shots reveal a menacing, onrushing modernity as cars and buses jam the nighttime streets of downtown Seoul, their blinding headlights casting pedestrians into harsh relief as they try to navigate the streets, their cacophonous horns creating a sense of discord. The following shot, however, reveals a quiet residential neighborhood of traditional *hanok* houses, whose tiled roofs and glowing windows suggest the ongoing vitality of traditional modes of living. A slow tracking movement brings viewers to the door of one of these houses, and a dissolve transports them inside. The first interior shot, a close-up, centers on a shiny electric iron gliding across a piece of clothing. As the camera pulls back, it reveals a seemingly cozy domestic scene: a mother plies the iron on the floor, as her young son does homework at a small desk and her husband immerses himself in a newspaper with a charcoal brazier warming his feet. The contented tone quickly sours, however. When the son requests assistance with his homework, the mother, occupied with her ironing, asks her husband to help him. He blithely ignores her, prompting his wife to scowl and mutter "How callous." "I'm busy with my manuscripts," says the husband as he gets up and leaves the room, avoiding her gaze. "You always say that," retorts the wife bitterly, as she puts down her iron and turns to her son. Clearly this is not the first such exchange, suggesting an ongoing conflict within what viewers would recognize as an arranged marriage (figure 10).

This scene introduces a debate about modernization that will run through the rest of the film. The debate is not one of tradition versus modernity. This middle-class nuclear family, with access to electricity, sufficient resources to buy labor-saving devices, and no cohabiting in-laws, is clearly embarked on a modern life.[1]

FIGURE 10. Mme Oh (Kim Jeong-rim) with her electric iron, husband, and son in the opening scene of *Madame Freedom* (1956). (Courtesy KOFA)

Rather, the tension is between a feminized cosmopolitan and a masculinist cultural nationalist vision of Korean modernity. *Madame Freedom* explores this tension through the melodramatic conflict of an unhappy marriage. Oh Seon-yeong, also called Madame Oh, embodies a vision of cosmopolitan modernity: she is a modern woman who welcomes the influx of Western culture as a means of escape from a family life she finds constraining. Embracing the technological modernity of the electric iron (like the ones featured in *Yŏwŏn*), she expresses a desire for a corresponding social modernity: she wants her husband's assistance in raising their son (a variation, perhaps, on Lee Tai-young's pink- and blue-trimmed aprons). Her husband, Professor Jang, serves as a figure of cultural nationalist modernity. Shielding himself from his wife's demands with the newspaper, he enjoys the masculine privileges represented by the traditional brazier, which warms his feet alone. Serene in his patriarchal role, he dismisses the idea that he should take on any share of woman's work and is blind to his wife's disaffection with the dynamics of traditional family life. He turns away from her (and her shiny electric iron) to immerse himself in the study of the nation's cultural heritage.

With this chapter I begin my inquiry into Cold War cosmopolitanism as a film style, focusing on how it is embedded in the characterization of the modern woman as she appears in Han's films. In crafting his film around the conflict between husband and wife, Han dramatized competing ideas about women's status that were playing out simultaneously in the debate over the revision of the Family Law. Was a woman in the 1950s still defined through her role as daughter, wife, and mother within a patriarchal family, and thus as a vessel of Confucian virtue and Korean national essence? Or was she an individual, as in the liberal West, someone whose status was determined by her own choices and actions, and thus a modern subject in her own right?

To see *Madame Freedom* as staging a debate, rather than articulating a unified position, is to understand something about Han's prowess as a commercial artist. It is to recognize *Madame Freedom* as an ideologically open text that appealed to a broad range of viewers and perhaps to conflicting beliefs within individual viewers. Han put a changing society up on screen and invited viewers to enjoy it from their own perspective. In a period of social transformation such as the 1950s, when many traditional values were being questioned but not wholly overthrown, such openness made good box office sense. It allowed a film to speak with multiple voices, some that went "with the grain" of a dominant discourse, and others that went "against the grain" to articulate emergent perspectives.

Through his female characters, Han translated the Cold War liberal ideology into what Mica Nava has called "visceral cosmopolitanism"—a structure of feeling in which a connection to the foreign is experienced at an immediate, personal level and thus accessible to ordinary women. In contrast to more elite forms of worldliness generated by international travel or higher education, visceral cosmopolitanism is an everyday experience in which the "allure of elsewhere and others" is encountered in the city street, the shop, and the dance floor. Accessed through commercial forms of culture, it is often experienced as feeling and desire and becomes a means of making sense of a rapidly shifting social order.[2]

Cold War cosmopolitanism found expression in Han's films via a new type of cinematic character: the female individual. In crafting his female characters, Han tapped into emergent ideas about women that were circulating widely in public culture—in US propaganda, in *Yŏwŏn* magazine, in the daily lives of working women, and in the public utterances of feminists such as Helen Kim and Lee Tai-young—but were not yet normative. Amidst the influx of Western ideas, Han's characters attempt to liberate themselves from patriarchal constraints and remake themselves as autonomous agents. They are members of an avant-garde, navigating the opportunities and hazards of a new society as it is taking shape around them. They are emblems of modern selfhood, the embodiment of what Steven Chung has called the "liberatory-utopian promises of postwar reconstruction,"[3] and they carry the ideals of autonomous personhood that America's cultural Cold Warriors were promoting as the foundation of modern life. Han's female characters thus served as one of the most important sites within postwar public culture where a vision of Cold War cosmopolitan feminism was articulated.

THE APRÈS GIRL

What happens when a middle-class married woman leaves her home? This is the question that *Madame Freedom* poses. Mme Oh is a professor's wife who takes a job at the Paris Boutique, a Western luxury-goods shop, and embraces the new Western culture that is sweeping through Seoul. Her pursuit of "freedom," along with her exploration of what that concept means for a woman, drives the plot and gives the film its title. The film depicts the development of a woman's capacity for agency and her growing willingness to exercise it in the public realm. After making her first independent decision to take the paying job, Mme Oh subsequently chooses to discontinue her unpaid domestic duties. She rarely returns home after work, instead spending her newfound leisure time in cafés and restaurants with her friend Mme Choi, who entangles her in a scheme to smuggle in the foreign luxury goods that she sells at the shop and has come to enjoy herself. As her independence of mind develops, Mme Oh violates social conventions at will, unafraid of the gossip her actions stir up. In keeping with her new financial and social autonomy, Mme Oh decides to pursue her own sexual pleasure. Unhappy in her arranged marriage, she enters into a dalliance with her neighbor Mr. Shin, a college student about to depart for America, who teaches her how to dance. While practicing this new American skill at a dance hall, she initiates an affair with her female boss's husband, Mr. Han. As all of this is unfolding, she increasingly treats her mild-mannered (and poorly paid) professor husband with disdain, lying to him about her activities and ignoring the pleadings of her dutiful young son, who spends the entire film doing homework. She is not a wholly sympathetic character. Meanwhile, Professor Jang embarks on his own, more chaste, relationship with an attractive young woman. The film reaches its climax when Mme Oh is caught in a hotel room with her married lover and slapped across the face by his angry wife. In a brief conclusion, a humiliated Mme Oh walks through the nighttime streets and returns to her home, where she submits to her husband's chastisement of her as a shameless woman.

Mme Oh is an *apure kol*, or "après girl." Heir to the colonial era's "modern girl," the après girl was one of the 1950s' most prominent cultural figures of modernity. The term was derived from the French expression *après guerre*, meaning "after the war," and it evoked the social and cultural changes ushered in by the Korean War. To be "après" implied a willed break from the Confucian virtues that had defined Korean womanhood for centuries and continued to have broad currency. The après girl was assertive rather than selfless, sexually bold rather than chaste, and active in public rather than sequestered in the home. As Charles Kim has shown, novelists, reporters, and essayists produced a catalogue of stock après girl characters who populated postwar magazines and newspapers. These included the masculinized "contemporary girl" who rejects the role of housewife and mother and instead pursues a materialistic lifestyle; the snooty "university student" who thinks she's smarter than a man; the "*gye* madam," or money-grubbing house-wife, who participates in a savings club and lends out money; and the "liberated wife," a middle-class or affluent housewife who pursues her personal pleasure as a consumer of leisure, entertainment, and imported goods.[4] Après girls engage in conspicuous consumption and spend their time dancing, going to the movies, and dating. Sexually emancipated, they date foreigners, pursue sex for pleasure rather than procreation, and seek to choose their own husbands rather than entering into arranged marriages.[5] Above all, the après girl challenged the foundational principle that women were inferior to men and thus subject to their authority.

Han Hyung-mo populated *Madame Freedom* with the full range of après girls. Part of the film's success derived from Han's ability to put this new social type up on screen in all her permutations. Mme Oh's friend Mme Choi is a "*gye* madam" who runs a money club. Her niece, Myeong-ok, is a self-important "university student" who embraces Western notions of love and romance and peppers her speech with English words. Miss Park, her husband's love interest, is a fashionable "contemporary girl" who works in an American office. It was Mme Oh herself, however, who captured public attention as the quintessential "liberated housewife." Mme Oh's decision to shed her familial obligations and pursue her individual feelings was a shocking violation of social norms that prioritized duty to others over indulgence of self. *Madame Freedom* was scandalous, and thus deeply attractive to audiences.

Mme Oh liberates herself by turning towards the world beyond Korea's borders. When she leaves her home for the first time, Mme Oh crosses a small but symbolic bridge that separates her home from the street. In doing so, she reveals her characterological DNA: Han is introducing into postwar cinema a female protagonist modeled on Ibsen's Nora, whose departure from home in *A Doll's House* (1879) made her a global icon of early feminism. Crossing the bridge marks Mme Oh's transition out of a private space marked as Korean and into a public space marked as cosmopolitan. In the street, Mme Oh ceases to be a "wise mother, good wife" tending selflessly to her husband and son's needs. Instead, she moves freely amid the colonial architecture of downtown Seoul, making her way towards a paying job at a shop named for the capital of France. Leaving her *hanok* behind, she banters with her handsome young neighbor, Mr. Shin, about the German poet Goethe, Western ideals of romantic love, and the possibilities for individual freedom. Modern technology displaces the washtub and washboard at which she had previously labored, as she allows herself to be photographed by Mr. Shin and swept away in an American car by her friend Mme Choi. As the film progresses, she continues to encounter "abroad" indirectly in her everyday life. Mme Oh's cosmopolitanism is intimate and emotional, sensory and tactile. She wears a fitted gray suit, perms her hair, and applies lipstick to her mouth (figure 11). She handles imported perfume and purses. She eats steak with a fork and knife. She listens to jazz and waltzes in the arms of men who are not her husband. She kisses her lover. In all these ways, she embraces the Cold War's "ideology of freedom" as a

FIGURE 11. Visceral cosmopolitanism: Mme Oh applies lipstick in *Madame Freedom*. (Courtesy KOFA)

structure of feeling rather than as a political imperative. As Mica Nava notes, such visceral cosmopolitanism is dialogic in nature, embracing the foreign as a source of "counter-identification" that exists in tension with a nationalist traditionalism associated with the masculine. A form of "psychic revolt," this type of cosmopolitanism expresses "a desire to escape *from* family, home and country" and into a space of greater personal freedom that is identified with the foreign.[6]

Professor Jang, in sharp contrast to his wife, is a scholar of Korea's national language. Given the suppression of the Korean language during the colonial era and the centuries-long use of Chinese characters among Sinocentric elites, Professor Jang's linguistic expertise has strong nationalist overtones. It also resonated with the postcolonial drive to teach *hangul*, the Korean alphabet, in the public schools and to use it exclusively in print culture.[7] In his spare time Professor Jang teaches Korean grammar to women who work in an American office. As a masculine authority figure, he guides them towards a deeper understanding of their national culture and, perhaps, offsets the lure of their American surroundings. It is through this class that he meets and enters into a chaste romance with Miss Park, one of his students. Neither Professor Jang nor Miss Park is an emblem of unadulterated tradition. Professor Jang allows his wife to choose whether to take the job at the Paris Boutique, and the elegant Miss Park wears the latest in Euro-American fashions and presumably speaks English with her American coworkers. Rather, they embody the ideal of "wholesome modernization," which emphasized the adaptation of select Western norms in public life while preserving the "essence" of Koreanness in the private realm of personal relations. Miss Park is distinguished from Mme Oh primarily by her attitude towards sexuality and autonomy. While Mme Oh rejects her husband's authority and pursues her sexual desires independently of him, the chaste Miss Park admires Professor Jang and eagerly submits herself to him as a student of Koreanness. For Professor Jang and Miss Park, as with the opponents of the reform of the Family Law, the submission of a woman's sexuality and autonomy to the authority of a man is inseparable from an essential Koreanness that must not be sacrificed. The maintenance of gender hierarchy forms the core of the "fine, beautiful customs" that must be preserved.

Representations of the après girl in print and on screen were often derisive, depicting her as frivolous and debauched. She was an emblem of cultural inauthenticity and national betrayal, much as the modern girl had been in the 1920s. Some scholars have argued that the après girl was a stalking horse produced by patriarchal nationalists who regarded any threat to male authority as a threat to the fledgling nation. As Chungmoo Choi has written, "South Korean male nationalists . . . turn misogynic eyes" towards what they regard as overly westernized women, "not only because these women challenge traditional patriarchal authority but also because their familiarity with (materially superior, masculine) American culture may lead them to collaborate with the dominating foreign forces." The ideological effect of the debased après girl, according to this reading, was to reaffirm the Confucian virtues that she violated and to maintain the subordination of women to the patriarchal family.[8]

I believe it is a mistake to accept this reading of the après girl as an exclusively reactionary construct. I want to recuperate her, instead, as a complex cultural figure whose meaning was not so singular and coherent. The après girl, I suggest, was a richly ambivalent cultural figure of modernity—a complex icon for the benefits, as well as the costs, of Korea's postcolonial, postwar, and Cold War modernity.

READING AGAINST THE GRAIN

Madame Freedom is a melodrama, and it conforms to many of the conventions initially established in nineteenth-century European literature and polished by Hollywood in women's pictures from the 1930s to the 1950s. A woman's experiences occupy the center of the narrative, which focuses on the loosening of family bonds. Emotions are privileged over dramatic action, with music helping to express those sentiments that can't be fully articulated, and themes of impotence, loss, and entrapment—within a social role, within a physical space—develop. Melodrama takes shape in periods of social unease. According to literary scholar Peter Brooks, "melodrama starts from and expresses the anxiety brought by a frightening new world in which the traditional patterns of moral order no longer provide the necessary social glue. It plays out the force of that anxiety with the apparent triumph of villainy, and it dissipates it with the eventual victory of virtue." Moral conflicts are at the heart of melodrama, as characters struggle with shifting social norms and challenges to once-secure ethical imperatives. "The ritual of melodrama," writes Brooks, "involves the confrontation of clearly identified antagonists and the expulsion of one of them."[9] Endings thus take on added significance, as the moment in which the social order is purged and the moral order affirmed. *Madame Freedom* localizes these global conventions, shaping their expression around the specificities of Korean culture and contemporary life in Seoul.

Many critics of the film, in keeping with Brooks's approach to melodrama, have emphasized the restoration of patriarchal authority that takes place in the film's final scene. It is an unambiguous scene of punishment, in which Professor Jang finally asserts his full masculine authority over his wayward wife. Physically barring Mme Oh from reentering the house, he angrily rebukes her for bringing shame on the family. "Driven by vanity," he chastises, "you have abandoned your family. You gladly exchanged your duties as a mother. With what honor did you come back?" Mme Oh passively accepts this condemnation and verbally takes responsibility for the disruption of the family. The scene visualizes this restoration of the patriarchal family order with great clarity: Mme Oh crouches at her husband's feet as he berates her (figure 12), and in the film's final shot she kneels on the ground to embrace her son while her husband towers above them both, standing in the middle of the little bridge that she had crossed with such eagerness at the film's outset. These are powerful images that reaffirm the Confucian principle of sexual difference and hierarchy and that validate the patriarchal authority of the father. Mme Oh's assertion of individuality is voided as she is sutured back into her familial relationships. Her cosmopolitan affiliations likewise fade as she stands in front of her *hanok*, dressed in a *hanbok*, and is confronted by her husband who also wears *hanbok* beneath his overcoat. Her full reincorporation into the family remains uncertain as she remains outside the home, however. The public street in which she once conversed about Goethe has been restored to its ancient status as a site of female humiliation and shame.

Many scholars have read "with the grain" of this ending, accepting Professor Jang as the film's mouthpiece who delivers its critique of the corrupting effects of liberal American culture. This is a dominant reading, one that the film makes easy to arrive at and that echoes scholars' reading of the après girl as a conservative foil. Steven Chung, for instance, reads this scene, and the film as a whole, as delivering "moral lessons, elaborate illustrations of the pitfalls of sexual and social freedom." He identifies the ending as an act of "conversion," in which the "remorseful" woman is restored to "cultural tradition" and her proper position within the domestic sphere.[10] Byun Jai-ran in turn, describing Mme Oh's downfall

FIGURE 12. Patriarchy restored in *Madame Freedom*'s final scene. (Courtesy KOFA)

as the film's "inevitable conclusion," argues that the film "adheres to the point of view of that generation's male moralists, who rebuke the sexual depravity of women." While the film depicts Mme Oh's escape from patriarchal domesticity, "the gender ideology in the film seems to be a new form of regulation imposed on liberated women rather than a liberation of women." Han, says Byun, treats Mme Oh as a "dangerous woman" who must ultimately be contained: it is "a film that tries to limit 'Madame Freedom' and warns people of the danger associated with her rather than praising the female protagonist." Other scholars have likewise argued that the film ends up reinforcing the very patriarchal values that Mme Oh had challenged: "the film is clearly a cautionary tale about the dangers of freedom and sexual desire on the part of women."[11]

In contrast to these scholars, I want to read against the grain of the plot's patriarchal conclusion. As Thomas Elsaesser has written, film melodramas invite a contrapuntal reading of style in relation to narrative because they invest so much expressive capacity in the formal register. Much of a melodrama's meaning, then, is expressed through the skillful deployment of film form, in which colorful nuances of style undercut the clarity of a black-and-white moral universe.[12] By paying attention to *Madame Freedom*'s style, we can see how the film is not simply a conservative critique of its female protagonist: while the film's narrative arc endorses a patriarchal vision of domestic containment, some of the film's other formal properties do not.

I want to explore here the meaning-making abilities of the film in two ways. I begin by charting the construction of the "textual spectator," which is to say the formal properties of the film that structure any viewer's relationship to the characters. I then consider how the film's meaning might have been constructed by a "historical spectator"—an actual person watching the film in South Korea in 1956—who had access to other texts and experiences that were available at the same time. Together, these approaches reveal a far more nuanced vision of the film's après girl protagonist than scholars have so far recognized.

The question of viewer identification is crucial to understanding *Madame Freedom*'s full meaning. Miriam Hansen, in her discussion of Shanghai cinema of the 1930s, argued that the "contradictions of modernity are enacted through the figure of the woman, very often, literally, across the body of the woman who tries to live them but more often than not fails." The woman's failure to navigate the transition to modernity—expressed at the level of narrative—is not, however, the key issue for Hansen. Rather, her significance as a character is that she offered new "models of identification for being modern." She offered new subjectivities to historical viewers, new ways for women in the audience to "imagine their own strategies of survival, performance, and sociality, to make sense of living in the interstices of radically unequal times, places, and conditions."[13] This question of identification is central to *Madame Freedom*'s meaning-making. Although Professor Jang stands in for postcolonial traditionalism's socially dominant view of Korea's path to modernity, the film makes it very difficult to identify with him. Rather, it is Mme Oh whom the film constructs as the viewer's primary object of identification and proxy.

I want to begin reading against the grain of the film's ending by situating Han's film in relation to the best-selling novel of the same title from which it was adapted. Written by Jeong Bi-seok and originally published in 215 installments in the *Seoul sinmun* between January and August of 1954, the novel was an immediate *succes de scandale*, boosting the paper's daily circulation by 50,000 and driving conversations throughout the city for months. When it was published in book form later that year it sold 140,000 copies, making it Korea's first best seller.[14] With its popularity, the novel did much to establish the après girl character in print culture. Many filmmakers were attracted to the novel because of its tremendous popularity, but Jeong decided to sell the film rights to Han and producer Bang Dae-hun because he valued them as skilled filmmakers and trusted that the film would not be a "failure."[15] And indeed, Han's film remains faithful to the novel in many respects, reproducing much of its story, narrative structure, characters, settings, and themes. Han follows Jeong's lead, for example, in casting Mme Oh as a revolutionary, Nora-like figure swept up in the social changes of the period. "Revolution does not necessarily mean that shots be heard and blood be spilled," wrote Jeong in the novel. "There can be bloodless revolution, peaceful revolution. Seventy years ago, a woman named Nora left behind her child and husband and ran away from the doll's house. At the time, it was one kind of revolution."[16]

Han's departures from the novel, however, are crucial to the film's meaning. One major point of departure involves the structuring of reader versus viewer identification. In the novel, Jeong deploys an authoritative third-person omniscient narrator who comments directly on the characters' thoughts and actions and firmly guides the reader's sympathies towards Professor Jang. The narrator consistently presents Professor Jang's thoughts and actions favorably, while assuming an overtly negative stance towards those of his wife. The narrator presents Mme Oh, for instance, as having only a very superficial understanding of the ideals of freedom and democracy, concepts that the novel takes pains to explore. The narrator describes Professor Jang as wanting "to teach proper democratic ideology to his wife," a lesson that Mme Oh does not understand because she "confused freedom and license." Where Mme Oh selfishly understands democracy as the freedom to engage in licentious behavior, Professor Jang affirms democracy as something that takes place within the family, and he puts forth an ideal of a more egalitarian relationship between husband and wife who yet retain much of their traditional social roles. Similarly, Mme Oh is "unaware of the importance of *hangul*," the Korean alphabet that is her husband's research specialty, and thus fails to realize the value of the "holy business" of her husband's work.[17] The narrator consistently contrasts the husband's proper understanding of modernization with his wife's improper one.[18] The strong voice of the narrator, and its overt condemnation of Mme Oh, makes it difficult for the reader to fully identify with Mme Oh and to see her in ways other than those that the narrator suggests.

In Han's film, however, the viewer has little choice *but* to identify with Mme Oh, despite her morally questionable behavior. Through the dexterous manipulation of film form, Han constructs a textual spectator that is closely aligned with his female protagonist. Han eschews the novel's strong third-person narrator, thereby eliminating the authoritative voice that articulates patriarchal Confucian values. Instead, the film delegates control of the narrative to Mme Oh. The film allocates most of the screen time to her, charting her transformation from dutiful "wise mother, good wife" into an après girl in great detail, and allowing her choices and actions to drive the plot forward. The film relegates Professor Jang to the subplot, where he has limited screen time and even less control over the main plot's momentum. Spending so much time with Mme Oh, the viewer learns the process of individual self-invention alongside her. She serves as the viewer's proxy: when she leaves the house and enters the city, she brings the viewer along with her. Watching her, the viewer learns how to order coffee in a coffee shop, how to flirt with a man, how to put on lipstick and powder, how to dance to Western music, how to eat Western food, and even how to lie to one's husband and dismiss his protestations against her behavior. Ultimately, the viewer learns how to escape the patriarchal constraints on womanhood. By encouraging this identification with Mme Oh through temporal duration and on-screen presence, the film constructs its heroine as a mediatory figure who guides viewers through the very same tumultuous social conditions in which they, too, are immersed.

The film also cultivates the viewer's identification with Mme Oh by privileging the female gaze through editing and point-of-view shots. In a number of important scenes, as Kathleen McHugh has pointed out, both "the gaze and its object are emphatically *female*." Mme Oh's gaze is privileged in the women's luncheon scene, in which a series of point-of-view shots depicts Mme Oh and her friend Mme Choi "looking closely at the lavish jewelry and stylish clothes of their fellow club members." A similar exchange of "female-to-female gazes" takes place in the Paris Boutique, when Mme Oh's female boss watches her make a lucrative sale and winks at her with approval, a look that Mme Oh returns with a smile of pleasure. Han creates parallel point-of-view shots in the scenes where Mme Oh and her niece watch each other interact with Mr. Shin, who is later revealed to be toying with both of them: Mme Oh watches disapprovingly as her niece kisses Mr. Shin in the street, and the niece later glowers as Mme Oh dances with him at a dance hall.[19] Finally, when Mme Oh and her lover are interrupted in the hotel room, it is a woman who charges in—the lover's wife and Mme Oh's boss—rather than Professor Jang, who has also learned of the affair. The spurned wife flips on the light in the darkened room and, seizing control of the camera, turns her furious, exposing gaze first upon the couple and then on each lover separately, both of whom visibly shrink and turn their faces away. (One can read Mr. Han's averted gaze as a textual acknowledgment of the 1953 adultery law that Lee Tai-young fought for and that for the first time criminalized the adulterous behavior of married men.) Her withering look is matched by a violent gesture, as she slaps Mme Oh across the face twice. Significantly, it is a female character who bears the powerful gaze of society that exposes and condemns this adulterous affair.

This privileging of the female gaze is another way that Han aligns the viewer with his female protagonist, while making it difficult for the viewer to identify with Professor Jang. Throughout the film, Han denies Professor Jang any correspondingly authoritative point-of-view shots of his wife. Unlike the women in the film, he is unable to control the camera's gaze. In many scenes with his wife, he either averts his gaze from her entirely or is deprived of a reverse shot to balance her gaze at him. Not until the final scene, when he chastises his wife, does the camera align generally with the husband's scornful look. Yet even here he is denied a fully subjective point-of-view shot, and the camera is positioned low on the ground alongside the crouching Mme Oh, capturing her upward look at him rather than his downward look at her. The viewer identifies here with Mme Oh's submission to patriarchal authority, rather than with the patriarchal male gaze itself. Han thus severely limits the camera's ability to fully express patriarchal subjectivity, impeding the viewer's ability to identify with male authority.

In privileging Mme Oh's subjectivity, the film reinforces her claim to autonomous selfhood. The careful deployment of film form succeeds in creating a unique and independent personhood that the viewer can recognize, thereby validating her experiences and her worldview. This alignment of the viewer with Mme Oh creates a cultural space in which viewers can inhabit, at least temporarily, an anti-patriarchal and cosmopolitan feminist consciousness. The film's style thus serves as an ideological counterweight to the final scene's work of narrative closure. This tension between style and narrative closure is itself historical evidence of the experience of modernity in the 1950s and the anxiety it generated. While the style allows the viewer to share in the expansion of a woman's possibilities, the narrative attempts to shut most of those possibilities down. Far from being a simple bearer of patriarchal ideology, then, the film should be read as historical evidence of the powerful challenges it was facing.

Han also made changes to the novel's plotting—specifically its ending—in ways that undermine its restoration of patriarchal authority. Author Jeong Bi-seok concluded his novel with a series of scenes in which Mme Oh fully and sincerely repents for her transgressions. In these scenes Mme Oh realizes that her husband has been right about the beauties of domesticity all along. It dawns on her that her husband was correct to see democracy not as individual license, as she had, but in terms of a household in which "the couple respects each other and collaborates." Embracing her previously abandoned domestic role, she realizes that "the home that she had thought was a house of slavery was, now that she thought of it, not a house of slavery but a paradise." She realizes that her "true freedom" was "in her living room" and not in "the street," and it dawns on her "that she could have enjoyed all the freedom she wanted in her living room since her husband was a progressive scholar." Undergoing a complete change of heart, she embraces all that she had previously rejected: her husband's authority, her home, her family, her role as wife and mother. The narrator amplifies Mme Oh's reversion: "Home! It didn't appear that women could have freedom or happiness away from home. Women's freedom and happiness can be achieved only on the foundation of marriage." This ending reasserts a core tenet of Confucian gender ideology: that a woman's existential happiness can only be achieved within the collective structure of the family, in which she holds a subordinate position. After this realization, Mme Oh for the first time suffers emotionally the consequences of her actions and cries over the loss of her children, whom her husband, in accordance with Confucian norms, has forbidden her to see: "losing her rights as a wife and mother," she laments, "was a bone-wrenching sorrow." The novel wallows in Mme Oh's suffering: it renders her "homeless," describes the "lump in her throat" and "her eyes brimmed with tears," and lingers over her feelings of "wretchedness" as she wanders the street.[20] It also reaffirms the gendered division of space by reentrenching Mme Oh in the domestic space of the home.

The novel reaches its climax in a grandiose scene in which Professor Jang delivers a speech in the highly symbolic National Assembly building. A noted linguist, Professor Jang has been called upon to speak about a proposed simplification of the Korean alphabet, a reform that he opposes on democratic grounds, arguing eloquently that a small number of people should not have the power to change the people's language when it is evolving naturally according to actual usage.[21] With this speech Professor Jang becomes a symbol of the new nation and defender of its culture. Far from being "feudal," as his wife has so often characterized him, he is presented as a figure of authentic democratic and progressive ideals who is yet cautious about changing Korea's long-standing culture. While reading about this upcoming speech in a newspaper, Mme Oh has an epiphany wholly in keeping with the novel's patriarchal sensibility: "I was the most vicious and stupid wife!" Later, as she watches her husband speak in this nationally resonant space, she sees him with new eyes: he is "majestic," "sublime," "noble," and one of the true "representatives of Korea's 30,000,000 citizens."[22] With this realization, Mme Oh undergoes a dramatic 180-degree transformation and embraces the very nationalist and patriarchal values that she had previously spurned. Her husband is restored to his position of patriarchal authority and redeemed in Mme Oh's eyes.

The ending of Han Hyung-mo's film is sharply different. There is no scene in the National Assembly, nor any patriotic defense of Korean culture. Neither is there any declamation of the tenets of patriarchal authority. At no point does Mme Oh express a renewed commitment to patriarchal ideals or express enthusiasm for her role as wife and mother, or even express any fondness for her husband. Above all, Mme Oh does not have an epiphany in which she sees her actions in a new light. She expresses regret for her actions only in the final thirty seconds of the film and only after getting caught in a hotel room with her lover, slapped in the face by his wife, and barred from her house by her husband. Even then, she can only deliver a single line of dialogue in which she takes responsibility for her actions without apologizing for them, and which she directs to her son rather than her husband: "It's all mom's fault." Mme Oh does physically submit to her husband's authority, wiping tears from her eyes and crouching at his feet as he chastises her, but she does so in a moment of extreme emotional duress and with no indication that she has actually changed her views. She submits because there exists no alternative course of action. In contrast to the novel, which devotes about thirty pages to Mme Oh's moral rehabilitation, the film's brief patriarchy-restoring ending feels quite rushed. In a film with a running time of over two hours, the final scene lasts only four minutes. The sudden reversal of her character from defiant to submissive happens so quickly that it rings somewhat false. The concluding minutes of screen time in which she is punished are hardly sufficient to counter the preceding two hours in which Mme Oh, with the viewer in tow, has been thoroughly enjoying herself. Despite the iconic power of the film's final shots, this abrupt act of narrative closure cannot fully counter the previous story time in which Mme Oh has acted as the viewer's surrogate, vicariously ushering her into a new modern lifestyle and mentality. The ending may be an ideologically necessary conclusion, but it also constitutes something of a rupture in the viewing experience.

Which brings us to the historical spectator. It is always difficult to make claims about how ordinary viewers would have understood a film at the time of its release. We do know, however, that Han's revised ending caught the attention of at least one viewer inside Seoul's Sudo theater, the novel's author Jeong Bi-seok. In an otherwise positive newspaper article in which he praised the film's overall fidelity to his novel and acclaimed it as "a great work," Jeong reserved his lone negative comment for the ending. "I am very displeased with the ending of the film," he wrote. "In the novel, Seon-yeong . . . goes through many tribulations before she is 'purified' and realizes the true worth of Professor Jang Tae-yeon." Jeong was clearly troubled by the absence of Mme Oh's genuine repentance, and he lamented that "the intention of the novel" in this respect had clearly not been kept "intact."[23] Given the tremendous popularity of Jeong's book and its publication only two years before the film's release, it seems safe to assume that many viewers likewise read the film intertextually, mentally comparing Han's ending to the novel's, in which case what might have struck historical viewers—just as it struck the novel's author—was not so much the restoration of the husband's patriarchal authority as the flimsiness and insincerity of the wife's submission to it. Perhaps it was the absence of her genuine moral "purification" and her refusal to celebrate her husband's authority that resonated with viewers most deeply. While the reassertion of sexual hierarchy is powerfully made at the visual level in the final shots, the absence of any verbal assent to these values by Mme Oh is quite notable. In comparison to Mme Oh's explicit and repeated assertions of her renewed faith in patriarchy in the novel, her near silence in the film could be read as forced submission to, but not belief in, patriarchy.

As Scott Bukatman reminds us, however, historical spectators are not slaves to narrative closure. The experience of reception is vital to a film's meaning. Referring to women in Hollywood screwball comedies of the 1930s, Bukatman weighs the expressive power of extended screen time against the privileged position of the ending, and concludes that "5 minutes of 'good' behavior" by women at the end of a film "hardly obviates or obliterates the previous 85 minutes of their wreaking madcap havoc." The shocking sight of a powerful woman violating patriarchal norms, he suggests, likely had a greater impact on viewers' consciousness than did the brief, perfunctory scenes of punishment. Bukatman quotes Molly Haskell on the inability of Hollywood narratives to fully contain the power of the women up on screen:

> Sure, they had to be punished every so often, particularly as women's real-life power in society and in the job market increased . . . As women represented real threats to male economic supremacy, movie heroines had to be brought down to fictional size, domesticated or defanged. But even so, and in the midst of mediocre material, [these stars] rose to the surface and projected, through sheer will and talent and charisma, images of emotional and intellectual power.[24]

Feminist scholar Janey Place makes a similar argument about the treatment of women's sexuality in film noir. She argues that the "potent stylistic presentation" of the *femmes fatale*—via lighting, costume, cinematography—made a greater impression on viewers than did their obligatory punishment at the end. "It is not their inevitable demise we remember," writes Place, "but rather their strong, dangerous, and above all, exciting sexuality." Despite film noir's regressive ideology at the level of narrative, the "uniquely sensual visual style" through which they put powerful women on display often "overwhelms" these narratives completely.[25] These critical observations apply directly to Mme Oh, who both enters public life as a wage-earning worker at the moment that her husband is unable to maintain the family's middle-class status and displays a bold sexuality that threatens his authority. "Domesticated" and "defanged" as she is by the ending, the film can't quite undo the sheer volume of images devoted to her "will and talent and charisma."

Han's abrupt ending may have made it possible for viewers to experience *Madame Freedom* in a divided way. Film scholars have long noted Mme Oh's simultaneously "dangerous and desirable" appeal to viewers.[26] I want to suggest something different, namely, that the restoration of the familial patriarchal order at the end may have *allowed* female viewers—who were understood to be the primary audience for melodramas—to identify with Mme Oh's assertions of female autonomy, by protecting them from the psychic consequences of that identification. In other words, the punishment of Mme Oh at the end of the film in some sense enabled the prior scenes of Mme Oh's transgressive behaviors, by giving the viewer a free pass of plausible deniability. The restoration of traditional gender roles in the final scene is not necessarily the true expression of the film's meaning, but can instead be seen as a rhetorical device. If the body of the film allowed the viewer to temporarily inhabit Mme Oh's assertive individualism—to "try it on," as it were—the patriarchal ending allows the viewer to step back out into a more familiar female subjectivity. The ending is thus not necessarily a conservative endorsement of patriarchal control, but rather an acknowledgment that patriarchy is still a powerful force in society.

Film viewers in the 1950s—*Madame Freedom*'s historical spectators—would have had plenty of experience recognizing the ideological reversal of the abrupt ending and choosing whether to embrace it as central to the film's meaning or disregard it as peripheral. Korean cinema had been subject to censorship since the early twentieth century, and these regulations shaped the endings of many films. Colonial-era films, which were subject to Japanese censorship laws, often had tacked-on endings that affirmed Japanese imperial values or articulated support for the colonial enterprise. Choi In-kyu's *Street Angels* (1941)—the film that launched Han Hyung-mo into a film career—stands as a fine example. While the body of film largely sidesteps colonial ideology in its story about the creation of a group home for orphaned Korean boys, a brief moment in the final scene depicts the boys gathered below a Japanese flag and pledging allegiance to the Empire. This ending provides political cover for an ideologically ambivalent film that could be seen as asserting the viability of self-governing Korean institutions, and brings it into alignment with censorship rules forbidding any advocacy of Korean independence. This brief episode is very efficient: the image of Korean children bowing to a Japanese flag condenses the dense web of imperial ideology, and especially the idea of Korean-Japanese unification, into a single, instantly legible image. Such a tacked-on ending opened the film up to multiple readings by diversely situated viewers. Those who supported the colonial enterprise, such as censorship officials, could focus on the ending and project its values back onto the body of the film, while those who valued the film's vision of a Korean community free from Japanese oversight could disregard the ending and focus on the body of the film alone. Politically inflected films of the postwar 1950s often had similarly abrupt endings that papered over ideological contradictions. *Piagol* (1955), for instance, tells a nuanced story about a female North Korean partisan guerilla who proves herself morally stronger than her male comrades. When the film ran into trouble with Rhee's censorship office for being too sympathetic to its North Korean characters, director Lee Kang-cheon solved the problem by inserting an ideologically correct ending. Like *Street Angels*, its final shot resorted to the condensed shorthand of an icon. It superimposed a fluttering ROK flag—redolent with associations of anticommunism and opposition to North Korea—over a shot of the heroine walking out of the mountains, visually affirming that she has renounced communist ideology and is on her way to joining the South Korean nation. These addendums allowed filmmakers to explore controversial characters and stories in depth simply by adding a brief, ideologically correct ending.

Madame Freedom ran into its own censorship difficulties, based on its sexual content. Forced to meet the censors' demands, Han trimmed the offending scenes and cut several minutes from the film's running length. But Han also, like Choi In-kyu and Lee Kang-cheon, concluded his film with an instantly legible iconic image—kneeling woman, standing man—that, like the Japanese or ROK flag, functioned as visual shorthand for a dense web of meaning. Han Hyung-mo called attention to the ideological work of the ending when he publicly defended his movie against the censors by characterizing it as an "educational" film that could teach viewers a "lesson" about the consequences of depraved behavior.[27] Scholars who have taken Han's characterization at face value as an expression of the film's conservative intent have ignored its instrumentality as a defense against censors' demands to cut the film. We can read the "educational" ending as self-serving on Han's part, allowing him to depict his heroine's social transgressions in great detail by briefly condemning them at the end.

THE FEMININE '50s

Madame Freedom launched the "feminine '50s" as a distinct moment in Korean cinema history. The film's success at the box office stimulated an outpouring of modern melodramas that depicted women grappling with the social and economic transformations of modernization. Strong, independent-minded women had appeared in several films released in the preceding eighteen months, such as Han's *The Hand of Destiny* (1954), Lee Kang-cheon's *Piagol*, and Park Nam-ok's *The Widow* (1955). But it was *Madame Freedom* that proved the commercial viability of the woman-centered modern drama. The film's success emboldened other directors, who began producing a steady flow of films featuring après girl characters who challenged patriarchal norms in the realms of work, family, and sexuality. Popular with viewers, these women's pictures dominated theaters for the rest of the decade.

Alongside the visual culture of *Yŏwŏn* magazine, these films cemented the figure of the modern woman as a central mechanism through which the transformations of postwar society were debated. Many of these films depicted what Eunsun Cho has called "women out of familial order": women who venture into public life and take on social roles beyond the familiar ones of filial daughter, self-sacrificing mother, powerful mother-in-law, and chaste widow.[28] As après girls and Korean Noras, they struggle to become the modern selves that Ibsen's heroine aspired to. Some of these women succeed admirably. In Lee Yong-min's *Holiday in Seoul* (1956), Yang Mi-hee plays a childless obstetrician in a happy companionate marriage who protects vulnerable women from suffering at the hands of men: she defends one pregnant young woman from abuse by her father and a seducer, and saves the life of an older woman, whose husband is a murderer, during a difficult childbirth. Other characters fare less well. When a naive coffee-shop waitress (Um Aing-ran) in Gwon Yeong-sun's *A Drifting Story* (1960) puts her ideas about free love into practice by having sex before marriage with a man who doesn't truly love her, she gets pregnant, has an abortion, becomes a prostitute, loses her mind, and ends up killing herself. Still others occupy a middle ground, such as Sonia (Choi Eun-hee) in Shin Sang-ok's *Flower in Hell* (1958), a worldly and morally corrupt prostitute who creates the life she wants for herself, yet ends up dead at the hands of her lover. Taken together, these films create a continuum of modern female characters whose lives, and fates, vary.

Han Hyung-mo holds a privileged position within the "feminine '50s." Between 1954 and 1967 he directed more than a dozen modern dramas featuring après girl characters who systematically violate Confucian gender precepts and counter-identify with liberal Western values. He produced the largest and most consistent body of films that feature Korean women as individuals. Han's characters were not sociologically representative, as many of them belonged to the numerically small middle or elite classes. They did, however, offer visions of future possibility, ways of being a Korean woman that were becoming imaginable if not yet common in the 1950s. As he did with *A Jealousy* (1960), Han popularized some of the ideas that feminists such as Helen Kim and Lee Tai-young were expressing in more intellectual venues, although as a filmmaker working in the classical Hollywood vein, Han focused on the exploits of individual women rather than, as Kim and Lee did, the collective improvement of the lives of women as a social class.

Although Han's films cross many genres, their après girl characters share certain qualities. Many of them reject sequestration within the domestic realm and freely inhabit urban space. They ride in cars, stroll the streets, visit parks, and go to country clubs. Some, such as In-sun (Kim Ui-hyang) in *The Pure Love* (1957) and Margaret (Yoon In-ja) in *The Hand of Destiny*, live on their own. Those who do live among family often push back against the authority of the male relatives who try to control them. Most of these women have jobs and quite a few have professional careers, including Song-hui (Kim Ui-hyang) in *Men vs. Women* (1959), who is a doctor. Many of them stand out for their assertions of individual autonomy. Like Mme Oh they drive the plots, by committing murder, treating patients, and hiring new employees. Sometimes these women behave admirably, as when the doctor Song-hui risks her safety to tend to a sick child. Other times they are rude, self-centered, morally compromised. And that is often precisely the point: it is the mastery of their own will and the fierceness of their inner drives that make these women notable, not the morality of their behavior.[29] Han liberates his characters from the demands of "womanly virtue" (*p'udok*) and frees them to be selfish. Because they are not defined by their virtue, they are free to participate in public life without fear of sexual humiliation, which has long served as the rationale for domestic confinement. While this inversion of normative behavior was often treated as comedy, the very existence of such characters was regarded as remarkable. According to his colleague Kim Kee-duk, Han was unusual among Korean directors in portraying "active women" who were "aggressive or enthusiastic," rather than the familiar women who were "passive and always dependent on men's lead." Such women were very rare "in our society and in our lives," says Kim, and Han's depiction of them had "no precedent."[30] Their independent action was often matched by their independent minds. Like the young Helen Kim who defied her father's pressure to marry, they ably resist social conformity. This quality receives its most sustained exploration in *My Sister Is a Hussy* (1961), in which Sun-ae (Moon Jung-suk) rejects the social rules of femininity, resisting her family's encouragement to marry and mocking her suitors for their overinflated egos; even when she does marry, she defies her husband's expectations and continues to follow her own path.

Sexuality often serves as the arena in which these après girls assert their independence. In a patrilineal society that values women for their ability to produce male heirs, sexuality becomes a logical arena for asserting female agency. A married woman who is sexually active outside the confines of her marriage threatens the purity of her husband's line and by extension the entire social order. She thus becomes a source of social, as well as personal, anxiety. In Han's films, writes Kim Sun-ah, "patriarchal oversight and the prohibitions against sexual promiscuity, adultery, and homosexuality were routinely rejected."[31] Han's female characters flirt (*Hyperbolae of Youth* [1956]), seek love marriages (*Poor Lovers* [1959]), pursue men they find attractive (*A Female Boss* [1959], *The Pure Love*), engage in extramarital sex (*The Hand of Destiny*), have affairs (*Madame Freedom*), and express homosexual desire (*A Jealousy*). At a time when romantic love was still on the margins of social acceptability, Han showed women taking the initiative to pursue their romantic interests outside of the mechanisms of arranged marriage. These violations of patriarchal sexual norms across Han's many films serve as a metonym for the characters' larger challenge to the Confucian principle of female submission.

As in *Madame Freedom*, the female characters in Han's other films are often punished for their assertions of individuality and independence. Sometimes, like Mme Oh, they are punished with humiliation and a return to patriarchal authority. Other times they are punished with violent deaths, as in *The Pure Love* and *The Hand of Destiny*, or with acts of violence such as rape, as in *Men vs. Women*, or physical beatings, as in *My Sister Is a Hussy*. Still other times these punishments take the form of "happy" endings that recontain independent-minded women within the patriarchal marriages and homes that they sought to avoid, as in *A Jealousy*, where Jaesoon is cured of her lesbianism and restored to heterosexual "sanity." But as in *Madame Freedom*, these punishments and "happy" outcomes are often delivered in abrupt, sudden-reversal endings, the significance of which sinks under the weight of the lavish deployment of screen time and formal resources that have privileged these women stylistically throughout the preceding hours of screen time. Such punishments are rarely accompanied by expressions of genuine remorse by the women, and thus often fail to fully persuade. As in *Madame Freedom*, these endings can be read as rhetorical devices to provide ideological "cover" for the preceding depictions of female autonomy.

Han's emphasis on punishment is most significant for what it replaces: female suffering. Suffering was a crucial dimension of Confucian femininity, what Lee Tai-young called the "deep pain that was inscribed in our bones" and what Helen Kim identified as "the typical unhappiness of the Korean woman."[32] The valorization of such suffering was deeply ingrained in Korean culture, as seen in the popular folktale "The Story of Chunhyang," which David James describes as one of the "master myths of Korean culture" and an "all but sadomasochistic" story about a young woman who willingly suffers imprisonment and torture to protect her virtue.[33] The aestheticization of female suffering was alive and well in 1950s cinema, as evidenced by the success of Lee Gyu-hwan's *Chunhyang Story* (1955), which was Korea's first blockbuster. The films of Shin Sang-ok, the other major director of women's pictures during the late 1950s–early 1960s, often seemed to celebrate female suffering. Several of Shin's films made during these years reach their emotional climaxes in scenes of deep female anguish. Shin's wife and muse, actress Choi Eun-hee, suffers from unrequited love for the son she gave away in *It's Not Her Sin* (1959), puts the happiness of others ahead of her own in *A Sister's Garden* (1959), tearfully resigns herself to never marrying the man she loves in *Dongsimcho* (1959), and forcefully represses her sexual desire in *The Houseguest and My Mother* (1961). These women suffer because they adhere to traditional ideals about motherhood, virtue, sacrifice, and self-abnegation. When faced with the opportunity to claim greater individual freedom, they willingly choose to embrace patriarchy's constraints instead. Shin renders their suffering noble and admirable. As the male romantic lead in *A Sister's Garden* observes, "They say a woman looks most beautiful when she is drenched in sadness, and that is so true." Shin's masterpiece, *The Houseguest and My Mother*, is a moving elegy for a body of virtues rooted in Confucianism's "fine, beautiful customs." It is a postcolonial traditionalist tour de force, one that honors a self-sacrificing woman's choice to preserve traditional values within the private domestic sphere, even as the world outside modernizes. Shin depicted female suffering most ostentatiously in *Seong Chunhyang* (1961), a lurid retelling of the folktale that presents gruesome scenes of the heroine's physical and mental pain in widescreen Technicolor.

Han largely liberated his après girl characters from the logic of suffering. By and large, Han's women do not agonize over past actions; they do not lie awake at night fretting over future decisions; they do not fearfully anticipate the social condemnation of others. They do not succumb to wasting illnesses. They do not spend time in jail. Above all, they rarely shed tears.[34] (*Men vs. Women* is one exception, in that the après girl doctor does suffer in the second half of the film after being raped.) Han's romantic comedies, such as *Hyperbolae of Youth* and *A Female Boss*, eschew female suffering in keeping with their adherence to genre convention. But even in films where female suffering would be generically appropriate, Han pares it down. *The Hand of Destiny* is a film noir melodrama featuring a female North Korean spy named Margaret (Yoon In-ja) who falls in love with a South Korean police detective. In the final scene, her cover is blown and she faces imminent death. Instead of creating an extended scene in which she wallows in her misery, begging for her life and apologizing for her treason, she requests that her lover shoot her ("I don't want to die by an enemy bullet. Please . . . kill me by your hand") and then kisses him—a shocking scene at the time, and Korea's first on-screen kiss. In films that do revel in suffering, Han shifts that burden onto his male characters. In *The Pure Love*, for instance, it is the male protagonist who spends much of the film blind and in jail, wrongly accused of murder and praying to God for relief. Han deploys lighting and mise-en-scène in ways that elevate his suffering and infuse it with an aura of spiritual ennoblement. His female love interest, in contrast, remains free, her distress paling in comparison to his spectacular—and stereotypically feminine—suffering. Han's lone foray into historical drama, *Prince Hodong* (1962), depicts two women rescuing the eponymous hero after he has been imprisoned in a dungeon, suspended from the ceiling by his arms, and flogged into unconsciousness. The women, one of whom spends much of the film in drag as a highly competent male soldier, then complete the secret mission that the hero failed to accomplish because he was sidetracked by love.

In freeing his female characters from suffering, Han freed them from *han*, the distinctly Korean psychic condition of anger, resentment, and fatalism rooted in the country's history of invasion, colonization, division, and war.[35] Throughout

Korean film history, and especially within the work of cultural nationalist film-makers such as Im Kwon-taek, women have often served as embodiments of *han*, representing the nation as a feminized victim. As Joshua Pilzer has written, suffering women were "powerful figures in the consolidation of national identities and class sensibilities and in the consolidation of modern masculinities that arise to administer or protect the suffering woman." As such, they "often legitimized whole new regimes of gendered domination."[36] Han Hyung-mo likewise liberated his female characters from the conventions of *shinpa* melodrama, which presented women as passive victims of forces beyond their control and appealed to viewers' emotions by emphasizing their protagonists' tears and suffering.[37] While *shinpa* films spoke to women's real experiences of class and gender oppression, they embodied a conservative film style that provided an outlet for women's expression of *han* without imagining any alternatives to women's suffering. Han's rejection of the figure of the suffering woman was thus a significant intervention in a long-standing cultural discourse about Korean women's essential nature.

Han's rejection of *shinpa* conventions and female *han* was crucial to his assertion of feminine individualism. According to Oh Young-sook, it was precisely this rejection of the logic of female suffering that marked Han's films as modern for his audiences.[38] Han's female characters are punished for their own individually chosen actions, rather than succumbing to a collective and unavoidable fate. They are not victimized by forces beyond their control, so much as punished for their audacious efforts to assert control over their own lives. Ultimately, if seemingly paradoxically, Han's choice to depict brief scenes of punishment rather than extended scenes of suffering had feminist undertones: like his choice of abrupt endings, it allowed him to elaborate the possibilities of female individuality at length, while providing him with a veneer of compensatory conformity to still-dominant patriarchal values. As film scholar Yu Chi-na notes, "There must have been a special kind of pleasure" for postwar women "in seeing the new, dangerous women on screen, no matter that they were always punished in the end."[39] One can also read the punishment in his films as the price his female characters willingly pay for their assertion of individual autonomy, the coin that they must expend in order to purchase their freedom. This price is part of the transaction that Han's female characters enter into as individuals, in contrast to the suffering that women endure as a consequence of their existential status as women.

The après girls with which Han populated his films were not an exclusively South Korean phenomenon. In 1953, Japanese writer Ono Saseo published an essay, "[These] Jazz-Crazed Times," whose main character is an *apure musume*—or après girl.[40] In 1956, two years after the publication of Jeong Biseok's novel *Madame Freedom* and the same year that Han released his film version, the Japanese magazine *Chuo koron* serialized a novel about a professor and his wife who each pursue an extramarital affair; as with Mme Oh, the wife's sexual appetites, long dormant in her unhappy marriage, are ignited through her encounter with a younger man.

That same year, the Japanese women's magazine *Fujin koron* published a special issue devoted to "women's desires." As Jan Bardsley has explored, the magazine limned a new social type that had emerged at war's end: the "exceptional postwar woman." According to Bardsley, the magazine defined this new woman as one who gave "rein to her desires, whether they are for sexual pleasure, money-making, self-assertiveness, public stature, or personal growth." A product, in part, of the occupation's wide-ranging gender reforms, she had a "foreign-influenced approach to life." Eager to step outside her historic confinement within the home, she sought out paid employment, civic engagement, and her own sexual and social liberation. She was a member of Japan's *apure* generation, and she displayed a distinctly "postwar morality" that violated long-standing behavioral norms for women.[41] Portrayed as ambitious, materialistic, masculine, and promiscuous, she was a source of social anxiety and an object of derisive satire. She was also an object of intense interest.

A variation on the après girl likewise appeared in Hong Kong cinema in the late 1950s and early 1960s. Grace Chang and Linda Lin Dai, big stars at MP&GI studio, regularly performed as modern women who were breaking out of traditional social roles by embracing Western popular culture, embarking on careers, pursuing love on their own terms, and engaging in new levels of material consumption. These films presented upbeat visions of a feminized, Free Asian modernity in which women's expanding opportunities paralleled Hong Kong's social and economic development. Unlike many South Korean films, which cast the modern woman as a scandalous figure who threatened core national values, these films presented their female characters, especially those played by Grace Chang, as able to finesse the balancing act between exciting modern woman and good Chinese girl. Produced with lavish studio resources and echoing Hollywood's genres and story lines, they presented capitalist modernity in a largely positive way. The après girl, it turns out, was a transnational figure as well as a cosmopolitan one—a multivalent icon embodying the shifting gender roles and transforming societies across East Asia.[42]

5

Film Culture, Sound Culture

Setting, Cinematography, and Sound

In *Madame Freedom*'s (1956) penultimate scene Mme Oh dances with her married lover, Mr. Han, in a Western-style hotel room. It is an intimate study of erotic desire, as the lovers hold each other close and gaze into each other's eyes, murmuring sweet nothings. Romantic music emanates from an unseen source, guiding the couple's movements and stimulating a passion that breaks all the rules of respectable behavior. A gliding camera gracefully tracks their dance around the room and enhances the rhythm of their bodies, while Western décor, including a symbolically blazing fireplace and a large bed, helps visualize the characters' feelings and suggests the modernity of their actions. It is a masterfully constructed scene in which setting, cinematography, and sound work together seamlessly to express the final moments of Mme Oh's morally ambiguous freedom (figure 13).

This chapter explores *Madame Freedom* through the lens of poaching, which was introduced in chapter 3 as one of the defining features of *budae jjigae* cinema. The hotel room scene is constructed out of bits and pieces of "elsewhere," from the Latin music on the soundtrack to the Scotch plaid upholstery of the club chairs to the passionate embrace so reminiscent of Hollywood. This subtle cinematic pastiche is evident throughout the film.

Poaching was a central mode of South Korean cultural production during the 1950s. Michel de Certeau developed the concept of poaching as a way to explore the agency of cultural consumers in relation to the much greater power of cultural producers. Through poaching, active consumers transform a text from a closed system of fixed meanings into a "reservoir of forms," a more or less open pool of resources that consumers can draw upon to construct new meanings that address their specific social situations.[1] Henry Jenkins has extended this line of thought,

FIGURE 13. *Budae jjigae* cinema: Mme Oh and her lover, Mr. Han, dance to Latin music amidst a hotel room's Western décor. (Courtesy KOFA)

suggesting that textual poachers have the ability not just to make new meanings, but to become full-fledged cultural producers in their own right: by taking bits of existing texts and reassembling them, they can create new texts that engage with, but are not identical to, their source material.[2] For both de Certeau and Jenkins, poaching entails transformation and reinvention. It involves removing something from its original context, resituating it, and investing it with new meanings—turning American Spam, as it were, into a component of Korean *budae jjigae*. The concept of poaching intersects with Homi Bhabha's notion of mimicry to remind us that even within highly unequal relations of power, there can still be agency on the part of weaker parties, and that acts of copying often combine admiration with a sense of pugnacious challenge. In colonial and postcolonial contexts, especially, poaching can result in both "resemblance and menace."[3]

Poaching, of course, is central to the work of imagination and creation. As Jonathan Letham argues in "The Ecstasy of Influence"—an essay constructed out of passages culled from other writers—"appropriation, mimicry, quotation, allusion, and sublimated collaboration consist of a kind of *sine qua non* of the creative act, cutting across all forms and genres in the realm of cultural production."[4]

Plagiarism and creativity, in other words, go hand in hand. Film historian Miriam Hansen has argued that poaching has long been a central tactic among non-Western filmmakers eager to explore the modernization of their societies. In the 1920s and 1930s Hollywood offered filmmakers around the world a ready-made language of "vernacular modernism": its films served as reservoirs of stories, characters, and cinematic conventions that could convey the varied experiences of modernity, from its "liberating impulses" to its "pathologies." In poaching from these reserves, local filmmakers indigenized Hollywood conventions, combining them with local forms of cultural expression and with other imported idioms, and using them to represent their new social and material conditions. Hansen emphasized cinema's ability to convey the "sensory-reflexive horizon" of modernity—new sights and sounds, new states of mind, new bodily experiences—and to make that vicariously available to moviegoers. By doing so in crowded public theaters, films fashioned modernity as a collectively shared social condition, rather than as mere individual experience.[5]

As a number of scholars have shown, poaching was a widespread practice among Golden Age filmmakers. Working within what Kathleen McHugh has described as a "global network of cultural influences," they made films characterized by a rich aesthetic hybridity and deep veins of ambivalence. Filmmakers routinely borrowed elements from Hollywood films—iconic images, generic conventions, character types—via acts of creative appropriation and cross-cultural adaptation that reworked their meanings to suit new contexts and audiences. Such acts of "strategic 'thievery,'" as Hye Seung Chung and David Scott Diffrient dub them, helped fuel the robust cultural production of the 1950s and 1960s. They also expressed what Andre Schmid has called, in a different historical context, South Korea's fraught geopolitical location "between empires."[6]

Poaching involves the act of reception as well as production, and so it invites attention to film history as well as to film form. What interests me in this chapter is the textual poaching in Han Hyung-mo's work, specifically *Madame Freedom*. Where in the film can we see the formal traces of other cinemas? The simple fact of poaching is less interesting to me, however, than the historical and cultural specificity of the act. What were the conditions obtaining in Korean film culture of the 1950s that made textual poaching a compelling creative strategy? What kinds of aesthetic reserves did Han tap into, and what were the historical conditions that made them available? Ultimately, this chapter explores how poaching made possible the expression of sentiments and ideas that might otherwise have been difficult to convey.

I focus here on Han's textual poaching in relation to postwar Korea's film culture and sound culture. I take the term *film culture* from Alan Higson, who uses it as a way to move beyond the national limits of *film industry* and *national cinema*.[7] Film culture is a transnational category, in that it includes all the films in circulation within a given market, foreign as well as domestic. As a concept, it makes visible the cosmopolitan dimension of film consumption that exists in most countries. Film culture is also a transmedia category that includes material and discursive factors that affect the production, distribution, exhibition, and reception of films, such as import regulations and newspaper reviews. I am using *sound culture* as a parallel concept to refer to the foreign and domestic music in circulation within South Korea, as well as the factors that shaped its production, distribution, and consumption, such as radio stations and listening venues. Both film culture and sound culture, in turn, are subsets of the larger public culture discussed in chapter 3.

Colonialism, the Korean War, and the Cold War had rendered South Korea's film and sound cultures surprisingly cosmopolitan by the 1950s, rich with material that had originated elsewhere. Han treated these film and sound cultures as reservoirs of aesthetic possibility from which he could poach at will. By doing so, he produced a cinematic style that was cosmopolitan both in flavor and in its material groundings. He was also able to assemble the textual material necessary to imagine South Korea's integration into the Free World. In *Madame Freedom*, South Korea's growing bonds to the larger noncommunist world find expression not so much through dialogue as through the visual and aural registers of film form—that is, through a distinctly cosmopolitan style. The connection to the Free World becomes, for the viewer, something seen, heard, and felt, rather than apprehended intellectually. This sense of union slips under the mind's radar as it is absorbed through the senses, accompanied by cinematic pleasure.

This chapter focuses on Han's relationship to Japanese films, Hollywood films, and recordings of Western music. It argues that Han created an emotionally and sensuously rich representation of modernity by appropriating elements of setting, cinematography, and sound from texts that were already in circulation within South Korea. It poses two questions about film style. First, how did Han use these stylistic elements expressively: what meanings do they carry within *Madame Freedom*? Second, how can we read these stylistic elements as historical evidence: what can they tell us about South Korea's historical-material situation as a modernizing country?

CONDITIONS OF POSSIBILITY FOR POACHING

In the years after the Korean War, filmmakers were searching for an expressive language capable of conveying their contemporary experience of modernity. To many filmmakers, existing Korean styles seemed exhausted and outmoded, incapable of conveying the new world that was taking shape around them. Cinematographer and director Kang Beom-gu spoke of this turn away from indigenous styles in an interview many years later. "As for Korean topics or modes of expression," recalled Kang, "back then, they were regarded as a little old fashioned, and weren't highly regarded." On top of that, the limited domestic film production in the late 1940s and early 1950s meant that "there weren't many Korean films that we could use for reference."[8] Filmmakers instead looked outward to the cinemas of others countries for stories, genres, characters, and styles that could help them explore their own society with fresh insights.

The accessibility of new cinematic languages within postwar film culture, however, was constrained by geopolitics. The Cold War had rendered the communist film cultures of the Soviet Union, China, and North Korea illegitimate as sources of creative inspiration and as models of modern film language. During the occupation years, the US military government halted the production of leftist films and removed from circulation all films from communist countries.[9] Syngman Rhee's government extended these prohibitions and implemented a censorship system that forbade the expression of anything that could be regarded as sympathy towards communism in general and North Koreans in particular.[10] The experience of colonialism, in turn, rendered Japan's cinema highly problematic as a source of expressive language. Rhee sought to delegitimize Japan as a model of modernity that South Korean cultural producers should look towards, and he made the eradication of "Japanese things and ways" (*wae-saek*) an important part of his cultural decolonization efforts. Japanese popular culture was effectively banned by means of censorship laws that prohibited "unhealthy and immoral" works of art, a category that encompassed Japanese popular music and publications.[11] Japanese films were regarded as particularly threatening, given their historical use as conveyors of imperial ideology and the extremely high quality, and thus attractiveness, of contemporary productions. As a result, Japanese films were not legally imported into Korea for commercial exhibition until 1998. Rhee's government also limited the representation of Japan in Korean films, banning Korean-Japanese romances, the inclusion of footage shot in Japan, and most uses of the Japanese language.[12] The complete erasure of Japan from postwar film proved impossible, however, and throughout the 1950s and 1960s Japanese cinema continued to have a subterranean presence within Korea's film culture.

American models of cultural modernity, in contrast, were widely available and publicly championed within postwar film culture. The provision of South Koreans with a language for thinking about modernity was, in fact, a central objective of the cultural Cold War. USIS newsreels, documentaries, and educational films were widely exhibited via mobile units and screened in most commercial theaters before the feature presentation. These films presented attractive visions of Americanized modernity: they educated Koreans about American history, culture, and institutions; showcased American reconstruction efforts in Korea; highlighted modern developments within South Korea; and promoted Cold War values such as democracy and freedom.[13] South Korean writers and filmmakers, as discussed in chapter 3, were closely involved in producing and localizing this material for Korean audiences. Working together, Americans and South Koreans constructed America as an acceptable embodiment of modernity within South Korea's film culture.

This search for a politically acceptable cinematic language of modernity inter-sected with a fairly cosmopolitan film culture and sound culture. While Hollywood films dominated the commercial market, they shared that space with smaller num-bers of films from other countries, including the United Kingdom, France, Germany, Italy, Sweden, Austria, Spain, Taiwan, Hong Kong, Venezuela, Argentina, Brazil, and Mexico.[14] Some of these films had an impact far beyond their small attendance fig-ures. Neorealist pictures from Italy, such as *Bicycle Thieves* (1948, Vittorio De Sica) and *Paisan* (1946, Roberto Rossellini), found favor with film critics who appreciated their social criticism and directors who admired their low-budget artistry, although they often played to half-empty theaters. French melodramas, in turn, were popular with filmmakers and audiences alike.[15] The commercial market did not comprise the entirety of Korea's film culture, however: a robust black market in films oper-ated throughout the late 1940s and 1950s. This involved films from Allied countries that had escaped confiscation by the Japanese in 1941; films from communist coun-tries that had escaped confiscation by the US military occupation government in 1946; contemporary commercial films from Japan, Taiwan, and Hong Kong that were smuggled into Korea; and American documentary and features film that were stolen from the US Army Picture Service in South Korea.[16] Korea's sound culture likewise contained music, both live and recorded, that had originated in diverse countries and was accessible through commercial, military, and black markets.

SETTING: CREATING A GENDERED GEOGRAPHY OF MODERNITY

Han Hyung-mo made films that imagined modernity in spatial terms. He often created a gendered geography of modernity, using physical settings to express how modernity was inhabited differently by women and men. Han made metropolitan films at a time when the city was associated with progress and when it was the site in which Korea's ties to other countries were most visible. He often announced these urban settings in his films' opening shots. The credit sequence for *A Female Boss* (1959), for instance, features a bird's-eye view of the iconic Myeongdong rotary in Seoul, surrounded by multistory buildings and bustling with automobiles, while *Hyperbolae of Youth* (1956) opens with a panorama of Busan's waterfront followed by a montage of busy street shots. These cities, in turn, are home to myriad smaller public spaces that female protagonists inhabit with ease and in which they often engage with bits of foreign culture. In *The Hand of Destiny* (1954) Margaret works in a bar, attends a bicycle race and a boxing match, and plays miniature golf. In *My Sister Is a Hussy* (1961), Sun-ae and her sister stroll through a city park and patronize a photography store. In *Hyperbolae of Youth* Mi-ja enjoys a picnic with American food at a crowded beach. *Men vs. Women* shows a female obstetrician, Dr. Yun, walking through the urban streets during the day and night, working in a Bauhaus-style hospital, and performing surgery in a technologically advanced operating room. Han's female characters lay claim to the city, with all its associations of modernity, as a social space they can legitimately inhabit.

In *Madame Freedom* Han creates settings that express Mme Oh's efforts to live outside the familial order and that open up space for a critique of patriarchy; they also allow for the imagination of alternative social relationships. In its mapping of story and character onto space, *Madame Freedom* bears a strong resemblance to a film by Japanese filmmaker Ozu Yasujiro. Ozu is often hailed as the quintessentially Japanese director. In his large body of films made between 1927 and 1962, he captured the rhythms and emotions of daily Japanese life by means of a distinctive style built around the static shot and slow editing tempo. While some scholars have read his films as repositories of traditional Japanese values and aesthetics, recent scholarship has emphasized the extent to which his postwar films explore Japan's transformations under the influence of America. Alastair Phillips argues that Ozu's home drama films, such as *Late Spring* (1949), *Early Summer* (1951), and *Tokyo Story* (1953), grapple directly with Japan's postwar social changes, including increased urbanization, new patterns of work, and changes in family structure. Phillips proposes that, far from being expressions of unvarying tradition, these films capture the experiences of postwar modernity as it was unfolding.[17]

Phillips suggests that Ozu played out the tensions between tradition and progress by constructing dynamic relationships between women and space. Ozu repeatedly crafted films about modern young women who negotiate between long-standing social expectations for marriage and submission to the patriarchal family on the one hand, and new opportunities for work, pleasure, and independence on the other. Phillips argues that Ozu used setting to grapple with women's shifting social roles, creating a gendered spatial logic that is central to the films' structure: they are simultaneously domestic films that privilege the spaces of the home and urban films that depict the city as a site of new opportunities for work and leisure. While Ozu's modern young women live in traditional Japanese houses, they also occupy Western-style living spaces, work in modern offices, socialize in urban cafés, walk through city streets, and achieve even greater mobility on trains. The constructions of "female social space" are central to the films' depiction of the tensions surrounding modernity, insofar as they serve as stages for female friendship, which in turn offer opportunities for open debates about the competing values of tradition and modernity. In these films, Phillips suggests, "feminine space becomes *the* field in which the contemporary and the traditional were fought over."[18]

Madame Freedom echoes the story and gendered spatial logic of *The Flavor of Green Tea over Rice* (1952), which predates the publication of Jeong Bi-seok's serial novel by two years and the release of Han's film by four. Both *Madame Freedom* and *Green Tea* tell the story of a middle-class urban housewife who inhabits the overlaps between tradition and modernity and between Asian and Western cultures. Like Han's Mme Oh, Ozu's Satake Taeko feels bored with her husband and stifled in her arranged marriage, and she, too, seeks pleasure and excitement outside her home. She also has a niece who dismisses arranged marriages as old-fashioned and sets out to forge her own relationships based on love. Both films tell their stories by locating their protagonists within a series of physical spaces marked as modern and/or Western and by showing how, when occupying these spaces, these women behave in ways that violate traditional gender norms. Both films present these spaces as creating new opportunities for women: for paid work, for the development of a new social identity, for consumption, for leisure, for female friendship, and for individualism. Physical settings help define what modernity offers a woman and what its costs might be.

By comparing specific scenes we can see how Han, like Ozu, creates a network of spaces in which patriarchal values are called into question. Both *Madame Freedom* and *Green Tea* include early scenes in which the female protagonist, having left her home, drives through the city in the back seat of a taxi. The scenes include a pair of shots that are similar in size and composition, with the protagonist, dressed in traditional clothes, sitting on the right side of the frame in a medium shot as a female friend, dressed in stylish Western attire, sits on the left. Each scene locates the women within an urban space that is both modern (there are multistory buildings, buses, and cars visible through the windows) and host to an American military presence: a PX (post exchange military department store) in *Green Tea* and US military jeeps in *Madame Freedom*. The films thus bestow automobility upon their female characters, enabling them to navigate modern, urban, Americanized space confidently and safely, rather than being overwhelmed or threatened by it. This automobility enables the women to escape from family obligations and pursue pleasure instead: in *Green Tea*, Taeko and her niece talk about going to a French movie starring Jean Marais, while in *Madame Freedom* Mme Choi whisks Mme Oh off to a women's luncheon.

Each film creates a domestic space that expresses the tensions between husband and wife, and between Japanese/Korean and Western culture. The room associated with the husband in each film—a home office—is visually aligned with traditional and national culture. In *Green Tea*, Mr. Satake wears a kimono while sitting on a tatami matted floor. In *Madame Freedom* Professor Jang wears a padded *hanbok* while he works on his Korean manuscripts, a graduation photograph on the wall identifying him as a scholar—a high-status position in Confucian culture—and a scroll with Chinese characters signaling Korea's history of Sinocentrism. The rooms associated with the wives, in contrast, are identified with Western culture. In *Green Tea* Taeko broods over her unhappy marriage in a bedroom decorated with visually overwhelming Western décor, including a bed, chairs, chintz upholstery, a tall bureau, and flowered wallpaper. *Madame Freedom* identifies the living room as the wife's space. While the furniture is Korean, Madame Oh uses this space to store her new Western-style clothes, to put on her makeup, and to use her shiny electric iron, making this room a site of incipient westernization. In both films the visual contrast between the westernized space of the wife and the Korean/Japanese

FIGURE 14. The Western-style clothes shop in Ozu Yasujiro's *The Flavor of Green Tea over Rice* (1952).

space of the husband suggests that the wife is challenging her husband's authority from within the home, by creating a culturally separate space for herself.

Both films remove the unhappy wife from this home and send her into a commercial shop that sells Western-style fashions. Compositionally these spaces are very similar, with plate-glass storefront windows, double glass doors, glass display cabinets, a saleswoman to the left, and a mannequin dressed in Western clothes (figures 14 and 15). These shops are run by competent businesswomen who take the upper hand with their husbands. In both, the wives encounter the material objects of Western culture and imbibe the values associated with it, including the freedom that comes from earning one's own money. Within this feminized social and professional space, the protagonist is encouraged to pursue her individual desires in ways that erode the authority of her husband: Madame Oh flirts and makes dates with men, while Taeko plots a secret vacation away from home.

Both films locate their female characters within a series of public commercial spaces devoted to leisure and entertainment. In *Green Tea*, various female characters eat at a noodle shop, attend a bicycle race and baseball game, and visit a pachinko parlor. In *Madame Freedom*, Mme Oh spends time in restaurants, a coffee

FIGURE 15. A similar layout in *Madame Freedom*'s Paris Boutique. (Courtesy KOFA)

shop, a nightclub, and a hotel room. In each of these public spaces the women shed their roles as "wise mother, good wife" and affirm alternative identities as friends and lovers. In one pair of scenes, the wives attend a social gathering with a group of female friends: Mme Oh a luncheon of school alumnae, and Taeko a trip to a spa with her girlfriends. Although neither of these spaces is markedly Western, both films suggest that when women socialize together they encourage each other to push at the boundaries of acceptable feminine behavior. These female social circles are presented as an alternative to the family, linking women to each through consumption, leisure, and the bonds of friendship. In *Madame Freedom*, the women smoke cigarettes, drink beer, comment on each other's expensive jewelry, discuss the need to earn their own money, and make plans to go dancing with men who are not their husbands. In *Green Tea*, they drink sake, one of them to excess; Taeko lies to her husband about her activities when he calls on the phone, and all the women mock him as a dullard. In each film, these female social spaces create opportunities for overt critiques of patriarchy, as the women complain about the "tyranny" and "harsh" authority of husbands. In each film, a woman voices the wish to be free of this authority: "What's the use of husbands?" asks Mme Choi in *Madame Freedom*, while Taeko laments, "I wish my husband would go far away." Within these settings women can express their disaffection with patriarchy and forge same-sex relationships that stand as alternatives to the arranged marriages in which they are suffering.

After depicting these female forays into the public sphere, both films include a somber scene in which the husband returns home from work only to be informed by a maid that the wife is absent. Like the shots set in the taxis and shops, these shots are compositionally very similar: the husband stands to the right and the maid faces him on the left, with both characters separated from each other and isolated within rectangular spaces created by doorways, gridded screens, and other architectural elements. Each film also includes a subsequent shot that reveals the emotional cost of the wife's abandonment of the home. In *Madame Freedom* the young son articulates his own sadness and suggests the negative impact of his mother's actions: "Mom always comes home late, I hate it." In *Green Tea*, Ozu uses poignant music, rather than dialogue, to express the husband's sorrow. These scenes function as critiques of the women's behavior, expressing the feelings of loss that modernity's disruptions generate. They are also powerfully affecting and contribute to each film's ideological complexity.

Han, like Ozu, uses physical setting to define what it means for a woman to become modern. In both films this transformation entails increased mobility within urban space, a remaking of the home to satisfy women's desires, challenges to patriarchal authority, and the assertion of a woman's individual will. For male characters, it means emotional loss. While the visual and thematic parallels between Han's and Ozu's films are striking, the historical-material relationship between these two films is much less clear. If style is a form of historical evidence, of what historical relationship are Han's settings evidence? Was Han familiar with Ozu's work? Did he ever see *Green Tea*? Did he intentionally poach stylistic elements from that film? The attempt to answer these questions does not turn up a definitive answer. It does, however, point to the secret history of Japanese cinema's presence within postwar South Korean film culture.

JAPAN IN POSTWAR KOREAN FILM CULTURE

It would not have been possible for Han to see *The Flavor of Green Tea over Rice* in a Korean theater, given the de facto ban on the import and exhibition of Japanese films. Despite this absence, however, Japanese films continued to have what Jinsoo An has called a "phantom" presence within postwar Korean film culture.[19] This presence was both a legacy of colonial relations and a result of postwar conditions.

Japanese films certainly existed as a memory for Han, a result of the intertwining of the Korean and Japanese film industries during the colonial era. It is quite possible that Han encountered Ozu's earlier films in a Korean theater when he was in his teens and twenties. Korea served as an important market for Japanese films during the colonial period, and Japanese studios owned the best theaters. The colonial Japanese population constituted the primary audience for these films, and it was large enough to make Korea a profitable market. Shochiku, the studio that produced Ozu's films, had been a major player in the Korean film industry since the 1910s, and since Ozu's films were good earners for Shochiku in Japan in the 1930s and 1940s, it seems likely that they played in Korean theaters as well, where a young man interested in a film career might have seen them.[20] It is also possible that Han encountered Ozu's films in the four years he was in Tokyo studying cinematography during the Pacific War.

South Korean filmmakers of the 1950s were also engaged with contemporary Japanese cinema, to a surprising degree. Despite the widespread resentment of the Japanese, many filmmakers felt a shared professional and creative bond with their Japanese counterparts. The shared experiences produced by the colonial encounter often made the films of Japan seem more culturally proximate than those from America and Europe that filled local theaters.[21] Korean filmmakers kept abreast of postwar developments in Japanese cinema by reading Japanese books, technical manuals, and film magazines, including *Kinema Junpo*, *Scenario*, *Eiga Geijutsu*, and *Eiga Hyoron*, which were carried into Korea by travelers and smuggled in through the black market. Screenwriters, directors, cameramen, lighting directors, and others devoured these publications, gathering together and sharing them as in a study group.[22] These print publications became an important part of South Korean film culture and one of the most important ways that Korean filmmakers advanced their professional education. Filmmakers and technicians who could read Japanese occupied a privileged position within the South Korean industry. Screenwriter Kim Ji-heon recalled years later that South Korean filmmakers were "very much" influenced by Japanese films, which they considered to be much more "advanced" than their own productions. Kim considered Japanese writers to be his "teachers" because their screenplays were full of original ideas and techniques, and he described his relationship with them as "almost like a comradeship" because of the shared history of living and studying together during the colonial era. Kim rejected a narrow sense of nationalism in favor of the artist's more cosmopolitan perspective, asserting that "if you do film, there is no border" because filmmakers of all nationalities have "film as a common ground."[23]

Han Hyung-mo was among those in the industry who could read Japanese. Committed as he was to stylistic and technological innovation, he almost certainly read contemporary Japanese film magazines, in which case he would likely have come across *Green Tea*: these publications carried numerous articles about the film in 1952, along with reviews, stills, production photographs, and even the entire script.[24] Han might also have encountered *Green Tea* or print coverage of it while in Japan: he made several trips to Japan during the 1950s to avail himself of advanced film technology and services that Korea lacked, including one in 1954 that might have afforded him an opportunity to see Ozu's film or read print coverage of it. (After attending the Asian Film Festival in Tokyo in 1957, Han was reportedly able to travel to Japan quite freely).[25]

This illicit engagement with Japanese print culture led directly to widespread poaching of Japanese screenplays. Cold War cultural entrepreneur Oh Young-jin was among the first to identify and condemn this practice, asserting in a 1958 newspaper article that 50 percent of the films being planned or in production "were stolen from the narratives of French or Japanese films." By the early 1960s such poaching had become a widespread practice and an open secret within the industry, with one observer estimating that 80 percent of Korean films contained material plagiarized from Japanese sources. Lee Hyung-pyo, who worked as a writer and director during this period, recalled that Korean screenwriters read the scripts published in Japanese film magazines and "copied those scenarios exactly," with the result that South Korean movies were "exactly the same as the Japanese ones." He was blunt in his evaluation: "So that's stealing." According to a 1999 documentary, producers would hire screenwriters who could read Japanese, who then rushed to get hold of the latest film magazines and competed with each other to translate the scripts as quickly as possible. Sometimes prints of Japanese films were smuggled into South Korea, which meant that filmmakers could copy their visual style as well their narrative elements.[26] One of the most famous and influential South Korean films of the early 1960s, Kim Kee-duk's *Barefoot Youth* (1964), plagiarized the screenplay of Ko Nakahira's *Purity Stuck in the Mud* (1963) and may also have copied elements of that film's visual style.[27] Given the paired institutionalized practices of smuggling and textual poaching, it is thus possible that Han Hyung-mo saw a print of Ozu's *Flavor of Green Tea over Rice* that had found its way into South Korea.

A number of conditions made such poaching an attractive option for filmmakers. The booming South Korean film industry generated a huge demand for stories, but lacked the screenwriting talent to meet that demand. Financial motives also came into play: copying an existing script was much cheaper than paying a screenwriter to produce an original one. Shared histories created their own incentives. Lee Hyung-pyo pointed to cultural proximity and the similarities of "lifestyle and emotions"—rooted in the experience of colonialism—to explain the attraction of Japanese films.[28] The two countries also shared the more recent experience of navigating an American modernity introduced through military occupation. Both countries found their patriarchal gender norms, and the custom of arranged marriages in particular, challenged by the influx of Western ideas.[29] Japanese films were also attractive because they performed much of the work of localizing American cultural trends: a Japanese youth film, for example, was easier for Korean filmmakers to digest than the James Dean original. As in the colonial era, Japanese films served as portals through which American cinematic conventions entered into Korea. These layered, shared experiences of Japanese colonialism and American political and cultural hegemony, in combination with the uneven development of the Korean film industry, created conditions in which poaching from Japanese films became an easy and attractive option. Japanese films offered Korean filmmakers a reserve of stories and characters through which they could imagine their own experiences of modernization and social transformation. The fact that poaching from this reserve was both widespread and controversial suggests the ambiguities of Korea's postcolonial, Cold War relationship with Japan.

While Han may have been inspired by the settings in Ozu's *Flavor of Green Tea over Rice*, he certainly did not poach the film's plot wholesale. The endings of the two films are substantially different. Ozu's film ends with the unambiguous redomestication of the wayward wife, as Taeko realizes the error of her ways and verbally proclaims the wisdom of her husband's views on marriage—much as in Jeong Bi-seok's novel. Her transformation takes place in the kitchen of her home—a room she had not previously occupied—as she goes about making her husband the simple dinner he desires, the green tea over rice of the film's title. Doing so involves stepping around a large can of American Wesson oil and rejecting the packaged white bread and packaged ham stored inside the enormous refrigerator, and instead immersing her hands in a simple bucket that holds a pleasingly odiferous pickling paste. Taeko's return to her proper role as wife thus involves a degree of re-Japanization as well as redomestication, as she embraces the traditional foods that her husband craves. Han's version of the story, of course, includes no such visual restoration of Mme Oh to a nationally inflected domestic sphere and no verbal assent to her husband's patriarchal authority.

While Ozu's film may have offered a catalogue of settings that Han could use to signal Mme Oh's movement into the public sphere and into a modern sense of selfhood, it did not offer a full panoply of stylistic moves to capture her experience of modernization. For that, Han had to look to the era's other great modern cinema—Hollywood.

CINEMATOGRAPHY: HOLLYWOOD AND THE FEELING
OF MODERNITY

Madame Freedom's visual style differs significantly from that of *Flavor of Green Tea over Rice*, most notably in its cinematography. Ozu, of course, was famous for his highly restrained use of camera movement: he typically positioned his camera low to the ground and moved it very little. Although *Green Tea* has more camera movement than many other Ozu films, it is still quite modest. *Madame Freedom*, in contrast, was groundbreaking in its use of mobile cinematography. From the opening moments to the last shot, there is hardly a scene that doesn't involve a tracking, following, craning, or otherwise moving camera. This movement is breathtaking in its relentlessness and its visual prominence. While the camera had certainly moved in earlier films, no Korean director had ever achieved the ceaseless movement that Han did in *Madame Freedom*.

In South Korean film culture of the 1950s, different styles of cinematography had clear national associations: South Korean filmmakers identified a static camera with Japan and a mobile camera with America. When Hollywood films came rushing back into South Korea in 1945, after a hiatus of several years during World War II, they impressed filmmakers with their elaborate movements in which a camera, located on a cherry-picker-like crane, glided fluidly up and down and side to side. This delicate, sophisticated camera movement struck them as the stylistic element that most distinguished Hollywood films from their colonial Japanese predecessors. Remembering those years, Kim Kee-duk made the contrast with Japanese cinema explicit. He observed that the "camera moved about so freely in Hollywood films. But people like Ozu Yasujiro in Japan stuck to a fixed camera."[30] The terms "fixed" and "free" suggest a layer of meaning beyond mere cinematography: to be "fixed" was associated with the past and the constraints of colonialism, while to be "free" was associated with a sense of future possibility that modernization was opening up.

Most colonial-era Korean films of the 1930s and 1940s had indeed displayed limited camera movement, in keeping with the dominant Japanese aesthetic. While they include some panning, tracking, and tilting shots, these movements tended to be modest in scope and utilitarian in function: they were typically deployed in the service of the narrative and functioned as an alternative to editing. They did not, by and large, call attention to themselves, nor were they richly expressive. Rather, they were used to reveal landscapes and large spaces, to show a group of people, to locate characters within a physical space and follow them as they moved through it, and to link characters to each other and to objects. Such limited camera movement was part of a Japanese-derived stylistic repertoire that valorized a stately pace, emphasized long takes and compositions in depth over editing, and eschewed close-ups in favor of long shots and high-angle camera positions.[31] This Japanese-inflected style of cinematography continued as the default in most South Korean films of the 1950s. According to Kim Kee-duk, the fixed camera was regarded as the "textbook" style. Cinematographers and directors believed that ostentatious camera movement would be confusing to viewers, and unless there was "a strong reason for it," says Kim, they regarded it as "a great taboo." Camera movement was also constrained by the lack of equipment. No In-taek describes how the "dolly" shots in the 1955 period film *Sad Story of an Executioner* were created using pillows: "we sat a [camera] man on a cushion and pulled him back . . . [while] the lighting team sat on the cushion crouching and holding reflectors and moved along with the camera."[32] Colonial legacies and postwar shortages thus combined to make dramatic camera movement a rarity.

Han Hyung-mo, as a brilliant technician and master cinematographer, pushed against these constraints. Seeking greater visual mobility for *Madame Freedom*, Han arranged for the construction of Korea's first camera crane. The story of the crane's construction has become legendary within the film industry. According to art director No In-taek, Han brought his camera to a machine shop for repair and made the acquaintance of three men who had money to invest and were interested in film production: Bang Dae-hun, Eom Mun-geun, and Lee Rae-won. Han persuaded them to finance his film, and together the three investors created Samsung Productions. Given their experience with machining tools, Han asked if it was possible to manufacture a crane according to his specifications. When they assented, Han gave them the design of what he wanted, and within a week he had his crane. The result was a long, ladder-like contraption with a platform at one end that held the camera and two operators, and a heavy steel counterweight at the other that allowed the platform to be raised and lowered. This was attached to a rotating, turntable-like base that enabled the camera platform to swing horizontally. This base, in turn, could be mounted on a wheeled dolly. The entire apparatus thus enabled the camera to move in three directions smoothly and simultaneously: up and down, side to side, and backwards and forwards. While the crane mechanism was custom-built by Han's investors, the dolly was improvised out of a handcart that rested on four US Army helicopter wheels, most likely purchased on the black market. Han's elegantly mobile camera, so vital to *Madame Freedom*'s exploration of South Korean modernity, literally rested on resources poached from the US Army.[33] *Budae jjigae* cinema, indeed.

Han used this piece of technology to produce highly expressive camera movements that were central to *Madame Freedom*'s exploration of modernity. Where Han employed Ozu-like settings to convey a new geography of modernity, he used a style of cinematography poached from Hollywood to express the *feeling* of modernity. Contemporary viewers understood this link between movement and modernity, with newspapers noting that the film's "flexible camera movement" contributed significantly to its "exact portrayal of the modern lifestyle."[34] More precisely, mobile cinematography was central to the film's ability to convey what Miriam Hansen called the "sensory-reflexive horizon" of modernity. In Han's hands, camera movement captured the sensuous and emotional dimensions of modernity. Han used it to express the heady rush of Western culture into postwar Seoul, and in freeing the camera from the tripod, he translated a dynamic social reality into a visceral cinematic experience. Han's camera movements gave form to the freedoms so intensely desired in the 1950s and yet also feared. The result was an immensely appealing sense of movement and excitement.

Han employed an "excessive" style of cinematography in *Madame Freedom*, which is to say that the camera's movements exceed the demands of the narrative and call attention to themselves. Such excess expands the camera movements' expressive capacity. The film's single most famous shot is a minute-and-a-half-long crane shot that depicts Mme Oh's entry into a Western-style dance hall with her neighbor Mr. Shin (video 1). Han uses a spectacularly mobile camera to fully explore this quintessentially modern space. The shot begins as a medium shot of a trumpeter soloing on a stage in a large dance hall. The camera slowly dollies backward, revealing first a complete band and then a crowded floor of men and women dancing in each other's arms. From here the camera rises and pivots to catch Mme

VIDEO 1. Clip from *Madame Freedom*.
To watch this video, scan the QR code with your mobile device or visit
DOI: https://doi.org/10.1525/luminos.85.1/

Oh and Mr. Shin as they enter the club to the left of the stage. It then cranes down
and dollies back to follow them as they walk through the club, and then cranes up
again as they sit down at a table to the right of the stage. The shot ends, finally, with
a pan to the left that recenters the shot on the band and thus returns the camera to
where it began. The scope of the camera's movement reveals a vast set that includes
a stage, dance floor, tables, columns, and about thirty people. It is a fully realized
physical and social space. This shot was a technical masterpiece and a newsworthy
display of technological modernization. Working in the bombed-out remains of
the Yongsan train station, Han took several days to set up and execute the shot, with
reporters and photographers from numerous publications—including *Yŏwŏn*—
present to document the crane at work.[35]

The shot comes at an important moment in the narrative. This is Mme Oh's first
date with her handsome young neighbor, her first visit to a Western-style place of
leisure, and her first attempt at Western dance. The camera's movement is strongly
associated with Mme Oh, although it is not an optical point-of-view shot from
her perspective. Her presence in the nightclub motivates the shot, and the camera
expresses her emotional state: her awe at entering such an exotic space for the first

VIDEO 2. Clip from *Madame Freedom*.
To watch this video, scan the QR code with your mobile device or visit
DOI: https://doi.org/10.1525/luminos.85.2/

time and her curiosity about everything in it, from the musicians to the dancers to
the decoration of the space itself. More importantly, the camera's mobility works
as a visual metaphor for the story arc of her liberation: it offers a visual correla-
tive to her physical movement out of her home, her social movement out of her
role as wife and mother, her cultural movement out of Confucian values, and her
existential movement into a new sense of herself as an autonomous individual and
sexual being. The camera movement thus helps to express her transformation into
a modern woman. It expresses the personal freedom that is Mme Oh's defining
characteristic.

Other scenes also contain highly expressive camera movements. In a brief but
stunning shot that introduces the Paris Boutique, Han uses mobile cinematography to construct the viewer as a modern, urban, desiring subject in his/her own
right—a position that is similar to but distinct from that of Mme Oh (video 2).
The shot begins with the camera positioned above a street bustling with jeeps and
buses. It cranes down to reveal a block of shops crowded with signs, moves later-
ally at eye level across a sidewalk jammed full of pedestrians, and comes to rest in

front of the shop's plate glass window. Western luxury goods, including high heel shoes and a man's plaid shirt, completely fill the screen as the frame of the shot aligns with the frame of the window. This camera movement stands out because it is wholly disembodied, unmotivated by any character's movement or emotional state: it exists for the viewer alone. The mobility that has been associated with Mme Oh here belongs to the viewer and by implication to the society of which the viewer is a part.

With this crane shot, Han constructs the viewer as a modern subject who feels a range of sensory emotions: visual command over an urban street, a social sense of being immersed in urban space, the physical feeling of being jostled by passersby, the psychic state of anonymity, and, perhaps most powerfully, a covetous desire for the Western goods in the window. This sense of urban modernity was enhanced by a sense of realism: only half the people on the sidewalk are hired actors, and the rest are real people who happened to be on the street in the fashionable neighborhood of Myeongdong as the scene was being filmed.[36] This shot thus immerses the viewer in a very real, very fashionable landscape and vicariously transforms the viewer into one of the well-dressed pedestrians. When the camera pauses in front of the store's display window, it is as if the viewer is pressing his/her nose up against the glass and admiring those high-heeled pumps. The shot thus animates the desire for small luxuries that was widespread amidst the intense poverty after the war. Han's mobile camera produces in the viewer the exhilarating feelings of being modern that Mme Oh is in the process of seeking out. In its combination of urban immersion, anonymity, visuality, and desire, this crane shot positions the viewer as a South Korean version of the nineteenth-century French *flaneur*, the quintessentially modern subject who strolls the city, gazes at what is new and different, and takes pleasure in the sights on display. Like the crane shot in the nightclub, it immerses the viewer within what Miriam Hansen called the "sensory-reflexive horizon" of modernity.

This shot, like that in the dance hall, was itself a modern event. It was the first shot Han filmed using his crane, and it entailed constructing a ninety-foot-long rail in the middle of the street, onto which Han installed the dolly, crane, and camera. The act of filming turned into a public event, with crowds gathering to observe the wonderful new piece of modern and heretofore foreign technology that Han was mastering and indigenizing. This shot also became central to the marketing of the film. Because the crane shot was so new to South Korean cinema and the setting so fashionable, Han included this shot in the film's preview trailer, convinced that it would pique the public's interest. It did, and among the filmgoing public the mobile camera became, according to No In-taek, "a hot topic at the time."[37]

Many other characters in the film are also associated with camera movement, thus suggesting visually that Madame Oh is not alone in her desire for escape and transformation. Virtually all of the main characters in the film are engaged in some version of her quest, and they, too, are presented via camera movements.

Miss Park, for instance, is introduced via a tracking shot into her face as she talks to Professor Jang on the telephone in her modern office, which is followed by a second tracking shot as she walks back to her desk. While these camera movements are modest, they establish her ease and comfort within a westernized physical and cultural space: they reveal that she wears chic Western fashions, is adept at using modern office technology like a telephone and a typewriter, works with an American man, and is not above flirting with a married man. As the romantic relationship between Miss Park and Professor Jang progresses, the camera moves with them, accompanying them on walks through the city's parks. The couple is accorded two spectacular crane shots outside Miss Park's home. In the first, Professor Jang is dropping Miss Park off after a chaste date: as they linger on the street, the camera eases down from a twenty-foot-high overhead shot to frame the couple in an intimate two-shot, which becomes a deep-space shot as Miss Park departs up a staircase and glances coyly back at the professor. This camera movement expresses the couple's growing intimacy, with the move in to closer framing visually expressing their emotional closeness. This shot is mirrored by a second one later in the film, when Miss Park tearfully tells Professor Jang that she is ending the relationship because it will only cause suffering for others. Now the camera begins in the intimate two-shot of Miss Park and Professor Jang, and cranes up, back, and away before stopping about twenty feet in the air. Here the emotional resonances are the opposite, as the camera movement conveys the sadness of both characters at their separation.

Paying attention to the expressive use of camera movement alters our understanding of the film's character system and story. No longer is this a film about Mme Oh as a unique figure encountering modernity and remaking herself in the process. Instead, we can see how virtually all the adult characters are engaged in some version of self-modernization. The camera's constant movement, especially with the "excessive" crane shots, is a formal device through which Han expresses modern desires—for sexual freedom, for individual autonomy, for new experiences, for emotional authenticity—that extend beyond Madame Oh and into the other characters. We can thus read these crane shots as visual metaphors for a collectively held desire for movement and change. The film becomes less a study of one woman's transgressions and more a film about a society in transition.

The only character who is not represented by a moving camera is the film's lone innocent casualty of modernity, Mme Oh and Professor Jang's young son. In a pattern repeated throughout the film, a dramatic crane shot involving one of the parents is immediately followed by a resolutely static shot of the boy alone at home, sadly studying or sleeping at his low Korean desk. Unlike the adult characters, this child cannot partake of the freedoms afforded by Western modernity. He remains the dutiful Confucian son, even as his mother and father experiment with new social identities, and as such he serves as an emblem of that which may be lost if the Confucian social order crumbles. By using an Ozu-like style

VIDEO 3. Clip from *Madame Freedom*.
To watch this video, scan the QR code with your mobile device or visit
DOI: https://doi.org/10.1525/luminos.85.3/

of cinematography—a static camera positioned roughly at the eye level of someone sitting on the floor—Han expresses these "old-fashioned" values visually. And like the previously discussed scene of Professor Jang feeling sadness at his wife's absence, these are emotionally powerful shots that contribute to the film's ideological complexity. Han, however, is not deeply interested in the son's experience, and the camera does not invite the viewer to share his perspective for more than a few seconds. While the son does function as an object of the viewer's pity and thus helps to construct Mme Oh as a "bad mother," the film is not very interested in a character who is not caught up in the possibilities that modernity offers.

The film's sophistication lies in the way that it so perfectly marries form to content: it uses camera movement to express social roles destabilized and in flux, and to capture the accompanying surge of feelings and desires. This marriage is made most clear in the film's penultimate scene, which is built around a nearly three-minute-long crane and dolly combination that captures Madame Oh as she is about to consummate her love affair with her boss's husband (video 3). The shot begins with the camera positioned high outside an illuminated hotel room at night, looking down and through the window as Madame Oh and her lover

Mr. Han dance cheek to cheek. The shot parallels the earlier crane shot in the nightclub, in that it explores the consequences of Mme Oh's decision to go out in public rather than stay at home. In a technically masterful movement that predates by four years the famous opening of Alfred Hitchcock's *Psycho* (1960), the camera slowly cranes down through a seemingly closed window and into the hotel room. It follows the couple as they dance around the Western-style living room, towards a symbolically blazing fireplace, and past an open doorway through which a bed is prominently visible. The camera pauses as the lovers nuzzle and embrace, their passion building, and then moves into a close-up as Mme Oh closes her eyes and lifts up her face to receive a lengthy kiss. As the lovers turn their faces away from the camera, the frame centers on Mme Oh's white hands massaging her lover's dark-suited shoulders, suggesting that it is *her* passion that is driving this action forward. At this point the camera discreetly moves away from the couple, only to slide over to the bedroom doorway again and pause before the bed, thus signaling that this is where they will soon end up. Like the crane shot in the nightclub scene, this is an instance of cinematographic excess that uses dramatic camera movement to express the new freedoms that modernity enables. And like the shot of Professor Jang bidding a longing farewell to Miss Park, it is immediately followed by a static shot of their son alone at home.

For Han, this lengthy camera movement was vital to the scene's emotional impact. Han believed that when there is a cut from one shot to another within a scene, it creates the possibility that the building tension will be "interrupted." So he told his crew, "let's make it happen in one cut" so that "the emotional flow is not broken."[38] Han used the moving camera here to express the emotional complexity that accompanied women's shifting gender roles: the scene conveys a sense of anxiety as well as liberation. To the extent that the camera tracks the movements of the lovers' bodies and moves closer as their feelings become more intense, it visualizes their growing intimacy and passion. However, the camera movements also have a voyeuristic dimension. The shot begins outside the hotel room, peering in through the window like a Peeping Tom, and at various moments it moves independently of the lovers, as when it looks into the bedroom. These movements suggest the existence of an unseen observer and thus the possibility of being watched—and judged. The disembodied camera movement, which suggested a widely shared consumer desire in the earlier shop-window scene, here suggests the possibility of surveillance. If the disembodied camera movement implies the existence of "society," which includes the viewer, then this scene raises the possibility of social condemnation of the lovers' actions. Han's editing reinforces this possibility. He crosscuts this scene with one of Professor Jang reading a letter informing him of his wife's betrayal, and concludes it with a pair of sharp cuts to shots of Mr. Han's wife (and Mme Oh's boss) barging into the hotel room as the lovers embrace on the bed, flipping on the lights, and slapping Mme Oh across the face, twice. Through this editing pattern, the disembodied camera movement retroactively takes on the condemnatory perspective of the betrayed spouses, who are revealed to have known about their spouses' actions.

No In-taek remembered this shot, like the film's other instances of mobile cinematography, as being "a big issue" within the industry at the time. Other cinematographers wanted to know how Han had passed a large camera, crane, and dolly through a seemingly closed window and into a hotel room. The trick, which was standard practice in Hollywood and perhaps Japan as well, was to remove the glass from the window and build the exterior wall out of two pieces that could be pulled apart as the camera seems to go "through" the window and into the room. Han perhaps learned this technique from reading foreign film manuals and magazines.[39]

HOLLYWOOD IN POSTWAR SOUTH KOREAN FILM CULTURE

Han's style of cinematography, in addition to being thematically expressive, can also be read as historical evidence of South Koreans' relationship to Hollywood during the colonial and postcolonial periods. Han's intentional textual poaching of this style of cinematography from Hollywood films was recognized by his peers. Han openly admired Hollywood's mobile cinematography and made clear his intention to make it his own. According to Noh In-taek, the art director on *Madame Freedom*, Han was inspired by the sweeping camera movements he had seen in a Hollywood Western and set out to "graft" that camerawork onto his own film.[40] Kim Kee-duk, in turn, recalled that the paired crane shots of Miss Park and Professor Jang were inspired by the famous Atlanta train station shot in *Gone with the Wind* (1939) in which "the camera pulls back endlessly," an emotionally dense shot in which the camera's movement captures both the material carnage of war and Scarlett O'Hara's subjective feelings of horror as she perceives it.[41]

Such textual poaching was enabled by Han's deep familiarity with Hollywood films, which had been an essential part of Korea's film culture since the 1910s. According to Brian Yecies and Ae-gyung Shim, the ten years from 1926 through 1935, which coincided with Han's childhood and adolescence, saw the import into colonial Korea of 5,626 non-Japanese films—of which 5,078 were American. By 1934 Hollywood films had achieved a dominant market share of as much as 62%. Exposure to Hollywood films was not the only issue, however: equally important were the meanings that adhered to these films within the colonial context. While both Japanese and American films were easily accessible, Korean viewers had a strong preference for American films. Japanese films were shown in theaters that catered to Japanese audiences composed of colonial officials, military personnel, businessmen, and expatriates. Korean-owned theaters that catered to Korean viewers, in contrast, typically shunned Japanese films, with the result that "twenty million Koreans were watching foreign films almost exclusively." In other words,

Korean audiences chose to watch American films instead of Japanese ones. At a time when Japanese and American films filled theaters, the choice of which film to watch may very well have carried political implications. American films were no doubt popular in Korea, as in most other parts of the world, for their intrinsic entertainment qualities and high production values. They also seem to have been valued for their extrinsic quality of simply being not Japanese. At a historical moment when Japanese films were often imbued with imperial values, American films may have taken on extra meanings through the absence of that content. As Yecies and Shim surmise, "One might ask whether the watching of thousands of Hollywood films during the Japanese colonial period constituted, for Korean audiences, a form of passive resistance, or at least a temporary escape from their harsh reality."[42] Hollywood films thus likely carried a layer of meaning that was constructed by viewers located in the historically specific condition of colonial spectatorship. Japanese authorities banned the import and screening of Hollywood films completely after the attack on Pearl Harbor in 1941, when Japan was at war with the United States. By the time the legal imports resumed in 1946, Hollywood films had been absent from Korean theater for a period of less than five years

American films swept back into South Korea's film culture following liberation. Korea's film market was in an initial state of chaos after the colonial film system collapsed, and a black market emerged that made older Hollywood films, as well as those from the Soviet Union and Europe, available in theaters. The US military government soon established control, suppressing the screening of Soviet and leftist films and confiscating films that had not been approved by its Department of Public Information.[43] The legal import and distribution of Hollywood films began in April 1946, with the establishment of a Seoul branch of the Central Motion Picture Exchange (CMPE), which was headquartered in Tokyo. The CMPE was a partnership between the US military, the US State Department, and the major Hollywood studios, and it served as the exclusive importer of Hollywood films into South Korea from 1946 until 1951. The CMPE had a dual mission. Politically, it was part of SCAP's (Supreme Command of the Allied Powers) reorientation efforts in the occupied territories, and it distributed only films that the Army had approved for that purpose. The Army's Civilian Affairs Division selected films with an eye towards selling democracy, educating Koreans about American history, culture, and values, and encouraging identification with the US. Using film, it hoped to establish America as a model for South Koreans to emulate as they made the transition from colony to independent nation. The CMPE was thus an instrument of the cultural Cold War, as well as of postwar reorientation. The entertainment value of these films was crucial, and the Hollywood studios purposefully selected films that could "avoid the flavor of propaganda." These films also served as "bait" to draw Koreans into theaters where they would see official newsreels and informational/propaganda films that extolled the American presence in South Korea and the fight against communism. Commercially, the CMPE worked to restore

Hollywood's access to the East Asian markets that had been closed to the US during World War II. It reintroduced Hollywood films into South Korean theaters and carved out a privileged market position for them, setting low ticket prices that drew in large audiences and establishing single-feature screenings that ensured profitability for theater owners. As a result of this joint effort between Washington and Hollywood, American movies saturated South Koreans theaters after 1946 and assumed a dominant position within the market. Once securely established, this favorable market position was maintained after the CMPE shut down operations in 1951 and South Korean companies took over the profitable business of importing and distributing Hollywood films.[44]

The CMPE and South Korean importers maintained a steady flow of Hollywood films into South Korean theaters throughout the late 1940s and early 1950s. About 145 Hollywood films were approved for exhibition during the occupation years of 1946–48, and about 84 in 1949–53. After the conclusion of the Korean War, this flow turned into a torrent, with 1,264 Hollywood films imported between 1952 and 1961.[45] Many of the most popular films were released multiple times. The Hollywood films imported during these years were drawn from studios' backlog of productions from the 1930s and 1940s, as well as from current releases. They came from across the genre map, and included musicals, Westerns, melodramas, films noir, comedies, and war films. Some of the films were B pictures and lesser-quality productions from both major and poverty-row studios; others were among the best films Hollywood ever made.

As in other dimensions of the cultural Cold War, gender played a significant role in the choice of films to import. As Sueyoung Park-Primiano has shown, one of the goals of the Army's Civilian Affairs Division was "to promote the equality of women as part of American democracy," and as a result quite a few of the films included in the reorientation program in the late 1940s contained powerful depictions of American women. These included *The Farmer's Daughter* (1947), which tells the story of a Swedish American woman elected to Congress and which was "likely selected for release in South Korea for its strong portrayal of a woman at home, at work, and in the service of the public, all topics identified as suitable by the CAD."[46] Later imports presented women as working professionals (*Woman of the Year* [1942]), hardy pioneers (*Shane* [1953]), factory workers (*Carmen Jones*, 1954), sexual aggressors (*Written on the Wind* [1956]), glamorous socialites (*Rear Window* [1954]), and strong-willed individuals who stand up to patriarchal Asian men (*The King and I* [1956]).[47] Hollywood films thus sometimes complemented Washington's efforts to "modernize" Korean women's social roles, and Korean filmmakers likely looked to these films for inspiration as they crafted the après girl characters who figured so prominently in the "feminine '50s" productions.

Korean filmmakers embraced these Hollywood pictures as sources of new ideas, treating them as style manuals and storytelling guides. For Ma Yong-cheon, who worked as the assistant lighting director on *Madame Freedom*, Hollywood films stimulated filmmakers' "interest in film and their dreams." Unlike Japanese films, they served as inspirations rather than as models to be copied exactly, because they were "incomparable to Korean movies in their tremendous extravagance and large scale." No South Korean filmmaker had the resources to reproduce what he saw in a typical Hollywood film, and elements of décor that were common in Hollywood films, such as rugs and chandeliers, barely existed in postwar South Korea. Instead, said Ma, "ambitious filmmakers took a studious approach." They watched for technical and formal innovations, taking notes "that the lighting worked this way in a scene and the camera angle worked this way in another scene, and the camera moved this way for such an emotional expression." The basic techniques of classical Hollywood style, including continuity editing, had already been absorbed via Japanese cinema in the 1930s and 1940s. Lee Hyung-pyo, who began his career working with USIS and UNKRA before becoming a screenwriter, cinematographer, and director, recalled that Korean filmmakers looked to Hollywood films as a "textbook" of more advanced techniques. "In the '50s," said Lee, "we mostly watched foreign films. Because we were trying to learn something." The films of Billy Wilder and Marilyn Monroe, *Love in the Afternoon* (1957), *Some Like It Hot* (1959)—these were "splendid" films that Lee said "inspired" him, and he applied the lessons learned from them to his own films, "tweaking" them as necessary. Lee went even further in explaining his relationship to Hollywood. "What is art?" asked Lee rhetorically. "Art is imitation. Aristotle said so. . . . Imitating something is art. What we learn, directly and indirectly, subconsciously, these are all imitations. . . . So I was influenced a lot from the American movies. From topics to directing or even usage of music. . . . Then camera technique. And then composition, screen, all of them I learned from those American movies." Cinematographer and director Kang Beom-gu recalled that Hollywood films offered models for how to combine social engagement with popular appeal. He remembered that *On the Waterfront* (1954) made a big impression on South Korean filmmakers in the 1950s who were attracted by its story about an ordinary man who resists an oppressive authority. They saw the film as a powerful work of social criticism that also worked as commercial cinema, with big stars, good acting, and a dramatic story.[48] One can see signs of the lessons learned across 1950s cinema, as in Shin Sang-ok's recreation of Deborah Kerr and Burt Lancaster's surfside kiss in *From Here to Eternity* (1953) in his film *Flower in Hell* (1958).

Han Hyung-mo seems to have poached not so much specific scenes from Japanese and Hollywood cinema as elements of style. The appeal of Japanese cinema for Korean filmmakers lay in its familiarity. They valued Hollywood cinema, in contrast, for its difference. These films offered a formal language for expressing ideas that broke with the legacies of Japanese colonialism and that involved new ways of thinking and living. Han drew on both of these vernacular modernisms in order to convey the complexities of South Koreans' experience of layered modernity in the 1950s. While he shared with Ozu a spatial vocabulary for depicting women's changing social ambitions, he looked to Hollywood cinematography, in turn, for a vocabulary to capture the exhilarating emotional dimension of modernity, its anxieties as well as its freedoms and desires. These two cinematic vocabularies intermingled in *Madame Freedom*, creating—like *budae jjigae*—a uniquely South Korean work of film art.

SOUND AND MUSIC

Han was as creative in his use of sound as he was with the visual elements of cinematic style. Most Korean films in the 1950s were shot silent and had their sound and dialogue dubbed in during postproduction. But while most of these films have fairly simple soundtracks, Han used sound and music in sophisticated ways. Like cinematography, sound was a dimension of filmmaking in which Han was an important modernizer. Here, too, Han acted as a textual poacher, taking what he needed from Korea's rich sound culture. Of particular interest to me here are Han's political uses of sound: how he used sound and music to express South Korea's affiliations and disaffiliations within a Cold War landscape. Han used sound and music to create a soundscape of modernity that suggested South Korea's integration into, and cultural contiguity with, the Free World.

Han began working creatively with sound effects in his first feature film, *Breaking the Wall* (1949), which told a story of family conflict set during the Yeosu-Suncheon Rebellion of 1948. Han took great pride in the film's innovative sound design, which he achieved by poaching from Hollywood films:

> Since it was the first military film in Korea, I had a hard time in recording the sound of gunshots. First, I copied 10,000 gunshot sounds from Western movies produced in America. From this, I selected 1,000 bullet sounds and I used them in the sound film containing the dialogue. It took over 40 days to complete just the sound edit.[49]

Han doesn't say exactly how he copied this improbably large number of gunshot sounds, but it is possible that theater owners or importers let him record directly from the films in their possession. This episode allows us to see how poaching involves indigenization rather than mere copying, and how the meaning of sound changes as it moves out of American films and into Korea's film culture. The sounds of these gunshots were taken from Hollywood Westerns, where they had perhaps been fired at a "savage" Indian or a cattle rustler who was blocking the spread of "civilization" on the American frontier. In poaching these sounds, Han stripped them of their nineteenth-century frontier associations and repurposed them to dramatize a twentieth-century South Korean story about a family riven by the ideological conflict with communism—a very different struggle between "savagery" and "civilization" and one that implies the existence of a very different "frontier." The film's most poignant sound was perhaps found at the film's climactic moment, when the communist partisan shoots his brother-in-law in the chest at point blank range—a melodramatic sound designed to prove the moral bank-ruptcy of communism.

Han was pioneering in the use of music as well, employing it in many different capacities over the course of his career. Han helped launch the musical as a South Korean genre with *Hyperbolae of Youth*, which incorporated musical numbers into its romantic comedy story line. Han made music a central narrative element in *I Am Alone* (1958), a melodrama whose story is built around the writing, com-posing, performing, broadcasting, and hearing of the eponymous song. Han fre-quently included scenes of characters dancing to music in settings that varied from a stately theater in *Because I Love You* (1958) to a seedy nightclub in *The Heaven and the Hell* (1963). Han began including stand-alone musical performances in *Breaking the Wall*, which included a special appearance by the popular singer Hyeon In.[50] His last two films are full to the brim with musical performances. In *Let's Meet at Walkerhill* (1966), he uses the narrative device of two country bump-kins traversing Seoul in search of a lost daughter and girlfriend to survey Seoul's popular music scene. Han's final film, *The Queen of Elegy* (1967), was a biopic of singer Lee Mi-ja that dramatized the hardships of her life and her path to stardom, and it, too, consisted largely of performances set in nightclubs, radio studios, and concert halls.

Madame Freedom's sound design is quite extraordinary. Han embedded his characters within a soundscape of modernity that he created by combining bits of foreign sound and music poached from South Korea's sound culture with other, indigenous sounds. This soundscape works in tandem with and complements Han's settings and cinematography. Dialogue plays an important role in the film as sound. Characters regularly insert English words and phrases into their speech, with the younger, more Americanized ones doing so more frequently: Mr. Shin says "Good morning" and "I love you" to Mme Oh and offers her "whiskey," while she asks him to teach her the "skate waltz." Miss Park orders "coffee" at a café with Professor Jang and gives him a "present." He, in turn, refers to her as "Missu" Park, using a Korean pronunciation of the English honorific. The value of these words resides in their sound as well as in their meaning: what matters most is that they are English words and thus mark the speaker as conversant, literally, with American culture. Han's incorporation of select English words stands in implicit contrast to the ban on the public displays of the Japanese language, which was an important factor in keeping Japanese films out of Korean theaters, and by extension with the efforts to limit Chinese characters within print culture.[51] The sound of the English words, like the sound of the gunshots in *Breaking the Wall*, carries its own political associations, suggesting an affiliation with America that is displacing the colonial relationship with Japan and the even older cultural relationship with China.

Han uses sound effects to embed his characters in urban modernity. This can best be seen in the Paris Boutique, which functions as a key node in the film's soundscape as well as its spatial system. In the many scenes set here, Han suffuses the shop with a muted cacophony of honking car horns and traffic noises. This urban symphony carries into the shop from the street, despite the closed doors that might logically keep it out. These traffic sounds are pervasive and surround the characters, functioning as an auditory complement to the Western goods on display. Han uses sound to create a richly layered sensory environment in the shop, in which the visual and the aural complement each other and work together to express the experience of modernity in multiple modalities. These sound effects may have been poached from Hollywood films, like the gunshots in *Breaking the Wall*. They may also have been taken with permission from recordings made freely available by the US State Department's Voice of America (VOA), which kept a recording library that included fifty-six records of sound effects that commercial filmmakers could borrow. Many filmmakers used this library to create their soundtracks, borrowing sounds of industrialization, transportation, and modern violence: according to sound designer Choi Hyeon-rye, the most popular effects were "the sounds of a car, airplane, guns, and machinery." For Lee Kang-cheon's *Piagol* (1955), an anticommunist film about North Korean partisans behind the lines in South Korea, sound designer Lee Sang-man used the VOA's gunshot sounds in a scene where the brutal communist captain kills a wounded comrade and again at the end when the heroine kills the captain before turning herself in. Choi used the library extensively when he created the soundtrack for Shin Sang-ok's *Flower in Hell*, which featured the sounds of car horns honking, doors slamming, and tires screeching; police sirens wailing; trucks accelerating and shifting gears and crashing; the whistling and chugging and clacking of steam trains; and ultimately, the exchange of handgun shots and machine-gun fire. Choi reports that filmmakers had access to sound-effects recordings from the colonial era, but they were mostly the sounds of sliding doors, wind, and rain—in other words, culturally Japanese sounds and sounds of nature.[52] While filmmakers used these Japanese sounds, they did not help them represent postwar modernity. For modern sound, they used American resources.

Han's use of music in *Madame Freedom* was even more nuanced. Working with his highly skilled music director Kim Yong-hwan, Han produced a remarkably rich tapestry of music: the film incorporates about thirty-five distinct pieces of music, some only a few seconds long, others several minutes in duration. Three songs appear as musical performances; the rest are heard on the soundtrack as diegetic and nondiegetic music. The variety of musical traditions used in the sound design is remarkable. Han includes one Korean *trot* song, "Saturday for Avecs," which is performed in an extended musical number by the well-known singer Baek Seol-hui at the women's luncheon. *Trot*, similar to *budae jjigae*, is a hybrid Korean cultural form with roots in American, European, and Japanese musical traditions; John Lie describes it "something of a halfway house . . . new and different enough to be interesting, old and familiar enough to be soothing."[53] Han also includes American popular standards by George Gershwin and Richard

Rodgers, a bit of blues written by African American composer W. C. Handy and performed in a hot jazz style by African American trumpeter Erskine Hawkins, and several big band arrangements reminiscent of Glenn Miller. One song has its origins in Mexican folk music, another in the traditions of the European gypsies. There is an Eastern European waltz and a Czech polka, plus a wide variety of Latin music, including Argentine tango, Mexican bolero, and Cuban mambo. The film includes music produced by writers, composers, and performers from around the world: Mexican songwriters Manuel Ponce and Consuelo Velazquez, Spanish-born Cuban bandleader Xavier Cugat, Cuban-born Mexican band leader Damaso Perez Prado, Hungarian-French composer Joseph Kosma, Anglo-Italian conductor Annunzio Paolo Mantovani, and Russian-Jewish American crooner Eddie Fisher. Much of this music is diegetic: the characters play records in their room, hear their neighbor's music in the street and in their own home, work in an office where music plays in the background, listen to music in cafés, are serenaded by a singer over lunch, and dance to live and recorded music in dance halls. The film's characters thus inhabit an extraordinarily cosmopolitan musical world—into which Han invites the film's viewers.

Han's technical skill with music is on full display. Han creates nondiegetic sound bridges to ease the viewer across cuts and from one scene into the next, as when Mme Oh departs her home for the first time and crosses into the street, a key transition that is unified through a jaunty tune. This music will reappear alongside the dramatic crane shot into the Paris Boutique's window, suggesting the optimistic possibilities of her work outside the home. He inserts short pieces of nondiegetic music to help convey the meaning of a scene. When Mme Oh secretly watches Mr. Shin kiss her niece in the street, a burst of dark and dramatic music, heavy on strings and oboe, accompanies her scowling look and suggests that she is feeling a combination of social disapprobation and jealousy. Han blurs the distinction between music and the human voice, as when Madame Choi's suicidal collapse on a dance floor is accompanied by shrieking strings that mimic the sound of human cries. Han and his music director clearly selected the music with deep knowledge. They add emotional depth to individual scenes by choosing songs whose lyrics—sometimes heard, other times not—are aligned with story events. When Miss Park, for instance, initiates her relationship with Professor Jang by arranging a date over the phone, the music and lyrics of Dee Lippman's "That's the Chance You Take" can be heard in the background. This song is about taking a chance with a new love that may bring laughter or tears, both of which Miss Park will experience in her relationship with Professor Jang. While most members of the film's audience were unlikely to understand these English lyrics, the song significantly enriched the emotional content of the scene for those sophisticated few who did.

Han uses all this music expressively. Han opens the film with a bit of musical foreshadowing, before the story even begins. He bookends the film with a distinctive rendition of Joseph Kosma's "Autumn Leaves," which features descending

VIDEO 4. Clip from *Madame Freedom*.
To watch this video, scan the QR code with your mobile device or visit
DOI: https://doi.org/10.1525/luminos.85.4/

piano scales and arpeggios that mimic the falling leaves of the song's title and thus suggest the ending of something. We first hear the song during the opening credits, where it sets a somewhat somber tone that gradually dissipates. The song returns, however, in the film's concluding scene, as Mme Oh walks through the nighttime streets after being caught in the hotel with her lover and while she is being berated by her husband. The first usage thus foreshadows Mme Oh's experience of romantic loss and moral decline that by the end of the film has come to fruition.

Han puts music in the service of his exploration of an emerging social modernity. Two brief pieces of music set the story in motion and introduce its theme of westernization. In the film's second scene, following the brief squabble with his wife over helping with his son's homework, Professor Jang has retreated into his office to work on his manuscripts (video 4). His scholarly work on the Korean language is soon interrupted, however, by music wafting in through an open window: a brief burst of W. C. Handy's "Saint Louis Blues," followed by a longer portion of Franz Lehar's "The Merry Widow Waltz." Professor Jang tries to ignore the music, but cannot—it is too present. These songs function like aural counterparts to the shiny electric iron in the previous scene, and they, too, suggest that Western culture is already insinuating itself, unbidden, into the Korean home before Mme Oh takes her job. Paying attention to music, as to cinematography, reveals the film's complex attitude toward modernization: music tells the viewer that the influx of Western culture and values is unstoppable and not simply a matter of one woman's choices. Unwilling to confront this intrusion himself, Professor Jang instructs his wife to send their son to tell the neighbor, Mr. Shin, to turn the music down; the boy agrees, since the music is disturbing his studying as well. Mr. Shin lowers the volume, but only after the boy makes clear that the request comes from his mother rather than his father. The music thus implies an erotic relationship between Mr. Shin and Mme Oh before they ever occupy the same visual frame. While this Western music alienates the male members of the household as they try to fulfill their socially respectable roles of scholar and student, it introduces the possibility of a new social identity—lover—for Mme Oh.

As the story progresses, "The Merry Widow Waltz" develops into a musical motif that marks Mme Oh's growing romantic relationship with Mr. Shin. Each time it returns, Han toys with the distinction between diegetic and nondiegetic music: what initially seems to be soundtrack music is shown to emanate from Mr. Shin's record player (a sound trick that John Ford used to great dramatic effect in *Stagecoach* [1939]). The song proves irresistibly attractive to Mme Oh, drawing her out of her role as wife and mother and enticing her into defiantly modern acts. When she hears it in the street one evening after walking home with Mr. Shin, she pauses and thinks fondly of the young man, who has just complimented her on her beauty. The next time she hears it, she diverts from her homeward path and enters Mr. Shin's home, where she asks him to teach her how to dance. She hears it a third time as she sits angrily in her house following her husband's derailment of her date with Mr. Han, and again the song lures her into Mr. Shin's home. Once there, she boldly asks for a drink of whiskey and for further dance instruction: she wants to enact with her body the ideas of romance that are present in the music and so notably absent from her marriage. As their dance hold turns into a cheek-to-cheek embrace, Mr. Shin dips her low and out of the frame for what seems to be a passionate kiss, until they are interrupted by the sound of her son's voice calling Mme Oh back home. In this scene, sound orchestrates Mme Oh's shifting relationship to her home and the social roles she must play there: "The Merry Widow Waltz" lures her out of her home and her role of wife and mother; the sound of her son's voice, in turn, reels her back in.

Han creates a second musical motif to signal Professor Jang's developing extramarital relationship with Miss Park. Here Han uses music less as an enticement to modern action, and more as an expression of modern feelings. This motif is composed of multiple iterations of a lush and romantic light-classical orchestration of strings. The motif is introduced as diegetic music when Mr. Shin teaches Mme Oh to dance in his room, which then wafts over into the adjoining house as a dejected Professor Jang returns from work to find his wife absent and his son untended. In this initial appearance, the music conveys the husband's sad sense of abandonment as his wife sheds her domestic role. The music reappears when Miss Park and Professor Jang stroll together in a park, and then again as an accompaniment to the dramatic descending crane shot as Professor Jang tenderly bids Miss Park good night outside her house. These iterations suggest their growing feelings for each other and the possibility that this freely chosen and emotionally satisfying relationship might replace Professor Jang's failed arranged marriage. The motif's final reprise comes in the form of George Gershwin's "Someone to Watch over Me," which accompanies the parallel ascending crane shot outside Miss Park's house as she breaks off the relationship with Professor Jang. Here the lush strings—as well as the implied but unheard lyrics—suggest the sadness of these platonic lovers as they give up the possibility of "watching over" each other with tender care.

Han creates a third musical motif to mark his characters' embrace of a modern *enjoi* lifestyle centered on dance. When his characters are in the act of dancing, talking about dancing, or even thinking about dancing, Latin music can usually be heard on the soundtrack. When Mr. Shin calls Mme Oh from a café and invites her to go dancing, the famous tango "La Cumparsita" can be heard in the background. When Mme Oh goes to the dance hall with Mr. Shin, the band performs the mambos "Cherry Pink and Apple Blossom White" and "Que Rico el Mambo." When Mme Oh waits impatiently for Mr. Han in a café so they can go dancing, she listens to the bolero "Bésame Mucho." And in the hotel room where Mme Oh and Mr. Han go to consummate their affair, they dance to Pablo de Sarasate's "Gypsy Airs." Latin music marks Mme Oh's movement out of a social order and identity centered on the home and into a public space that operates according to different rules. With its invitation to dance, the music suggests new possibilities for an embodied life. It signals leisure rather than endless domestic chores, the satisfaction of individual desires rather than dutiful service to others, and the possibility of romance with a freely chosen partner. Its exotic, foreign sound serves as an invitation to inhabit, if only temporarily, a new world that has suddenly opened up within Seoul.

Like the settings and the mobile cinematography discussed earlier, the presence of all these Western songs on *Madame Freedom*'s soundtrack was a result of textual poaching. Most South Korean filmmakers in the 1950s had neither the money nor the equipment to compose, perform, and record original songs. Instead, they used preexisting music—from foreign albums, Korean rerecordings of foreign albums, and soundtracks of foreign films—and transferred it to the film's soundtrack.[54] *Madame Freedom*'s music director, Kim Yong-hwan, who worked in radio as well as film, was known as the best in the industry for "selecting the songs."[55] All the Western songs in *Madame Freedom* were taken, without permission, from other sources. Kim poached widely from contemporary music to create the soundtrack for Han's film. He took "Autumn Leaves" from a recording by pianist Roger Williams that was released in the United States in 1955 and became a number one hit, selling over two million copies.[56] He used Erskine Hawkins's 1950 recording of "Saint Louis Blues," Eddie Fisher's 1952 recording of "That's the Chance You Take," Perez Prado's 1955 recording of "Cherry Pink and Apple Blossom White" with Billy Regis on trumpet, Leo Diamond's 1955 recording of "Melody of Love," David Rose's 1954 recording of "Someone to Watch over Me," and Xavier Cugat's 1951 recording of "Gypsy Airs." Many of these songs were hits that topped the Billboard charts in the United States and found popularity in other parts of the Free World. These acts of textual poaching often involved material poaching, as well: as was the case with the US military helicopter wheels that formed the foundation for Han's crane, many of these recordings would have been acquired on the black market.

Madame Freedom's soundtrack constitutes a survey of music that was popular in the United States and the West in the 1940s and 1950s. As such it functions as an aural expression of Cold War cosmopolitanism. With its globally sourced songs, it gives musical form to the idea of South Korea's integration into a free world that includes America, Europe, and Latin America. The soundtrack creates, for the film's characters and its viewers alike, an experience of temporal and cultural contiguity with the West. Through music, Han creates Seoul as a city that is fashionably up-to-date with cultural trends in New York, Mexico City, Havana, and London. The soundtrack's contemporaneity ushers its auditors into a temporality of cultural modernity that is shared with the inhabitants of those Western metropolises. Han uses music to embed South Korea as one node within a network of modern locales. E. Taylor Atkins has commented on the powerful ability of music to create a shared sense of time. Writing about the global popularity of jazz earlier in the century, he noted that the music "represented nothing more profoundly than the coevalness of modern time: as they listened and danced to jazz, people imagined that they were experiencing modernity simultaneously with their counterparts in distant lands."[57] Han's cosmopolitan soundtrack accomplishes something similar. It allows the film's characters—and viewers—to experience their incorporation into the Free World system as pleasure, imagination, and emotion. Such a claim of coevalness has political implications in a postcolonial society, suggesting that the "backwardness" that Japan invoked to justify its colonial project has been overcome.

Such poaching of popular Western songs was, like the remaking of Japanese films and the borrowing of Hollywood techniques, standard film industry practice in the 1950s. Particularly popular were the songs of Rodgers and Hammerstein, who were at the peak of their success in the United States in the 1950s and whose Asia-Pacific-themed musicals were major producers of Cold War Orientalism.[58] In *The Widow* (1955), for instance, director Park Nam-ok uses an orchestral version of "Some Enchanted Evening" from *South Pacific* (1958) to express a young widow's romantic longings, weaving it throughout the film as a motif that reappears at key moments. Shin Sang-ok used the same song to similar effect in *A Sister's Garden*

(1959), and he concluded that film and *A College Woman's Confession* (1958) with a medley of music from Jerome Kern and Oscar Hammerstein II's *Show Boat* (1936, 1951) that included a few bars of "Ol' Man River." Shin also used Perez Prado's "Mambo #5" in *Flower in Hell*, and reportedly included George Gershwin's "Rhapsody in Blue" in the soundtrack of his first film, *The Evil Night* (1952).[59] In each of these films, Western popular song signals the modernity of the films' characters, especially its female ones, as they try to renegotiate their place in the world.

Filmmakers' use of Western music must be understood within the broader context of postwar sound culture. By the 1950s Koreans had some familiarity with Western music. Members of the educated middle class had embraced European classical music during the colonial era, and American jazz, blues, and dance music had gained popularity as a "modernist counterculture" to imperial Japanese culture.[60] The US military became a major disseminator of American music during and after the Korean War, through live USO and Eighth Army Shows, the Armed Forces Korea Network (AFKN) radio station, and as a source of pilfered records.[61] Yet it was not always easy for ordinary Koreans to hear Western popular music in the 1950s: most ordinary Koreans did not have access to the US military base shows, few foreign albums were legally imported, those available on the black market were expensive, and Korean radio stations did not play many Western songs. One major venue for this music was the music cafés in downtown Seoul, which attracted more educated patrons such as college students, writers, poets, musicians, and members of the film industry. Each café specialized in a different type of music—the Dolce, for instance, played "light music" such as movie soundtracks and songs by Elvis Presley, Paul Anka, and Pat Boone.[62] These cafés often shared their albums with filmmakers. Han took more than songs from these music cafés, however: he also took Kim Jeong-rim, the actress who plays Mme Oh. Kim was a hostess at the famous Renaissance café in Myeongdong, which specialized in Western classical music. Han valued Kim not for her acting ability, which was limited, but as a minor celebrity and real-life après girl strongly associated with Western culture and lifestyle. She was an object of interest in her own right—a "center of curiosity," as one member of the film's crew described her—and Han counted on her to pull in viewers.[63] Other films also drew inspiration from the music cafés, including Gwon Yeong-sun's *A Drifting Story* (1960): set in the fictional Madonna café, it featured American album covers prominently in its decor and hosted a soundtrack full of Western songs. These movies functioned as widely accessible vehicles for popular Western songs, and thus as integral parts of Korea's sound culture as well as its film culture. By bringing this music into his films, Han made it available to a far larger audience than could frequent the downtown music cafés, while also embedding it in a Korean context rather than the English-language world of AFKN. The presence of these exotic songs likely contributed to the films' appeal, serving as a crucial part of the entertainment they provided for audience members, who should thus be understood as "auditors" as well as "viewers." Historians of Korean popular music have argued that Western music was not very popular among Koreans in the 1950s.[64] Locating movies within Korea's sound culture, however, suggests that this music was more accessible to Korean audiences than the history of live performances and broadcast radio suggests.

Han's poaching of Western music in *Madame Freedom* was not appreciated by all the film's viewers. One newspaper reviewer, for instance, complained about "the appropriation of unnecessary songs and dances, which are a poor imitation of American movies."[65] The reviewer here implies that such acts of poaching are undignified and untrue to Korea, not unlike what a critical viewer might see Mme Oh herself as doing: senseless copying of a foreign model that is not appropriate for Koreans. Such a comment implies a cultural nationalist framework: a South Korean movie should express an exclusively South Korean cultural world. But that is not what *Madame Freedom* does.

The Free World exists in *Madame Freedom* as an absent but structuring space. Travis Workman has written about the role of such unseen spaces—what he calls *topos*—in postwar Korean melodramas, focusing on the traumas of the Korean War that are not represented directly on screen but that undergird many story lines and characterizations.[66] In *Madame Freedom* and other Cold War cosmopolitan films, the Free World is just such a topos: a place that is not directly represented but whose existence is continually suggested by visual and aural style. While the film's narrative remains focused on Mme Oh's peregrinations through Seoul, its formal properties suggest the presence of a larger world that invests her actions with additional, unarticulated meanings. Through setting, cinematography, and sound, the film suggests South Korea's affiliations with the unseen capitalist, democratic, Western world beyond its borders.

6

———

Consumer Culture and the Black Market

Mise-en-Scène

Han Hyung-mo's films are marked by a distinctive mise-en-scène. They are visually dense and lush, their frames full of alluring objects that catch the eye, with Western material culture, especially consumer items, often taking pride of place. This dimension of Han's style is apparent in *Madame Freedom*'s (1956) Paris Boutique. We first see the shop's interior after the remarkable mobile camera shot, discussed in the previous chapter, in which the camera sweeps down across a bustling sidewalk and comes to a rest up against the shop's display window. A cut brings the viewer into the boutique, with the camera now peering into a glass display case filled with an array of enticing objects: a jar of Ponds cold cream, a box of Coty face powder, bottles of perfume, pressed powder compacts, lipsticks, men's shirts, a cardigan sweater. Each item, vividly rendered via a crisply focused cinematography, attracts the viewer's attention and solicits an acquisitive desire. Into this still life enters Mme Oh, neatly coiffed and prettily made up, as she kneels down and removes a bottle of perfume, as if to hand it to the viewer (figure 16). The Paris Boutique is an oasis of commercial plenitude, filled with distinctive consumer objects and representations of them, from Chanel's rectangular perfume bottles to men's fedoras. In a period of postwar scarcity, Han's mise-en-scène provides the visual pleasure of material abundance. The shop is also a cosmopolitan oasis: all of the items on display are of foreign origin. The dialogue highlights their Western provenance as Mme Oh tells one customer that "the perfume and powder are from France, and the others are all from America," and offers another, in English, a set of "American Max powder." The sales clerks and customers, dressed in Western clothes and sporting the latest in hats, gloves, and purses, bring the shop's inanimate goods to life as they discuss them, handle them, pay for them, and wrap them up.

144

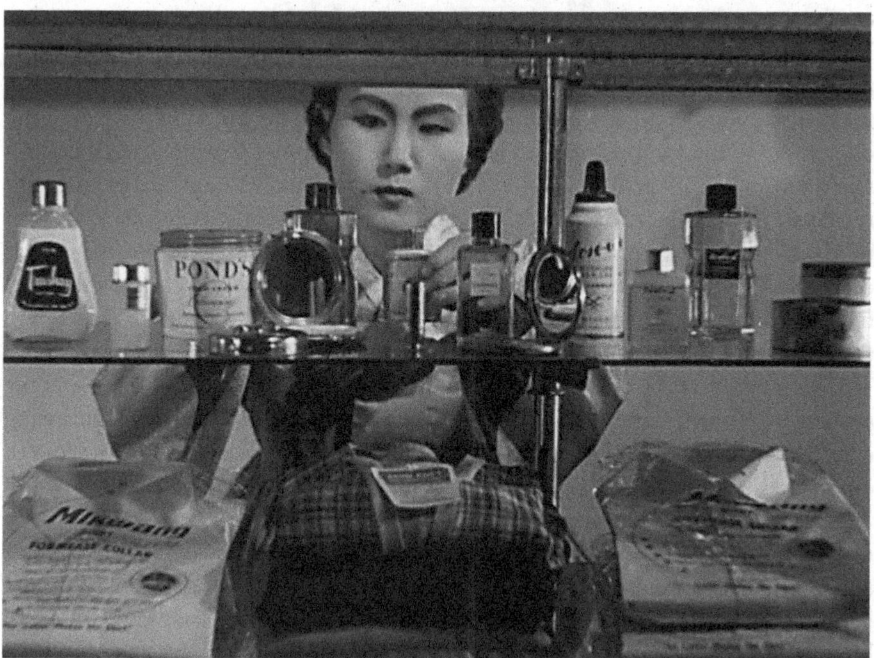

FIGURE 16. Han Hyung-mo's mise-en-scène: an oasis of commercial plenitude in *Madame Freedom*. (Courtesy KOFA)

Mise-en-scène refers to everything that the camera films: setting, costume, décor, props, lighting, color, and the composition of all of these within the frame. Han's mise-en-scène was a key component of his Cold War cosmopolitan period style, part of what made his films so popular with viewers, attractive to investors, and inspiring to his colleagues. Like many of his films, *Madame Freedom* deploys a mise-en-scène that mirrors the glamour and visual density of Hollywood. I want to read Han's mise-en-scène, however, as more than an instance of neocolonial mimicry by interpreting it in two ways, as I did with setting, cinematography, and sound in the previous chapter: as an expressive element creatively deployed to construct meaning within the films themselves, and as historical evidence that reveals something significant about Korea's experience of postwar modernization. Han's films served as advertisements for, and products of, an emerging consumer capitalist modernity. They offered visions of a material lifestyle that was widely desired but not yet widely achieved

Thomas Elsaesser has argued persuasively that mise-en-scène is central to the expressive powers of the melodrama and key to its ideological complexity. He suggests that at their core, melodramas work through the "sublimation of dramatic conflict into décor, colour, and composition of frame." Writing about postwar Hollywood, he describes melodramas' mise-en-scène as richly expressive of the pressure, repression, and social alienation experienced by the individual within the claustrophobic social atmosphere of the American family. Individual material objects—a fountain, a mirror—symbolize and metaphorically condense characters' inarticulate inner lives, visualizing their interpersonal conflicts and fraught relationship to social conventions. Mise-en-scène thus serves as visual expression of ideas and feelings that cannot be articulated openly at the level of story and dialogue. This tension between mise-en-scène and narrative is central to melodramas' ability to serve as what Elsaesser calls "critical social documents," allowing them to cast doubt visually on the very ideologies that they reinforce narratively.[1] Thinking about Han's mise-en-scène textually, we can see how it often works the same way, pushing against the ideological thrust of the narratives and expressing characters' distance from dominant norms and values even as the stories seem to embrace them.

Cultural anthropologists and consumer studies scholars, in turn, can help us think about Han's mise-en-scène as a form of historical evidence that reveals something about the world beyond the films. These scholars have focused on the social function of consumer goods and acts of consumption, calling attention to how they work in modern (and modernizing) societies as a "system of human communication" that is "charged with cultural meaning."[2] Carefully chosen consumer objects can locate their possessor within a social order, enabling her to make, according to Robert Oppenheim, "claims about who one is in the world."[3] As products of modernization themselves, they can serve as an "idiom" for thinking through what Daniel Miller calls the "problems of modernity" and for negotiating the new and unfamiliar worlds and identities that modernization creates.[4] Such objects thus serve both a creative and a mediatory function, enabling their owners to invent new social identities through which they engage shifting social conditions. Arjun Appadurai expands the analytical framework of consumer culture even further when he invites us to investigate "the social life of things." He urges us to explore how material artifacts are embedded within networks of social, cultural, political, and economic relations. The meanings of objects, he writes, are inscribed in their "trajectories": "it is the things-in-motion that illuminate their human and social context."[5] To understand the full range of meaning that an artifact carries, he suggests, we must recover its ties to the networks that made its production, circulation, and consumption possible. Such recovery becomes even more essential when these networks cross national and cultural boundaries.

Cultural historians of the Cold War have emphasized the extent to which consumer goods in the 1950s carried ideological meanings about the rewards of capitalist democracy. The postwar years were the heyday of international trade exhibitions, which provided a platform for the United States to trumpet the fruits of its humming industrial economy. These consumer goods—from washing machines to cars—were imbued with the ideas of freedom, equality, abundance, leisure, and the just rewards of hard work, a political message that Vice President Richard Nixon articulated clearly in his 1959 "kitchen debate" with Nikita Khrushchev at the American National Exhibition in Moscow.[6] Hollywood movies were intimately linked to this political symbology, and the State Department valued them as visually enticing advertisements for the products of American industry.[7] It was, in part, this linkage of mise-en-scène to Free World economic ideology that led the State Department to work with the big eight studios, via the Central Motion Picture Exchange (CMPE), to facilitate film exports into postwar Asia.

Thinking about the expressive capacity of mise-en-scène invites us to ask: what role did it play in Han's depiction of gendered modernity? As with the modern girl in the earlier part of the century, the postwar après girl was characterized by her interaction with foreign consumer goods. When Mme Oh's independent-minded niece awaits her lover in a coffee shop, she reads *Reader's Digest*. When Miss Park goes on a date with Professor Jang, she orders coffee. When the heroine of *Hyperbolae of Youth* (1956) participates in the *enjoi* lifestyle, she drinks Coca Cola. When the heroine of *A Female Boss* (1959) asserts her right to monopolize a public phone in defiance of the men waiting in line behind her, she feeds her dog a Fig Newton cookie. Han was certainly not alone in associating the après girl with Western objects: the heroine of *Holiday in Seoul* (1956), for instance, daydreams of riding in a streamlined motor boat after she sees an advertisement for one in an American magazine. Han's films do stand out, however, for their sheer abundance of consumer items and for the central role that they play in expressing character and theme.

Thinking about style as historical evidence leads to a different question: How was it possible for Han to create such a rich mise-en-scène so soon after the Korean War, during a period of widespread poverty and limited economic growth? In what kinds of networks were these consumer items embedded? *Madame Freedom* hints at an answer in its subplot about Mme Oh's involvement in a smuggling scheme run by her friend Mme Choi. This subplot invites us to investigate the connections between the film's vision of capitalist modernity and the trajectories—legal and illegal—through which consumer goods entered Korea.

This chapter explores mise-en-scène from three perspectives. The first section offers textual analyses of *Madame Freedom*, *Hyperbolae of Youth*, and *The Hand of Destiny*. Beyond simply marking the après girl's modernity, Han's use of setting, props, and décor helps characterize women who are engaged in the work of self-making. Anthony Giddens has argued that the construction of "self-identity" is a core feature of modernity. As traditional, collective social identities lose some of their vitality and relevance, individuals take on the task of active self-development, constructing an individuated personal identity by making choices from among a range of options. Such constructions of self-identity are stimulated by globalization, which opens channels for the inflow of information from other cultures and facilitates the formation of social relationships of unprecedented geographic scope. The work of self-making is also enabled by commodity capitalism, which makes possible the cultivation of "lifestyles" that "give material form to a particular narrative of self-identity."[8] We can see this dynamic in Han's films. Through their consumer-capitalist mise-en-scène, they show women creating and inhabiting new individual identities that depart decisively from Confucian social identities. Working through Elsaesser's mechanisms of symbolism, metaphoric condensation, and sublimation, material objects in Han's films convey the cultivation and performance of a modern female self.

The middle portion of the chapter explores the material dimensions of Cold War cosmopolitanism by exploring style as historical evidence. It investigates the "social life" of Han's mise-en-scène by showing how the material artifacts out of which it was composed were embedded in transnational economic and military networks. It traces the historical development of these networks, revealing their roots in the Japanese colonial system and their expansion via the construction of the US military base system in the Pacific. The influx of consumer goods through these networks, in turn, fueled the growth of a vast black market that made American and other foreign goods widely available to those South Koreans who could afford them. Han's mise-en-scène, when taken seriously as historical evidence, sheds light on how consumer capitalism emerged in postwar Korea and the central role played by the black market as a social and economic institution.

The chapter's final section brings us back to the metaphor of *budae jjigae* cinema by investigating poaching as a widespread material practice within the commercial film industry. It explores how filmmakers relied on resources procured from the black market and US military bases to bring their films into existence and to achieve the high-quality production values that attracted viewers. This section brings the expressive and historical dimensions of mise-en-scène together. It reveals how the US military functioned, ironically, as a South Korean cultural institution, inadvertently supplying Han and other filmmakers with some of the resources they needed to make films that depicted female self-making with such tactile vividness.

In focusing on mise-en-scène as an essential element of Han's style, we can understand Cold War cosmopolitanism as a vein of material culture, one that was brought into existence by the transnational networks that carried into South Korea a flood of goods from various parts of the Free World.

HAN'S STYLE OF MISE-EN-SCÈNE

Han Hyung-mo participated in crafting his films' mise-en-scène to a degree that was unusual at the time. His involvement may have arisen out of his wide-ranging aesthetic interests, which extended well beyond cinema. As a youth, Han's first passion had been painting, and he worked for two years designing sets for the

Sintaeyang Theater Group.[9] Later, when his film career began to slow down in the early 1960s, Han took a two-year break and turned to architecture, designing and building Western-style houses—similar, perhaps, to the homes featured in *Yŏwŏn*'s pages—which he then sold. As his colleague Kim Kee-duk recalled, his creative ambitions and modern sensibilities found expression in "a certain upscale house which nobody had seen the likes of before." His commercial instincts were as astute here as elsewhere, and his houses were as popular as his films: "Because he had very keen eyes and was fashionable, once he built his own house, people went for it."[10]

Han worked closely with his regular art director, Lee Bong-seon. Lee was an unrivaled figure in the film industry, a first-generation art director whom colleagues regarded as possessing a "very modern sense" of aesthetics.[11] Lee's roots were in the consumer-oriented arts of capitalism. Lee and Han had met as youths in colonial Manchuria where they both worked in a department store (most likely a branch of Japan's Mitsukoshi chain), Lee as an art assistant and Han as a sign painter.[12] Han brought Lee into the film industry, where he began working on films for which Han was the cinematographer. He served as art director on Han's *Breaking the Wall* (1949), *The Hand of Destiny*, *Madame Freedom*, *A Female Boss*, and other films. Lee continued working with department stores after the Korean War, taking charge of the interior designs of Seoul's Midopa, which had been damaged during the war, and Shinsegye, which had been home to the Eighth US Army PX. He also worked with an event management company that staged political events, including a birthday celebration for Syngman Rhee. Han had such respect for Lee's skill, and such appreciation for the material and financial constraints within which Lee worked, that he often adjusted his shooting plans to accommodate the sets as Lee had constructed them. Lee's commercial orientation is evident in his use of what today would be called product placement: Lee had a side job creating logos for liquor companies, and he sometimes incorporated signage for his clients' products into his set design, as he did when he placed a large, flashing neon sign for Crown Beer in the middle of a nightclub stage in Han's *A Female Boss* (figure 17).[13]

Working together, Han and Lee used mise-en-scène to explore the idea of women's self-development through the tools that capitalist modernity was making available. They deployed setting, décor, props, and other material artifacts to convey the idea that women could lead lives that departed drastically from dominant norms. In *Madame Freedom* and *The Hand of Destiny*, consumer objects become a means through which the heroines create new lifestyles and express new subjectivities. They are tools through which the après girl characters manufacture the modern ideal of an individual, authentic self.

In *Madame Freedom*, Han creates a Korean version of a Western icon of modernity: the shop girl. The young woman presiding over an emporium of material delights appeared across late-nineteenth and early-twentieth-century Western

FIGURE 17. Product placement: a flashing neon sign for Crown Beer in *A Female Boss* (1959). (Courtesy of KOFA)

literary and visual culture as part of what Lise Sanders has described as the "heated debate about the nature of social, sexual, and moral practice for women employed in the public sphere."[14] Han's arrangement of Mme Oh amidst the setting of the shop (see figure 15 in chapter 5) echoes classic Western imagery, such as James Tissot's painting *The Shop Girl* from his "Women of Paris" series (1883–85) (figure 18). Like Tissot, Han uses the glass window and door to link his shop girl to the modern city outside and to suggest that she, too, is on display, part of the array of visual spectacles that the city offers to sidewalk strollers. Tissot's shop girl, cradling a wrapped package in her arms and gazing directly at the viewer, suggests that her life is defined by participation in commercial networks rather than by motherhood, while the exchange of glances between a man on the street and another shop girl gestures towards new forms of interaction with the opposite sex. The tumble of ribbons on the counter, in turn, hints at erotic *dishabille*. In postwar Korea, as in 1920s–30s Japan and turn-of-the-century Paris, the shop girl was a familiar type of modern woman, and she appeared in the pages of *Yŏwŏn* as the "Hope of Our Workplace" and as a defender of the dignity of women's work.[15] Like other working women, her presence in the commercial public sphere was facilitated by the US military: shop girl was one of the many jobs opened up on the bases for Korean women, who frequently staffed post exchange stores and Korean concessions.

The primary "action" that takes place in the Paris Boutique over the course of the film is Mme Oh's self-transformation, through her engagement with consumer goods, from a "wise mother, good wife" into a professional woman and "liberated wife." Grant McCracken has written about consumer goods as "instruments of the self," expressive tools through which people engage in the inherently modern

FIGURE 18. Icon of modernity: *The Shop Girl*, from James Tissot's series, "Women of Paris, 1883–1885." (Courtesy of Art Gallery of Ontario)

"enterprise of self-creation" and "express new notions of gender."[16] For Daniel Miller, this self-making always implies a relationship to a social world, with consumer goods acting as forms "in which we construct our understandings of ourselves in the world."[17] As a shop girl and a consumer herself, Mme Oh undertakes precisely such a project of personal reinvention. When she first arrives, she wears a *hanbok* and styles her hair in the traditional bun worn by married women, but over time she begins to wear Western fashion and hairstyle. This external change visualizes her more profound inner transformation. Like countless Western literary female consumers before her, Mme Oh is engaged in a project of shedding a self-abnegating identity rooted in the family and crafting a new identity as an autonomous individual. The shop functions as an educational space in which Mme Oh learns how to be modern: how to be a saleswoman (rather than an unpaid domestic laborer), how to flirt with men (rather than be an attentive wife), how to recognize the latest fashion (rather than maintain sartorial customs), and how to participate in a market economy (rather than manage a household economy). While in this space she receives encouragement from other women who spur her on to master these new skills, attitudes, and behaviors: she earns her boss's praise not for being demure, but for actively increasing sales, selling the most expensive items, and providing excellent service. The qualities for which she is now valued are public and commercial, not private and familial. Mme Oh's embrace of a cosmopolitan consumer identity entails spurning a woman's traditional role as a producer of Korean household goods, a rejection that becomes apparent when she sneers at the handmade tie that Miss Park gives her husband as a gift. Such a homely item, along with the female subjectivity that it symbolizes, no longer has any appeal for the modern Mme Oh.

Emboldened by her new sense of herself as a professional woman, Mme Oh also boldly rejects as "uncivilized" Mr. Han's teasing comment that women who "decorate themselves" with the shop's cosmetics gradually develop a "prostitute-like nature." She asserts instead that "makeup is an absolute necessity for the beauty of a woman's life and mind." While this exchange constitutes a bit of foreshadowing of her affair with Mr. Han, it also links a woman's outer, bodily transformation via consumer goods to a more profound inner one. Through makeup, a woman can symbolically lay claim to an autonomous life and mind not defined through her relationship to a man. This exchange resonates with the long history of cosmetics used as instruments of self-definition for women as they shed purely domestic identities and enter the public sphere.[18] It is precisely through consuming the goods that she sells, and imbibing the meanings that they contain, that Mme Oh transforms herself into a self-possessing individual.

As part of her new identity as a shop girl, Mme Oh becomes a disseminator of modern ideas and a purveyor of a lifestyle that gives them material form. In addition to selling consumer goods, she also schools her customers in their use and in the ideals and practices they embody. "What is this thing called bed perfume?" asks one perplexed male customer. "It's perfume you can spray on your bed," answers Mme Oh with a smile, as his female companion gives him a knowing nudge. Mme Oh is not just selling a toiletry here: she is selling the concept of sex as a sensuous and pleasurable experience, and not just an exercise in marital duty undertaken for the purpose of extending the male family line. Through this consumer object, Mme Oh redefines an everyday feature of Korean life—sexuality—and infuses it with new meanings. Mme Oh is dispensing what Laurel Kendall has called "embodied modernity": an experience of being modern that takes place at the level of bodily sensations and practices.[19] The Paris Boutique functions as a "schoolroom" for embodied modernity, teaching people how to express new versions of themselves by consuming new kinds of material goods.[20] As she educates her customers, Mme Oh also educates the film's viewers, who are just as likely to be unfamiliar with bed perfume. In this role, Mme Oh becomes a kind of alter-ego for Han Hyung-mo and Lee Bong-seon, displaying consumer goods and their associated values in an attractive way.

The shop's goods help Mme Oh renegotiate her social relations. When deployed as gifts, they become instruments of female empowerment, enabling Mme Oh to usurp some of the markers of male privilege. When her handsome neighbor Mr. Shin comes by the store before his departure for America, she gives him a shirt and tie from the store's stock—*not* a handmade gift. Previously angry with him for "sporting" with her affections, she now gently teases him for his inability to afford such things himself. Smiling at his visible discomfort, Mme Oh claims for herself the power to bestow expensive foreign gifts on a romantic partner, a power that has heretofore been possessed only by the shop's male customers. The shirt and tie serve as metaphorical condensations of Mme Oh's new subjectivity as a woman who has liberated herself from the constraints of normative gender roles. By giving them to Mr. Shin she claims a new position in the social hierarchy, placing herself above a high-status male college student on his way to America.

Han's consumer goods–based style of mise-en-scène reaches its apogee in his domestic interiors, which reimagine the postwar home as a site of what Kristin Hoganson has called "cosmopolitan domesticity."[21] Han makes the contrast between traditional and modern domestic spaces the visual centerpiece of *Hyperbolae of Youth*. Han structures this romantic comedy around a trading-places story line. Two young men, once friends in college and now of vastly different economic fortunes, become reacquainted in a doctor's office where they have sought treatment for their respective stomach ailments: the rich man, Bu-nam (Yang Hun), is suffering from the effects of overeating, while his poor friend, Myeong-ho (Hwang Hae), suffers from malnutrition. The doctor proposes an unusual cure: each man should move in with his friend's family and live and eat as they do. The body of the film depicts the misadventures that follow, playing them for comedy and romance, since each young man has an attractive sister. Han stages the story in contrasting domestic spaces that express each family's degree of social modernity and their corresponding values. The poor family, led by a widowed mother, lives in a leaky, one-room shack that resembles a *hanok*. The space is small and sparsely furnished, and the few material objects that do exist are functional rather than decorative. Furniture is minimal and consists mostly of thin *yo* mattresses, a small bureau, and a small *soban* table-tray. This single room is used for eating and sleeping, both of which are done on the floor, while cooking and household chores are conducted outside or on the *maru*, a small porch. The traditional décor harmonizes with its inhabitants' traditional behavior. The home is a site of work done in traditional ways: the daughter Jeong-ok (Ji Hak-ja) irons clothes using a charcoal-heated iron, while Bu-nam learns to split wood with an axe and haul water in a bucket. The home is infused with a sense of Koreanness, evoked by a portrait of the father, who was kidnapped by North Koreans during the war, and by the sweeping natural vistas of Busan harbor and the surrounding mountains. When Bu-nam asks Jeong-ok why she is darning a sock rather than simply buying a new one, she responds with a nationalistic defense of frugality: "Imagine if everyone wore their socks for an additional fifteen days. It's a problem that Koreans pretend to have a lot when they actually don't." In sharp contrast, the wealthy family lives in a spacious house that has separate bed- and living rooms and is full of Western-style furniture and objects, including a piano, a record player, and a telephone. This house is a place of leisure, where the daughter Min-ja (Lee Bin-hwa) dances to Western music, eats fresh fruit, and wheedles money from her father to go clothes shopping. It is suffused with an air of cosmopolitanism: "Your house is like a restaurant, coffee shop, and a dance hall all in one" notes Myeong-ho. "I just feel like I'm in a different country."

Han makes the moral valences of these two households abundantly clear. The daughter in the poor family is dutiful and hardworking, and her widowed mother attends a Christian church and exemplifies the endurance that postwar Koreans deeply admired.[22] A portrait of Jesus looks down on them from the wall. The daughter in the rich family, in contrast, is rather spoiled, and her father is a corrupt importer who lies to avoid paying taxes. The arc of the film's narrative breaks down these distinctions, however, as the rich siblings come to appreciate the values of their poor counterparts, and the poor siblings learn to enjoy Western-style leisure. In the end, the health of each man is restored by embracing the strengths of the other family. A happy medium is achieved when the two couples fall in love and, after agreeing to "forget about outdated tradition," get married in a double ceremony. The penultimate scene depicts both families ensconced in the rich family's living room, visually suggesting that while traditional values are admirable, progress and happiness are represented by the Western-style home.

Han's most sophisticated meditation on consumer culture, female empowerment, and cosmopolitan domesticity can be found in *The Hand of Destiny*, a generic hybrid that combines elements of film noir and melodrama. Set in Incheon during the Korean War, it tells the story of Margaret (Yoon In-ja), a fashionable and affluent bar hostess who is also a secret agent working for a North Korean spymaster. One night, Margaret comes to the aid of a man, Yeong-cheol (Lee Hyang), who has been beaten and falsely accused of theft, and she invites him into her well-appointed apartment, where he tells her he is a poor student who must work as a manual laborer to support himself. They fall in love and Margaret begins to support him financially: she buys him new clothes, takes him out on dates, and urges him to give up his job so he can focus on his studies. The melodramatic moral conflict emerges as she experiences a contradiction between her feelings of love for Yeong-cheol and her work as a spy, and it deepens when she discovers that he is a counterintelligence officer. The film reaches its climax when Margaret, under orders from her spymaster, reluctantly brings Yeong-cheol at gunpoint to an isolated location in the mountains. When the spymaster commands her to shoot Yeong-cheol, she turns her gun against the spymaster, who dodges Margaret's bullet and shoots her instead. As Yeong-cheol cradles her dying body, the lovers kiss—the first in Korean film history. She asks him to call her by her Korean name, Jeong-ae, which is a sign—like the *hanbok* and white lace headscarf she wears— that she has renounced both communism and the morally tainted Westernized lifestyle it supported to become a good Korean woman.

As with *Madame Freedom*, the film's narrative arc and much of its dialogue invite a reading that reinforces patriarchal values, as it charts the transformation of the "impure," Westernized, and traitorous Margaret into the good, self-sacrificing, Korean Jeong-ae, who must nevertheless be killed as punishment for her misdeeds. The film can be seen as reinforcing nationalist sentiments by making a male representative of the South Korean state serve as the agent of her transformation. The film echoes the Cold War's humanist ideology, as well, by giving Margaret dialogue in which she renounces the Communist Party's "hate, scheming, and the startling defilement of man" in favor of the "freedom" to express her full humanity through expressions of love and generosity towards another.

An against-the-grain reading that focuses on the expressive capacities of style leads to a significantly different interpretation. The distribution of screen time suggests that the film's primary interest lies less in the spy plot, which takes up less than a third of the film's running time, and more in Margaret's après girl lifestyle and her relationship with Yeong-cheol. What the film expresses quite forcefully, in large part through its domestic mise-en-scène, is that Margaret is an extraordinarily powerful women who is engaged in a romantic relationship that inverts the socially normative gender hierarchy. Margaret's home is a shockingly antipatriarchal space that serves as a stage for her performance of modern ideas about female autonomy and sexuality.

The film's opening scene introduces the viewer to Margaret's apartment, one of the most visually dense and ostentatiously modern domestic spaces in Han's oeuvre. Chock full of exotic foreign goods, it is clearly marked as cosmopolitan (figure 19). "It's a patchwork of what we'd seen in Japanese and American

FIGURE 19. Cosmopolitan domesticity: Margaret's apartment in *The Hand of Destiny* (1954). (Courtesy of KOFA)

books and magazines," recalled Lee Bongseon's assistant Noh In-taek.[23] Its decor includes Western-style furniture, including an upholstered couch and chair, a coffee table, a bed, bookshelves, and a vanity with a large round mirror; boldly patterned textiles used for curtains and upholstery; decorative items on the wall, including a mechanical owl clock with moving eyes; a fluorescent desk lamp; a telephone; a radio; and a bottle of Seagram's whiskey. Margaret's dialogue calls attention to this opulent décor, and she hints that it is the product of a disreputable line of work—"I may live like this, but please don't doubt my sincerity"—which Yeong-cheol assumes is prostitution. As in *Madame Freedom*, where the items for sale in the Paris Boutique are linked to smuggling, and in *Hyperbolae of Youth*, where the wealthy family's home décor is the product of corruption, Margaret's décor is linked to criminality and moral degradation, the products of her work as a spy and a café hostess.

The visual presentation of the apartment, however, undercuts the moral condemnation of the dialogue and narrative closure. The opening scene's cinematography and editing emphasize the importance of the décor and invite the viewer to gaze at it openly (video 5). A series of relatively long takes puts the décor on display at a leisurely pace that allows the viewer to absorb all its components and

VIDEO 5. Clip from *The Hand of Destiny*.
To watch this video, scan the QR code with your mobile device or visit
DOI: https://doi.org/10.1525/luminos.85.5/

understand how they relate to each other spatially. After Yeong-cheol enters the apartment, he gazes around the room with an expression of bewilderment, motivating a series of strong point-of-view shots that display select decorative items in close-up, including a print of a Gauguin nude. (*Yŏwŏn* would reproduce a similar Gauguin painting in its April 1961 issue.) Yeong-cheol acts here as a proxy for the viewer, allowing us to openly ogle what most contemporary audience members would have regarded as a fantastically luxurious and exotic home. Members of the film's production crew were certainly in awe of the set and its decoration: "We didn't live with all that furniture set up like that," recalled Kim Kee-duk, referring to his childhood spent in a *hanok*. The scene presented "a lifestyle, an environment that we could not see in our own society." Other crew members, when they saw the finished film, exclaimed "wow, look at these new things."[24] The rooms are clean, the décor is in good shape, and the lighting is bright enough to reveal the space in its entirety. The film thus presents the apartment as attractive and comfortable, rather than tawdry or menacing, despite Margaret's disparaging comments. One item of décor stands out in particular: a round, oscillating fan prominently positioned between Margaret's and Yeong-cheol's heads so that it seems like a third party to their conversation. Electric fans were very desirable items in this period, much sought-after during Korea's hot and humid summers; for contemporary viewers, it would likely have suggested physical comfort rather than decadence. Like the apartment as a whole, it suggests a welcome refuge from the rubble-strewn and violent street from which Yeong-cheol has just escaped.

The lifestyle Margaret lives within this apartment is as radically new as its decor. At a time when most Korean women lived with their parents, husband and children, or in-laws, Margaret lives alone and entirely outside a patriarchal familial structure. In her apartment full of Western objects she has neither mother-in-law nor man to constrain her actions, nor children to whom she must devote herself. As an economically independent working woman, she purchases her material goods to satisfy her own needs, rather than anyone else's—an unusual display of female consumer autonomy.[25] More shockingly, she uses her Western-style domestic space to entertain and seduce a man whom she finds attractive at first sight. After spending the night with Yeong-cheol in her Western-style bed and presumably having sex with him, Margaret expresses no shame and Yeong-cheol no condemnation. Yeong-cheol, in fact, goes out of his way to tell Margaret that her morally dubious work is not an obstacle to his love for her: "You have every right to be loved," and later, "What's so bad about being a prostitute? You helped a poor and hungry student who was working his way through school. And with no strings attached. Why shouldn't you receive praise from God himself for your pure heart?" Through consumer capitalism, Margaret has created a lifestyle—expressed both in her material surroundings and her intimate relations—that expresses a new way of being a Korean woman.

As a melodrama, the film is centrally concerned with the dynamics of the relationship that is nurtured within this cosmopolitan space. Multiple scenes depict an inversion of the normative heterosexual gender hierarchy. Time and again, and in ways large and small, Margaret asserts power over Yeong-cheol who, although impoverished, is of higher social status due to his identity as a man, a student, and an agent of the state. From the outset she takes on the masculine role of seducer while Yeong-cheol assumes the female quality of sexual reticence. She finances his entry into the *enjoi* lifestyle, taking him out to a boxing match, a bicycle race, and a game of miniature golf. Having said she would assist him financially, she gets angry when she finds him working after he has promised to stop. Margaret essentially renders Yeong-cheol a kept man—and he shows no signs of being anything but grateful.

Margaret asserts her power most overtly in an early sequence of scenes that is constructed around Western consumer objects. The sequence begins on the docks at the port of Incheon, where Margaret watches hundreds of American GIs disembark from a troop ship, an intense look on her face (video 6). She is surrounded by material artifacts (and visual icons) of Western power and modernity. She leans nonchalantly against a large American car, wearing a tailored suit with decorative stitching and holding a white, woven purse (identical to the one Jane Russell

VIDEO 6. Clip from *The Hand of Destiny*.
To watch this video, scan the QR code with your mobile device or visit
DOI: https://doi.org/10.1525/luminos.85.6/

holds as she boards a ship in Josef Von Sternberg's 1952 film *Macao*). A large
military ship is visible behind her, its phallic smokestack paralleling her upright
body and suggesting her strength. Although she is a woman in a decidedly masculine space, she radiates self-possession and confidence. A moment later Margaret
notices Yeong-cheol resting after unloading crates from a boat and walks over to
him, assuming a position above him in the frame. After eyeing his torn and dirty
work clothes, she spirits him away from the waterfront, guiding him into the back
seat of her car with an authoritative grip on his arm. Margaret's actions, like the
mise-en-scène that surrounds her, suggest her power: she seeks out the man she is
attracted to, tells him to leave his work, and takes him away for her own unstated
reasons. Where does Margaret take him? Shopping. In a brief montage sequence,
we see Margaret escorting Yeong-cheol out of a clothes store dressed in a new
double-breasted suit. They stop to gaze into a shop window crowded with shoes
and purses, and in a dissolve Yeong-cheol's worn-out shoes are replaced with a pair
of two-tone spectator Oxfords. Smiling, Margaret tells him, "I've caught you in my
spell" as she again takes him by the arm. This is a reverse Pygmalion scenario, in
which Margaret remakes her lover according to her own desires, visually transforming him from a dirty dockworker into a respectable middle-class man. It is

an exercise of female power conducted through the medium of consumer goods—akin to what Mme Oh does when she gives Mr. Shin clothes he can't afford to buy for himself. In purchasing and gifting the suit and shoes, Margaret lays claim to Yeong-cheol in a way that a man typically lays claim to a woman—through the bestowal of expensive gifts. Consumer goods become gendered instruments of power in her hands.

When they return to Margaret's apartment, the inversion of the normative gender hierarchy continues. After closing the door with a Western-style lock and key (an exotic system of closure at the time) Margaret says to Yeong-cheol, only half-jokingly, "You are totally and completely my prisoner." When he stands in front of Margaret's large vanity mirror, gazing at himself and adjusting his tie—i.e., primping—Margaret looks at him admiringly and says, "The clothes look great on you." Margaret again assumes an authoritative gaze, as she did at the waterfront when she spied Yeong-cheol from a distance. Assuming a traditionally male prerogative, she eroticizes and objectifies Yeong-cheol through her look, admiring him as her creation and as the fulfillment of her own desires.

Margaret retains her position of dominance over Yeong-cheol through to the end of the film. Although she eventually renounces communism, and by implication her Western lifestyle, she doesn't actually give up her autonomy or her power over her lover. Refusing to die from the spymaster's bullet, she asks Yeong-cheol to shoot her—and he complies. Although Yeong-cheol holds the gun, it is Margaret who decides how it will be used. At the crucial moment, she looks at Yeong-cheol unflinchingly via a strong point-of-view shot, while he squeezes his eyes shut in anguish and turns his head away as he pulls the trigger. To the very end it is Margaret who commands the authoritative gaze.

Han was not alone in using mise-en-scène to think through the gendered dimensions of postwar modernity. For many filmmakers in the 1950s and early 1960s, the material trappings of domestic life served as a privileged means of visualizing ideas relating to changing gender roles, westernization, and consumption. Directors working in a realist style and interested in exploring masculine subjectivities also used domestic mise-en-scène expressively, albeit in a very different way. An alternative to the Hollywood-inflected Cold War cosmopolitan style, realism was at once a product of the limited resources available to filmmakers, who turned to exterior locations, minimalist props, and stories about working people out of necessity, and also a sign of the creative influence of European cultural trends such as Italian neorealism and French existentialism, which gave intellectual cachet to expressions of despair.[26] Kim So-dong's *The Money* (1958) and Yu Hyun-mok's *Aimless Bullet* (1961) present the opposite of the empowered woman's cosmopolitan home. Here, threadbare domestic interiors speak vividly of emasculation. These films imagine modernity as masculine loss and psychic collapse, which are manifest visually through the pointed absence of foreign consumer goods and material comforts. While the homes in these films are culturally

Korean spaces, they have been voided of all potency. Efforts to improve quality of life—through theft, black-marketing, and trading in Western goods—lead only to deepening despair. Postwar transformations have turned the male protagonists of these films into patriarchs *manqué*, unable to fulfill their traditional gender roles of providing materially for their families and anchoring them in society. The emptiness of their homes visualizes the experience of modernity as profound powerlessness.

(The tension between realism and cosmopolitanism as competing styles and attitudes towards postwar modernity came to a head in 1958, when officials at the Ministry of Education rejected the selection of Kim Sodong's realist film *The Money* as Korea's submission for the fifth Asian Film Festival in Manila on the grounds that it "portrayed the wretched shadowy side of Korea," and replaced it with Han's upbeat romantic comedy *Hyperbolae of Youth* [1956]. This decision prompted complaints from some film critics, who regarded Han's film as a lesser work of art.)[27]

Director Kim Ki-young, in contrast, used domestic interiors to explore women's empowerment via a horror-derived style. In his expressionistic masterpiece *The Housemaid* (1960), Kim makes a bourgeois family's Western-style house the setting for his critical vision of westernization and the revolution in gender roles it was unleashing. Newly constructed at the wife's urging, the two-story house is stocked with the high-status consumer goods that Han's houses often contained, including a modern kitchen with a refrigerator, a TV, a Western-style bedroom set, and an upright piano. This modern décor expresses the changing gender roles of the inhabitants: while the mother works sewing clothes to finance their new lifestyle, the minimally employed husband cooks dinner for the family and serves his wife in bed after she falls sick from overwork. Kim offers up a nightmare inversion of Han's cosmopolitan homes and self-making women, in which a materialistic housewife and a sexually aggressive servant destroy the entire family. The house's staircase—which functions both as a marker of Western-style architecture and a symbol of the family's upwardly mobile ambitions—becomes the central stage for the enactment of the dark side of westernization, which Kim represents as marital infidelity, abortion, murder, and suicide. In this cosmopolitan domestic space, female-driven consumption and westernization appear as a kind of self-destructive madness. Rather than articulating contemporary feminist critiques of the patriarchal family, as Han's *A Jealousy* (1960) does, or imagining an alternative to it, as *The Hand of Destiny* does, *The Housemaid* depicts the erosion of masculine authority as a gothic nightmare.

THE SOCIAL LIFE OF MISE-EN-SCÈNE

In order to fully understand the meanings that Han's mise-en-scène conveyed, we need to consider the "social life" of the objects out of which it was composed.

This entails recovering the transnational networks in which these artifacts were embedded and through which they entered Korea and became available to Han and his art director Lee Bong-seon. At the same time, by exploring the social life of Han's mise-en-scène, we can see it as historical evidence that sheds light on certain aspects of Korean life beyond the boundaries of the film text, specifically the role of the black market as a social and economic institution.

Consumption was a vexed issue in the 1950s. "Frugality itself, as a public moral value," notes anthropologist Laura Nelson, "has deep roots in South Korea."[28] Grounded in Confucian respect for education over commerce, frugality as a national cultural value was further nurtured by Christian missionaries and by colonial-era nationalists seeking economic independence. Discourses about consumption, says anthropologist Laurel Kendall, "have a long history as moral discourses," with "moral disapprobation" accruing around acts of "getting and spending."[29] These cultural values persisted into the mid-twentieth century, when poverty imposed frugality on many, albeit in tension with widespread aspirations for modernization. As historian John Lie has noted, "material longings loomed large" in the 1950s, and "the impressive material culture" that Americans brought into Korea came to stand for modernity in toto. "Few South Koreans in the 1950s escaped the sweet lure of material plenty represented in Hollywood films," he observed, as "imported luxury goods became the most visible marker of modernity and prestige."[30] This social tension in the moral meanings of consumption percolated through Han's films, often manifesting in the formal tension between narrative and style.

Han's mise-en-scène was rooted in the fledgling consumer culture that was taking shape in Korea's cities in the 1950s. Consumer culture, of course, is a distinctly modern phenomenon, one that developed historically in tandem with industrial modernization, colonialism, and global capitalist expansion. As Korea experienced different types of modernity in the twentieth century, it likewise experienced different forms of consumer culture. In the 1930s, Seoul was home to a thriving consumer culture that was created as an adjunct to Japanese colonialism.[31] Four department stores—three of them owned by Japanese—sold a wide array of primarily Japanese manufactured goods and catered to middle-class Japanese and Korean women, making them one of the few public places where colonizer and colonized intermingled. Like virtually all of Korea's economic institutions, the department stores were thoroughly integrated into Japan's imperial economy and subject to the "fundamental imperialist goal of controlling Korea for Japanese national purposes."[32] The consumer culture that took shape in the 1950s was different in many ways. Korea, of course, did not have an industrial economy capable of producing a broad range of consumer goods. What it had instead was an import economy, divided into legal and illegal sectors. Both of these sectors were embedded in US-centered Cold War transnational networks that partially overlaid colonial-era networks.

Korea's primary trading partners in the legal import economy were the United States and Japan.[33] Washington encouraged trade with Japan throughout the 1950s, both to support its Cold War policy of restoring Japan's economic strength and as a means of stretching the value of American aid dollars, since goods imported from nearby Japan were often cheaper than those from more distant countries. Given Rhee's bitter resentment of the Japanese, however, this trade was conducted on a limited and sporadic basis. This legal import economy focused on immediate consumption and was largely funded by US aid, which provided the foreign exchange needed to import reconstruction materials and bulk foodstuffs to sustain the population. Imports consisted overwhelmingly of agricultural commodities, fertilizer, and petroleum products which were then processed and sold by local businessmen. This aid-and-import system sustained a corrupt political apparatus, as Rhee bestowed lucrative import licenses upon politically allied businessmen, who kicked back a portion of their substantial profits into his political machine.[34] (Han gestures towards this practice in *Hyperbolae of Youth*, when the wealthy father lies to the tax collector about how much money his company has earned processing fertilizer.)

Only a small percentage of Korea's legal imports consisted of consumer goods, and these were subject to quotas and high tariffs that elevated their retail prices considerably. These imports proved both desirable and controversial. They were a point of conflict between American aid officials, who sought to maintain the focus on reconstruction, and members of the ROK government, who benefited from the lucrative profits and tax collections they generated. They also engendered ire among Korean manufacturers, who resented easily available foreign goods for undermining the nation's struggling efforts to industrialize.[35] Consumers often felt differently. Given the scarcity of domestically produced consumer goods and the poor quality of those that did exist, these imports were in high demand among the urban middle class. The influx of relief supplies during and after the Korean War had helped create this consumer market by training Koreans to prefer foreign goods over locally produced ones.[36] These legal imports of bulk commodities and manufactured goods contributed to Korea's social modernization and laid the foundation for a nascent consumer economy. They did little, however, to establish a material foundation for industrial modernization.

Legally imported luxury items turned up frequently in Han's films and those of other directors, where they served as visual shorthand for modernity. Foodstuffs were a significant import category. Imports of bananas, for example, increased from $11,000 in 1956 (when they appeared in *Madame Freedom*'s adulterous hotel room) to $200,000 in 1959. Imports of coffee (a favorite beverage throughout 1950s cinema) fluctuated, from about $12,000 in 1957 to $78,600 in 1959. Electric irons (featured in *Madame Freedom*'s opening scene) were imported to the tune of about $40,000 per year, as were fluorescent lamps (visible in Margaret's bedroom in *The Hand of Destiny*), which peaked in 1958 at $170,000. While women's clothing was not imported at all and handbags were a tiny item (only $4,000 worth in 1958), men's clothes were imported in much larger quantities, including items like felt hats and trench coats ($360,000 and $40,000 worth, respectively, in 1956), which attired Han's noirish characters in *The Heaven and The Hell* (1963). Musical instruments, like the grand piano featured in *I Am Alone* (1958), were a big category, with over $600,000 worth being imported between 1955 and 1959. Clocks and watches, the latter a regular feature of men's costumes, were an even bigger import, with over $3.2 million worth imported between 1955 and 1959.[37]

The US military played a crucial role in financing the import of these consumer goods. While all imports had to be paid for with foreign exchange, such as American dollars or Japanese yen, US regulations prohibited the use of its aid dollars for the import of what it regarded as "luxury"—that is, nonessential, nonproductive— goods. These had to be paid for with Korea's own foreign exchange, which could only be generated through the sale to foreigners of Korean goods and services. The US military provided a vital source of this foreign exchange through its purchases of large quantities of Korean hwan. The UN command spent these hwan on "offshore procurement" (i.e., buying goods and services from Korean suppliers to support US, UN, and ROK troops) and to pay the wages of its Korean civilian employees. These hwan purchases generated much of the foreign exchange necessary to import consumer and luxury goods. During FY 1956, for example, sales to the US Army generated $28 million, which was $5 million more than the earnings from Korea's own exports.[38]

Operating alongside this small legal consumer-import economy was a much larger illegal one: the ubiquitous black market. In Korea, the black market consisted primarily of the illegal trade in US military scrip, which was used on the bases instead of dollars, and the sale of goods that had entered Korea without paying import duties. Like the legal economy, the black market was fueled by goods brought into Korea from the United States and Japan and was intimately connected to the US military. This postcolonial black market emerged with the arrival of Americans at liberation in 1945, became institutionalized during the US military occupation government of 1945–48, and expanded exponentially during and after the Korean War, as the US military presence became a permanent feature of Korean life. By 1954 the black market had become, according to the *US News & World Report*, an "established institution in Korean life," and would remain so until at least the late 1980s when South Korea liberalized its trade laws and began legally importing more foreign goods.[39] While the size of the black market in economic terms is impossible to determine, in 1959 the UN's Office of the Economic Coordinator estimated that "merchandise valued at from 25 to 50 billion hwan"— or $50 million to $100 million at the official exchange rate—"reaches the market annually through illegal channels."[40] This is roughly 15 to 30 percent of the total value of all the legal imports (both aid-financed and privately financed) coming into Korea.[41] Given that the overwhelming majority of legal imports were bulk commodities and reconstruction materials, this suggests that most consumer items available in Korea came through black market channels.

The black market took a range of physical forms. It included the small shops in the camptowns outside US military bases, as well as the large open-air markets that emerged in Seoul during the Korean War, which consisted of "hundreds of long tables . . . placed so closely that the aisles permit only one person to walk comfortably." In the southern port city of Busan the black market was ten times bigger and occupied a space about a mile square; when it burned down in 1954, it made news around the world.[42] Extending far beyond these distinct locales, the black market also encompassed the middle-aged street vendors on "nearly every street corner" in major cities, the storefront shops in many smaller towns, and the sprawling Namdaemun (South Gate) and Dongdaemun (East Gate) market areas in Seoul.[43] These latter were known colloquially as "goblin markets," from a Korean folktale about a magical creature who could make any desired object appear. In practice, there was little distinction between the legal and the black markets. Department stores regularly carried "tremendously large stocks" of black-market goods alongside Korean-made and legally imported items, and there was little effort made to disguise the illegal origins of these goods.[44] As large as these open displays were, an even larger portion of the black market remained invisible. As one Eighth US Army official observed, "It is like an iceberg, . . . For every part you see, there is two-thirds as much more underwater—or under the counter, as the case may be."[45]

Goods available for purchase on the black market, according to one American journalist, included "almost every consumer item that can be bought in New York," including watches, toys, books, carpets, cigarettes, and fountain pens. Foodstuffs were common, and *budae jjigae*'s American ingredients—Spam, hot dogs, processed cheese—remained popular up through the 1980s; by 1960, three tons of coffee were entering the black market every day.[46] Japanese foodstuffs, such as Asahi beer, were openly displayed on the street.[47] Black-marketers retailed the bulk commodities that had been imported with US aid dollars, US military supplies, and building materials needed for reconstruction. With weary admiration the Americans tasked with eliminating the black market agreed that "if you want anything, they can get it for you. You may have to wait a day, but they can get it."[48]

Black-market goods entered Korea from abroad through two major avenues, the first of which was smuggling. The full scale of smuggling was unknown, since data was collected only on that small fraction of operations intercepted by the poorly equipped ROK authorities. Americans working with the ROK Customs Bureau, however, regarded the smuggling problem as being "staggeringly enormous in scope." Data collected for 1953–57 showed that while the number of annual interceptions fluctuated from a low of 865 to a high of 5,855, the value of the intercepted goods rose steadily, with a total value for the five-year period coming to about 7.3 billion hwan (or $14.6 million at the official exchange rate). The majority of smuggled goods—an estimated 70–80 percent—were brought into Korea from Japan. Hong Kong was a distant second as a source of goods (14 percent), followed by the United States (7 percent) and Taiwan (2 percent). The majority of these smuggled goods were presumably of Japanese manufacture, and many of them had been legitimately purchased in Japanese department stores; however, Japan was a regional smuggling hub and host to a large US military force, so goods from other areas, including Hong Kong, Okinawa, and the United States likely passed through Japan on their way to Korea. The components of women's fashion, which comprised such a central element of Han's mise-en-scène, comprised a significant proportion of these smuggled goods. An ROK report identified textiles as the highest-value smuggled item in 1957, accounting for almost half of the total value of intercepted goods. This category was followed by accessories (11 percent), which included things like jewelry, and cosmetics/toiletries (9 percent). (Food/drink/tobacco products accounted for 7 percent and constituted the only category in which the United States was the major point of origin.) As one US report noted in 1958, "the presence in the 'market' of large quantities and complete lines of many items such as ladies' shoes, makes it quite apparent that this type of smuggling is a large scale operation." This smuggling data, like Han's gendered geography of modernity discussed in Chapter 5, points toward Japan's submerged presence in postwar cinema: the fashionable, Western-style costumes worn by Madame Oh in *Madame Freedom*, Margaret in *The Hand of Destiny*, and Min-ja in *Hyperbolae of Youth* were likely made from Japanese fabric. (The black market extended north as well: in 1955, Americans estimated that $3–5 million worth of goods were being smuggled out of South Korea and into North Korea annually, much of it by ROK intelligence officers.)[49]

The Korea-Japan smuggling trade flowed through networks rooted in both colonial-era and Cold War ties. A half-century of imperial economic integration, combined with physical proximity, rendered Japan easily accessible to the many skilled seamen in southern Korea's fishing industry. Colonial-era migrations, in turn, had created in Japan a sizable *zainichi* population. These were ethnic Koreans who had moved to Japan during the colonial era in search of opportunity or were later conscripted as industrial workers and imperial soldiers during the Pacific War. Widely discriminated against after 1945 and with a precarious legal status, they were consigned to marginal sectors of the economy. Numbering about six hundred thousand, they played an outsized role in Japan's own black market and the cross-straits smuggling trade.[50] The Cold War expansion of US military power created additional networks that sometimes overlapped with colonial-era ones. The Americans involved in smuggling, although few in number, included members of the US military who traveled between Korea and Japan. In 1956, for instance, more than thirty Korea-based GIs who were in Japan for rest and recreation were arrested after purchasing golf clubs and other items at US military stores on behalf of Japanese and *zainichi* black-marketers. American GIs also smuggled goods into Korea directly from America: late in the Korean war, for instance, an

Air Force clerk was caught trying to "carry into Korea 16 duffel bags loaded with powder puffs, face powder, face cream, zippers, wool mufflers, and cloth" via Air Force planes.[51]

US military installations constituted the second major avenue, after smuggling, through which black-market foreign goods entered Korea. As with smuggling, no one really knew the true volume of goods coming through this portal, although ROK officials estimated that prior to 1961, US goods accounted for about 30 percent of the goods in the black market. Given the amount of relief goods that had poured into Korea, including military surplus, it was sometimes difficult, however, to determine if any given item had been black-marketed or legally acquired. There were a variety of ways by which these American goods were poached from US military bases and found their way into the black markets. There was a good deal of direct theft by individual Koreans, known as "slicky boys" in the Army slang of the day. Pervasive stealing from Americans began with liberation. American homes were regular targets: thieves emptied bedrooms while their inhabitants slept, removing guns, wallets, and valuables from under pillows, and they stripped houses left alone for a few hours of their furniture. In the postwar years teenage boys, many of whom had lost their parents and families during the war, worked in fast-moving teams, distracting a GI at the front of his jeep or truck in order to steal the contents in the back. "Korean boys," reported one journalist, "jump aboard Army supply trucks and toss off bundles to confederates before the startled drivers know what is happening." In one engineering compound in the late 1950s, the Americans padlocked the toilet paper holders in the bathrooms to prevent thefts of the tissue by Korean "lady friends" who spent the night.[52]

One can read such acts of poaching as attempts to assert some power within a vastly unequal relationship. For some poachers, their actions, like other "weapons of the weak," no doubt expressed feelings of resentment against the quasi-imperial presence of the Americans and their not-infrequent expressions of racism. And the brazen young men who liberated goods from military trucks and warehouses no doubt felt an element of pride in their own skill at stealing from under the noses of the big, powerful Americans. Yet poaching was also a dangerous activity that often culminated in acts of violence against Koreans, as GIs took it into their own hands to punish the thieves whom the ROK government did so little to prosecute.[53] Local newspapers were full of stories of Korean men, women, and children being shot at and assaulted by American soldiers. In 1958 a group of officers and enlisted men stationed at ASCOM Depot caught a fourteen-year-old boy taking personal items out of their rooms; they beat him, shaved his head, daubed him with tar, stuffed him into a three-foot shipping crate, loaded him onto a helicopter, and flew him to the Uijeongbu airbase twelve miles north of Seoul, where he was unpacked and set free.[54]

Han's films, and those of his colleagues, were full of objects that may very well have entered Korea through the portal of the US military bases. Electric fans, such as the one so prominently placed in Margaret's living room in *The Hand of Destiny*, were often stolen from US civilian and military offices. The Office of the Economic Coordinator (OEC)—that is, the head of the entire UN aid mission to South Korea—reported that twenty electric fans disappeared from his buildings in July and September 1958, a rash of thefts that prompted another bureaucrat to request 170 feet of chain and seventeen locks to secure the fans in two other buildings. (In 1958 the newly launched Goldstar company, predecessor to today's LG *chaebol*, began manufacturing an electric fan, Korea's first domestically made appliance.) The OEC's chief port operations advisor in Incheon had his bedroom robbed of thirty-five records and a portable hi-fi record player, similar, perhaps, to the one Mr. Shin has in his room in *Madame Freedom*. Office equipment, including type-writers and telephones, similar to the ones Miss Park uses, were so frequently stolen from US and ROK installations that the American brass finally asked the phone company to stop installing stolen phones. (The first Korean telephone began manufacture in 1961.) Gasoline was a big black-market item originating on US and ROK military bases, with observers estimating that stolen fuel accounted for fully two-thirds of the amount used to run the country's cars—including those, presumably, that appeared on screen.[55]

Pilferage, or the large-scale theft of commercial goods and military supplies, took poaching to a higher level. "Pilferage from freighters, warehouses, trains and trucks" was "extensive," according to *US News & World Report* in 1954. In one instance, "an entire set of rail cars" loaded with "steel reinforcing bar . . . was rolled out of [a] . . . supposedly secure compound" in the middle of the night while Army Corps of Engineers bureaucrats slept nearby. In Busan, a tunnel was dug under an army warehouse, which was entirely emptied in one night of all the construc-tion materials it held, including refrigerators—a domestic appliance found in both military housing and Kim Ki-young's *The Housemaid*. Korean guards were often involved in such thefts, and they frequently had American partners. In 1958 the average loss of US military supplies was estimated at $96,000 per month, or over $1 million annually. Large-scale diversions of military supplies were sometimes facilitated by the US military customs clearance officers who approved import requests. Partnering with Korean businessmen working on US military construc-tion projects, these bureaucrats would sign off on requests for building materials far in excess of what was necessary for the job, with the extra materials fetching handsome profits on the black market.[56]

The military's network of over 150 commercial stores constituted a third major military channel through which American goods entered the black market. Post exchanges (PX), which are similar to department stores, stocked about 14,500 dis-tinct items in an effort to maintain something akin to the American standard of living for GIs. Because the PX was open to select civilians, they also stocked "a bewildering array of luxury items of little or no use to the military itself." A typical PX carried food, candy, liquor, cigarettes, men's and women's clothes, toiletries, shoe polish, women's cosmetics, household appliances, sports equipment, and fabrics. All of these goods were diverted, at one time or another, into the black market. Coca Cola, which like American beer could not be legally imported, was a popular PX item on the black market—as it was in Han's films. The volume of Coca Cola thefts from Eighth Army Headquarters at the Yongsan garrison surprised even the military's distributors: "My depot has been sending to that bulk sales outfit every day 800 cases of Coca Cola. There's no business in the world that can handle that flow. If you go right outside the gate, you can see little boys on bicycles taking Coca Cola up the street."[57]

Thefts from these stores were common, often perpetrated by some of the thousands of Koreans who worked as cashiers, clerks, stock boys, and guards. In her novel *The Naked Tree* (1970), set during the Korean War, Park Wan-so includes a scene in which Korean women employed at the PX make off with a load of goods:

> The cleaning women entered [the employee break room], pushing a large trash box in front of them. They hitched up their skirts, pulled down their underwear, took out endless tubes of toothpaste and bars of soap from the trash box, and stacked them up on their calves, tying each row tightly with an elastic band. They heaped up the goods tier after tier, pulled up their underwear, and in no time they were fat with a layer of goods reaching from their calves, over their buttocks, to their waists. They pulled their skirts down, put on their coats, and swaggered out.[58]

More typically, however, the PX goods that ended up on the black market began as legitimate purchases. GIs often used PX goods to pay for sexual services and gave them to Korean girlfriends, laundresses, houseboys, and friends, who in turn sold them to black-market vendors. Korean cashiers and clerks, many of them women, often bypassed point-of-purchase regulations designed to stop the flow of legally purchased goods into the black market. The American PX managers, in their turn, had little incentive to police legitimate purchases that ended up on the black market, since each PX was a self-supporting commercial enterprise whose profits supported the GI welfare fund.[59]

Korean women were important facilitators of the influx of PX-based American goods into the black market and thus key actors in producing a modern and cosmopolitan standard of living for those who could afford it. In addition to working as PX employees, Korean women who married GIs were legal dependents and as such authorized to shop at the PX. With the assistance of Korean base employees such as cashiers, taxi drivers, and gate security guards, some of these wives would engage in a practice known as "racetracking," which involved rushing from one post store to another, making numerous small purchases to evade control systems, and then quickly reselling the items to a black-market middleman. The network of civilian Korean employees facilitated efficient black-market shopping: "The word about new items at the PX gets to the Korean wives before our people know about it," observed one American tasked with eliminating the black market. "As soon as the new items appear, the Korean wives are at the PX in force." Some of these marriages—out of a total of about 575 in 1959—were in fact business partnerships, entered into for the sole purpose of diverting goods out of the posts. Such marriages could be quite lucrative, since Korean women continued to have access to the PX for up to a year after their husbands returned to the United States. Korean wives received a lot of attention from US authorities, who sometimes kept them under surveillance. They stood out among the mostly white and black male customers at the PX, and their excessive purchases were easy to track; it also proved easy to compare the value of a wife's monthly purchases to the salary of her husband and determine if she was spending beyond her legally earned means. In 1959, military police broke up a black market ring consisting of four Korean wives who were keeping one village well supplied with PX bicycles and women's clothing, with one of the wives reselling about $500 worth of goods each month. The military's educational material urged GIs not to get caught in the "black market trap" set by Korean seductresses, warning, "Every soldier is their prey. Watch 'em!"[60]

The Army/Air Force Post Office (APO) channeled American consumer goods directly into the hands of GIs, bypassing the PX system altogether. Some GIs would ask family and friends at home to ship them items that could then be sold or otherwise transferred to Koreans. The Sears Roebuck catalogue circulated widely throughout Korea in the 1950s, a stimulus to both fantasy and actual consumption. For American civilians who did not have PX privileges, it was a vital source of clothing and supplies.[61] Koreans with contacts on the US bases would often ask their American friends to order things from the Sears catalogue on their behalf and have them shipped right to the bases. As with other black market channels, the APO route was often tied up with sexual relations between American men and Korean women. In GI circles the catalogue was known as the "moose-manual," with *moose* being the dehumanizing slang term for a Korean woman, derived from the Japanese term *musume*, which means girl. "It's inevitable that the girlfriend will ask you to order from the United States items which are unavailable locally," warned the author of one Eighth Army information bulletin. "Using the so-called 'moose-manual' mail order catalogues as a guide, she will point out what she wants."[62] This use of mail order catalogues to buy American clothes and goods began during the Korean War. According to Pat Frank, a writer on an UNKRA documentary film project, "the Sears Roebuck catalogue was the most widely circulated English language publication in Korea. . . . When a soldier was wooing a Moosie-Maid, he would borrow the catalogue from the company clerk and hie himself to his girl's house, and they would spend hours deciding whether she would look best in Sweater VT-2385, or VT-2387. A steady stream of postal money orders flowed to the mail-order houses Stateside, and a steady river of packaged durable goods poured back."[63]

The last major channel for illegally moving American goods into the Korean market involved the sale by GIs of their personal belongings before they transferred out of Korea. Sometimes these personal goods included such large and expensive items as pianos, which were status symbols among middle-class Koreans and could be sold for "fabulous prices," and American cars, so common in 1950s films, which some GIs brought with them only to discover that the streets of Korean cities were too chaotic to navigate. By 1958 Korean authorities required that all GI vehicles be completely dismantled before they could be sold.[64]

Recovering the "social life" of Han's mise-en-scène makes visible the black market as a complex social, political, and economic institution, one that was tightly integrated into the transnational networks through which consumer goods flowed. The meanings that this institution carried for Koreans varied, and that variety inflected the many postwar films that touched on the black market through their narratives, characterizations, and mise-en-scène.

Many of the black market's meanings were negative and drew on the deeply rooted moral discourse of frugality. The transnational and illegal dimensions deeply offended those with strong nationalist sentiments and interests. Some regarded the fawning over foreign goods as a sign of national humiliation and self-abasement. The author of a 1959 ROK report on smuggling chastised his fellow citizens for having an "unwholesome national spirit" that led them to "admire foreign manufactured goods unconditionally" and to prefer to "use smuggled goods rather than the domestically produced" ones.[65] The black market helped fuel the rage against political corruption that culminated in the April Revolution of 1960 and the installation of president Yun Bo-seon, an "austerity minded" figurehead who publicly supported the "post-revolution student campaign against the widespread smoking of U.S. cigarettes sold on the black market." That same year nationalist university students seized more than fifty jeeps, most of them owned by National Assembly legislators, arguing that Korea already had too many cars for a nation that did not produce any gasoline and that too much money was being diverted into the black market to buy fuel.[66] These negative associations were clearly visible in those postwar films that linked black-marketing with criminality and corruption, such as Kim Sodong's *The Money* and Shin Sang-ok's *Flower in Hell* (1958). The association of the black market with women, in turn, clearly inflected the après girl characters, who were so strongly defined by their fondness for Western goods. In *Madame Freedom*, for instance, Mme Choi's participation in the black market leads to her arrest, public humiliation, and suicide.

The black market was also an ordinary part of postwar Korean life that was maintained by a wide swath of society. For the many Koreans without regular jobs or with poorly paying ones—a category that included refugees, veterans, members of families without male wage earners, civilian employees of the US military bases, and even ROK military officers—the poaching and selling of American goods offered a desperately needed source of income. For consumers and businesses hamstrung by the paucity of domestic manufacturing, the corrupt diversion of aid supplies, and the limits on legal imports, the black market often provided the only access to high-demand consumer goods and such basic reconstruction supplies as hammers. Americans as well as Koreans patronized the black market. Civilians such as CIA staff, economic advisors, construction supervisors, missionaries, and private relief workers all shopped for the goods they needed to do their jobs and maintain a reasonably comfortable quality of life. While US military brass went to great lengths to quell black-marketing, quite a few Americans viewed the underground economy with sympathy. Regarding poaching as a legitimate means of survival in trying times, they saw the "slickied" goods as just another form of foreign aid and saw their own black-market purchases as unofficial "offshore procurement."[67] Yu Hyun-mok taps into this "everyday" aspect of the black market in *Forever with You* (1958), in which he depicts the criminal activities of its young male protagonist as an unfortunate but wholly understandable consequence of poverty and limited life options. In *The Widow* (1954), Park Nam-ok treats black-market goods in a morally neutral fashion as part of the everyday life of a young widow and her sex-worker neighbor, who struggle to get by as best they can.

Consuming black-market goods became a small way for ordinary Koreans to claim a place for themselves at the table of capitalist modernity and to assert that they, too, belonged in the Free World alongside the more economically advanced residents of Japan and Hong Kong. Anthropologist Grant McCracken views consumer objects in relation to "displaced meaning," which he defines as treasured ideals that are impossible to fulfill in ordinary life and so are displaced onto distant spaces or times. America was the site of such displacement for many Koreans, the place where the ideals of modernity, democracy, freedom, education, and material comfort resided. For McCracken, consumer goods can serve as "bridges to displaced meanings," insofar as they enable the consumer to "contemplate the possession of an emotional condition, a social circumstance, even an entire style of life, by somehow concretizing these things in themselves." In this way consumer goods become "objective correlatives" of values that are hard to achieve in reality. In the 1950s, the possession of American consumer goods enabled Koreans "to rehearse" a much larger set of attitudes and feelings about their own modernity that they were not always able to inhabit in their everyday lives.[68] As newspaper columnist Lee O-young wrote in the early 1960s, "Each time I drink Coca-Cola, I think about American civilization," whereas drinking *makgeolli*, a humble rice wine, evoked for him only Korea's history of poverty and "oppression."[69] Such condensed symbolism and displaced meaning suffuses Han's films.

The black market functioned as a contact zone where Koreans and Americans interacted with each other outside the bounds of official state and military partnerships: as business partners and violent antagonists, as occupiers and resisters, as victims and victimizers, as customers and employees, as wives and lovers, as poachers and hosts. It encapsulated a complexly ambivalent relationship that Shunya Yoshimi, writing about local attitudes towards US military bases in Japan, has characterized as one of "desire and violence."[70] Which brings us back to

The Hand of Destiny and the scenes set at the Incheon waterfront, where Koreans and Americans are shown as occupying a shared physical space.

As Margaret leans against the large American car before whisking Yeong-cheol away for the shopping trip, she watches a troop of American soldiers disembark from a ship. Carrying heavy duffel bags and rifles, they line up in rows as a rousing military tune plays on the soundtrack (video 6, earlier in the chapter). (This footage was itself poached from a newsreel.)[71] When she returns to the waterfront in a later scene, she walks in front of train boxcars clearly labeled "USA" and "US Army." These shots do little narrative work, as neither the soldiers nor the train cars play any role in the story (although presumably Margaret is reconnoitering troop movements as part of her spy work). One of the few such direct representations in postwar cinema of the large US military presence, these shots offer what Elsaesser would call a "metaphoric condensation" of the postwar history of Korean consumer culture. While the southern city of Busan was the major entry point for goods smuggled in from Japan, the northern city of Incheon was the gateway for American goods. Virtually all the material imported into Korea by the US military passed through Incheon, from where it was transported via train to the nearby ASCOM Depot, the central storage facility and transportation hub that warehoused PX goods and military supplies before they were distributed to bases throughout the country.[72] In locating Margaret at the Incheon waterfront and train yard, Han positions her at ground zero for entry of American consumer goods into the country. In occupying this space, Margaret seems to be absorbing for herself some of the power associated with America—a power which she immediately exercises over Yeong-cheol via the purchase and gifting of consumer goods. Margaret's steely expression as she leans against the car now reads less as a spy's penetrating gaze and more as a woman's frank acknowledgement of the foreign source of the ideas and objects that enable her to reimagine her way of being in the world.

POACHING AS FILM INDUSTRY PRACTICE

Shin Sang-ok's *A Flower in Hell* includes a scene of pilferage from a US military base. A noir-melodrama set, like *The Hand of Destiny*, in and around the ASCOM Depot area, the film revolves around a prostitute who works in the camptown, her gangster boyfriend, and his plan to rob a military supply train. Like *The Hand of Destiny*, this film's mise-en-scène is full of black-market goods. The scene in question is set on a US military compound at night, and it cuts back and forth between events taking place inside a service club, where Korean prostitutes and scantily clad performers entertain GIs, and in the yard outside, where the Korean gangsters cut through a barbed-wire perimeter fence and steal a load of goods. Three of the prostitutes are in league with the gangsters: at a preordained time, they leave the club and lure the patrolling military police away from the gangsters. While the women flirt with the MPs, the scene cuts back to the club interior, where the camera ogles a feather-clad erotic dancer, traveling up and down her body in close-up and pausing at her hips as she makes sexually suggestive motions. Meanwhile the gangsters, having located a stack of pallets, transfer the booty onto a pushcart and spirit it away.

Kang Beom-gu, the cinematographer who shot the scene, recalled that many young Koreans in the 1950s saw the Americans living among them as both powerful exploiters and as a resource to be exploited. This exploitation had both sexual and economic dimensions. "All the stylish" and "pretty" young women, says Kang, including those who graduated from "good colleges," took "US soldiers and officers as lovers," which was, of course, "devastating" for young Korean men like himself. But many of these young men were engaged in their own profitable relationships with the Americans. "Our young people lived off the US soldiers" in the 1950s, says Kang. "If you didn't do that back then, you couldn't live. The young people deliberately gave their lives to the U.S. Army, like prostitutes . . . and emptied their pockets, as well." *Flower in Hell*'s scene of theft, Kang suggests, was a thinly fictionalized depiction of a common practice with which Kang was quite familiar: "Back then," he said, "breaking into the US army base was, if there's a wire fence like this you cut it and make all the guards drunk and put some women with them so they wouldn't look this way."[73] This scene speaks to the complexity of postwar power relations between Koreans and Americans. At the outset the American GIs exert their dominance over Korean women via a militarized male gaze that reduces the women, in classical Laura Mulvey fashion, to segmented and sexualized body parts. By the end of the scene, however, the Koreans have seized the upper hand, the women by distracting the naïve MPs and the men by making off with a large quantity of military goods. Significantly, it is the act of poaching that transforms a scene of sexual exploitation *of* Korean women by Americans into a scene of material exploitation *by* Korean men of Americans. Poaching functions here as an assertion of power against the Americans.

Kang Beom-gu's comments invite us to recognize filmmaking as a material practice that was intimately bound up with the US military and the black market. The black market was not just a source of consumer goods and reconstruction materials. It was also essential to the development of South Korea's film industry. Kang's obvious familiarity with the techniques of stealing hints at the reliance of the film industry itself on the very type of poaching that this scene depicts. As discussed in chapter 3, the postwar film industry was plagued by shortages of virtually all the resources necessary for commercial film production. Filmmakers responded with admirable creativity, creating nighttime stars by attaching shards of shattered reflector bulbs to black fabric with "cooked sticky rice," and improvising camera movements by hoisting cameramen up and down with rope.[74] They also responded by availing themselves of the relative bounty of the US military, treating military bases as pools of material resources upon which they could draw.

Sometimes filmmakers accessed these resources through legal means. The portable Eyemo cameras that many filmmakers used had often begun their social lives with the US military, which used them to shoot wartime newsreels, before being turned over to the Korean Office of Public Information, which rented them to commercial filmmakers. When Han shot on a location without access to electricity, he would sometimes send a crew member to the Eighth Army construction and engineering battalion to borrow a generator for the day. Other filmmakers rented lighting equipment from the still photography studios at the Yongsan garrison. They also accessed military resources via the black market, including hard-to-get film stock, which was purchased in complete reels and in short pieces left over from newsreel productions that were then spliced together. Steenbeck and Moviola editing tables, in turn, "floated out" from the US Army film department.[75]

Han Hyung-mo produced the distinctive style of his films in part by tapping into the resources of the Eighth US Army and the black market. For example, as Mme Oh walks home through the city streets at night at the end of *Madame Freedom*, a light snow drifts down, settling on her hair and clothes as she kneels at her husband's feet and embraces her son (see figure 12 in chapter 4). This snow was created from a variety of materials, all of them poached from Eighth Army supplies. For the snow on Mme Oh's head, Han and his art team used Lux laundry soap, which was only sold at the PX and which the art team liked because the flakes "look like scales of carp. Very light and flat" (figure 20). When they couldn't get Lux, which was difficult to find and expensive, they would crumble into powder the Styrofoam packing material that "was brought in with foreign goods." For snow in the background, they used down feathers from GI sleeping bags. Han's mobile cinematography—produced by a crane that rested on four US helicopter wheels—was likewise indebted to the black market. When it came time to light interior scenes, Han's crew sometimes poached the power supply from the Korea Electricity Corporation, bribing the company to add another transformer to the electricity pole just outside the building and running a line into the set. (Like other forms of poaching, this could be dangerous: technicians were sometimes hurt when a transformer exploded.) Han's soundtrack most likely relied on poached albums: American records stolen from GIs' personal belongings and from PXes appeared frequently on the black market, and music director Kim Yong-hwan was known to ask US soldiers to bring him back albums from Japan when they went there for R&R. This is an instance where one can see the Eighth Army as a facilitator of cultural flows within America's Cold War alliance, creating a channel for the flow of recorded music among the United States, Japan, and Korea. The cars that appeared so prominently in postwar films often had ties to the military: because privately owned cars were rare in Seoul, Han would send a crew member (and translator) to stand outside the gate to the Eighth Army headquarters at Yongsan and ask GIs if they could rent their car, sometimes hanging around for days at a stretch until they got the make they wanted. Eventually something akin

FIGURE 20. Boxes of Lux and Ivory Snow soap flakes for sale at a Busan PX in 1951. (Courtesy NARA)

to prop-rental houses emerged, stocked with household goods disposed of by GIs who were finishing their tour of duty.[76]

Han also used poached material to build his sets. The cave interior which provides the setting for the final scene of *The Hand of Destiny*—and which constitutes part of the Korean nature to which Margaret returns—was constructed out of heavy paper that the Americans used as packing material. Plywood was rare and expensive in the 1950s, so Han's art department built sets out of wooden boxes used for shipping relief supplies. (Plywood would become a significant export industry in the late 1960s.) The set for Margaret's luxurious apartment, for instance, was built from "construction materials and boxes from the US Army base." The art team "gathered up cleaner plywood from that and made doors and windows," and used painted cotton cloth nailed to the wooden frames for the walls.[77]

Han and his crew members also engaged in small-scale importing/smuggling themselves, bringing in props and other materials via the Asian Film Festival's transnational networks. Whenever Han or other filmmakers, producers, or actors went abroad for the festival, "they bought bags and bags of stuff, using it later for making films." One year Han brought back Japanese Shiseido cosmetics as gifts for his actresses, which greatly endeared him to them and which they used during filming, since there were no professional makeup artists. The actors, in turn, sometimes offered their own personal goods for use as props. All the items on display inside the Paris Boutique's glass case, for instance, were items "that actors bought when they went overseas, things that Han Hyung-mo borrowed." Several of the decorative items in Margaret's apartment in *The Hand of Destiny*, including the fluorescent desk lamp and owl clock, were Han's personal items that he had purchased in Japan, suggesting again the possibility of reading his après girl characters as alter-egos for himself as a self-consciously modern Korean subject who inhabits Western-style spaces. Creating domestic spaces like Margaret's apartment laid the groundwork for Han's work designing and building Western-style homes in the early 1960s. He also purchased in Japan the boldly patterned textiles used for her curtains and furniture upholstery, which were unknown in Korea at the time. These fabrics were so precious that the art team, instead of cutting them, taped and pinned them to fit the furniture so that they could be reused; they appeared again in the rich family's home in *Hyperbolae of Youth*.[78] This fabric is typical of the presence of Japanese artifacts in 1950s cinema: vital to the vision of Korean modernity that these films projected, but without obvious markers of their national origin.

By rediscovering the ties between the fledgling film industry and the black market, we can see how the US military functioned in the 1950s, paradoxically, as a cultural institution. For the film industry, military bases functioned as pools of material resources that enabled the production of movies made by, for, and about Korean people. The fostering of local cultural production was an unintended consequence of the expansion of US military power into Korea. Acts of material poaching made it possible for Korean films to begin to approach the production values of Hollywood films. Such acts of mimicry, however, were always undertaken with the goal of competing against Hollywood films and reclaiming from them a share of audiences and box office earnings. Emulation and competition went hand in hand. As the pilferage scene from *Flower in Hell* suggests, poaching could be an assertion of power against Americans as much as an act of cultural affiliation with them. Like the black market itself, the production of *budae jjigae* cinema was a cultural space of cooperation and contestation with a much more powerful partner/rival.

Ultimately, understanding the social life of things in Han's films allows us to recognize foreign consumer goods as densely compressed symbols for the emerging web of relationships that was binding Korea to the United States, Japan, and the rest of the Free World. When we see the electric iron, the can of Coca Cola, or the bottle of Chanel perfume, we should infer the diverse social, economic, and military networks that made their appearance on screen possible. These objects are the visual traces of the country's colonial past and its Cold War present. They are textual evidence of an aid- and import-based economy and the political corruption it bred, of colonial-era migrations that created a disenfranchised *zainichi* population in Japan, of a network of US military bases that spanned the country and the region. They are the material and visual residues of transnational relationships of conflict, cooperation, assistance, exchange, theft, and resistance. They are the material tips, as it were, of a vast geopolitical iceberg. To read style as historical evidence is to be able to perceive these networks and relationships beneath the polished surface of Han's films. It's all there in the shot of Margaret leaning against the car at the Incheon waterfront, if you know how to look.

7

A Commitment to Showmanship

Spectacle

The opening scene of Han Hyung-mo's *Hyperbolae of Youth* (1956) is set in a medical clinic on a Saturday afternoon, where three nurses hum in unison as they tidy up the examining room and a doctor dressed in shorts prepares to go to the beach with a friend. When the nurses (the popular singing trio the Kim Sisters) remind the doctor (the legendary music composer Park Si-chun) about a promise he made, the doctor turns to his friend—and by implication to the audience—and says, "I'll show you something fun. Wait." He picks up a guitar and launches into Eddie Fisher's hit song from 1954, "I Need You Now," as the nurses sing along, first in Korean and then in English (figure 21). Dynamic editing and camera movement enhance the syncopation of the scene, as do the movements of the identically dressed nurses, who walk, wave their hands, and enter the frame in time to the music. Fluidly shifting visual compositions add to the sense of orchestration, as the nurses line up by height, wend their way through the room, and form a triangle around the doctor's friend. At three minutes long, the scene allows the viewer to enjoy the song in full. This is a stand-alone performance, completely unintegrated into the film's narrative: the song is unmotivated by the story, which has not yet begun, and the nurses make no further substantive appearance in the film. The jaunty song and the amusing image of a guitar-playing doctor and singing nurses do, however, introduce the film generically and thematically, preparing the viewer for a quasi-musical comedy—with songs composed by Park Si-chun—that revolves around the contrast and ultimate harmonizing of Korean and Western values.

Such moments of visual and aural pleasure constitute one of the signature elements of Han's Cold War cosmopolitan style: as film scholar Cho Junhyoung has

FIGURE 21. A penchant for spectacle: the Kim Sisters, accompanied by composer Park Si-chun, sing Eddie Fisher's "I Need You Now" in *Hyperbolae of Youth* (1956). (Courtesy of KOFA)

noted, Han had an "obsession for spectacle." Many of his films contain moments in which the forward movement of the narrative pauses and the viewer is invited to gaze upon, and often listen to, something that is inherently interesting. I am interested in "spectacle" as a particular mode of address that a film makes to its viewer. Spectacles are moments of heightened visuality in which the viewer is invited to look at something whose intrinsic qualities justify the viewer's attention. Tom Gunning has argued that such moments of spectacle solicit the viewer's "attention and curiosity through acts of display." They are "attractions" that embody an aesthetic of showing rather than telling, and they draw the viewer's gaze directly rather than channeling it through the narrative mechanisms of character motivation or psychology. These are brief interludes of exhibitionist *presentation* that interrupt the viewer's otherwise voyeuristic immersion in the fictional *representation* being enacted on screen. Laura Mulvey has argued that in Hollywood films such female-centered spectacles often construct a male gaze that objectifies and eroticizes the female body, and this aspect is certainly at play in *Hyperbolae*'s opening scene, which presents the nurses as physically attractive and inviting of the viewer's gaze.[1]

The nature of Han's spectacles extends far beyond the erotic, however. A number of his films, including *Hyperbolae*, open with displays of bustling urban modernity that suggest postwar development and progress. *My Sister Is a Hussy* (1961) puts nature on display in sweeping Cinemascope shots of mountain vistas. *Let's Meet at Walkerhill* (1966) and *The Queen of Elegy* (1967), like *Hyperbolae of Youth*, present viewers with musical performances by popular singers. Han's displays of film form could themselves function as spectacle, as with the exuberant camera movements in *Madame Freedom* (1956) and the lavishly materialistic mise-en-scène in *The Hand of Destiny* (1954). Han's preferred spectacle, however, was the modern Korean woman-in-public, and he regularly paused his narratives and invited viewers to look at one of his après girl characters doing, or being, something remarkable. Han regularly presented the modern woman as something worth looking at—and thinking about. While some of these moments involved titillating scenes of female sexuality, as with Korea's first on-screen kiss in *The Hand of Destiny* and the S-sister relationship in *A Jealousy* (1960), the modernity of these acts mattered as much as their sexual nature. Han's orientation towards spectacle was part of what his colleagues saw as his larger commitment to "showmanship" and "service." Han liked to give the viewer as much entertainment value as possible, and he saw these spectacles as an added attraction that he could provide. Audiences responded favorably: according to Han's colleague Kim Kee-duk, "When people watched *The Pure Love* they would say, 'Ah, that's Hong Kong' . . . [and] when they watched the mambo dance, they would say 'Ah, how new.'"[2] This commitment to entertainment was an innovation within the film industry. Prior to Han's debut as a director, filmmakers favored a quasi-pedagogical aesthetic that valued the cinema as an instrument of moral uplift and mass "enlightenment." Han's aesthetic of spectacle helped to shift that orientation, and he nudged other filmmakers in the same direction.[3]

This chapter explores Cold War cosmopolitanism as a function of Han's poaching from contemporary South Korean public culture. Paying attention to spectacle in Han's films allows us to see the kimchi part of the "*budae jjigae* cinema" metaphor, namely, the ways in which Han crafted his films by engaging deeply with local cultural fashions, which were themselves often cosmopolitan in nature. In his effort to infuse his films with a ripped-from-the-headlines quality of contemporaneity, Han drew extensively from various domains of Korean public culture and presented this material to the viewer as interludes of spectacle. Numerous scholars have noted that *Madame Freedom* drew on the postwar craze for Western social dance and the sexual scandals that ensued.[4] Han's poaching extended far beyond the realm of social dance, however. His films serve as a kind of catalogue of postwar public culture, a visual and aural record of the many cultural tools that Koreans were using to make themselves modern.

This chapter focuses on four films, each of which uses a different Free World–inflected cultural form in combination with a modern Korean woman as its central spectacle: Japanese judo in *My Sister Is a Hussy*, Latin mambo in *Madame Freedom*,

European-inspired fashion in *A Female Boss* (1959), and traditional Korean dance in *Because I Love You* (1958). As expressive elements within the films, these spectacles construct their female characters as active and often powerful participants in modern public life: athlete, performer, professional, and cultural emissary. They also perform the cultural work of claiming cosmopolitan modernity for South Korea, in diverse ways. Read as historical evidence, these spectacles—like the mise-en-scène in the previous chapter—reveal the transnational networks in which South Korea was becoming embedded. Rather than looking at the inflows of consumer goods, however, this chapter focuses on the flows of people into—and out of—Korea as cultural performers and producers. Han's spectacles, when read as a form of historical evidence, illuminate a range of transnational networks—colonial, military, commercial, diplomatic, biographical—that fueled postwar public culture. They also reveal some of the ways in which Koreans were stepping out and making themselves visible on the Free World stage. As such, these spectacles are signs and products of Korea's colonial legacies and its increasing enmeshment with the Free World.

JUDO: *MY SISTER IS A HUSSY*

Spectacle and narrative are two modes through which commercial fiction cinema addresses its viewer. Narrative tends to be the more dominant, inviting the viewer to be drawn into the intimate lives of strangers. Spectacle tends to be secondary, with its intermittent pleasures of exhibitionism. A number of film scholars have focused on the tension between narrative and spectacle, akin to that between narrative and mise-en-scène. Kristin Thompson regards spectacle as a form of cinematic "excess," which she defines as any element of a film that exceeds the demands of the narrative and thus escapes its "unifying impulses." Such excess, she argues, can have a liberatory effect by temporarily diverting the viewer's attention away from the story and its embedded ideologies, denaturalizing its assumptions and revealing individual narrative events as mere convention rather than existential truth. Richard Dyer and Thomas Elsaesser, in turn, have focused on musical numbers as form of spectacle, suggesting that, by privileging sensory and aesthetic pleasure over the narrative's ideological coherence, they can create a space in which different values are affirmed.[5] Paying attention to spectacle, then, is yet another way to read against the grain of narrative and recognize the articulation of alternative meanings in moments of visual pleasure.

My Sister Is a Hussy offers perhaps the most extreme instance of tension between spectacle and narrative in Han's oeuvre. The film tells the story of two adult sisters who have been raised by their single father, a martial arts instructor who has trained them in judo. Temperamentally the two sisters are quite different: the protagonist and older sister, Sun-ae (Moon Jung-suk), is strong-willed and ill-humored, while the younger sister, Seon-hui (Um Aing-ran), is easygoing and accommodating. A romantic comedy of sorts, the film charts the love lives of the two sisters. While Seon-hui has a fiancé, Sun-ae one has no interest in marriage—echoing her previous role as Jaesoon in *A Jealousy*. Her father (Kim Seung-ho), concerned about her future, arranges for Sun-ae to meet a series of potential suitors, but she rejects them all. Through a series of comic misadventures, Sun-ae ends up falling in love with a friend of her sister's fiancé, and the two couples marry in a joint ceremony. Sun-ae, however, has a difficult time adjusting to married life and does not treat her husband (Kim Jin-kyu) with respect. Her father teaches her a lesson about a wife's proper role, and by the final scene Sun-ae has become a domesticated and subservient wife. The arc of the narrative moves through the three stages common to many of Han's films: a woman behaves in a transgressive manner that challenges patriarchal authority, she is punished, and she is restored to patriarchal authority and the domestic sphere.

The spectacle in this film consists of displays of judo, which was just becoming an object of widespread public interest. Developed in Japan by Kano Jigoro in the 1880s, judo is a modern martial art that involves throwing, grappling, and striking. It was introduced through colonial routes into Korea, where it became incorporated into the imperial military and educational systems; by the 1920s and 1930s, it had gained some popularity among Koreans. After liberation, rather than being banned as "Japanese things and ways" (*wae-saek*), it was indigenized as an "invented" Korean tradition. Newspaper articles claimed Korea as the ancient birthplace and subsequent exporter of judo to Japan, where it was transformed into a modern sport and, by some accounts, rendered "impure." With the memory of its colonial origins repressed, "Korean judo" was ideologically cleansed and disentangled from what one journalist called the "brutal martial arts of the Japanese Empire."[6] The sport became enlisted in the service of South Korean nationalism during Rhee's presidency through the hosting of intraregional competitions, the founding of the Yudo (Judo) College of martial arts, and the incorporation of judo instruction into the Air Force Academy's curriculum. At the same time, the sport served as a means for Koreans to make themselves visible on the Free World stage, as judo masters traveled to the United States as teachers, delegations were invited to Europe, and Korean teams participated in international competitions in Japan. The sport served as an instrument of Korea's integration into the Free World, as the Korean Judo Association joined the Judo Union of Asia and the European-based International Judo Federation. Public interest in judo peaked around 1960–61 with the announcement that it would be included in the 1964 Tokyo Olympics and thus provide an opportunity for South Korean *judokas* to demonstrate their skill in this most visible and prestigious global venue. The announcement led to a sense of national excitement and widespread newspaper coverage, some of which endowed the sport with a Western aura by noting its popularity in Europe and America. Han's film capitalizes on this enthusiasm, incorporating a visually dynamic bit of Korean public culture that had complex associations with colonialism, nationalism, and cosmopolitanism.[7]

Han uses judo in *My Sister Is a Hussy* to create feminist spectacles in which a woman physically contests the Confucian principle of female inferiority (*namjon-yŏbi*). Sun-ae, in keeping with her prickly personality, uses judo to beat up every man who displeases her. Each of these encounters is treated as a privileged spectacle as the narrative pauses, the camera pulls back to a long shot, and the wide Cinemascope screen displays in full these surprising scenes of female physical prowess. Spectacle works here to challenge Confucian gender ideology by repeatedly offering evidence of a woman's physical superiority to a man. The visual excitement, emotional intensity, and sheer unexpectedness of these spectacles works to displace the abstract ideal of the Confucian principle.

The first explosion of female force arrives with the introduction of the main characters, and takes up the question of women in public. The film opens with the sisters, attired in Western-style dress, enjoying themselves in a public park; modern women, they are claiming the right to inhabit public space unaccompanied by a protective man. When two men make unwanted sexual suggestions, Sun-ae pretends to be interested and suggests they go to a secluded area, but when they arrive she turns her judo skills against the men. Sun-ae flips both men, who end up lying in a heap on the ground, and the two sisters walk away laughing. Rather than being forced out of public space by threats against their sexual virtue, the women physically defend their right to be there. Han takes care to present their violence as a legitimate act of self-defense against male harassment. One can imagine the thrill that this scene must have given some female viewers, who no doubt shared similar experiences as they moved into public life. A second scene of female judo expertise revolves around the issue of arranged marriage. When a suitor, invited to the house by Sun-ae's father, replies to her questions with some sexual innuendo about enjoying indoor sports involving two people, Sun-ae takes this as an invitation to do judo with him. She quickly throws him to the ground and then smirks as he crawls away on his hands and knees, his groveling, like the prone bodies of the men in the park, visually enhanced by the wide screen. Again, one can imagine this scene providing delight to those female viewers, growing in number in the 1950s, who wanted to choose their own husbands.

The third spectacle of judo revolves around the duties of a wife. Newly married, Sun-ae sits on the floor in a Western dress looking in a mirror and applying makeup, a classic image of the modern woman as narcissist (video 7). When her husband calls her from another room, she ignores him. Her behavior contrasts sharply with the preceding scene, in which her sister, dressed in a *hanbok*, lovingly tends to her husband. When Sun-ae's husband complains that she is not taking care of him and demands that she get his shirt, she refuses and snaps, "I'm not the maid," thereby raising the issue of wifely servitude. Asserting his masculine authority, he slaps her. Sun-ae does not submit, however, and instead she kicks

VIDEO 7. Clip from *My Sister Is a Hussy*.
To watch this video, scan the QR code with your mobile device or visit
DOI: https://doi.org/10.1525/luminos.85.7/

him and flips him twice, leaving him moaning on the ground as she, like Ibsen's
Nora, leaves the house. This is a genuinely shocking inversion of the gender hierarchy in which Sun-ae not only resists her husband's authority but asserts her own
superior physical strength. Unlike the previous judo scenes, the tone shifts away
from comedy towards something more foreboding, creating the implication that
Sun-ae has crossed some sort of line.

What follows is the most disturbing scene of punishment in all of Han's extant
films. When her father finds out what she has done to her husband, he decides to
teach her a lesson. He invites Sun-ae into the dojo and delivers a physically and
emotionally devastating beating. As he throws her onto the tatami mats over and
over, heightened sound effects of her body hitting the floor convey how much she
is being hurt. The father, who has heretofore been an exceptionally mild figure,
is now asserting his patriarchal authority in a brute, physical way. As Sun-ae lies
crying on the floor, he tells her that she needs to accept the role of a woman and
learn to "serve her husband." When she replies that she is not a "slave"—the same
term used by Helen Kim, Lee Tai-young, and Jaesoon in *A Jealousy* to characterize a woman's role in the patriarchal family—he beats her more. Towering over
her prone body, he says he would rather kill her with his own hands than let her
continue to behave in such a way. And indeed Sun-ae does appear to be dead,
although she eventually gets up and staggers out. The scene is long and brutally
violent, without a shred of humor or lightness. It presents one of the most sustained articulations of Confucian gender ideology—both visually and through
dialogue—in all of Han's films: a dead daughter is preferable to a disobedient wife.

After this spectacle of punishment, one might expect the film to conclude quickly
thereafter: the deviant woman learns her lesson, reconciles with her husband, and

lives happily ever after. Instead, the film continues with several more spectacles of female judo prowess. On her walk home alone, Sun-ae is assaulted in the street by the ruffians she beat up in the park. Sun-ae resists briefly, but then submits, as if she has decided to accept her subservient relationship to male authority. Suddenly her sister Seon-hui appears and rescues Sun-ae, flipping the men multiple times in arcing movements that Han captures elegantly within the Cinemascope frame. After the men limp away, Seon-hui chastises Sun-ae for letting herself be beaten up by delinquents and instead misusing her judo on her husband. This scene also feels like a plausible ending: having renounced judo herself and learned a lesson from her sister about the legitimate objects of female power, Sun-ae can live happily ever after with her husband.

Instead, she goes home and picks up her argument with her husband right where she left off. It turns out she is not repentant and has no intention of submitting to his authority. She kicks him out of their bedroom, throws his bedclothes after him, and forces him to spend the night in a separate room. Han's final spectacle of female physical power follows soon thereafter. During the night a burglar breaks into Sun-ae's room. Her husband, awakened by the noise, rushes and attacks him, only to knock out Sun-ae with a stray punch. The burglar quickly beats the husband into unconsciousness. At this point Sun-ae gets up, attacks the thief using her judo, and knocks him out—all the while wearing a flimsy white nightgown. A moment later her husband comes to and they embrace. Here is the film's real climax, and moral lesson: far from abandoning her physical power, Sun-ae must hold on to it and channel it appropriately, using it to defend her home and protect her husband, a visibly weaker creature who needs her help. (Two years late Kim Jin-kyu would play another man beaten into unconsciousness who needs to be rescued by a woman, in Han's *Prince Hodong* [1962].)

With this final verdict on female power rendered, the film can come to an end, and it does so with the obligatory scene of female domestication. In the brief coda, Sun-ae is wearing a *hanbok* (for the first time) and serves her husband (for the first time) a traditional Korean breakfast on a small *soban* table-tray. The husband compliments Sun-ae on her looks and her cooking, and praises her as a wise mother and good wife; she, in turn, helps put on and brush his coat, doing all the things her younger sister had previously done for her own husband. The final shots show her husband, now accompanied by her father, walking together in the public street as Sun-ae waves to them from the safety of her home. Not only have "proper" gender roles been restored, but the gendered separation of public and private spheres has been affirmed, and Korean forms of food and dress have replaced Western fashions and ideas of female autonomy.

Yet this brief moment of narrative closure fails to lock down the film's meaning. In fact, the very legitimacy of patriarchy as a hegemonic system has been called into question by the excessive quality of Sun-ae's punishment at the hands of her father. The beating that he delivers is so over-the-top that it becomes a spectacle of masculine brutality rather than of legitimate authority and thus undermines rather than affirms his patriarchal precepts. If a woman must be beaten nearly to death in order to accept her "proper" role in a marriage, it suggests that her submission no longer has any real legitimacy. A relationship sustained by force rather than consent is tyrannical, not consensual, and the excess of the father's violence reveals this. This ambivalence is reinforced by the star persona of actor Kim Seung-ho, who made his career playing "vanishing" and impotent patriarchs whose Confucian values have become outdated. Although his visual presentation and use of physical force in the dojo scene endow him with abundant potency, viewers familiar with his other films may have projected this aura of outmodedness onto the character he plays in this film as well.[8] The result is that the final act of narrative closure restores patriarchy, but not absolutely. Sun-ae has learned to hold her judo in check, not give it up, and her power remains latent. As her husband banters with her while she shines his shoes, she warns him, "If you tease me, I'll go back to being a hussy," implying that her submission to him is conditional and that violence against him remains a possibility. Because her superior physical power has been treated as spectacle, it cannot be forgotten—by her husband or the viewer. It has been displayed too frequently, too intensely, and too attractively for its meanings to be wholly sidelined.

Contemporary reviews capture the tension between narrative and spectacle as competing producers of thematic meaning and cinematic pleasure. The *Chosŏn ilbo*'s reviewer begins by commenting on the film's cosmopolitan dimension, observing that "judo fever" is high "in many countries including Europe, America, and Japan" and that the sisters live a "foreign" lifestyle characterized by "a leisurely household" and "time to spare." Alongside a photograph of the wedding ceremony, the reviewer praises the narrative's "happy ending" that shows Sun-ae "reeducated in the Eastern duties a woman must follow," thus reading the film's narrative closure as a rejection of judo's cosmopolitan and feminist associations.[9] The reviewer at the *Kyŏnghyang sinmun*, in contrast, emphasized the film's spectacle. Accompanied by a still of Sun-ae throwing a man onto the ground, this review expressed delight at the sight of "a huge man being taken down by the skills of a fabulous woman" and noted that in judo Sun-ae has become "better than men."[10] Each reviewer arrives at a markedly different interpretation of the female protagonist—submissive to men or superior to men—by privileging either narrative or spectacle as the film's primary expressive mode.

MAMBO: *MADAME FREEDOM*

One of the most compelling spectacles in all of 1950s cinema occurs in the middle of *Madame Freedom*: a mambo music and dance performance that brings the narrative to a grinding halt and solicits the viewer's full attention (video 1 in chapter 5). The scene begins with a close-up of a trumpeter as he plays the solo in "Cherry Pink and Apple Blossom White," a worldwide hit recorded in 1955 by the "king of mambo," Damaso Pérez Prado. As the camera crane pulls back and begins its own spectacular movement through the space, it picks up Mme Oh and Mr. Shin as they enter the dance hall and follows them to their table. Once they are seated, the eleven-man jazz band, heavy on brass and replete with bongos and maracas, launches into Pérez Prado's version of "Que Rico el Mambo." A woman hops down a set of stairs from the stage and begins to dance. She is an exotic vision: sheathed in a tight black dress slit to the thighs, she wears a flower in her permed hair and sports bare shoulders, legs, and feet. Her performance is mes-merizing. As she dances to a propulsive Latin beat, she raises her arms skyward, shimmies her shoulders, and swivels her hips, opening up her body to the cam-era's gaze. Diagonal rows of white fringe on her dress accentuate her curves and quiver enticingly when she shakes. The scene presents a richly sensuous depiction of a modern place and time: the elaborately decorated nightclub is filled with the sound of big-band Latin jazz, the sight of the dancer's luxurious costume and art-fully made-up face, the motions of her body, and even a vicarious sense of tactility as she touches herself. Long and medium shots reveal the dancer's body in full and include members of the band, who are themselves objects of visual and aural interest; close-ups of the dancer's body privilege the viewer's gaze, providing more intimate access than any member of the diegetic audience would be able to experi-ence. The performance's extended duration—a full three minutes, uninterrupted by dialogue—loosens its ties to the narrative and heightens the autonomous plea-sure of the scene.

As much as this performance functions as a stand-alone spectacle for the film viewer, it is also a spectacle for the audience within the film. Contra Laura Mulvey, Han edited the scene to privilege Mme Oh's gaze. The dancer is introduced only after Mme Oh turns to look at her, and Han cuts repeatedly to Mme Oh's reaction shots during the performance, revealing her face as it registers what seems to be a mix of wonder, confusion, and admiration. That she is profoundly affected by what she sees is indicated by the scene's pivotal position within the arc of Mme Oh's development: after watching it, she dances in public herself for the first time and pursues her own individual pleasures with greater enthusiasm. Spectacle here functions as a mode of pedagogy: as Mme Oh watches the dancer, she learns things that change the course of her life. What kinds of lessons did mambo convey? And how did mambo come to be in this Korean dance hall to begin with? I want to sug-gest that mambo was part of a curriculum in cosmopolitan modernity that the US military inadvertently introduced into Korea as it entertained its own troops. As a scene of education, the mambo performance outshines the earnestly nationalist yet visually dull lessons in Korean grammar that Mme Oh's husband, Prof. Jang, offers his female students.

Mambo was a global phenomenon in the 1950s, one of the most cosmopoli-tan sounds in a period when the Cold War was opening up new cultural circuits across the globe. According to cultural historian Gustavo Pérez Firmat, mambo was a profoundly transnational musical form, "conceived in Cuba, nurtured in Mexico, and brought to maturity in the United States." The Afro-Cuban musician and bandleader Pérez Prado was the individual most responsible for determining "its musical shape and its commercial success." In 1949 Pérez Prado left Cuba for Mexico City, recorded "Que Rico el Mambo," and launched the mambo craze across Latin America, which quickly spread to the United States after the song's release there in 1951. Mambo, according to Pérez Firmat, was a music of "ostentatious hybridness." It combined Afro-Cuban rhythms with a North American big-band jazz instrumentation that featured large woodwind and brass sections. A "bicultural creation" of Cuban and American musics, it was described at the time as a "stew of sounds"—*a musical budae jjigae*, as it were. Mambo reached its fullest flowering in the ethnically diverse neighborhoods of New York City and then spread around the world, carried by an array of media including live performances, recordings, radio broadcasts, movies, and magazines.[11]

Mambo involved more than just music. It was something to see as well as hear, a spectacle that merged the visual with the aural. Pérez Prado, like Han Hyung-mo, believed in showmanship[12] and he liked to prowl across the stage in a zoot suit, delivering his signature grunt and "punting the brass into action with a swift kick of his right foot."[13] Other mambo musicians of the day were known to "slither," "roll on the floor," and lie "prone on the ground" while playing their instruments. Dance played a central role in the global mambo phenomenon. According to Robert Farris Thompson, Afro-Cuban dancers, inspired by Hollywood's all-black musicals of the 1940s such as *Cabin in the Sky* (1943), developed mambo by combining the lindy hop's swing-outs and spins with the hip-centered movements of the rumba. As the dance migrated internationally, characteristic moves emerged, including "arms akimbo" stances, bodies that "quivered" in a shimmy, the shuffling of bare feet and the opening of mouths, and a woman's step dubbed "the head" that involved "standing in place, weaving one hand in space, then the other, while rattling the head with puppet-like suddenness." (This last move, according to Thompson, "announces the aura, of the coming of the spirit, among priestesses of the traditional religion of the Akan in Ghana.")[14] *Madame Freedom*'s mambo dancer was remarkably in step with these conventions as they developed in Havana, Mexico City, and New York. Barefoot and arms akimbo, she shimmies, quivers, and even does a version of "the head," closing her eyes as if being transported to another plane of existence.

The mambo craze hit Asia hard and was embraced with wild enthusiasm by listeners and dancers in Taiwan, Japan, and even Communist China. In the Philippines, President Ramon Magsaysay was swept into office in 1953, buoyed by CIA support and the song "Mambo Magsaysay," which he credited with giving his campaign its dynamism. In 1956 a Chinese-language version of Rosemary Clooney's novelty song "Mambo Italiano" became a hit under the title "Cha Shao

Bao," its lyrics localized to refer to different varieties of steamed buns. Mambo was controversial as well as popular. In China, Communist officials lambasted mambo as a vehicle for decadent "bourgeois ideology and sentiments." In Japan, provincial education officials complained that "mambo is an indecent, corrupt music that is designed to highlight sexual desires" and called for a ban. In Taiwan, a security agency banned the Chinese-language version of "Papa Loves Mambo"—whose lyrics in English include the line "Papa's lookin' for Mama, but Mama is nowhere in sight"—for being "unwholesome." Korea was no exception to the mambo craze, and the phrase "Hey! Mambo," derived from Clooney's song, became a popular catchphrase.[15]

Mambo formed part of the soundtrack for the new lives that were taking shape in postcolonial and postwar East Asia. It embodied a sense of the new, and it brought together a nascent postwar youth culture with the democratic values that the United States was promoting. The influx of mambo had a gendered dimension, suggesting in particular the transformation of young women's lives. In 1957, Hong Kong's MP&GI studio released *Mambo Girl*, a music- and dance-filled film that established Grace Chang's star persona as the "charismatic embodiment of modern feminine identity." Regarded by Jean Ma and other critics as the "single most representative work of postwar Mandarin cinema," the mambo-rich film stimulated the "cosmopolitan imaginary" of postwar Hong Kong film. In the films that followed, female stars such as Chang and Linda Lin Dai embraced popular Western music and dance, as well as the latest fashions and international travel, becoming the "point of access to a world beyond local borders" and ushering in a period of "cosmopolitan worldliness." The situation was similar in Japan where the youngest daughter of Emperor Hirohito was hailed as an icon of Japan's modern young women. In addition to bucking tradition by driving a car and marrying a commoner, she took a job as a radio DJ. Her theme song? A mambo titled "Princess Suga," written for her by Pérez Prado. Across East Asia in the 1950s and 1960s, writes Jean Ma, "cosmopolitanism had a feminine accent"—and a mambo beat.[16]

Given Korea's poverty after the war, which limited access to foreign recorded music, how did mambo enter Korea? Through which circuits, to use Andrew F. Jones's term, did this music flow? Kathleen McHugh points to the role of popular Mexican films. Mexican cinema in the 1940s and early 1950s was experiencing its own Golden Age, and dramas set in the mambo-saturated world of cabarets and nightclubs formed a rich vein of production. These films, many of them featuring Pérez Prado himself, served as one of the most important vehicles for mambo's global diffusion. As McHugh points out, Han Hyung-mo's staging of the mambo performance seems to be indebted to these Mexican films, echoing their setting, costuming, cinematography, style of dance, and, of course, music. While Korean film import records are spotty before 1956, the Mexican film industry was interested in Asian markets, and some Mexican films were imported in the later 1950s, so it is possible that Han saw some of these films in Korean theaters.[17] Mambo, however, flowed into Korea through multiple channels.

While the State Department sent Benny Goodman to South Korea in 1957 as part of its jazz-based cultural diplomacy effort aimed at nonaligned and decolonizing nations, it was the US military that created a capillary system through which mambo flowed into Korea.[18] Here again we see how the American armed forces functioned in Korea as a cultural institution. The US military served as a global disseminator of Western popular music. It was a sprawling, transnational entity with vast entertainment needs, and the ethnic diversity of its troops—a consequence, in part, of America's imperial reach into the Caribbean—created pathways for Latin music to flow into Korea. The Eighth US Army introduced mambo into South Korea just as it was taking off in the United States. During the early years of the Korean War, members of the Puerto Rican Sixty-Fifth Regiment created a band called the Mambo Boys and entertained soldiers across the country, often playing near the front lines and in theaters before film screenings. Similar live performances continued after the war as GI musical groups entertained troops; mambo was so popular that one soldier show featured a mambo version of the iconic Korean folk song "Arirang." AFKN radio, the US military network, played all the hit songs of the day, and military service clubs offered mambo and other dance lessons. The Far East Army and Air Force Motion Picture Service published 45 rpm records of popular songs, including mambos such as Pérez Prado's 1954 hit recording of "Skokiaan," which were played in service clubs and sold in military PX stores.[19] More spectacularly, the Eighth US Army hosted tours of big-name Latin bandleaders: Xavier Cugat toured US bases in Korea in 1953, and Pérez Prado himself arrived in September 1956—three months after *Madame Freedom*'s release—and performed for thousands of GIs. These celebrities also turned up on AFKN-TV (the US military TV network in Korea), which rebroadcast Pérez Prado's appearance on "The Ed Sullivan Show" in 1958. The EUSA also distributed American magazines, which covered the mambo phenomenon extensively, as part of its standard soldier-entertainment package, so images of mambo dancers and fashions circulated as well.[20]

While these iterations of mambo were aimed at Americans, quite a few Koreans had access to them as well. KATUSA soldiers (Korean Augmentees to the US Army), civilian employees of the military, and invited guests would have attended Xavier Cugat's and Pérez Prado's shows; Korean waitresses and dance partners were always present in military service clubs; Korean radio and TV sets picked up AFKN's broadcasts; and American records and magazines found their way easily into Korean hands through the black market and other channels. The mastery of mambo by Korean musicians, who sometimes played alongside Americans in US military bands, was apparent by mid-decade. When a Korean singer performed for UN servicemen in 1956 as part of a "Korea's Night" culture show, she sang "Arirang," of course, but also "Mambo, Mambo," which she delivered, according to

Stars and Stripes, with an "Eartha Kitt inflection" that left the "predominantly male audience howling for an encore."[21]

Mambo also flowed into Korea from Japan, where its tremendous popularity was likewise linked to the US military. A sizable American population during the occupation (1945–52) and Korean War (1950–53) years stimulated the emergence of Japan's lively jazz scene. Singer Misora Hibari had her biggest hit in 1954 with the song "Omatsuri Mambo," and by 1955 American critics in Japan were complaining that mambo was appearing in practically every musical stage show, whether thematically appropriate or not, and homegrown Latin-music bands such as the Tokyo Cuban Boys and the Tokyo Mambo Orchestra had become well established.[22] Unlike in Korea, where he performed only military engagements, Pérez Prado played to ninety thousand ecstatic fans during a single week of his month-long tour of Japan in 1956. He was the guest of honor in a three-hour parade, and the subject of a two-hour TV show. The musical border between Japan and Korea, like the one surrounding the US military bases, was porous. Korean newspapers commented on the mambo craze in Japan, and southern Korean cities and towns picked up Japanese radio and TV broadcasts.[23]

What kinds of meanings might *Madame Freedom*'s mambo scene have conveyed to its audiences? As with other of Han's cosmopolitan spectacles, this mambo performance entailed a degree of mimicry, as the dancer reproduces a set of moves that clearly originated elsewhere. In doing so, she is also claiming and recirculating some of their meanings. Jazz music in general carried powerful associations with individual creativity and freedom. This made it attractive to cultural Cold Warriors, who embraced it as "emblematic of the radical differences in human liberty between the 'free world' and the communist realm."[24] As a form of dance, mambo also carried a specifically gendered set of associations relating to female sexuality. Mambo had an improvisatory dimension that conveyed a sense of sexual freedom. This was expressed through the seemingly "uninhibited" quality of the bodily movements, the "expression of ineluctable bliss" on dancers' faces, and the insistence, in both music and dance, on a near-continuous sexually ecstatic experience. This aesthetic of improvisation also communicated a sense of individual freedom that was not found in other forms of social dance. As partners separated on the dance floor, the woman was liberated from the man's guiding lead, leaving her "free to dance around her partner" just as "he was free to dance around her." This linkage of sexuality and freedom led observers around the world to characterize the mambo as "primitive."[25] In the Korean context, this primitivism took on a Picasso-like modernist quality that suggested the possibility of liberation from what some dancers no doubt regarded as the dead weight of tradition.

The nightclub performer in *Madame Freedom* communicates precisely this modern-primitive sense of sexual freedom. She channels an exuberant and mischievous sexuality, combined with a powerful vision of female autonomy. In one repeated gesture she stands with legs apart and thrusts her hand towards her pubic area, arching her back and opening her mouth into a pleasantly surprised "O" as she gazes upward with ecstatic pleasure. The move has an unmistakably autoerotic dimension and offers a compelling vision of female sexual pleasure independent of any male participation—the ultimate après girl gesture. Like the judo spectacles in *My Sister Is a Hussy*, this stand-alone musical number asserts a counterweight to the reassertion of patriarchal control at the film's conclusion. With its loose ties to the surrounding story, it is able to express an alternative set of values that celebrate rather than condemn female sexual autonomy. And because the mambo dancer is not a character within the narrative, the vision of energy and abundance that she embodies is not subject to the narrative's conservative closure: the film does not condemn her behavior through dialogue or visual suggestion. Instead, the scene offers a rich sensory experience that expresses ideas of women's sexual autonomy and pleasure in ways that remain apart from the ideological containment of the narrative, even as it directly challenges Confucian ideals of female self-denial.

Mambo in Korea, as elsewhere in Asia, thus took on a set of gendered associations with personal freedom, release from male authority, and a female sexuality liberated from the demand to reproduce the patriarchal family. With these associations the word *mambo* escaped the realm of music and dance and became a free-floating synonym for modern. At a time when Korean women rarely wore pants, for instance, the slim-fitting cropped pants that fashionable young women began to wear were quickly dubbed "mambo pants." Apparently inspired by Audrey Hepburn's costume in *Sabrina* (1954), which was created by French designer Givenchy, mambo pants shocked Koreans who thought them overly sexual in the way that they revealed the shape of a woman's backside and legs.[26] As such they were embraced by filmmakers seeking costumes for their après girl characters, such as the charismatic prostitute Sonia in Shin Sang-ok's *Flower in Hell* (1958).

It is these lessons in personal freedom and sexual autonomy that Mme Oh imbibes from the mambo performer. Immediately after watching her, Mme Oh ventures out onto the dance floor herself, taking first Mr. Shin and then Mr. Han into her arms. She finds the dancing intoxicating and liberating, and increasingly seeks it out it as the movie progresses. As she dances in public, Mme Oh performs her growing sense of autonomy and independence, her willingness to break from social norms, and her desire for sensuous bodily pleasures. Like many other fictional characters and social actors in Asia during the 1950s and 1960s, she physically enacts an expanding sense of her own possibilities via the mechanism of Western social dance.

Part of *Madame Freedom*'s "cinema of attractions" quality derives from the presence of celebrities. Han often poached well-known personalities from the larger arena of public culture, which he treated as a reservoir of human resources to be tapped at will. The mambo scene featured two prominent cultural figures: dancer Na Bok-hui, who was known as "No. 1 in the Korean Mambo World," and trumpeter and band leader Park Ju-geun, who was an important figure in the postwar

Korean jazz scene.[27] As celebrities, they function as a form of cinematic excess. Because their identities are rooted outside the confines of the film, they threaten to pull the viewer's attention out of the narrative flow and onto themselves as autonomous performers. They appear in a presentational, rather than representational, mode: they are simply themselves, rather than pretending to be fictional characters. Park and Na were particularly high-status performers, and thus attractive to Han, because they performed primarily for Americans in what were known as Eighth Army shows. Until the mid-1960s, the live music scene in Korea ran on two parallel tracks. On one track were performers who sang Korean-language songs for Korean audiences in Korean venues, such as nightclubs, theaters, and even the Midopa department store.[28] Han borrowed celebrities from this track, including composer Park Si-chun, who appeared as the doctor in *Hyperbolae of Youth*, and the singer Baek Seol-hui, who performed in *Madame Freedom*'s luncheon scene. On the other track were performers like Park and Na, who performed mostly Western music for American audiences in US military venues. There was some overlap of these tracks, as performers on the Eighth Army circuit sometimes played in the best Seoul theaters or appeared on Korean radio, but not much. Performers on the Eighth Army circuit had a significantly higher status due to their association with Americans, their access to the US military bases, their ability to use English, their immersion in Western musical culture, their often higher levels of education, and their higher earning power. In incorporating Na Bok-hui, Park Ju-geun, and Baek Seol-hui into his film, Han bridged these two domains of musical public culture. Han's showmanship in *Madame Freedom* thus involved not just presenting a compelling scene of music and dance, but also in making high-status performers available to a broad swath of the Korean population, who might not have been able to see them otherwise.[29]

The Eighth Army shows played a major role in Korea's culture and economy. From the mid-1950s to the mid-1960s, the fifty to eighty thousand troops stationed around Korea created an enormous demand for entertainment.[30] The US military bases were home to an estimated 264 service clubs, many of which wanted live entertainment several nights a week, far more than military troupes and the USO could provide. To meet the demand, the US military turned to Korean musicians, singers, and dancers. The Eighth Army shows were a large-scale phenomenon, providing employment to many Korean entertainers and a large percentage of the live entertainment for GIs. In October 1954, for example, 25 separate Korean show units, which together employed 363 people, gave 556 performances to 170,000 GIs, or almost 50 percent of the total audience.[31] At a time when the average annual per capita income was less than $125, top-rated show groups were paid that much for a three-hour show, which meant that entertainers—many of whom were women—were able to achieve a measure of comfort in their lives and support other family members. Music historians estimate that the military spent about $1 million annually on Korean entertainers, although earnings for some years were much higher. The *Seoul Kyung Jae* newspaper reported, for instance, that entertainers in 1959 earned \$2.8 million, which was more than the value of all the domestically manufactured products that Korea sold to the ROK and UN Armed Forces in 1958.[32] (Korean entertainers were paid out of the Eighth Army Major Command Welfare Fund, which was funded, in part, through income generated by PX stores—which meant that purchases of PX goods for resale on the black market helped pay the salaries of Korean entertainers as well as providing income to the black-marketers.)

The US military inadvertently facilitated the professionalization of popular music through its bureaucratic system of auditions, ratings, and performance reviews. This was similar to what the Asia Foundation intentionally sought to do with the film industry and publishing. The Americans who served on audition committees helped shape the shows' content and performance style according to American tastes. The performers, in turn, learned how to perform a range of Western popular music, so as to appeal to the military's diverse population. The singer Miss K, for instance, imitated Elvis Presley by holding the microphone stand at an angle; Miss Kim Hye-kyeong sang in the style of Nat King Cole; the Western Jubilee band specialized in country music; and the MBC band played jazz.[33] Performers learned how to sing in English, even if they didn't understand the words, and how to be entertaining and physically attractive, according to American standards. They learned, in other words, how to create a visual spectacle as well as an aural one. The shows also facilitated the professionalization of Korean managers and talent agents, who emerged to help the hundreds of performers navigate the military's entertainment system. Na Bok-hui's and Park Ju-geun's polished performances in *Madame Freedom* were products of this system. So were those of the Kim Sisters, the singing nurses in the opening scene of *Hyperbolae of Youth*.[34] Na's experience on the Eighth Army Show circuit no doubt contributed to the air of professionalization that she brings to Han's film. For all her exuberant sexuality, she comes across as a well-trained performer rather than an object of exploitation. The sexual autonomy that she mimes is paralleled by the professional autonomy that she radiates.

These Eighth Army shows make visible the complex role that mimicry played in the development of postwar Korean public culture. As these Korean musicians, singers, and performers gave their customers what they wanted, they laid the foundations for an indigenous popular music that would flourish in the 1960s and that was less beholden to Japanese music than were the Korean-language "trot" songs of the 1950s. Mimicry functioned as a tool of cultural redefinition: by copying American music, Koreans freed themselves of some of their colonial legacies. As David Scott Diffrient has argued in relation to Korean "remakes" of Western and Japanese films, such acts of copying were a crucial part of postwar cultural reconstruction.[35] Mimicry can be understood as a stage in cultural development, especially in the case of a small country navigating between more powerful empires. It is how cultural producers learn a body of skills that can later be put in the service of more fully localized cultural production. The Eighth Army shows thus functioned as what Pil Ho Kim and Hyunjoon Shin have dubbed cultural "incubators": they served as a training ground for Korean musicians of a cosmopolitan bent who were seeking new idioms for expressing distinctly postwar and postcolonial identities.[36]

Han Hyung-mo was a secondary beneficiary of these incubators, which produced a field of local talent upon which he could draw. In seeking to give his viewers the best "service" possible, he sought out performers who had been professionally nurtured by the Eighth Army shows, as well as stars from the Korean-language circuit. His musical spectacles of Eddie Fisher songs and mambo dance were thus enabled, in diverse ways, by the entertainment infrastructure created by the US military.

FASHION

Han Hyung-mo opened *The Pure Love* (1957) with yet another kind of attraction: a virtual fashion show. Set on a beach, the scene starts out in spectacle mode, with a series of panning and tracking shots across a crowded beach that mimic the gaze of a strolling person. It presents the viewer with an engaging vista of ocean, sand, umbrellas, a water skier, and plenty of men and women in revealing bathing suits. Bodies are on display. The act of looking is emphasized when several sunbathers begin frantically pointing towards the sea, which prompts a cut to a point-of-view shot of a boating accident. After a brief scene in a hospital, the film returns to the beach for a montage sequence in which the female accident victim, In-sun (Kim Ui-hyang), looks for, finds, and goes on several dates with her rescuer, a painter (Seong So-min) (video 8). Over the course of this sequence, In-sun appears in seven extremely fashionable outfits. These include mambo pants, a white square-neck T-shirt worn snug atop matching short-shorts with a contrasting black belt, and a flesh-toned maillot with spaghetti straps, a ruffle along the top that accentuates her amply supported breasts, and a small decorative flower at the thigh. This fashion display is structured as a leisurely series of long and medium shots that are filmed straight on and allow the viewer to examine the costumes closely. Diegetically, these revealing Western-style clothes establish In-sun's character as a sexually adventurous après girl who actively pursues a man in whom she has a romantic interest. At the same time, the number of outfits and the visual attention devoted to them constitutes a spectacle that far exceeds the demands of the narrative. One or two would have sufficed for sketching her character; seven outfits constitute cinematic excess that commands the viewer's attention in its own right. Sexualized display is clearly part of this spectacle. But something more is going on.

In-sun works as an airline stewardess, a glamorous job that in the 1950s carried associations with capitalist and cosmopolitan modernity.[37] Travel is a key

VIDEO 8. Clip from *The Pure Love.*
To watch this video, scan the QR code with your mobile device or visit
DOI: https://doi.org/10.1525/luminos.85.8/

element of her après girl characterization. She lives alone in an apartment decorated with an airline poster of Manila and a miniature airplane, and, when not dressed in fashionable outfits, sports a smart, professional uniform. Her flight to Hong Kong creates an opportunity for a brief touristic interlude in which the city's exotic sights—a sampan-crowded harbor, rickshaw-lined streets—are displayed for the viewer's pleasure. Her international travel extends the associations between modernity and female mobility that *The Hand of Destiny* and *Madame Freedom* forged with the automobile (an association that *Yŏwŏn* would likewise make in its "Miss Earring's World Adventure" travel series in 1961). International travel was also a component of Korea's Free World integration, as the Asia Foundation's support for international conferences attests. When the Minnesota-based Northwest Orient Airlines added Seoul and Busan into its pan-Pacific flight route in 1954, the airline became both a symbol of South Korea's engagement with the Free World and a means to achieve it. When *Yŏwŏn* published a photo essay on modern office etiquette in its second issue as part of its exploration of the working woman, it used a female travel agent as its subject and positioned a Northwest brochure directly in front of her, alongside posters of London, Hong Kong, and Washington, DC.[38] And when Asia Foundation president Robert Blum traveled to South Korea and writer Kim Mal-bong traveled to America, they flew on Northwest Orient as well.

With *The Pure Love* and other films, Han incorporated into his film a particularly dynamic dimension of South Korean public culture: fashion. In the context of postwar South Korea, I am using the term *fashion* to refer to the embrace of Western-style women's clothing that calls attention to itself for its currency with contemporary styles in Europe and America (although as Steven Chung has noted, the *hanbok* was undergoing its own fashionable transformation in this period).[39] All clothing functions as an expressive medium that conveys information about the wearer's identity in terms of age, gender, occupation, and other defining categories. Traditional clothing, or what Ted Polhemus and Lynn Procter have dubbed "anti-fashion," emphasizes the wearers' collective, social identity and their adherence to long-standing shared values. "Fashion," in contrast, is defined by its newness. It is a statement of belief in the positive value of change. According to Malcolm Barnard, every fashionable item of dress "is a challenge and a contestation of the *status quo.* . . . . It is the embodiment of difference, change, and of things not staying the way they are." For Grant McCracken, fashion serves as an expressive medium "through which social change is contemplated, proposed, initiated, enforced, and denied." Fashion conveys the ideals of individual self-expression, and of voluntary affiliation and disaffiliation with social groups, thus contributing to the construction of self-identity that Anthony Giddens regards as central to modernity.[40] In postwar Korean cinema, fashion functioned as a kind of billboard announcing the wearer's commitment to social change enacted at the level of the individual woman.

Han was among the first filmmakers to make fashion a central part of his style, and it figured prominently in the "feasts for the eyes" that he provided for his viewers. He regularly drew upon the emerging worlds of professional and street-level Korean fashion to create his spectacles, and as a result became known in the film industry for his "cutting edge" and "scandalous" costumes.[41] Other filmmakers followed his cue, and the prominent use of Western fashion became a distinctive feature of postwar film style, where it served as a visual cue for a female character's attitude towards the sweeping changes that were remaking postwar Korea.

By dressing actresses in up-to-date Western fashions, Han and other directors claimed glamour for Korean women. Long the exclusive property of white women in Hollywood films and Western fashion magazines, glamour signifies affluence, sophistication, and worldliness. By making their actresses glamorous, filmmakers asserted that Koreans can rightfully occupy that elevated cultural space alongside Western women. The use of fashion as spectacle can also be read as a reaction against Japanese colonial visual discourse. As Michael Robinson, Todd Henry, and Youngna Kim have shown, spectacles of modernity such as neon street signage and industrial expositions were common in colonial Seoul, but they served to construct primarily the Japanese as truly modern.[42] The mass of Koreans, in contrast, were constructed as what E. Taylor Atkins has called Japan's "primitive selves"—a developmentally stagnant branch of a shared racial stock—and colonial officials directed considerable resources to public displays of the archaeology and folk culture of Japan's "backward cousins."[43] Clothing figured prominently in visual ascriptions of Korean backwardness, and Hyung Il Pai has shown how the colonial tourist industry symbolized this "Old Korea" via photographs of Korean women dressed in traditional *hanbok* and posed in rural settings.[44] As in Western colonial discourse, the denial of coevalness via visual constructions of the colonized woman as "traditional" helped to reinforce colonial hierarchies of power and justify foreign rule as an instance of a "civilizing mission." The panoply of fashionably dressed Korean women in postwar films can thus be read not simply as copies of Western femininity or titillating erotic displays, but also as a reaction against a colonial visual culture that used "traditional" costumes to signify Koreans' inferior status. Glamour and fashion served as postcolonial tools for extracting Korea from Japan's anthropological temporality and asserting claims of coeval modernity instead.

The 1950s was a transitional period during which many Korean women began wearing Western-style clothes for the first time. Although Korean men had adopted Western-style uniforms and suits at the turn of the century, most women continued to wear *hanbok* throughout the 1940s. The *hanbok*, which literally means "Korean clothing," is composed of two main parts: the *ch'ima*, a long, bell-shaped wrap skirt that ties across the chest or hangs from shoulder straps, and the *jŏgori*, a long-sleeved short jacket that falls just below the breasts. This loose-fitting outfit visually obscured the shape of a woman's body, but also threatened to reveal it in embarrassing ways. Because the wrap skirt was unsecured in the back, the wearer had to use one hand to bring the fabric forward to prevent her backside from being exposed, while the short jacket threatened to reveal her underarms if she raised her arms too high. The *hanbok* thus hindered a woman's movements, physically reinforcing Confucian ideals of feminine grace and modesty. As women moved into public life, they often found Western clothes more practical for working, riding public transportation, and even walking in the streets, as well as more comfortable than the flowing *hanbok*.[45] By the end of the 1950s Western clothes had become the norm for younger urban women, while the *hanbok* was reserved for married women and over the course of the 1960s became marked as ceremonial clothing.

Widespread poverty during and after the war stimulated the speed and scope of this sartorial transformation. Relief goods sent by American churches and charitable organizations provided the largest source of clothing, and Koreans modified military surplus items such as uniforms, blankets, and parachutes into practical garments.[46] High-heeled shoes and accessories such as purses came into Korea through black-market channels, and many a Korean girlfriend ordered outfits from the Sears and J. C. Penney "moose manual" catalogues. Educated and affluent women were among the earliest adopters. Helen Kim noted that Ewha students, aided by donations from a group of "Ewha Friends" in Wichita, Kansas, quickly converted to an "all Western style" of skirts and slacks while seeking refuge in Busan during the war.[47] Women who had close contact with American men, including entertainers, dance partners, girlfriends, and sex workers, were also among the first to embrace Western styles, which emphasized the sexual dimensions of a woman's body through tight bodices and cinched waists. Such beguiling clothes were often a pragmatic choice for Korean women whose livelihoods depended on American men. Such fashionable outfits, noted William Armour Murdoch, an Eighth Army civilian employee, made it "difficult to refrain from entering into a friendly or romantic relationship with those too many women, who were unfortunate enough to be alone in life after losing their husbands and brothers in the war so recently over." Professional women, in turn, embraced Western fashion as a means to signify readiness to conduct business. Murdoch vividly recalled meeting a Korean executive in an industrial company that was contracting with Eighth Army engineers: she wore "a tailored knee-length pink wool suit, with full lace overlay. She had a pink leather handbag; pink medium height shoes and neatly coiffed black hair."[48]

Media played a role in this transformation as well, with Hollywood movies stimulating the desire for new fashions and seamstresses producing variations of outfits seen in *Vogue* and *Harper's Bazaar*.[49] *Yŏwŏn* also functioned as a fashion manual, and the introductory photo essays almost always included a spread in which Korean or Western women modeled the latest in Western clothing, accessories, and hair styles. The magazine published an extensive dictionary of Western fashion terms that spread across two issues in 1958, giving readers a vocabulary for talking about the images they saw and explaining to their dressmakers exactly what they wanted, and it published sewing patterns in virtually every issue.[50] These included guides for making garments that reshaped the body along Western lines—such as "bullet" bras, which featured a wire spiral centered on the nipple that created an axis perpendicular to the chest, and which In-sun seems to be wearing in *The Pure Love*—as well as instructional articles explaining how to wear these new garments (figure 22). The embrace of Western fashion thus entailed revising Korean femininity by, for example, emphasizing a woman's sexual identity over her role as a preserver of cultural norms. This interest in physical transformation extended to the body itself, and the magazine published articles and advertisements about plastic surgery—especially eye surgery—designed to literally remake women's bodies along Western lines.[51] In *Yŏwŏn*'s pages, the transformation of the female body appeared as part and parcel of the modernization of Korean society.

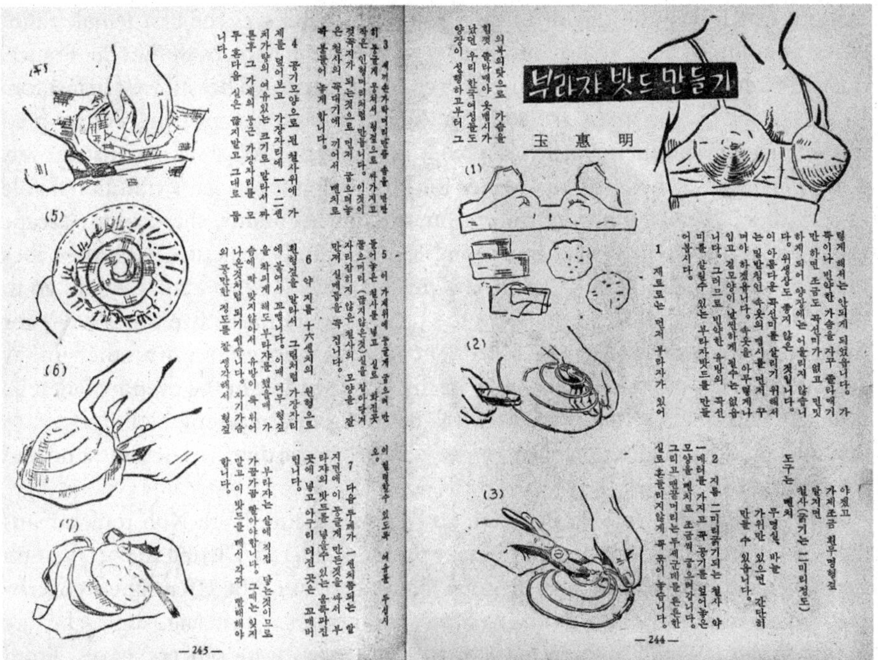

FIGURE 22. Revising Korean femininity: pattern for a "bullet" bra in *Yŏwŏn*. (February 1958)

Nora Noh

In the 1950s Nora Noh (1928–) emerged as Korea's first fashion designer. Fashion—along with magazine publishing, higher education, the law, and music—marked a site within public culture where exceptional Korean women could launch professional careers. Noh operated across the worlds of fashion, women's magazines, Eighth Army shows, beauty pageants, and film, and her career reveals the interconnections among these varied realms of public culture that centered on women and that had ties to the world beyond Korea's borders. In her 2007 autobiography and a 2013 documentary film, Noh reveals how she used fashion to invent herself as a new kind of Korean woman—professional, breadwinner, cosmopolitan—in part by traveling along the transnational routes and seizing the creative and economic opportunities that the Cold War was opening up.[52] In making new kinds of clothes for her customers, Noh tailored new identities for them—and herself—as professional women.

Noh was a second-generation "modern girl" and real-life après girl who helped invent Korean fashion as part of postwar public culture. She was born Noh Myeong-ja in 1928 to affluent parents who embodied colonial-era modernity. Her father was the founder of Korea's first radio station, the Kyeongseong Broadcasting

Station, which went on the air in 1927, and her mother was the first female radio news announcer. Her stylish mother, who bought her own clothes in France, dressed Noh in Western-style clothes as a child and nurtured her interest in fashion. In 1944 at age 17, Noh married a young soldier in order to escape being conscripted into the Japanese imperial army as a "comfort woman." What she got instead was a mother-in-law who conscripted her into the daughter-in-law's traditional role of servitude. Even though she came from an affluent family, she couldn't escape the drudgery prescribed by a traditional Korean family structure. Noh describes her "days of living as a daughter-in-law" in this way: "At 4:30 a.m., I would go to the farm over the hill to get milk for the baby, prepare meals five times a day for the mother-in-law who had given birth, prepare lunchboxes for my brother-in-law and sister-in-law, and prepare a table for my father-in-law in the evening when he drank."[53] Recognizing that liberation was ushering in a new era, Noh decided to take a chance on the unknown, and in 1947, at age 19, she divorced her husband and set out to create a new life.

Like the Kim Sisters, Na Bok-hui, and Park Ju-geun, Nora Noh took advantage of opportunities that the US military presence offered. During the occupation period, she taught herself English, got a job as a typist in the US military government's Department of Health and Welfare, and became a translator in the beauty parlor at the PX store, where most of the customers were officers' wives. From there she moved on to a job as secretary to an American banker, a position that involved planning and attending receptions. Noh made her own culturally hybrid dresses for these events, using her mother's old *hanbok* and kimonos left behind by departing Japanese as the raw material for her original creations. The American wives delighted in her work and spread the word that she was a talented designer. When her banker boss heard that Noh, like so many other young Koreans, aspired to attend school in the United States, he arranged for her to study in California. Noh's travels outside Korea provided the foundation for her professional development. Noh took her impending departure as an opportunity to reinvent herself. When she applied for her passport in 1947, Noh Myeong-ja rechristened herself as Nora Noh: like Lee Tai-young and earlier generations of Korean feminists, she found inspiration in the rebellious Nora of Ibsen's *A Doll's House*. In the United States, Noh studied fashion at the Frank Waggon Technical College and worked with the Taback of California clothing company. In 1949 she returned to Korea, motivated in part by a nationalist desire to help her young country develop. With the encouragement and support of her American friends, she opened a small boutique in her family's house, where she began making dresses for the wives of US military officers and foreign diplomats. Noh's decision to become a fashion designer in the late 1940s was quite courageous because, as she later said, "women who enjoyed wearing Western clothes were rare, and there weren't many places that women could go wearing Western clothes."[54]

Like the GIs who constituted the audiences for performances by Na Bok-hui, Park Ju-geun, and the Kim Sisters, the elite foreign residents of Korea constituted an initial customer base on which Noh was able to draw at the early stage of her career. As such, they allow us to see the importance of Americans as early consumers of Korean cultural production and a market for some of the new nation's fledgling cultural industries. As with the black market and the Eighth Army shows, the US military served as an important cultural-economic force. By buying Korean-designed clothes and shaping and attending shows by Korean musical performers, American military personnel and their wives helped jump-start a few sectors of commercial public culture.

With the outbreak of war in 1950, Noh's developing career became further enmeshed with the US military. The Eighth Army shows that were so important for Korean singers, musicians, and managers also created opportunities for Noh, who began designing costumes for performers. The Army's demand for a steady stream of fresh material proved a boon to Noh, who was kept busy by performers needing to change their costumes as often as they changed their song lists. Noh also used her English skills to help the performers deliver the high-quality performance that the Army required, translating song lyrics into Korean so performers could understand what they were singing, and marking songs' emotional peaks and valleys so singers could make their delivery more expressive. The Eighth Army shows were "such a good chance for me," said Noh, who soon was able to build herself a bigger shop with its own small production facility.[55] Noh continued to avail herself of Eighth Army resources after the war—as Han Hyung-mo did for building his sets—when she began making costumes for a Korean theater troupe. For a production of *Hamlet*, for instance, she made the queen's costume out of some shiny silver paper that had been used to wrap American weapons, and Hamlet's costume from a US Army blanket.[56] In 1953 she staged a mini–fashion show for the American NBC television network as a way to demonstrate that Korean culture was still alive during the war: as a professional woman, she served as a symbol of Korean strength and creativity during difficult times. In 1955 Noh opened her own boutique in Myeongdong, the same fashionable neighborhood in which *Madame Freedom*'s luxury goods shop would be located a year later. At age 27, she had become her family's breadwinner.

Creatively, Noh was oriented towards Europe, and she introduced Paris fashion trends into Korea. She indigenized Western fashion, enabling elite Korean women to feel themselves on par with their Free World contemporaries without being indebted to foreigners or becoming entangled in the black market. In 1956 she spent six months studying fashion in France and Spain, where she took in current design collections. Once again, her travels outside Korea proved crucial for her professional development. Noh drew on these European experiences when she staged Korea's first fashion show that same year. The show, like so much of Noh's career, had a distinctly cosmopolitan air. Noh taught her models how to walk and move their bodies in the manner of Parisian runway models, while they displayed outfits—day dresses, evening dresses, suits, coats, even a wedding dress—inspired by the works of Christian Dior, Coco Chanel, Cristobal Balenciaga, and Nina Ricci that she had seen in Europe. Noh married the cosmopolitan style of her work to her nationalist sentiments, as she proudly made some of the outfits from the first high-quality wool produced by a Korean textile company, Goryeo Wool. Noh went on to stage additional runway shows in 1957 and 1958, as well as a private show for a "US Wives Club" in 1959. The fashion show was a new cultural form in Korea, and other producers of public culture quickly embraced it. Noh's shows appeared on TV and in the pages of *Yŏwŏn*, which sponsored and devoted extensive coverage to the 1957 show held on the roof of the Bando Hotel. These shows were not without controversy, however, and they ignited opposition from the same orthodox Confucianists who resisted Helen Kim's and Lee Tai-young's efforts to revise the Family Law. Noh continued her international travel (via Northwest Orient Airlines) and her involvement in new forms of feminized public culture when she designed costumes and chaperoned contestants to the Miss Universe beauty pageants held in California in 1958 and 1959.[57] As Korean popular singers moved out from the Eighth Army shows and into Korean venues in the 1960s and 1970s, Noh moved with them, creating controversial miniskirt and hot-pants outfits, inspired by British and French fashions; during these same years she expanded her business into the US market, opening showrooms in Hawaii and New York and establishing an American subsidiary.

Noh understood her work as a designer as not just the foundation for her own individual career, but as an expression of her liberal and feminist values. Like Helen Kim and Lee Tai-young, Noh understood her work to be in the service of Korean women's liberation. "What I tried to do," said Noh recently, "was to make the people who wore my clothes move around freely and become confident upon wearing them. Back then, from right after liberation, there was almost no position for women in Korea. Just look at us—we had no freedom of marriage or freedom to go out in the society, or freedom of jobs. For us to accomplish something during those times required courage. So I did it all out of the thought that the women who would plant such awareness would wear the clothes and be active with confidence and demonstrate their abilities." "Once you are comfortable in your clothes," said Noh, "you can move around freely. Then your thoughts are eventually liberated, too."[58] Pioneering female journalist Chang Myeong-su hailed Noh for "breaking free from all the chains of tradition that have tied the minds and bodies of the women in this country," and celebrated her for fighting "the stubborn tradition of *namjon-yŏbi* (the superiority of male over female) and achieving the life she wanted."[59] For Nora Noh and her like-minded peers, fashion was a modernizing enterprise.

Fashion in Film

Noh began designing costumes for films in 1954, and for the next twelve years she was an important figure in the film industry. She worked closely with director Shin Sang-ok on his cycle of women's pictures, and helped shape the personae of two of the era's biggest female stars, Choi Eun-hee and Um Aing-ran.[60] Noh had great leeway in designing film costumes, and she advised many young actresses on how to present themselves on screen. Her film work and custom couture business often overlapped: she used actresses as models in her fashion shows, and film directors often scouted her shows for new acting talent, with future director Lee Bong-rae (*A Petty Middle Manager*, 1961) even serving as the announcer for Noh's first show in 1956.

Films of the 1950s stand out for the ways they use Western-style costumes to express a range of meanings about women's experiences of modernity. Han Hyung-mo was one of the first directors to foreground Western clothes. When in *The Hand of Destiny* he dressed Margaret in a then-exotic striped men's bathrobe as she entertained her soon-to-be lover, he forged a conceptual link between Western clothes and Western values that would become standard throughout the 1950s. Park Nam-ok used Western costuming in *The Widow* (1955) to signify economic security: her war widow protagonist wears a *hanbok* when she struggles with poverty, and only dons Western-style clothes—already worn by her wealthy antagonist and a sex-worker friend—when she opens her own dressmaking shop and embarks on the road to financial independence. *Holiday in Seoul* (1956) deploys fashion as part of its celebration of the professional woman: the heroine is a Western-trained obstetrician who wears an elegant vertically striped sleeveless dress and matching short-sleeved coat. *The Love Marriage* (1958) creates a visual metaphor for a compromise "arranged love marriage" when a young woman dons a *hanbok jŏgori* over a strapless Western gown as she prepares to meet a suitor; here costuming suggests the possibility of harmonizing Western and Korean approaches to marriage. *Hyperbolae of Youth* creates a sharp contrast between characters who wear *hanbok* and those in Western dress; many other films depict women moving fluidly between these two styles. Such costuming suggests that modern and traditional values exist along a continuum, rather than in strict opposition to each other, and that women can locate themselves at different points along that continuum at different moments in their lives. Characters who embrace modern ideals sometimes wear *hanbok*, some of which have been modernized with new fabrics (nylon in *A Sister's Garden* [1959]) and patterns (polka dots in *The Widow*). This diversity of clothing styles implies individual choice and thus a degree of agency on the part of female characters, suggesting that they are actively navigating the processes of social modernization.

Even women's pictures that express skepticism about Westernization at the level of the narrative invariably pause for a moment of spectacle in which Western-style clothes are directly presented to the viewer's gaze as an object of visual interest and pleasure. In Gwon Yeong-sun's *A Drifting Story* (1960), Um Aing-ran plays a naïve young coffeehouse waitress who becomes a prostitute after an accidental pregnancy leads to an abortion. When she returns to her job to give notice, she walks in wearing an elegant black Western-style suit, accessorized with high-heeled shoes, a purse, scarf, gloves, and sparkly jewelry. Narratively, the film condemns this character's choice: the virtuous manager (dressed in a *hanbok*) chastises and slaps her, and the young woman later kills herself. Visually, however, the film treats her costume as an object of intense visual interest. As if in a fashion show, Um's character pauses upon entering the coffee shop and strikes an elegant pose, which the camera captures in a long shot that reveals her outfit in its entirety. The viewer is directed to admire the outfit by other characters, who gaze at her intensely, and by closer-in shots that allow the viewer to inspect the costume's details. Shin Sang-ok's *A Sister's Garden*, which depicts the entry into public life of its "virtuous" protagonist (Choi Eun-hee) as a series of shameful humiliations, nonetheless poses her full-length in a polka dot New Look–style frock designed by Nora Noh. That film's ambivalent attitude towards fashion, and the modern values it implies, is made clear through the character of the "selfish" sister (Choi Ji-hie), a professionally ambitious fashion designer who mortgages the family home in order to open a shop in Myeongdong. While the narrative is critical of this Nora Noh–like character, Shin used Noh's shop as a set and incorporated poached footage from one of her fashion shows.[61]

By the turn of the decade, the embrace of Western fashion by modern young women had become such a convention that it was ripe for repurposing into reaction and critique. In the male melodrama *A Coachman* (1961), which tells the story of the old Confucian patriarchy giving way to a younger, more modern version, director Kang Jae-jin treats sartorial transformation as a sign of moral—and cultural-national—corruption. The film includes a scene in which a young working-class woman (Um Aing-ran) dons a Western suit for the first time, an outfit she hopes will trick an affluent businessman into marrying her. Kang presents Um as struggling painfully in her high-heeled shoes and grotesquely swinging her hips in an exaggerated sexual manner. While the seduction works, the businessman turns out to be a violent gangster who beats Um's character after having sex with her. Kang's film treats the fashionable, and victimized, woman as a symbol of Korea's heedless rush to Westernization, a process that it equates with cultural inauthenticity, self-prostitution, and humiliation. Yet even in this film the spectacle of fashion is present: the suit that Um wears was designed for the film by Nora Noh.

This treatment of fashion as spectacle solicited a distinct mode of spectatorship, in which female viewers were invited to withdraw their attention from the narrative—and its often-conservative lessons—and focus on the Western costumes instead. In a recent interview Um Aing-ran suggested that such a mode of spectatorship was quite common among postwar women, who were attracted to her films by her Nora Noh–designed costumes rather than the stories. "When the films were released," said Um, "people would be like, 'hey, let's go see what Um Aing-ran is wearing, let's go see what she is carrying,' as if they were window shopping in the department store." As film viewers, their primary desire, said Um, was "to look" —not necessarily to lose themselves in a story.[62] These viewers went to the movies to consume clothes and accessories vicariously, and perhaps as a guide to their actual consumption.

A Female Boss

Han Hyung-mo worked with Nora Noh on only one film, *A Female Boss* (1959), which presents the fashionable, professional woman as its central spectacle. The film stars Jo Mi-ryeong, who had walked in Nora Noh's inaugural fashion show, as Joanna Shin, the publisher of a *Yŏwŏn*-like magazine called *Sin yoja*, or *The Modern Woman*. (This is the same title as the feminist magazine that Helen Kim helped found in 1920.) Like *My Sister Is a Hussy*, *A Female Boss* is a carnivalesque romantic comedy that upends patriarchal gender relations. Joanna is a strong-willed woman with feminist inclinations: she works at an enormous desk—like the ones visible in *Yŏwŏn*'s "Twelve Modern Korean Women" series—below a work of calligraphy that inverts the Confucian principle of *namjon-yŏbi* to read "women are superior to men," and she answers her telephone with an assertive "This is the Modern Woman." Throughout the film Joanna asserts her authority as a businesswoman, as when she usurps the privilege of paying for an expensive dinner from her older, wealthier uncle. While the subplot, in a nod to the real crisis besetting the publishing industry, charts Joanna's efforts to secure paper stock to keep her magazine afloat, the main plot follows her romantic pursuit of an employee whose conservative masculinity she finds irresistible. Mr. Kim (Lee Su-ryeon) resists her increasingly bold advances, only to succumb when she promises to give up her job. The film ends with the obligatory five minutes of patriarchy-restoring closure in which Joanna sits at home, while her now husband works at her big desk beneath a restored calligraphy painting that proclaims "men are superior to women." An agent of wholesome modernization rather than retrograde orthodoxy, Mr. Kim promotes a working-mother journalist to the role of business manager and launches a *Yŏwŏn*-like photo series on the working woman. Nevertheless it is clear that *The Modern Woman*—as well as the modern woman—has been brought securely under a man's control.

The film's display of fashion cuts against this conclusion by presenting the professional woman as an attractive spectacle and inviting the gaze of young female viewers inclined to against-the-grain modes of spectatorship. Han does not pause the narrative for a single fashion-show-type scene, as he did in *The Pure Love*. Instead, he distributes the spectacle of fashion through almost every scene, borrowing a trick from Hollywood films such as *Rear Window* (1954, imported

FIGRUE 23. A Nora Noh costume in *A Female Boss* (1959). (Courtesy of KOFA)

into Korea in 1957), in which Grace Kelly plays a fashion magazine editor who appears in a series of stunning outfits designed by the legendary Edith Head.[63] Han offers an extravaganza of Nora Noh designs, presenting Joanna and her female employees in more than a dozen outfits that survey contemporary Parisian fashion trends. Joanna, for instance, appears in a Balenciaga-inspired empire-waisted black and white dress paired with a short-sleeved kimono-style coat and matching hat (figure 23). The chief editor (Yoon In-ja) wears a Chanel-like little black dress with a Chelsea collar, complete with a double string of pearls. The business manager (Sim Suk-il) appears in a slim-fitting gray jersey dress with a wrap bodice, three-quarter sleeves, and long black gloves. Several outfits are fully accessorized from hats to shoes, and the women sport a variety of au courant hairstyles, including a bob and a flip. A party scene creates an opportunity to display multiple elaborate Noh designs at once. The film thereby offers its viewers a visual experience akin to browsing through an issue of *Vogue*, an education in style that is enhanced by the Cinemascope frame that captures the costumes in motion as the women move across wide open spaces (as if in a fashion show) and offers up sartorial details for careful inspection. The European flavor of these clothes is enhanced by the settings in which they appear, which contain such decorative items as a globe and a mounted pair of exotic bulls' heads, thereby suggesting that fashion is integral to the cosmopolitan lifestyle of this new social type.

The film positively associates fashion with modernity from its opening frames. The credit sequence depicts Seoul's bustling Myeongdong rotary and a street packed with automobiles, images redolent of postwar progress and (literal) social mobility. Superimposed on these shots are the film's title and an image of an elegantly attired Joanna, making clear that she is the female boss in question. A jaunty tune on the soundtrack—Perry Como's "Magic Moments," a hit from 1958—signals the genre will be comedy. The first scene begins with a slow tracking shot of men walking along a crowded sidewalk, their bodies filmed from the knees down in a manner reminiscent of the opening of Hitchcock's *Strangers on a Train* (1951) and Han's own *The Hand of Destiny* (video 9). After a moment the camera halts and tilts upward to reveal, in stages, the white high-heeled shoes, then the full skirt and jacket, and finally the face, hat, and gloved hands of Joanna as she monopolizes a public telephone. (This shot is a variation, perhaps, on the camera movement that accompanies the introduction—"reading from top to bottom"—of Grace Kelly and her striking black-and-white New Look dress in *Rear Window*.) The camera lingers on Joanna in a medium shot, giving the viewer time to inspect her chic outfit, then tracks slowly along a line of waiting men and women, before coming to rest on the handsome but disgruntled face of Mr. Kim, who is himself dressed in a not-unfashionable bomber-style jacket that signals he might be an appropriate mate for Joanna. Joanna blithely ignores the men's attempts to dislodge her from the phone, instead cooing at her tiny dog, Mario, as she feeds him a black-market Fig Newton and asserting her rights: "This is a pay phone. As long as I am using it, it is my right to talk on." Angered by this behavior, Mr. Kim kicks Mario, prompting a conflict that ends when Joanna stalks off into a taxi, leaving Mr. Kim to his telephone call and the revelation that he is unemployed and looking for a job.

While this meet-cute introduction is rife with class tensions, it also stages the familiar conflict between a cosmopolitan feminist and a cultural nationalist. Mr. Kim, as he explains later, is outraged that Joanna is feeding expensive American cookies to her dog when many Koreans don't have enough to eat. Joanna, in turn, ostentatiously refuses to conform to Confucian gender norms. Her disaffiliation

VIDEO 9. Clip from *A Female Boss*.
To watch this video, scan the QR code with your mobile device or visit
DOI: https://doi.org/10.1525/luminos.85.9/

from these norms is signaled sartorially by the contrast between her fashionable Western-style suit and the anti-fashion of the two *hanbok*-clad women waiting in line. It is also signaled through her actions. By talking on the phone at such length and refusing to yield to the men's requests, Joanna violates the expectation that women should be quiet, self-denying, and deferential. More importantly, her refusal to vacate this small patch of sidewalk serves as a claim to public space and the masculine privileges of freedom and autonomy that go along with it. Because Joanna, like Han's other modern-woman characters, is not defined by her sexual virtue, she is not ashamed by encounters with men in public space. This opening scene prefigures that of *My Sister Is a Hussy*, in which the two sisters use judo to defend their right to enjoy a city park unmolested, even as it foreshadows its own ending when Mr. Kim takes charge of Joanna's desk and telephone.

The fashionable newness of the professional women's clothing communicates their eagerness to challenge the patriarchal status quo. The film presents the magazine office as a space in which professional women simultaneously display their fashionable clothes and exert their authority over men. In one extended sequence, the chief editor (dressed in a belted shirtdress) and the business manager (in a button-front blouse and slim skirt) interview a series of men for the position into which Mr. Kim will ultimately be hired. The women comment on the men's physical appearance and marital status, ask questions that reveal the applicants' ignorance and overinflated sense of self, and otherwise treat the men with thinly veiled contempt—inversions, one suspects, of experiences encountered by postwar women as they entered the workforce. Although the women are described as "bitches" by their male coworkers, Han uses editing to indicate that they are delivering a well-deserved comeuppance: mid-scene he cuts away to a wordless shot of Joanna's teenage sister (Seo Ae-ja), dressed modestly in a long-sleeved frock trimmed with oversized rickrack, being visibly discomfited as she is aggressively ogled by a hallway full of men waiting to be interviewed. A similar exercise of female authority occurs during a party at Joanna's house. The chief editor, dressed in a sleeveless, boat-necked chiffon dress with a full skirt, puts an older male editor (Kim Hee-gap) in his place with a stern look after he mocks her style of dancing to Xavier Cugat's "The Brand New Cha Cha Cha." At work and at leisure, then, the fashionable professional woman upends the normative social relations between men and women. One can imagine that these scenes, by combining the pleasures of fashionable looking with feminine self-assertion, appealed to educated young female viewers who were beginning to imagine new futures for themselves.

In addition to her professional success, Joanna expresses her modernity by assuming the traditionally male role of sexual pursuer. This is evident in a nightclub scene in which Joanna slow-dances with Mr. Kim to the song "Johnny Guitar," pressing her body close to his while he registers both emotional discomfort and passive acquiescence due to her status as his boss. The song, which features a classical guitar motif, extends the film's Latin subtext (Balenciaga, bulls' heads, cha-cha-cha, Mario) and serves as a thematically appropriate extratextual reference. Peggy Lee wrote the song for Nicholas Ray's *Johnny Guitar* (1954, screened in Korea in 1958), a baroque Western starring Joan Crawford in a gender-bending role as a powerful business woman who aggressively pursues a handsome man (Sterling Hayden) who is her social and economic inferior. As in Han's film, Crawford's costume—pants, shirt, necktie, cowboy boots—visualized her character's challenge to contemporary notions of femininity, and prompted Bosley Crowther to seethe in the *New York Times* that Crawford was "as sharp and romantically forbidding as a package of unwrapped razor blades"—a sentiment seemingly shared by Mr. Kim as he dances stiffly with Joanna.[64] This nightclub scene is immediately followed by one in which Joanna—whose dress features two sharp handkerchief points at the neckline—urges Mr. Kim to remain in her apartment past curfew; a large bed in the background makes her intentions perfectly clear.

Finally, costume plays a role in the patriarchy-restoring ending, casting doubt on the work of ideological closure via a clothing-based joke. The final shot of the film shows Joanna dressed, for the first time, in a plain *hanbok* (indicative of her married status) and smiling as she crochets a tiny outfit and looks lovingly off-screen at what the viewer assumes is a baby (video 10). When the camera pans

VIDEO 10. Clip from *A Female Boss*.
To watch this video, scan the QR code with your mobile device or visit
DOI: https://doi.org/10.1525/luminos.85.10/

left, however, it reveals not a child but her beloved Mario, the small dog to which she indulgently fed a Fig Newton in the opening scene. This pan to the dog, in combination with Joanna's mirthful expression, wordlessly suggests that perhaps she is making the outfit for him, an idea that immediately undercuts the notion of Joanna as a contented housewife. Perhaps the viewer should see her happiness in the domestic sphere as akin to crocheting clothes for a dog, that is, something silly. By incorporating this purely visual joke, Han makes it possible for the viewer to read against the conservative act of narrative closure, and regard it as a convention rather than a truth: we all "know" that the transgressive heroine must be restored to the domestic sphere, but that doesn't mean we need to take it seriously.

TRADITIONAL DANCE AND *BECAUSE I LOVE YOU*

Han's *Because I Love You* was one of two Korean films entered into the sixth annual Asian Film Festival, held in Kuala Lumpur, Malaya, in 1959. The Asian Film Festival was a Cold War cultural institution (see chapter 2), and the participation of Korean filmmakers in it was the result of concerted efforts by Rhee's government and the Asia Foundation (TAF). International competitions such as film festivals, sporting events, and beauty pageants served as instruments of Free Asian integration, as they educated noncommunist countries about each other and fostered the development of transnational institutional ties and collectively held standards. Rhee and TAF also valued these events as platforms for making South Korea visible on the Free World stage. Film figured prominently in these visibility efforts. Between 1957 and 1960, at least nine Korean films were shown at the Asian Film Festival, with more screening at festivals in Berlin, San Francisco, and other Western cities. *Because I Love You* won a special prize at the Kuala Lumpur festival, making it one of the first Korean films to take home an international award, and it was among the first generation of Korean films to be commercially exported within Asia.[65] (While no print of the film exists, a copy of the script was found during the researching of this book which, when read in combination with publicity materials, reviews, and other documentation, provides a substantive, although not complete, picture of the film.)[66]

Because I Love You reveals a new dimension of Cold War cosmopolitanism: the display of Korea's cultural traditions on an international stage as a way of forging bonds with other anticommunist states. As such, the film achieves a synthesis of the competing cosmopolitan and cultural nationalist impulses coursing through postwar social and cultural life. It offers a vision of postcolonial traditionalism enlisted in the project of Cold War bloc building. Given the loss of the film itself, I explore Cold War cosmopolitanism less through the cinematic form of the spectacles themselves and more through the institutional structures through which these spectacles were produced and distributed.

Indigenous forms of culture can take on cosmopolitan shadings when they become self-conscious expressions of a nation's "cultural heritage" that is shared with people beyond the nation. *Because I Love You* narrates—and enacts—precisely such an act of international sharing. The film is structured around the spectacle of traditional Korean dance that is performed outside the country's borders for non-Korean audiences. Through display of this national art form, the film asserts that Korea possesses an indigenous culture worthy of recognition and respect by others. Spectacle here functions as a passport to the world stage and a mechanism for soliciting foreign interest in South Korea. Through spectacle, the film stakes a claim for Korea as a participant in the cosmopolitan realm of "world cultures," and contributes to the Cold War goal—shared by Washington and Seoul alike—of making Korea visible abroad.

In contrast to many of Han's other films, *Because I Love You* associates femininity with tradition, as did many postcolonial traditionalists. It does so with a twist, however: Korea's cultural heritage is borne by a professional woman who has achieved prominence in public life as a teacher and performer, not by a private woman who remains sequestered in the domestic sphere and lives these traditions as part of her everyday life (as in Shin Sang-ok's *The Houseguest and My Mother* [1961]).

Because I Love You tells a decidedly cosmopolitan story centered on international travel and cultural exchange. The film opens with the return of a young newspaper reporter, Min-ho (Yun Il-bong), from Malaya, where he has fallen in love with a local dancer, Wol-Yun (Landi Chang). He informs his widowed mother

Seong-ae (Kim Sun-seong), a well-known performer and teacher of traditional Korean dance, that she and her daughter Ok-kyong (Seo Ae-ja), along with the rest of their dance troupe, have been invited to Singapore in a cultural exchange program sponsored by his newspaper. The mother initially refuses because it would be too painful a reminder of her late husband Chang-min (Kim Jin-kyu), also a dancer, who died in Malaya during World War II after being conscripted into the Japanese imperial army. She later relents, and the three family members travel to Singapore. During her big performance at the National Theater in Singapore, Seong-ae sees her presumed-dead husband in the audience and collapses on stage. When everyone gathers around her bedside, the husband reveals his story: he was wounded during the war and nursed back to health by a Chinese-Malayan woman Li-Li (Chen Yan), whom he married out of gratitude. Together they had a daughter, who has now become a dancer. With a shock, the young lovers discover they are half-siblings and thus cannot marry. The two wives later decide between themselves with which family the husband should live. The Chinese-Malayan wife is willing to give him up, but at the last moment the Korean wife decides he should stay in Singapore. In the final scene, the Korean mother, son, and daughter drive away to the airport as the Korean husband, his Chinese-Malayan wife, and their daughter tearfully wave goodbye.

Because I Love You was unusual among Han's oeuvre, and 1950s films more generally, for being set in large part outside Korea. The film expands upon the urban automobility displayed by the female characters in *Madame Freedom* and *The Hand of Destiny* and showcases transnational mobility within the Free World. Where In-sun's international travel in *The Pure Love* is subsumed to her characterization as an après girl, Seong-ae's travel forms the spine of this film's narrative. As with *Breaking the Wall* (1949), his first feature film, *Because I Love You* engages explicitly with Cold War ideology: it is infused with the ideals of Free Asia bloc-building. Its story about Koreans traveling to Malaya resonates with the Asia Foundation's vigorous promotion of international travel as a tool of Korea's integration into the Free World. Several scenes are set in and around airplanes, which in the 1950s served as icons of globe-trotting sophistication. Screenwriter Park Seong-ho's dialogue somewhat bluntly imbues travel with the bloc-affirming value of international friendship: as the young journalist Min-ho tells his mother and sister, "My trip to the different countries in Southeast Asia made me realize how much they care about Korea. They all have hope for our independence and prosperity." Park's script expanded this rhetoric of friendship by invoking family ties as a metaphor for relations among Free Asian nations. An early version established this metaphor by having Min-ho remark upon his return from "our China" that "interacting with the Taiwanese is just like interacting with siblings." The film proceeds to literalize this metaphor through the father's bigamy and the revelation that the young Korean and Malayan lovers are half-siblings. In the end, the film sustains the binational marriage of the Korean husband and his Chinese-Malayan wife rather than the nationally homogenous Korean-Korean marriage. The Cold War thematics of international travel, friendship, and family formation overwrite the World War II backstory of Japanese colonial exploitation and suffering, a process of historical progression that the script renders explicit through the son's frequent exhortations to his mother to "let go of the past" and embrace new opportunities in the present.

In addition to highlighting travel, Park sprinkled the script with multiple small acts of cultural exchange, as when the Korean mother gives the Malayan family a *hanbok*-clad Korean doll, and when the Malayan mother, in turn, offers the journalist son a "local Southeast Asian delicacy" to eat. The young lovers embrace each other's culture more fully in anticipation of their marriage, as when Wol-Yun dresses in a *hanbok* to meet her future mother-in-law and Min-ho is revealed as being able to speak Mandarin like "a Chinese person." Most importantly, the film locates the export of traditional Korean dance at the center of its plot. Again, Park's bluntly written dialogue makes this export motif explicit, as when Min-ho appeals to his mother's nationalist sentiments in urging her to undertake the trip to Singapore. "Mother," he says, "for all these years you've devoted yourself to preserving Korean dance for the next generation, and at the same time worked to introduce Korean dance to the world. This upcoming goodwill visit to Singapore is for the glory of our country." His appeal succeeds, and the mother agrees to the trip "for the sake of the nation, and to also see your beloved."

Han stages this theme of cultural export via extensive dance performances. The display of traditional dance begins even before the story itself commences: according to Park's script, the credit sequence features a group of Korean girls "vividly expressing the uniqueness of Korean folk culture" through their performance of a fan dance. Later scenes revolve around extended dance performances, including one set to the folk song "Arirang" and another based on the folk tale "Chunhyang."[67] The film turns these nationalist displays of Korean culture into a full-blown international exchange by balancing them with equivalent performances of Chinese and Malayan dance. Min-ho, for example, falls in love with Wol-Yun while watching her perform an ethnic Uyghur dance from China's far west Xinjiang province. She later performs a traditional Malayan candle dance, and the climactic show, billed as a Grand Sino-Korean Dance Performance, shows her performing a Chinese chopsticks dance. As it does with travel, Park's screenplay explicitly associates this exhibition with Free World integration, as when Seong-ae observes, "I hope our dance exchange program will enhance the friendship between our two countries." The film extends this logic of cultural exchange to include its spectators by staging the dance scenes in a spectacular, presentational mode that reproduces the visual experience enjoyed by the diegetic audiences. These extended dance performances dominate the film and occupy about half its running time.[68] The film likewise opened up to its viewers the spectacle-based pleasures of international travel, specifically the touristic viewing of sights. In addition to staging scenes inside and adjacent to an

FIGURE 24. Traditional dance as international exchange in *Because I Love You* (1958). (Courtesy of KOFA)

airplane, the film displays the dancers at some of Korea's most famous architectural landmarks, including Changdeokgung and Gyeongbokgung palaces (figure 24). These are in turn paralleled by scenes of bustling Singapore streets and lush Malayan countryside.[69] The film was thus an *act* of cultural exchange as much as a *representation* of it, introducing its own spectators as well as its characters—Korean and non-Korean alike—to foreign sights and forms of culture. Through dialogue, gift exchanges, dance performances, and touristic vistas, the film represented and promoted the growth of mutual understanding among Free Asian people.

It was this display of traditional dance that so appealed to the jury at the Asian Film Festival in Kuala Lumpur in 1959 and led it to bestow a special award for choreography upon the film.[70] The Korean judge, a professor at Ewha Womans University, emphasized the nationalist ideal of cultural authenticity when he noted that while films from other countries also included dance, many of these were "too Westernized" and thus not worthy of special recognition.[71] This spectacular display of traditional Korean culture led to further international visibility when *Because I Love You* was commercially exported across Southeast Asia and invited to screen in a 1959 film festival in Frankfurt, West Germany, where it introduced the cultural heritage of Free Korean, Chinese, and Malayan people to Free Germans.[72]

While *Because I Love You* shared the Asia Foundation's cosmopolitan agenda, it seems to have been more directly inspired by Rhee's efforts to wage the cultural

Cold War on his own terms. In the mid-1950s, Rhee began sending displays of Korea's traditional arts and modern development to the United States, Europe, Australia, and other parts of the Free World.[73] Rhee devoted particular attention to Southeast Asia, which had previously figured in Korea's colonial imagination as an exotic imperial outpost.[74] This initiative grew out of the Asian People's Anti-Communist League (APACL), which Rhee launched in 1954 as a bloc-building mechanism designed to strengthen ties among the avowedly anticommunist countries in the region (see chapter 1). In its Statement of Principles, the APACL pledged to promote social and cultural exchanges among its members, a goal that was strengthened by the passage of a resolution at its 1956 Manila conference (which Helen Kim helped to plan) that singled out the "native dances of member groups" as particularly worthy of showcasing.[75]

In the mid-1950s, Rhee launched a sustained cultural diplomacy initiative designed to foster friendship and build ties with the people of Southeast Asia. It began with athletic delegations. The Korean national baseball team participated in the Second Asian Baseball Championship in the Philippines in 1955, which was followed by a visit from a professional golfer in 1956 and a girls' high school basketball team. South Vietnam, in turn, hosted visits from Korean boxing and football teams.[76] The effort expanded in 1957 with the dispatching of a large-scale Artists Mission to the region, which included the Seoul Symphony Orchestra and performers of Korean folk music and dance. The tour was a resounding success: the Vietnamese press reported being "astonished" at the quality of the performances, and the Korean legation in Saigon was thrilled to present Korea's "flourishing culture" to "other Asian nations which up until now have been almost totally ignorant of the artistic side of Korea."[77] Rhee's minister plenipotentiary Choi Duk Shin, invoking both anti-Japanese and cultural nationalist sentiments, urged the president to expand this initiative: Korea's diplomats must "devote much greater efforts for [the] introduction of Korean culture to the peoples in Vietnam and her neighboring countries so as to make them realize that Japanese culture is no more than simple imitation of ours." Choi also reported that South Vietnamese President Ngo Dinh Diem had requested additional exhibitions of Korean culture: "the cultural treasures" that Diem had seen during his recent state visit to Seoul "must be displayed [in Saigon] for all the people who have no knowledge of Korean culture."[78] In response, Rhee sent a second Cultural Goodwill Mission to Southeast Asia in 1958. This tour bypassed Japan, as did its predecessor, to visit only APACL members, including Vietnam, Thailand, the Philippines, Hong Kong, Taiwan, and Okinawa. It consisted of 136 people, including 64 symphony orchestra members, 30 choir members, 7 Korean classical musicians, 4 dancers, and 31 marine honor guards. It also included exhibitions of anticommunist photographs from the Korean War, modernist paintings, handicrafts, and costumes.[79] With these two missions Korea joined the ranks of nations, including China, the Soviet Union, and the United States, that were waging the cultural Cold War by sending performance troupes abroad for the purpose of forging international ties and polishing their image.

It seems likely that *Because I Love You* was inspired by these goodwill missions, which were extensively covered in newsreels made by the ROK's Taehan News and by the USIS's Liberty News.[80] As in his directorial debut, *Breaking the Wall*, Han turns the contemporary events of the Cold War into commercial entertainment. In making the film, Han and screenwriter Park Seong-ho seem to have poached several elements from these newsreels, including the Cold War rhetoric of promoting friendship and cultural exchange among the "free" people of Southeast Asia and Korea. The newsreels depict a series of enthusiastic cross-cultural encounters, as local leaders welcome the mission, Koreans bestow gifts, and audiences applaud exuberantly (similar scenes will appear in Han's film). They include performances of both traditional Korean performing arts and Beethoven's Fifth symphony, an admixture that suggests Koreans, in addition to possessing their own rich heritage, have mastered the forms of elite Western culture as well. As Han Sang Kim has noted, the Liberty News newsreel emphasizes the logistics and pleasures of international travel (as *Because I Love You* will also do): it depicts excitement-filled moments of departure and arrival, and shows the Korean artists on sightseeing trips to ancient heritage sites and vibrant modern cities. These touristic sequences make clear that the countries of Southeast Asia, like South Korea, are also modernizing while holding on to their traditions. Korean women, who figure prominently in the newsreels as cultural ambassadors (as in *Because I Love You*), extend their national iconicity by wearing *hanbok* onstage and off. (The *hanbok* in Han's film are somewhat less traditional in style, featuring split sleeves and diaphanous fabrics.) The newsreels make clear that the mission was a Cold War project: the group is given a send-off at the APACL's Anti-Communist Center of Seoul, it travels on an ROK Navy war ship, Korean marine guards present arms and march in military parades, and political leaders such as Ngo Dinh Diem and Chiang Kai-shek greet the mission upon its arrival in their countries. (Unable to reproduce these military and diplomatic spectacles, Han's film relies on dialogue to link its displays of Korean culture to Rhee's Free Asian political agenda.)

The protagonist of *Because I Love You* seems to have been modeled on the dancer Kim Paik-bong, who was a featured member of the 1958 goodwill mission. Like Seong-ae, Kim was a celebrated performer, choreographer, and teacher of Korean dance who operated a private studio in Seoul.[81] Kim's dances figured prominently in the newsreels, which show her performing a fan dance (a version of which is featured in the credit sequence of Han's film), a *geommu* sword dance, and a dance with a *janggu* hourglass drum (which appears in Han's film as well). As *Because I Love You* does, the USIS newsreel offers a moment of genuine cultural exchange when it presents a performance of a Filipino *tinikling* bamboo dance staged for the Korean visitors in Manila. Kim's dances are the exclusive subject of the second USIS film, "Kim Paik-bong Dancing in Bangkok," which features three dances performed in the courtyard of a Thai temple.[82] These extended performances are filmed in a presentational mode that reproduces the experience of watching the dances live (as in Han's film). These dances also suggest a kind of cultural exchange by combining Korean and Thai cultural spectacles, as Kim performs in front of an elaborately decorated temple flanked by two multistory statues of guardian *yaksha* spirits. Ultimately, as Han Sang Kim has noted, the newsreels offered Korean viewers a dual spectacle: of their cultural traditions (as presented in the shots of the performances) and of their Cold War cosmopolitan modernity (as presented in the shots of admiring audiences across Free Asia applauding those performances).[83] *Yŏwŏn* also covered the Goodwill Mission. Similar to what it did with the 1958 Miss Universe pageant, when it published a participant-observer article by Nora Noh, the magazine published a first-person travel essay about the mission written by Kim Paik-bong herself.[84]

In addition to drawing on Rhee's diplomatic missions, Han's film tapped into emerging transnational networks within Asia's film industries. *Because I Love You* was made via a cosmopolitan mode of production. It was one of Korea's first international coproductions, a collaboration between Im Hwa-su's Korean Entertainment Company, which initiated the project, and Wong Cheuk-hon's Liberty Film Company of Hong Kong.[85] Both industries contributed personnel, with actors from Korea playing alongside those from Hong Kong. Korea's Park Seong-ho wrote the screenplay and Han Hyung-mo served as cinematographer and one of two editors, as well as director.[86] Intended as a prestige production aimed at Korean and Southeast Asian markets, the movie was filmed in multiple countries: primary shooting took place in Hong Kong's Wah Tat studio, with additional location shooting in Seoul and possibly Singapore and Malaya.[87] Im Hwa-su, a wealthy Korean producer and exhibitor, provided a lavish production budget, part of which went towards renting a commercial airplane for use as a set. Hong Kong producer Wong Cheuk-hon, in turn, assembled the Chinese cast and crew, rented the Wah Tat studio, and managed the logistics of shooting in Hong Kong; he also distributed the film in Hong Kong and Southeast Asia.[88]

This cosmopolitan mode of production must be seen in relation to developments within the Korean film industry, the Hong Kong industry, and the Asian Film Festival, each of which valued cross-border cooperation for distinct reasons. *Because I Love You* was one in a series of Korean–Hong Kong coproductions initiated by Im Hwa-su in 1957 with *Love with an Alien*. A former black-marketer and well-known as a thug, Im had close ties to Syngman Rhee and worked to bring Korean film culture into alignment with Cold War ideology, pressuring artists to attend Rhee's rallies and later producing the state-funded election film *Syngman Rhee and the Independence Movement* (1959). Im launched Korean Entertainment Inc. in 1955 with the goal, according to one of its founders, of elevating the quality of Korean cultural products to an "international standard of entertainment" and exporting them abroad. He valued coproductions as an opportunity for Korean technicians to gain experience working with Hong Kong's advanced equipment and as a way to penetrate overseas markets; he also believed they would lead to closer "friendships" with fellow noncommunist nations.[89] Rhee supported Im's commercial ambitions and publicly praised *Because I Love You* in the context of increasing the nation's film exports.[90] (After the April 1960 Revolution that ousted Rhee, Im was arrested for embezzling funds secretly provided by the government to support participation in the Asian Film Festival; he was later hanged by the Park Chung-hee government.)[91] Screenwriter Park Seong-ho shared this politicized view of coproductions and regarded *Because I Love You* as a chance to work with the "free people" of Hong Kong to "maintain the anticommunist front line together." An internationally minded nationalist, Park viewed the production as an opportunity for Koreans to stop living like "frogs in a well" and broaden their vision of the world, which he saw as a first step towards securing "the entire world" as a market for Korean films.[92] For Hong Kong producer Wong Cheuk-hon, coproductions offered fresh sources of capital to offset the loss of the mainland Chinese market in 1952 and the effects of currency restrictions in Taiwan in 1955. He was particularly interested in films set in the Free territories of Southeast Asia, as he sought to expand into these markets. Wong shared Im's anticommunist political orientation, and he cast the president of a pro-Taiwan anticommunist film organization in a minor role. The film also allowed Wong to get in on an emerging trend for female-centered, cosmopolitan dance films that was taking shape within Hong Kong's Mandarin-language cinema. Given these overlapping interests, it is little surprise that Wong responded enthusiastically to Im's invitation to collaborate, signing a contract within twenty-four hours.[93]

As much as it was shaped by the needs of the Korean and Hong Kong film industries, *Because I Love You*'s status as a coproduction was also shaped by the Asian Film Festival and thus, indirectly, by the Asia Foundation. Han Hyung-mo certainly had the upcoming 1959 Asian Film Festival in Kuala Lumpur in mind during production. According to screenwriter Park, Korea's inability to win a prize at the 1958 festival with Han's *Hyperbolae of Youth* —which one critic bemoaned as a "humiliating failure"—was much on the mind of the Korean crew as they shot the film, goading them to take special care with their work.[94] The Asia Foundation's direct involvement with the film was limited, but intimately connected to its cosmopolitan mode of production: in August 1958, the Seoul office gave Im's Korean Entertainment Company US$1,000 in exchange for *hwan*, specifically to enable location shooting in Kuala Lumpur.[95]

Jack James's decision to assist the film was in keeping with the Asia Foundation's desire to "to assist Koreans to bring their cultural achievements . . . to the attention of other members of the free world family of nations, and to gain a position of respect in this family."[96] It also reflected TAF's enthusiasm for international coproductions, which it had been encouraging since 1952 as a local initiative that aligned with US interests. TAF saw coproductions as one of the best means for achieving several of its goals, including transferring knowledge from more to less developed film industries, improving production values, increasing regional film exports, and encouraging mutual understanding among Free Asian peoples. TAF's work on behalf of coproductions began in the Tokyo office, where Noel Busch and John Miller assisted Japanese producers who were eager to partner with Hollywood for their own economic and professional reasons. Soon thereafter, Charles Tanner began meeting with Hollywood studio heads, producers, and directors to encourage coproductions from that end as well. After the Asian Film Festival's launch in 1954, TAF looked to it as the preferred instrument for promoting coproductions, enthusiastically supporting the initiatives of the Federation of Motion Picture Producers Association of Asia (FPA).[97]

The movement towards coproductions gained momentum in 1956. At the festival in Hong Kong (which Han Hyung-mo attended), FPA members passed a resolution encouraging coproductions and instituted a series of professional forums, suggested by TAF, in which they could be discussed. That same year, TAF proposed approving "travel grant requests from young Asian industries to enable them to participate in co-productions with, for example, more advanced Asian industries"; two years later, *Because I Love You* received such a currency exchange grant. The push for coproductions continued at the 1957 festival in Tokyo (which Han also attended), after which TAF film consultant John Miller applauded the rising number of such projects as the festival's most promising result. (This was the year Im launched his series of Korea–Hong Kong collaborations.) In 1958 (the year in which *Because I Love You* was made), TAF reminded all its representatives that coproductions contributed to the achievement of foundation goals and urged them to support the Asian Film Festival in whatever ways they could. By the 1959 Asian Film Festival in Kuala Lumpur (at which *Because I Love You* was awarded its prize), TAF staffer Cho Tong-jae reported that he was "amazed at the demonstration of kinship and friendliness by the Hong Kong and Free Chinese delegates toward Korean attendants" as a result of coproductions undertaken in the previous year. The growth of "friendliness" among Free Asian nations was, of course, a major TAF goal and a major theme of *Because I Love You*. In life, as in Han's film, the metaphorical ties of kinship among Asian people sometimes became literal: Cho couldn't help mentioning that the participants in one coproduction "became so friendly that one of the Hong Kong actresses bore a baby of a Korean actor."[98]

As a coproduction with a Hong Kong company, *Because I Love You* was one of the first Korean films to get commercial distribution in Southeast Asia, an objective shared by TAF, Rhee, and the film's producers. Two distinct versions of the film were released, each tailored to a different market. The Korean-language version, titled *Because I Love You* and edited by Han Hyung-mo, presented the World

War II–era scenes in flashback and was released in Seoul in December 1958.[99] Im Hwa-su entered this version into the Asian Film Festival as an exclusively Korean production under the title *Love for You*. The Mandarin-language version, also titled *Love for You*, was edited by Chiang Hsing-lung and presented the story events in chronological order. The marketing material for this version capitalized on the Asian Film Festival award while downplaying Korean involvement and highlighting the display of Chinese and Malayan dance. It localized the film by treating it as a star-making vehicle for the Singapore-born Landi Chang, whom it identified as a "renowned Southeast Asian dancer."[100] Aimed at the Southeast Asian market, this version opened in Singapore, Kuala Lumpur, and Hong Kong in the fall of 1959 and across Malaya in 1960 and 1961.[101] Han's film thus delivered its Cold War cosmopolitan message to one of the audiences that TAF, and American cultural Cold Warriors more generally, were most concerned about— overseas Chinese.

The marketing materials for both the Korean and Hong Kong versions, while downplaying their status as a coproduction, emphasized the cosmopolitan story line and international filming locations. Malaya figured prominently in reviews as a setting and a filming location, with one Hong Kong article breathlessly claiming that "the filming crew traveled over five thousand kilometers to capture the distinct scenery and landmarks for the big screen." Korean reviewers, while sometimes lukewarm about the film as a whole, praised the cultural exchange motif. One noted that the film was "saved" through its inclusion of the "sentiments of Malaya," while another noted approvingly that the filmmakers did "seem to have put a lot of effort into capturing the exotic scenery down there." Another, picking up on the travel and international friendship themes, astutely noted that the film looked best "if thought of as a Korea-Malaya friendship tourist film." As a "touristy" film, *Because I Love You* offered a vicarious trip to a fellow Free Asian country, a broadening experience that reviewers welcomed.[102]

Because I Love You offers a variation on the cosmopolitan impulses and aesthetics of the period. Although it features Korean dance as its spectacle, and thus taps into cultural nationalist sentiments, it treats traditional culture as a means of forging ties with other Free Asian people. In its story, themes, and settings, as well as its mode of production and distribution, and reception, Han's film harmonized with the combined nation-building and bloc-building efforts of Rhee's government and the Asia Foundation.

Han's spectacle-heavy, Cold War cosmopolitan style gave visual expression to Koreans' desire both to embrace Free World cultural trends and to make themselves visible to their Free World allies as the possessors of their own rich heritage. As a period style, it emerged out of a diverse array of transnational networks: colonial military and education systems, the US military entertainment complex, cultural diplomacy tours, international film festivals, coproduction agreements, and commercial distribution networks. It is thus historical evidence of Korea's growing enmeshment with the Free World. Han put the modern Korean woman at the center of this process. In centering his spectacles on female characters, Han extended the parameters of the modern Korean woman beyond the sexually liberated woman to include the physically powerful athlete, the professional performer, the competent businesswoman, and the international cultural emissary.

Conclusion

The 1950s came to an abrupt end in South Korea. Outraged by political corruption and authoritarian abuses, the student-led April Revolution of 1960 ousted Syngman Rhee from the presidency and introduced a thirteen-month period of democratic openness under Prime Minister Chang Myon. That interlude came to end, in turn, with a military coup on May 16, 1961, led by Park Chung-hee (1917–79), which ushered in three decades of rule by military generals. The Cold War cosmopolitan sensibility that Han Hyung-mo had captured on film came under immediate attack and quickly faded from public life. The postwar period was over.

"Austerity" became the new byword after 1960. Student activists campaigned for a "lifestyle reform" that targeted foreign goods and encouraged the consumption of domestic products in their place.[1] The military men who came in their wake took austerity to new levels and infused it with an aura of moral purity. "A week after their military revolt," *Time* magazine reported, "South Korea's generals were full of puritanical zeal. Khaki-clad troops with rifles patrolled the streets of Seoul, arresting jaywalkers and hauling prostitutes off to the cells. Caught dancing in a nightclub, 45 hapless young men and women were herded before stern military judges and sentenced to terms of up to a year in jail; when the police ran out of handcuffs, they lashed the prisoners together with ropes. To keep people at home nights, the authorities arrested 10,000 for violating the nightly curfew."[2] A. M. Rosenthal characterized the ruling junta as unified by the "conviction that everything that went before in South Korea's official life was slothful and decadent and the new way is the way of righteousness." The campaign against decadence—led by "men who prided themselves on leanness, hard muscles, fatigue uniforms"—was wide-ranging.[3] A new law banned the import of two hundred "extravagant" foreign consumer goods.[4] Smuggling and the black market were severely (if only temporarily) repressed and foreign goods were set ablaze in public spectacles that, like inversions of Han's films, attracted thousands of viewers. Condemned to the bonfires was the rich material culture of Han's mise-en-scène: "cosmetics, ornaments, Hong Kong brocade, alligator-skin handbags, Swiss watches, radios, phonographs and records, foreign-made suitings, American shirts and neckties, Japanese toys, imported liquor, American cigarettes and tobacco, imported cooking oils and seasonings."[5] Goods that couldn't be burned, such as machinery parts, were dumped into the sea. "American coffee vanished from Seoul tea rooms," noted *Stars and Stripes*, and "American whiskey, beer, and soft drinks also disappeared from bars and dance halls."[6] The generals targeted fashion as well, requiring civil servants to wear "austerity suits" and staging a public display of simple, functional dresses for women; *Yŏwŏn* dutifully covered the event with a photo spread.[7] A month after the coup, *Stars and Stripes* reported, "housewives are afraid to wear Western dresses or carry parasols no matter how hot the sun. Many have put away the high heel shoes which they had scrimped and saved so long to buy."[8] Park's rule was a reaction against the society and culture of the 1950s, and he set out to cleanse South Korea from what he regarded an excessive Western influence that had weakened the country.

Park launched a program of rapid industrial modernization and economic development that channeled the country's resources towards production for export, rather than for domestic consumption. For two decades the regime kept wages low, restricted imports, and maintained high consumer prices in an effort to ensure profits, and thus economic viability, for the emerging industrial conglomerates, or *chaebols*—which meant that few consumer goods were available. Park bolstered these economic policies with speeches extolling the spiritual and national rewards of frugality. According to Kyung-Koo Han, "government campaigns denounced extravagance and needless consumption as the enemy of the developing nation; production and thrift were praised as a source of national salvation." Under Park, writes Laura Nelson, "quotidian frugality was ideologically transformed into an act of popular patriotism."[9] Consumer culture in the 1960s and 1970s barely existed. Like labor rights and political opposition, it was repressed in Park's drive towards a fully industrialized modernity. Park's economic agenda was aided by increased regional integration. Having been educated in the colonial military system, Park lacked Rhee's visceral anti-Japanese sentiment and in 1965 he normalized relations with Japan, bringing South Korea's foreign policy into closer alignment with Washington's and opening up a stream of investment and aid that helped finance industrialization.[10]

The cultural nationalism and postcolonial traditionalism that had been one strain of 1950s intellectual life now became dominant, as Park deployed them to salve the social tensions that his policies generated.[11] Against the previous decade's feminized cosmopolitanism, Park promoted what Seungsook Moon has called an "androcentric" nationalism that rooted itself in Confucian gender ideology and elevated patriarchal "tradition" as the essence of Korean national identity.[12] Critical of Western liberalism—including individualism and democracy—and eager to legitimize both his presidency and his political repression, Park promoted traditional values of hard work, loyalty to the state, and self-sacrifice. He also sought to transform public culture. As Michael Robinson has noted, Park "mobilized the power of the state in the service of nationalist cultural construction."[13] Seeking to restore an "original, primordial" Korea untainted by foreignness, he created an Office of Cultural Properties and instituted the Cultural Asset Protection Law, which preserved heritage sites such as warrior tombs and shrines that gave form to militarist values and connected the nation to its mythological, male founders.[14] In his official cultural politics, Park was an anticosmopolitan: as Youngna Kim has written, Park's brand of nationalism advocated "a return to the past and an assertion of cultural identity uncontaminated by Euro-American culture."[15] This revivified patriarchal gender ideology affirmed women's essential identity as wives and mothers, even as young, mostly poor and rural women poured into the industrial workforce. The cosmopolitan woman-in-public lost her prominence as an icon of modernity within public culture, as she did in the pages of *Yŏwŏn*, which dramatically reduced its visual content and increased both the number of articles espousing traditional values and the number of photographs of men.

Cinema was not exempt from the changes sweeping through South Korean political, economic, and social life. The glamorous cosmopolitanism and women-centered narratives of Han Hyung-mo's films soon disappeared from theater screens. Women's pictures gave way to films centered on the experiences of men, including male melodramas that cast modernization as an experience of emasculation and status loss (*The Housemaid* [1960], *Aimless Bullet* [1961]); modernization comedies that narrated the displacement of old-style Confucian fathers by their younger, more modernized sons (*The Coachman* [1961], *A Petty Middle Manager* [1961], *Under the Sky of Seoul* [1961]); and more robustly "masculine" genres such as war pictures (*The Marines Who Never Returned* [1963] and Manchurian Westerns (*The Man with No Home* [1968]) that reduced women to secondary roles, often as victims. The affluent families of Han's films were supeseded by working-class heroes and heroines (*Tosuni: The Birth of Happiness* [1963]). Even Han, in a major departure from his earlier work, made a film about a struggling lower-middle-class couple duped out of their savings by a Korean American who entices them with tales of easy money made via black marketing (*A Dream of Fortune*, [1961]). Given the suppression of foreign goods, it is no surprise that the visually dense mise-en-scène of 1950s films gave way to a cinematic version of Park's politically inspired austerity. Gone were the European-style party dresses, the electric irons, the fresh bananas, the elaborate dance halls, and the miniature golf, replaced by a distinctly spartan mise-en-scène. Story lines often reinforced what Charles Kim has called the "optimistic developmentalism" of the Park regime, and more than one reached its happy ending by sending its female character to work in a factory (*Bloodline* [1963], *Tosuni*, *Coachman*).[16]

Lee Man-hee's *Black Hair* (1964) stands as an exemplary instance of 1960s filmmaking and a sharp contrast to Han Hyung-mo's aesthetic. Like Han, Lee was a commercially and critically successful director known for having a distinctive artistic vision, which he expressed primarily in war films and tragic male melodramas.[17] *Black Hair* is a gangster film that combines a highly stylized cinematography built around high- and low-angle shots with an "austerity style" mise-en-scène centered on shabby rooms and harsh, high-contrast lighting. While the male characters' actions drive the narrative, the female protagonist (Moon Jung-suk) suffers ceaseless degradation. A gangster's wife, she is raped, has her face slashed with a broken liquor bottle, becomes a prostitute, supports a heroin addict, is slapped by a customer disgusted by her looks, and nearly murdered by being pushed in front of a train. Once disfigured, her value is so diminished that she can be abused by men without compunction: "Since you can't fix your face," one man tells her, "you're better off dead." While the film could be interpreted as a critique of patriarchal ideology, it wallows in its depiction of a woman's entrapment within that ideology rather than imagining her escape from it. Moon's character is a far cry from the strong-willed and independent women she portrayed in Han's *A Jealousy* (1960) and *My Sister is a Hussy* (1961), who actively sought alternatives to what Helen Kim called "the typical unhappiness of Korean women." The film does have a transnationally inflected style, most notable in its rock-inflected soundtrack, visual nods towards expressionism and film noir, and bits of narrative business derived from Japanese *yakuza* films, including a finger-severing. But the optimism that characterized Han's films has been replaced with an air misery and violence, and the numerous acts of casual misogyny make clear that this is a man's world. It is a claustrophobic film, inward turning and dark, whose narrative unravels in a cramped basement gangster hangout, a warren of brothel rooms, narrow alleys, and cluttered hallways. One of the film's few open spaces is located beneath a hulking concrete structure—perhaps a highway overpass or a partially completed infrastructure project—that suggests the sacrifice of human needs to a brutal and barely understood project of modernization. Far from opening out to the larger world, the film offers a vision of contemporary South Korea as a dark, dangerous, and small place.

In his drive towards modernization, Park turned his attention to the film industry, and in 1962 the first Motion Picture Law was enacted, with subsequent revisions to follow. Park sought to stabilize, rationalize, and industrialize the work of filmmaking, while also protecting it from foreign competition and policing it ideologically. In addition to establishing and enforcing an import quota on foreign films, the law called for the centralization of filmmaking into large, highly capitalized companies and pushed out smaller production companies and independent producers. Han Hyung-mo was unable to make the transition to the new system, and his career declined in the early 1960s; he released his last film, *The Queen of Elegy*, a bio-pic of female singer Lee Mi-ja, in 1967. Shin Sang-ok's Shin Films was the only company able to satisfy the new criteria and register as a production company, and as a result it dominated filmmaking throughout the 1960s, a decade in which the quantity and overall quality of films increased substantially. By the early 1970s, however, the industry entered a sustained period of decline, strangled by regulation and losing market share to the imported pictures that dominated the box office despite their reduced numbers. After running into financial problem, Shin Productions was deregistered in 1975, and in 1978 Shin was "abducted" by North Korea and relaunched his career in Pyongyang.[18] The Golden Age of South Korean cinema, which began with *Chunhyang Story* in 1955 and *Madame Freedom* in 1956, was over by 1972.

After nearly three decades of stagnation, South Korea's commercial cinema began to rebound quite spectacularly in the late 1990s and has sustained its growth and quality for twenty years. This New Korean Cinema has significant similarities with Golden Age cinema, albeit ones not often recognized by South Korean filmmakers themselves.

Some of these similarities reside in the kinds of films being made. The most successful and respected directors working today—Bong Joon-ho, Park Chan-wook, Kim Ji-woon—are known as commercial auteurs: they make films with a coherent artistic vision that also manage to please audiences and succeed at the box office. Eschewing the rules of arthouse cinema, they make genre central to their creativity, playing with familiar conventions in unexpected ways and bringing new genres (science fiction films, monster movies) into the Korean industry. In this sense, they are heirs to Han Hyung-mo, who pioneered the well-made commercial film while introducing new genres and combining their conventions in fresh ways.

Other similarities can be found in the relationship to foreign cinemas, Hollywood in particular. Park Chan-wook, when asked recently about films that had influenced his creative vision, singled out works of classical Hollywood cinema such as Alfred Hitchcock's *Vertigo* (1958), which he described as "decisively influential," and *Johnny Guitar* (1954), which he identified as a film that he had enjoyed as a youth. When asked if earlier Korean films had been important to him, he mentioned only one, Kim Ki-young's *Woman of Fire 82* (1982). Bong Joon-ho, when asked the same question, responded in a similar fashion, waxing enthusiastic about postclassical Hollywood films such as *The French Connection* (1971) and *The Godfather Part II* (1974). He, too, singled out Kim Ki-young as the only postwar Korean director whose work he was familiar with, praising *The Housemaid* in particular.[19] Their responses make clear that Korean cinema has not experienced a linear form of development in which each generation of filmmakers absorbs the lessons of the previous one. Instead, that development has been marked by historical ruptures that cause filmmakers to look outside South Korea for inspiration.

The result, during the Golden Age and today, is a body of films marked by cultural and stylistic hybridity. As with their predecessors, the relationship of today's auteurs to foreign cinemas is both admiring and ambivalent, and in both periods directors have used what they learned from Hollywood to nudge American films out of their dominant position in South Korea's domestic film market.

Finally, the commercial auteurs of today have also sometimes drawn on the resources of the US military. Bong Joon-ho in particular has spoken of the importance of the US military's TV network to his film education. As a child he spent many hours watching American movies, cartoons, and TV shows on AFKN (Armed Forces Korea Network), which was aimed at American GIs but accessible to Korean viewers, who thus constituted an unintended "shadow audience" for its programming. Like many young people of his generation, Bong was enamored of American popular culture, and AFKN was his preferred means of accessing the mother lode of what he desired. AFKN was an American military institution that functioned, inadvertently, as a Korean educational institution, teaching young Koreans about film form and the world beyond their national borders. The network was an important part of Korea's film culture in the 1970s and 1980s, when this generation of filmmakers—routinely characterized as a cinephile generation with an omnivorous appetite for all kinds of films—was growing up. AFKN offered an escape from Korea's national media environment, which Bong saw as flooded with dreary propaganda and films of inferior quality and which was subject to strict censorship. AFKN thus provided its own kind of Cold War cosmopolitan culture, offering an education in genre via films from around the world.[20]

The hybridity of South Korean cinema in both the contemporary and the Golden Age periods has been well recognized by film scholars. This book has sought to deepen our understanding of that hybridity by revealing some of its historical and structural underpinnings. It has explored the connections between cinema and the Cold War, in part by showing how the project of incorporating South Korea into the transnational networks of Free Asia and the Free World had cultural consequences. The Cold War cosmopolitan aesthetic that loomed so large in 1950s film and public culture was one consequence—simultaneously intended and unintended—of that enmeshment.

INTRODUCTION

1. Quoted in Tony Rayns, "Poet of Time," *Sight and Sound* 5, no. 9 (September 1995): 13.

2. Steven Chung, *Split Screen Korea* (Minneapolis: University of Minnesota Press, 2014).

3. Lee Young-il, author of the first definitive history of South Korean cinema, omitted Han from his list of "key directors" of the 1950s, which consisted of Yu Hyun-mok, Shin Sang-ok, and Kim Ki-young. Lee Young-il and Choe Young-chol, *The History of Korean Cinema*, trans. Richard Lynn Greever (Seoul: Jimoondang Publishing Co., 1998), 118. More recently, Han was omitted from the twenty-two-volume series "Korean Film Directors" published by Seoul Selection and the Korean Film Council in 2007–9.

4. Jules David Prown, "Style as Evidence," in *Art as Evidence* (New Haven: Yale University Press, 2001), 52–68.

5. Prown, 52.

6. Charles R. Kim, *Youth for Nation* (Honolulu: University of Hawai'i Press, 2017). Kim Keong-il also explores the 1950s in his article "Modernity and Tradition in Everyday Life of the 1950s," *Seoul Journal of Korean Studies* 14 (2001): 263–97. In contrast, note the temporal gap between the titles of Brian Yecies and Ae-Gyung Shim's two books: *Korea's Occupied Cinemas, 1893–1948* (New York: Routledge, 2011) and *The Changing Face of Korean Cinema, 1960 to 2015* (New York: Routledge, 2016).

7. John Lie, *K-Pop* (University of California Press, 2015), 35.

8. See, for example, Kelly Y. Jeong, *Crisis of Gender and the Nation in Korean Literature and Cinema* (Lanham, MD: Lexington Books, 2011), 85, and Steven Chung, *Split Screen Korea* (Minneapolis: University of Minnesota Press, 2014), 70–71.

9. Sheldon Pollock et al., "Cosmopolitanisms," in *Cosmopolitanism*, ed. Carol A. Breckenridge, Sheldon Pollock, Homi K. Bhabha, and Dipesh Chakrabarty (Durham, NC: Duke University Press, 2002), 10.

10. Mica Nava, "Cosmopolitan Modernity," *Theory, Culture, and Society* 19, no. 1–2 (2002): 83, 93.

11. Antoinette Burton, *The Postcolonial Careers of Santha Rama Rau* (Durham, NC: Duke University Press, 2007), 32.

12. Christina Klein, *Cold War Orientalism* (Berkeley: University of California Press, 2013), 24–28.

13. Jessica Tan, "From Shanghai Modern to Cold War Hong Kong," paper delivered at the Association for Asian Studies annual conference, 2019; Andrew Rubin, *Archives of Authority* (Princeton, NJ: Princeton University Press, 2012), 47–73; Nicolai Volland, *Socialist Cosmopolitanism* (New York: Columbia University Press, 2017), 6; Laura E. Ruberto and Kristi M. Wilson, eds., *Italian Neorealism and Global Cinema* (Detroit: Wayne State University Press, 2007); Laura Harrington, "The Greatest Movie Never Made," unpublished manuscript; Jennifer Lindsay and M. H. T. Sutedja-Liem, eds., *Heirs to World Culture* (Leiden: Brill, 2012), 22; David B. Coplan, *In Township Tonight!* (1985; repr., Chicago: University of Chicago Press, 2008); Rob Nixon, *Homelands, Harlem and Hollywood* (New York: Routledge, 1994).

14. Kathleen McHugh and Nancy Abelmann, eds., *South Korean Golden Age Melodrama* (Detroit: Wayne State University Press, 2005); Theodore H. Hughes, *Literature and Film in Cold War South Korea* (New York: Columbia University Press, 2012), 95–97, 119–28; Han Namhee, "Desiring from a Distance," *Acta Koreana* 20, no. 2 (2017): 349–76; Kelly Y. Jeong, "The Spectacle of Affect," in *East Asian Transwar Popular Culture*, ed. Pei-yin Lee and Su Yun Kin, (Singapore: Palgrave Macmillan US, 2019), 235–60.

15. Kelly Y. Jeong, "The Quasi Patriarch," in *The Korean Popular Culture Reader*, ed. Kyung Hyun Kim and Youngmin Choe (Durham, NC: Duke University Press, 2014), 126–44; Chris Berry, "Scream and Scream Again," in *Seoul Searching*, ed. Frances Gateward (Albany: State University of New York Press, 2007), 99–114; Eunson Cho, "The Stray Bullet and the Crisis of Korean Masculinity," in *South Korean Golden Age Melodrama*, ed. Kathleen McHugh and Nancy Abelmann, 99–116.

16. Hye Seung Chung and David Scott Diffrient, *Movie Migrations* (New Brunswick, NJ: Rutgers University Press, 2015).

17. Chung, *Split Screen Korea.*

18. Charles K. Armstrong, "The Cultural Cold War in Korea, 1945–1950," *Journal of Asian Studies* 62, no. 1 (February 2003): 71–99; Tony Day and Maya H. T. Liem, *Cultures at War* (Ithaca, NY: Cornell University Press, 2010); Tuong Vu and Wasana Wongsurawat, eds., *Dynamics of the Cold War in Asia* (New York: Palgrave Macmillan, 2009); Lanjun Xu, "The Southern Film Corporation, Opera Films, and the PRC's Cultural Diplomacy in Cold War Asia, 1950s and 1960s," *Modern Chinese Literature and Culture* 29, no.1 (2017): 239–81; Gregg A. Brazinsky, *Winning the Third World* (Chapel Hill: University of North Carolina Press, 2017).

19. Sangjoon Lee, "The Emergence of the Asian Film Festival," in *The Oxford Handbook of Japanese Cinema*, ed. Daisuke Miyao (Oxford: Oxford University Press, 2014), 226–44; Michael Baskett, "Japan's Film Festival Diplomacy in Cold War Asia," *Velvet Light Trap* 73, no. 1 (2014): 4–18.

20. Jan Bardsley, *Women and Democracy in Cold War Japan* (London: Bloomsbury Academic, 2014); Mire Koikari, *Cold War Encounters in US-Occupied Okinawa* (Cambridge:

Cambridge University Press, 2015); Mire Koikari, *Pegagogy of Democracy* (Temple University Press: 2008).

21. Reinhold Wagnleitner and Elaine Tyler May, eds., *"Here, There, and Everywhere"* (Hanover, NH: University Press of New England, 2000).

22. Arjun Appadurai, *Modernity at Large* (Minneapolis: University of Minnesota Press, 1996).

23. Robert Palmer, *Deep Blues* (New York: Viking Press, 1981), quoted in Carlo Rotella, *Good with Their Hands* (Berkeley: University of California Press, 2002), 9. Rotella's chapter "Grittiness" (105–66) is a fine example of period style analysis applied to film and was an inspiration for this book.

1. POSTCOLONIAL, POSTWAR, COLD WAR

1. "Rail Yards at Seoul are Bombed," *Lodi News-Sentinel*, July 17, 1950; "Communiques Describing the Fighting in Korea," *New York Times*, July 22, 1950; Gil Yoon-hyeong, "U.S.'s Yongsan Bombing of 1950 Caused 1,587 Civilian Deaths," *Han'gyŏre*, July 16, 2010.

2. No In-taek oral history, *Han'guk yŏnghwa rŭl mal handa: 1950nyŏndae han'guk yŏnghwa* [To speak on Korean cinema: Korean cinema in the 1950s] (Seoul: Han'guk Yŏngsang Charyowŏn [Korean Film Archive]/Ichae, 2004), 104–8; Ma Yong-cheon oral history and No In-taek oral history, *1950nyŏndae han'guk yŏnghwa sŭt'ail* [Korean film style in the 1950s] (Seoul: Han'guk Yŏngsang Charyowŏn [Korean Film Archive, 2009), 3:187–89, 84.

3. Han Sang Kim, "Uneven Screens, Contested Identities" (PhD diss., Seoul National University, 2013), viii.

4. Kim Keong-il, "Modernity and Tradition in Everyday Life," *Seoul Journal of Korean Studies* 14 (2001): 263–97.

5. I borrow the concept of historical layering from Kim Brandt, who discusses "layered empire" in "Japan the Beautiful," in *The Affect of Difference*, ed. Christopher P. Hanscom and Dennis Washburn (Honolulu: University of Hawai'i Press, 2016), 261–85.

6. Carter J. Eckert, *Offspring of Empire* (Seattle: University of Washington Press, 2014), 128, 236; Michael E. Robinson, *Korea's Twentieth-Century Odyssey* (Honolulu: University of Hawai'i Press, 2007), 76–99.

7. Steven Hugh Lee, "Development without Democracy," in *Transformations in Twentieth Century Korea*, ed. Yun-shik Chang and Steven Hugh Lee (London: Routledge, 2006), 161; Charles R. Kim, *Youth for Nation* (Honolulu: University of Hawai'i Press, 2017), 9

8. Bruce Cumings, *Korea's Place in the Sun* (New York: W. W. Norton, 2005), 223–24.

9. Steven Chung, *Split Screen Korea* (Minneapolis: University of Minnesota Press, 2014), 11; Eckert, *Offspring of Empire*, 253–58; Kim, *Youth for Nation*, 9.

10. Gregg A. Brazinsky, *Nation Building in South Korea* (Chapel Hill: University of North Carolina Press, 2007), 32.

11. John P. Lewis, *Reconstruction and Development in South Korea, an International Committee Report* (Washington: National Planning Association, 1955), 17; Kim, *Youth for Nation,* 36, 33; United States Information Agency, *Korea: In the Common Interest* (Washington: Distributed by U.S. Information Service, 1955), 32; David C. Cole and Princeton N. Lyman, *Korean Development* (Cambridge, MA: Harvard University Press, 1971), 22; Charles

R. Kim, "Unlikely Revolutionaries" (PhD diss., Columbia University, 2007), 107–9; Robinson, *Korea's Twentieth-Century Odyssey*, 124.

12. Park Wan-so, quoted in Kim, "Modernity and Tradition," 272.

13. Cumings, *Korea's Place in the Sun*, 303.

14. Andrei Lankov, *The Dawn of Modern Korea* (Seoul: EunHaeng NaMu, 2007), 80.

15. Ninety-five percent of foreign economic aid in the years 1953–62 came from the United States; the remaining 5 percent came from UNKRA, which received two-thirds of its contributions from the United States. Edward S. Mason, *The Economic and Social Modernization of the Republic of Korea* (Cambridge, MA: Harvard University Press, 1980), 189, 182; Brazinsky, *Nation Building in South Korea*, 33.

16. Cumings, *Korea's Place in the Sun*, 302.

17. James Sang Chi, "Teaching Korea" (PhD diss., University of California, Berkeley, 2008).

18. Donald Stone Macdonald, *U.S.-Korean Relations from Liberation to Self-Reliance* (Boulder: Westview Press, 1991), 260; Katarzyna J. Cwiertka, *Cuisine, Colonialism, and Cold War* (London: Reaktion Books, 2012), 121; Lankov, *Dawn of Modern Korea*, 258.

19. Kim, "Modernity and Tradition."

20. Brazinsky, *Nation Building in South Korea*, 4, 116.

21. Mark Gayn, "What Price Rhee? Profile of a Despot," *Nation*, March 13, 1954, quoted in John Lie, *Han Unbound* (Stanford: Stanford University Press, 1998), 32.

22. Lewis, *Reconstruction and Development*, 33.

23. Gregory Henderson, *Korea, the Politics of the Vortex* (Cambridge, MA: Harvard University Press, 1968), 169.

24. Lee, "Development without Democracy," 159.

25. NSC 48.5, *Foreign Relations of the United States* (hereafter *FRUS*), *1951, Asia and the Pacific*, vol. 6, pt. 1 (Washington: U.S. Government Printing Office, 1977), 44. NSC 48.1, in *United States-Vietnam Relations, 1945–1967*, United States Department of Defense (Washington: U.S. Government Printing Office, 1971), 227.

26. U.S. Department of Veterans Affairs, "America's Wars," accessed April 7, 2018, www.va.gov/opa/publications/factsheets/fs_americas_wars.pdf; Kwang Sub Kwak, "The US-ROK Alliance, 1953–2004" (PhD diss., Southern Illinois University Carbondale, 2006), 90, 86, 87; Brazinsky, *Nation Building in South Korea*, 30.

27. Bill Smothers, "1958–1966, Korea," www.flickr.com/photos/smothers/albums/72157594443648942/page1, accessed September 18, 2019; Whitney Taejin Hwang, "Borderland Intimacies" (PhD diss., University of California, Berkeley, 2010), 54–60.

28. Sang-Dawn Lee, *Big Brother, Little Brother* (Lanham, MD: Lexington Books, 2002).

29. Odd Arne Westad, *The Global Cold War* (Cambridge: Cambridge University Press, 2005), 92.

30. Nils Gilman, *Mandarins of the Future* (Baltimore: Johns Hopkins University Press, 2003), 5, 10, 16.

31. Chang Yun-Shik, "Conclusion," in *Transformations in Twentieth Century Korea*, ed. Chang Yun-Shik and Steven Hugh Lee (Abingdon: Routledge, 2006), 365.

32. Gi-wook Shin and Michael Edson Robinson, *Colonial Modernity in Korea* (Cambridge, MA: Harvard University Press, 1999).

33. Kim, *Youth for Nation*, 11–12; Lewis, *Reconstruction and Development*, 33.

34. Wolsan Liem, "Telling the 'Truth' to Koreans" (PhD diss., New York University, 2010), 205; Chungmoo Choi, "Nationalism and Construction of Gender in Korea," in *Dangerous Women*, ed. Elaine H. Kim and Chungmoo Choi (New York: Routledge, 1998), 10–11; Hwang, "Borderland Intimacies," 106–8.

35. Eunsun Cho, "Transnational Modernity, National Identity, and South Korean Melodrama (1945–1960s)" (PhD diss., University of Southern California, 2006), 81–82.

36. NSC 48.5, *FRUS*, 43; NSC 48.1, *United States-Vietnam Relations*, 250.

37. Sergei Y. Shenin, *America's Helping Hand* (New York: Nova Science Publishers, 2005), 47–58.

38. Victor Cha, *Powerplay* (Princeton: Princeton University Press, 2016), 3.

39. Maria Hohn and Seungsook Moon, "Introduction," in *Over There*, ed. Hohn and Moon (Durham, NC: Duke University Press, 2010), 8.

40. Macdonald, *U.S.-Korean Relations*, 111–12; NSC 5514, *FRUS 1955–1957, Korea*, vol. 13, pt. 2 (Washington: U.S. Government Printing Office, 1993), 47.

41. Lee, "Development without Democracy," 160; Macdonald, *U.S.-Korean Relations*, 283; Cha, *Powerplay*, 12.

42. Geoff Jones, *Northwest Airlines* (Charleston, SC: Arcadia Publishing, 2005).

43. Charles Kraus, "'The Danger Is Two-Fold,'" *International History Review*, 39, no. 2 (2017): 256–73.

44. Press release, March 16, 1954, box P-14, file Asian People's Anti-Communist League Chinhae Conf. 1st, The Asia Foundation Records, Hoover Institution Archives (hereafter TAF).

45. Junghyun Park, "Frustrated Alignment," *International Journal of Asian Studies* 12, no. 2 (2015): 217–37; Victor Hsu, "Pacific Destinies" (MA thesis, Columbia University, 2016), 29, www.academia.edu/31528465; "Asian Peoples' Anti-Communist Conference, Minutes of the Opening Session," June 15, 1954, History and Public Policy Program Digital Archive, B-387-039, Documents Related to the Asian Anti-Communist League Conference, Papers Related to Treaty-Making and International Conferences, Syngman Rhee Institute, Yonsei University (hereafter APACL-SRI), http://digitalarchive.wilsoncenter.org/document/118328; "A Brief History of the Asian Peoples' Anti-Communist League," March 5, 1956, APACL-SRI, http://digitalarchive.wilsoncenter.org/document/118348; "Asian Peoples' Anti-Communist League Third Annual Conference: Speeches and Reports," March 27, 1957, APACL-SRI, http://digitalarchive.wilsoncenter.org/document/118361.

46. Nicholas John Cull, *The Cold War and the United States Information Agency* (Cambridge: Cambridge University Press, 2008).

47. NSC 48.2, *FRUS, 1949*, vol. 7, *The Far East and Australasia, Part 2* (Washington: U.S Government Printing Office, 1977), 1220; Memorandum for CIO, September 28, 1951, DTPILLAR, vol. 1_0040, Special Collections, Nazi War Crimes Disclosure Act, Central Intelligence Agency Electronic Reading Room (hereafter CIA).

48. Richard L. Walker, "The Developing Role of Cultural Diplomacy in Asia," in *Issues and Conflict*, ed. George L. Anderson (Lawrence: University of Kansas Press, 1959), 43–62; Gregg A. Brazinsky, *Winning the Third World* (Chapel Hill: University of North Carolina Press, 2017), 132–33. On China's waging of the cultural Cold War, see Lanjun Xu, "The Southern Film Corporation, Opera Films, and PRC's Cultural Diplomacy in Cold War Asia, 1950s and 1960s," *Modern Chinese Literature and Culture* 29, no. 1 (Spring 2017): 239–82.

49. USIS began in 1941 as a small group of overseas information offices; the Office of War Information, created in 1942, expanded USIS across Europe, Africa, and East Asia. Cull, *The Cold War and the United States Information Agency*, 14–16.

50. Kenneth Alan Osgood, *Total Cold War* (Lawrence: University of Kansas Press, 2006), 5, 215, 291, 292, 316.

51. Osgood, 303.

52. Summary of Board of Trustees Meeting, February 11, 1955, Robert Blum Papers, box 1, folder 10, Manuscripts and Archives, Yale University Library (hereafter RBP).

53. Memorandum for Director of Central Intelligence, October 8, 1965, DTPILLAR, vol. 3_0014, CIA; Memorandum, Committee for a Free Asia, September 27, 1951, DTPILLAR, vol.1_0040, CIA; Committee on Foreign Relations, United States Senate, *The Asia Foundation: Past, Present, and Future* (Washington: U.S. Government Printing Office, 1983), 1.

54. Hugh Wilford, *The Mighty Wurlitzer* (Cambridge, MA: Harvard University Press, 2008), 28.

55. Blum was educated at the University of California and the Graduate Institute of International Studies in Geneva, Switzerland, and taught international relations at Yale. During World War II he served in the OSS, where he oversaw counterintelligence operations in Europe. After the war he served as assistant to Secretary of Defense James Forrestal; joined the Economic Cooperation Administration (ECA) missions in France and Indochina; became chief of the U.S. Special Technical and Economic Mission to Cambodia, Laos, and Vietnam; and worked for the Mutual Security Agency as the deputy for economic affairs in Europe. By August 1953, he had taken over the presidency of the Asia Foundation, in which capacity he served until 1962. "Robert Blum," Asia Foundation, http://asiafoundation.org/people/robert-blum/, accessed May 20, 2019; Emma Best, "Robert Blum, the Spy Who Shaped the World," MuckRock.com, August 17, 2017, www.muckrock.com/news/archives/2017/aug/17/robert-blum-spy-who-shaped-world-part-1/, and August 18, 2017, www.muckrock.com/news/archives/2017/aug/18/robert-blum-spy-who-shaped-world-part-2/; Letter to Field Representatives, August 25, 1953, box 1, folder 8, RBP.

56. Robert Blum, "The Work of the Asia Foundation," *Pacific Affairs* 29, no. 1 (March 1956): 48 (a 1965 program summary lists offices in Afghanistan, Pakistan, India, Sri Lanka, Thailand, Malaysia, Laos, Cambodia, Vietnam, Hong Kong, Taiwan, Philippines, Korea, and Japan); Memorandum for Director of Central Intelligence, October 8, 1965, DTPILLAR, vol. 3_0014, CIA.

57. Summary of Board of Trustees Meeting, February 11, 1955, box 1, folder 10, RBP.

58. Summary Request for Renewal, September 9, 1957, DTPILLAR, vol. 2_0009, CIA.

59. Second Revised Administrative Plan, August 1963, DTPILLAR, vol. 3_0022, CIA; Project Outline, March 1955, DTPILLAR, vol. 2_0029, CIA; Request for CA Project Approval, 1964, DTPILLAR, vol. 3_0018, CIA.

60. Korea Program Budget 1958/59, box P-59, file Korea Budget 1957/58, TAF.

61. Meredith Sumpter and John Rieger, eds., *A Partner for Change: Six Decades of the Asia Foundation in Korea, 1954–2017* (Seoul: The Asia Foundation, 2017), 43–47.

62. Korea Program Budget, 1958/59, box P-59, file Korea Budget 1957/58, TAF; The Asia Foundation Plan for Korea, October 20, 1955, box P-61, file General-1954/55- Korea-Program, TAF.

63. International Conferences, box P-59, file Budget-AP's & Allocations, etc. 1955/56-Korea-Administrative, TAF; Proposed Budget for 1957–58, February 1, 1957, box P-59, file Budget (Master) 1957–1958 Korea Administration, TAF; NSC 5514, 47.

64. Osgood, *Total Cold War*, 305; Brazinsky, *Winning the Third World*, 134–39, 67; Brazinsky, *Nation Building in South Korea*, 71–100. Private organizations involved in US-ROK exchanges included: American-Korean Foundation, Korean Association of Voluntary Agencies, Rockefeller Foundation, MIT, University of Minnesota, Southern Methodist University, and Harvard-Yenching Institute; see, Liem, "Telling the Truth to Koreans," 207–73; Macdonald, *U.S.-Korean Relations*, 284; Kim, *Youth for Nation*, 70.

2. COLD WAR COSMOPOLITAN FEMINISM

1. Pak Ch'a Min-jŏng, *Chosŏn ŭi k'wiŏ* [Chosŏn's queers] (Seoul: Hyŏnsil Munhwa Yŏn'gu, 2018); Gregory M. Pflugfelder, "'S' is for Sisters," in *Gendering Modern Japanese History*, ed. Barbara Molony and Kathleen Uno (Cambridge, MA: Harvard University Press, 2005), 133–90.

2. Personal communication, Kyeong-sook Seo.

3. Park Seong-ho and Kim Seong-min, *A Jealousy* scripts, Korean Film Archive. Some of these scenes and lines of dialogue were flagged in the censorship script, yet retained in the shooting script; because the film itself has been lost, it is impossible to know for sure what exactly appeared in the final version.

4. Han's film was not entirely alone in depicting alternative relationships among women. The 1950s saw the flourishing of female *gukgeuk* theater, in which women actors playing male and female roles enacted romantic story lines onstage, formed intense bonds with each other offstage, and prompted passionate attachments from female audience members. While these plays told traditional stories, the cross-dressing actors expanded the gender repertoire by representing, and living, new forms of love between women. *Girl Princes* (dir. Kim Hye-jeong, 2012); Louise Benson, "The Korean Artist Exploring the Vanished Drag Act of the All-Female Opera," *Elephant*, September 17, 2018, https://elephant.art/siren-eun-young-jung/.

5. Cho Haejoang, "Living with Conflicting Subjectivities," in *Under Construction*, ed. Laurel Kendall (Honolulu: University of Hawai'i Press, 2002), 188; Nils Gilman, *Mandarins of the Future* (Baltimore: Johns Hopkins University Press, 2003), 31, 10.

6. Uchang Kim, "Confucianism, Democracy, and the Individual in Korean Modernization," in *Transformations in Twentieth Century Korea*, ed. Yun-Shik Chang and Steven Hugh Lee, (London: Routledge, 2006), 230.

7. Stevi Jackson, Jieyu Liu, and Juhyun Woo, introduction to *East Asian Sexualities*, ed. Jackson, Liu, and Woo (London: Zed, 2008), 16.

8. John Duncan, "The Problematic Modernity of Confucianism," in *Korean Society*, ed. Charles K. Armstrong (London: Routledge, 2006); Michael Robinson, "Perceptions of

Confucianism in Twentieth-Century Korea," in *The East Asian Region*, ed. Gilbert Rozman (Princeton: Princeton University Press, 1991), 204–25.

9. Jackson et al., *East Asian Sexualities*, 9.

10. Martina Deuchler, *The Confucian Transformation of Korea* (Cambridge, MA: Harvard University Press, 1992); Hyaeweol Choi, "Wise Mother, Good Wife," *Journal of Korean Studies* 14, no. 1 (2009): 1–34.

11. Hyun Jeong Min, "New Women and Modern Girls," *Journal of Historical Research in Marketing* 5, no. 4 (2013): 512.

12. Alys Eve Weinbaum et al., eds., *The Modern Girl around the World* (Durham, NC: Duke University Press, 2008); Youngna Kim, *20th Century Korean Art* (London: Laurence King, 2005), 64–87; Yeon Shim Chung, "The Modern Girl (*Modeon Geol*) as a Contested Symbol in Colonial Korea," in *Visualizing Beauty*, ed. Aida Yuen Wong (Hong Kong: Hong Kong University Press, 2012); Hyaeweol Choi, *Gender and Mission Encounters in Korea* (Berkeley: University of California Press, 2009); Theodore Jun Yoo, *The Politics of Gender in Colonial Korea* (Berkeley: University of California Press, 2008); Hyaeweol Choi, ed., *New Women in Colonial Korea* (New York: Routledge, 2012).

13. Lee Im Ha, "The Korean War and the Role of Women," *Review of Korean Studies* 9, no. 2 (2006): 89–110.

14. Yi Im-ha, *Yŏsŏng, chŏnjaeng ŭl nŏmŏ irŏsŏda* [Women, rise above war] (Seoul: Sŏhae Munjip, 2004), Table 3-1, 90, cited in Sujin Han, "Gender at Work: Working Women in Postwar South Korea, 1953–1960" (MA thesis, Harvard University, 2018), 21–22.

15. Kim Hyun Sun, "Life and Work of Korean War Widows during the 1950s," *Review of Korean Studies* 12, no. 4 (2009): 88.

16. Han, "Gender at Work," 28.

17. Census data cited in Han, 27; Letter from Choong Yang Choung, February 22, 1960, Committee of Correspondence files, Sophia Smith Collection, Smith College Archive (hereafter SSC).

18. Han, "Gender at Work," 14, 40; Kim, "Life and Work of Korean War Widows."

19. Seungsook Moon, "Regulating Desire, Managing Empire," in *Over There*, ed. Maria Hohn and Seungsook Moon (Durham, NC: Duke University Press, 2010), 54.

20. Katharine H. S. Moon, *Sex among Allies* (New York: Columbia University Press, 1997); Ji-Yeon Yuh, *Beyond the Shadow of Camptown* (New York: New York University Press, 2002); Grace M. Cho, *Haunting the Korean Diaspora* (Minneapolis: University of Minnesota Press, 2008).

21. Moon, "Regulating Desire, Managing Empire," 54; Whitney Taejin Hwang, "Borderland Intimacies" (PhD diss., University of California, Berkeley, 2010), 89–92.

22. Chungmoo Choi, "Nationalism and Construction of Gender in Korea," in *Dangerous Women*, ed. Elaine H. Kim and Chungmoo Choi (New York: Routledge, 1998), 17–40.

23. Kenneth Alan Osgood, *Total Cold War* (Lawrence: University of Kansas, 2006): 261–62.

24. Osgood, 255, 259–60; Laura A. Belmonte, *Selling the American Way* (Philadelphia: University of Pennsylvania Press, 2008), 136–58.

25. Data is for fiscal year 1961, when the national population was 25.77 million: Han Sang Kim, "Uneven Screens, Contested Identities" (PhD diss., Seoul National University, 2013), 210.

26. Foreign Service Despatch No. 324, June 15, 1955, RG 59, box 2246, file 511.95B3/5–255, National Archives and Records Administration (hereafter NARA).

27. Foreign Service Despatch No. 360, May 8, 1956, RG 59, box 2246, file: 511.95B3/1–356, NARA; Letter from Choong Yang Choung, Committee of Correspondence papers, SSC.

28. Memorandum for the record, April 30, 1952, DTPILLAR, vol. 2_0048, CIA; Memorandum for Deputy Director of Central Intelligence, April 14, 1952, DTPILLAR, vol. 2_0029, CIA; Letter to Board of Trustees, October 22, 1954, Robert Blum Papers, box 1, folder 9, Manuscripts and Archives, Yale University Library (hereafter RBP).

29. Memorandum from Mary C. Walker, January 9, 1956, box P-59, file Lee Mrs. Yi Haeng; Monthly Report to the Board of Trustees, May 1955, box 1, folder 10, RBP; Letter from Mary C. Walker to Helen Kim, June 12, 1956, and Letter from Mary C. Walker to the President, May 14, 1956, box P-59, file Chang Mrs. Grace & Chu Mrs. Grace K., all TAF.

30. Jaqueline Van Voris, *The Committee of Correspondence* (Northampton, MA: Sophia Smith Collection, Smith College, n.d.), 32, 56; Helen Laville, "The Committee of Correspondence," *Intelligence and National Security* 12, no. 1 (1997): 104–21; Hugh Wilford, *The Mighty Wurlitzer* (Cambridge: Harvard University Press, 2008), 149–66; Letter from Choong-ryang Chung to Anne B. Crolius, August 2, 1965, Committee of Correspondence papers, SSC.

31. Mire Koikari, *Pedagogy of Democracy* (Philadelphia: Temple University Press: 2008): 5. See also Susan J. Pharr, "The Politics of Women's Rights," in *Policy and Planning during the Allied Occupation of Japan*, ed. Robert E. Ward and Sakamoto Yoshikazu (Honolulu: University of Hawai'i Press, 1987), 221–52.

32. Hyaeweol Choi, *Gender and Mission Encounters in Korea*, 38, 43, 175. See also Theodore Jun Yoo, *The Politics of Gender in Colonial Korea*, 60, 79, 85–87. On the persistence of this tension in contemporary cinema, see Chungmoo Choi, "The Politics of Gender, Aestheticism, and Cultural Nationalism in *Sopyonje* and *The Genealogy*," in *Im Kwon-Taek*, ed. David E. James and Kyung Hyun Kim (Detroit: Wayne State University Press, 2002), 107–33.

33. Choi, "Nationalism and Construction of Gender," 14.

34. Theodore Jun Yoo has written about the legacies of colonial-era New Women: "Though the impact of Korea's modern women on patriarchal structures and ideas may have been negligible during the colonial period, their articulation of a new vision of Korean womanhood and the controversies they ignited by their personal example laid the foundations for an eventual reevaluation of gender and identity in Korea." Yoo, *Politics of Gender*, 199.

35. Helen Kim, *Grace Sufficient* (Nashville: The Upper Room, 1964): 30.

36. AhRan Ellie Bae, "Helen Kim as New Woman and Collaborator," *International Journal of Korean History* 22, no. 1 (February 2017): 120n30. On slavery and bondage in first-wave American feminist rhetoric, see Jill Lepore, *The Secret History of Wonder Woman* (New York: Vintage Books, 2015), 101.

37. Hyaeweol Choi, *Gender and Mission Encounters in Korea*, 92; Kim, *Grace Sufficient*, 38, 40, 43.

38. Yoo, *Politics of Gender*, 76; Lee Bae-yong, *Women in Korean History* (Seoul: Ewha Womans University Press, 2008), 253.

39. Yung-hee Kim, "In Quest of Modern Womanhood," *Korean Studies* 37 (2013): 44–78; Lee, *Women in Korean History*, 256; Kim, *Grace Sufficient*, 116, 198; Chun Chae Ok, "Kim,

Helen," in *Biographical Dictionary of Christian Missions*, ed. Gerald Anderson (New York: Macmillan Reference USA, 1998), 364.

40. Helen Kim, "Kim, Helen: Response," in *Ramon Magsaysay Foundation Award (1963)*, www.rmaward.asia/awardees/kim-helen/, accessed May 8, 2019; Kim quoted in Lee, *Women in Korean History*, 252; Kim, *Grace Sufficient*, 27–28.

41. Sonia Reid Strawn, *Where There Is No Path* (Seoul: Korean Legal Aid Center for Family Relations, 1988), 28–29; In Kyung Kim Pini, "A New God, a New Education, and a New Generation of Women" (PhD diss., Columbia University, 2002), 187.

42. Lillian Faderman, *Surpassing the Love of Men* (New York: Morrow, 1981).

43. Pini, "A New God," 118, 238; Kim Hwallan [Helen Kim], "Na ŭi saurok 1: injŏng kiptŏn pŏt ko Yi Chŏngae" [A record of my friends and teachers], *Kyŏnghyang sinmun*, October 11, 14, and 16, 1967, 5; Kim Hwallan, *Kŭ pit sok ŭi chagŭn saengmyŏng* [A small life within that light], 2nd ed. (Seoul: Ihwa Yŏja Taehakkyo Ch'ulp'anbu, 1999), 149.

44. Insook Kwon, "Feminists Navigating the Shoals of Nationalism and Collaboration," *Frontiers: A Journal of Women Studies* 27, no. 1 (2006): 39–66; Bae, "Helen Kim as New Woman and Collaborator," 107–35; Choi, *Gender and Mission Encounters in Korea*, 153.

45. Kim, *Grace Sufficient*, 171–72.

46. Lee, *Women in Korean History*, 257; "About Korea Times: Times History," www.koreatimes.co.kr/www2/common/timeshistory.asp, accessed May 8, 2019; Helen Kim, quoted in Lee, "Korean War and the Role of Women," 97.

47. Letter, Robert Blum to Helen Kim, n.d., box P-61, file General, Trip to Korea, R. Blum, TAF; "Mary Walker Mag Hasse—1911–2007," *FAWCO Forum* (Winter 2007–8), 2, www.fawco.org/about/publications/the-forum.

48. Approved Project form, September 19, 1956, box P-59, file Budget (Allocations & APs) 1956/57, Korea, Administration, TAF; Heather A. Willoughby, ed., *Footsteps across the Frontier* (Seoul: Ewha Womans University Press), 104; Korea Program Budget 1958/59, box P-59, file Korea Budget 1957/58, TAF.

49. "A Korean Educator," *Free World* 9, no. 2 (1960): 13; Gregg A. Brazinsky, *Winning the Third World* (Chapel Hill: University of North Carolina Press, 2017), 147.

50. Incoming Telegram, January 28, 1954, RG 59, box 2541, file unlabeled, NARA.

51. Committee of Correspondence papers, SSC.

52. Documents on Asian Peoples' Anti-Communist Conference, June 15, 1954, History and Public Policy Program Digital Archive, B-390-001, Documents Related to the Asian Anti-Communist League Conference, Papers Related to Treaty-Making and International Conferences, Syngman Rhee Institute, Yonsei University, http://digitalarchive.wilsoncenter.org/document/118345 (hereafter APACL-SRI).

53. Memorandum, Mary Walker to the President, September 21, 1956, box P-16, file Asia Anti-Communist Youth & Student Conf., Korea, TAF.

54. Letter from Chin Hang Kong, July 15, 1956, box P-16, file: Asia Anti-Communist Youth & Student Conf., Korea, TAF; Reports of the Committees, Asian Youth & Students Anti-Communist Conference, October 16, 1956, http://digitalarchive.wilsoncenter.org/document/118360, APACL-SRI.

55. Quoted in Haesook Kim, "Lee Tai-young (1914–1998)," in *Women in the World's Legal Professions*, ed. Ulrike Schultz and Gisela Shaw (Oxford: Hart Publishing, 2003), 457.

56. Strawn, *Where There Is No Path*, 62.

57. Kim, "Lee Tai-young (1914–1998)," 462, 463.

58. Strawn, *Where There Is No Path*, 186, 85, 88. The *Kyŏnghyang sinmun* and *Tonga ilbo* newspapers together published about forty articles by or about Lee Tai-young between 1950 and 1959.

59. Lee quoted in Strawn, *Where There Is No Path*, 23; Hyaeweol Choi, "Debating the Korean New Woman," *Asian Studies Review* 36 (March 2012): 61, 62, 65.

60. Henrik Ibsen, *A Doll's House*, trans. Henrietta Frances Lord (New York: D. Appleton, 1894), 141.

61. Hŏ To-san, *Han'guk ŭi ŏmŏni Yi T'ae-yŏng* [The mother of Korea Lee Tai-young], rev. ed. (Seoul: Chayu Chisŏngsa, 1999), 88.

62. Lee Tai-young, "Elevation of Korean Women's Rights," *Korea Journal* 4, no. 2 (February 1, 1964): 5, 8.

63. Strawn, *Where There Is No Path*, 99–100.

64. Yoo, *Politics of Gender*, 82–83.

65. Lee, "Elevation of Korean Women's Rights," 6–7.

66. Program Budget, 1957–58, box P-59, file Korea Budget 1957/58, TAF; Memorandum to the President, April 18, 1957, box P-61, file Media, Paper, General, Korea, Program, TAF.

67. Erin Cho, "Caught in Confucius' Shadow," *Columbia Journal of Asian Law* 12, no. 2 (1998): 146; Hŏ To-san, *Han'guk ŭi ŏmŏni Yi T'ae-yŏng*, 293–99, 286.

68. Letter from Hyung Cho, November 15, 1965, Committee of Correspondence papers, SSC.

69. Molony et al., *Gender in Modern East Asia*, 197; Lee, "Elevation of Korean Women's Rights," 7–8; Cho, "Caught in Confucius' Shadow," 148–50; Sanghui Nam, "The Women's Movement and the Transformation of the Family Law in South Korea," *European Journal of East Asian Studies* 9, no. 1 (2010): 67–86.

70. Lee, "Elevation of Korean Women's Rights," 8–9; Ki-young Shin, "The Politics of the Family Law Reform Movement in Contemporary Korea," *Journal of Korean Studies* 11, no. 1 (2006): 100.

71. Shin, "The Politics of the Family Law Reform Movement," 94–98; Nam, "Women's Movement," 70; Hŏ To-san, *Han'guk ŭi ŏmŏni Yi T'ae-yŏng*, 187.

72. Charles R. Kim, *Youth for Nation* (Honolulu: University of Hawai'i Press, 2017), 43, 45.

73. Partha Chatterjee, *The Nation and Its Fragments* (Princeton: Princeton University Press, 1993), 6, 9, 134.

74. For a summary of the changes, see Cho, "Caught in Confucius' Shadow," 148–50.

75. Lee, "Elevation of Korean Women's Rights," 9.

76. Jid Lee, *To Kill a Tiger* (New York: Overlook Press, 2010).

77. Quoted in Sun, "Life and Work of Korean War Widows," 100.

78. As it did in Japan: Christine R. Yano, "Diva Misora Hibari as Spectacle of Postwar Japan's Modernity," in *Vamping the Stage*, ed. Andrew N. Weintraub and Bart Barendregt (Honolulu: University of Hawai'i Press, 2017), 127–43.

3. PUBLIC CULTURE

1. "Capturing an Era with a New Audacity," DVD video extra, *Hyperbolae of Youth* (Seoul: Korean Film Archive; Tae Won Entertainment, 2006).

2. Kim Kee-duk oral history, in *1950nyŏndae han'guk yŏnghwa sŭt'ail* [Korean film style in the 1950s] (Seoul: Han'guk Yŏngsang Charyowŏn [Korean Film Archive], 2009) (hereafter *KFS 1950s*), 2:51, 115–16; No In-taek oral history, in *KFS 1950s*, 3:28–32.

3. Quoted in Oh Young-sook, "Realistic but Popular," in *Han Hyung-mo: The Alchemist of Popular Genres* (Seoul: Korean Film Archive, 2008), 57.

4. Jonathan Sanfilippo, "Uijjeongbu Restaurant Owners Take Pride in Army Base Stew," Yonhap News Agency, June 24, 2012, http://english.yonhapnews.co.kr/search1/2603000000.html?cid = AEN20120622000100315; Katarzyna J. Cwiertka, *Cuisine, Colonialism, and Cold War* (London: Reaktion Books, 2012), 121.

5. Michel de Certeau, *The Practice of Everyday Life* (Berkeley: University of California Press, 1984); Miriam Hansen, "The Mass Production of the Senses," *Modernism/Modernity* 6, no. 2 (1999): 59–77; Henry Jenkins, *Textual Poachers* (New York: Routledge, 1992).

6. Poshek Fu, "The Politics of Entertainment," paper presented at Harvard University Fairbanks Center, Cambridge, Massachusetts, March 2015; Patrick Iber, "Anti-Communist Entrepreneurs and the Origins of the Cultural Cold War in Latin America," in *De-Centering Cold War History*, ed. Jadwiga E. Pieper Mooney and Fabio Lanza (New York: Routledge, 2013), 167–86.

7. Arjun Appadurai and Carol A. Breckenridge, "Public Modernity in India," in *Consuming Modernity*, ed. Carol A. Breckenridge (Minneapolis: University of Minnesota Press, 1995), 10.

8. Steven Chung, *Split Screen Korea* (Minneapolis: University of Minnesota Press, 2014), 229–230n11.

9. Kim Keong-il, "Modernity and Tradition in Everyday Life," *Seoul Journal of Korean Studies* 14 (2001): 263–97; Charles R. Kim, *Youth for Nation* (Honolulu: University of Hawai'i Press, 2017); Chung, *Split Screen Korea*, 47–81.

10. Robert Blum, "Introduction: The Flow of People and Ideas," Robert Blum Papers, box 1, folder 7, Manuscripts and Archives, Yale University Library (hereafter RBP); George Lerski, "Programming in Plastic, Performing, and Literary Arts," May 18, 1962, box 1, folder 7, RBP; Korea Program Budget, 1958/59, box P-59, file Korea Budget 1957/58, The Asia Foundation Records, Hoover Institution Archives (hereafter TAF).

11. Lerski, "Programming in Plastic, Performing, and Literary Arts," RBP; Korea Program Budget, 1958/59, box P-59, file Korea Budget 1957/58, TAF; Blum, "Introduction," RBP. For more on TAF's cultural program, see Christina Klein, "Cold War Cosmopolitanism," *Journal of Korean Studies* 22, no. 2 (Fall 2017): 281–316.

12. Lerski, "Programming in Plastic, Performing, and Literary Arts," RBP; "About Us, Highlights," The Asia Foundation, Korea, http://asiafoundation.or.kr/wordpress/en/highlights/, accessed June 13, 2018; "Case Study #6: The Committee's Cultural Program in the Republic of Korea," box P-61, file General-1952/53-Korea-Program, TAF.

13. "The Asia Foundation Plan for Korea," October 20, 1955, box P-61, file General-1954/55-Korea-Program, TAF.

14. "Monthly Report to the Board of Trustees," July 1955, box 1, folder 10, RBP.

15. Lerski, "Programming in Plastic, Performing, and Literary Arts," RBP; "Case Study #6," TAF.

16. "Asia Foundation Plan for Korea," TAF.

17. Box P-148, file O Young-jin-Korea-Individual, TAF; Box P-61, file Media-Publications-Literature & Arts Weekly-Oh Yong-jin, TAF.

18. Memorandum from Cho Tong-jae, November 26, 1954, file Media-Publishers-General (reports)-Korea-Program, box P-61, TAF; Memorandum to the President, April 18, 1957, file Media-Paper-General-Korea-Program, box P-61, TAF; Memorandum from Cho Tong-jae, December 11, 1957, file Media-Paper-General-Korea-Program, box P-61, TAF; Korea Program Budget 1958/59, Communications; Program Budget, 1957–58, file Korea Budget 1957/58, box: P-59, TAF.

19. Gregg A. Brazinsky, *Nation Building in South Korea* (Chapel Hill: University of North Carolina Press, 2007), 51, 50–59. Several other US agencies also supported print culture by supplying currency for paper imports, restoring a paper manufacturing plant, providing direct subsidies to publications, and sending journalists to the United States.

20. Kim, *Youth for Nation*, 23.

21. Letter, Mary Walker to Kim Myung Yup, October 10, 1956; Letter of Agreement, April 29, 1957, box P-61, file Media-Publications-General-Korea-Program; Memorandum to the President, April 18, 1957, box P-61, file Media-Paper-General-Korea-Program; Letter of Agreement, January 8, 1959, box P-151, file Media-Publications-General-Korea-Program; Box P-148, file: Kim Miss Kwi-hyung (Yo Won Magazine)-Korea-Individual, all TAF.

22. Letter, Pokyu Hong Shin to Miss Raymond, January 20, 1957, Committee of Correspondence papers, Sophia Smith Collection and Smith College Archive (hereafter SSC).

23. Han'guk Yŏsŏng Munhak Hakhoe, *"Yŏwŏn" yŏn'gu* [Research on "Yowon"] (Seoul: Kukhak Charyowŏn, 2008), 58n5, 312.

24. Chung, *Split Screen Korea*, 221n30; Minutes of meeting with government officials and a top member of national federation of cultural organizations held on November 18, 1954, box P-61, file Media-Publishers-General (reports)-Korea-Program, TAF.

25. Kim, "Modernity and Tradition"; Eunsun Cho, "Transnational Modernity, National Identity, and South Korean Melodrama (1945–1960s)" (PhD diss., University of Southern California, 2006).

26. Rita Felski, *The Gender of Modernity* (Cambridge: Harvard University Press, 1995); Patricia Uberoi, "The Diaspora Comes Home," *Contributions to Indian Sociology* 32, no. 2 (1998): 305–36; Lila Abu-Lughod, ed., *Remaking Women* (Princeton: Princeton University Press, 1998); Deborah L. Parsons, *Streetwalking the Metropolis* (Oxford: Oxford University Press, 2000); Andrew N. Weintraub and Bart A. Barendregt, eds., *Vamping the Stage* (Honolulu: University of Hawai'i Press, 2017).

27. *Yŏwŏn*, October, November, December 1955; Hyaeweol Choi, *Gender and Mission Encounters in Korea* (Berkeley: University of California Press, 2009), 104.

28. *Yŏwŏn*, October, November, December 1955, May, June, October, November, December 1958.

29. *Yŏwŏn*, February, March, April, May, June, July, August, September 1958.

30. Quoted in Sujin Han, "Gender at Work" (MA thesis, Harvard University, 2018), 2.

31. *Yŏwŏn*, beginning May 1959.

32. Kim, *Youth for Nation*, 53; Han'guk Yŏsŏng Munhak Hakhoe, *"Yŏwŏn" yŏn'gu*.

33. *Yŏwŏn*, February–December 1961.

34. Christina Klein, *Cold War Orientalism* (Berkeley: University of California Press, 2003), 100–42.

35. On the transnationally mobile Asian woman as an emblem of modernity, see Brian Hu, "Star Discourse and the Cosmopolitan Chinese," *Journal of Chinese Cinemas* 4, no. 3 (2010): 183–209; and Alisa Freedman, Laura Miller, and Christine R. Yano, eds., *Modern Girls on the Go* (Stanford: Stanford University Press, 2013).

36. National awards include: National Film Director's Award (1957); Seoul Culture Award (*Hyperbolae of Youth*, 1956); Daejong Award for editing (*My Sister Is a Hussy*, 1961). Ministry of Education "excellent Korean films": *Madame Freedom* (1956), *The Pure Love* (1957), *Because I Love You* (1958), *A Female Boss* (1959). International award: Sixth Asian Film Festival Choreography Award (*Because I Love You*, 1958).

37. Lee Sang-yong, forward to *Han Hyung-mo: The Alchemist of Popular Genres. Madame Freedom* was exported to Hong Kong in 1957: "Yŏnghwa Chayubuin tŭng tae Hyanghang such'ul ŭl ch'ujin" [*Madame Freedom* and *Holiday in Seoul* are to be exported to Hong Kong], *Chosŏn ilbo*, February 10, 1957, 2, in *Sinmun kisa ro pon Han'guk yŏnghwa, 1945–1957* [Korean films in newspapers, 1945–1957], ed. Han'guk Yŏngsang Charyowŏn [Korean Film Archive] (Seoul: Konggan kwa Saramdŭl, 2004) (hereafter *KFN, 1945–57*). *Because I Love You* was exported to Hong Kong and Southeast Asia in 1959–60; see chapter 6.

38. No In-taek oral history, in *Han'guk yŏnghwa rŭl mal handa: 1950nyŏndae han'guk yŏnghwa* [To speak on Korean Cinema: Korean cinema in the 1950s] (Seoul: Han'guk Yŏngsang Charyowŏn/Ichae [Korean Film Archive]/Ichae, 2004) (hereafter *TSKC 1950s*), 109–11; Cho Junhyoung, "Han Hyung-mo's Movies and Life," DVD booklet, *Hand of Fate* (Seoul: Korean Film Archive, 2005); Kim Chong-wŏn et al., *Han'guk yŏnghwa kamdok sajŏn* [Dictionary of Korean film directors] (Seoul: Kukhak Charyowŏn, 2004), 654–55.

39. Brian Yecies and Ae-Gyung Shim, *Korea's Occupied Cinemas, 1893–1948* (New York: Routledge, 2011), 91.

40. Chung Chong-hwa, "The Technical Advancement of Cinematic Style in Korean Cinema," in *Han Hyung-mo: The Alchemist of Popular Genres*, 98n12; "Han Hyung-mo," DVD booklet, *Hyperbolae of Youth* (Seoul: Korean Film Archive, 2006), 28–29.

41. Cho Hye-jung, "Film Technology in Disarray," in *Korean Cinema*, ed. Kim Mee hyun (Seoul: Communications Books/KOFIC, 2007), 114.

42. Bruce Cumings, *The Origins of the Korean War* (Princeton: Princeton University Press, 1990), 2:259–67.

43. "Capturing an Era with a New Audacity."

44. Korean Film Archive, *Traces of Korean Cinema, 1945–1959* (Seoul: Munhak Sasangsa, 2003), 149–52; Han Hyung-mo, "Yŏnghwa kwŏn ŭl changbi wa kyohwan han nal" [The days when we exchanged film rights with equipment], in *Kun yŏnghwa sasim-nyŏnsa* [40 years of military filmmaking] (Seoul: Kukkun Hongbo Kwalliso, 1992), 57–62; "An Assault on Justice," in *Han Hyung-mo: The Alchemist of Popular Genres*, 135.

45. Memorandum from Charles Tanner, December 3, 1953, box P-148, file Oh Young-jin-Korea-Individual, TAF; "Capturing an Era with a New Audacity."

46. John W. Miller, "The Korean Motion Picture Industry," February 16, 1955, box P-60, file Media-Audio-Visual-Motion Pictures-General-1956-Korea-Program, TAF.

47. John W. Miller, "Paper on the Korean Motion Picture Industry," December 29, 1956, box P-60, file Media: Audio-Visual-Films-John Miller-Korea-Program, TAF. Sangjoon Lee

has published an edited version of this report: "On John Miller's 'The Korean Film Industry,'" *Journal of Japanese and Korean Cinema* 7, no. 2 (2015): 95–112.

48. John W. Miller, "Oegugini pon han'guk yŏnghwa" [Korean films seen by a foreigner], *Yŏwŏn*, October 1956, 34.

49. Lee Young-il and Choe Young-chol, *The History of Korean Cinema*, trans. Richard Lynn Greever (Seoul: Jimoondang Publishing Corp., 1988, 1998), 108, 263; Chungkang Kim, "South Korean Golden-Age Comedy Film" (PhD diss., University of Illinois at Urbana-Champaign, 2010), 41.

50. "President Lauds Domestic Films," *Korean Republic*, January 3, 1959, 1; T. S. Kim, "Moviedom Continues to Grow," *Korean Republic*, August 22, 1959, 5.

51. The *Korean Republic* reported that in 1958 Korea exported fourteen films: seven to Hong Kong, three to Taiwan, three to the United States, and one to Japan. "Domestic Movie Industry Enjoys Unprecedented Boom," *Korean Republic*, August [n.d.], 1959, in Theodore Richard Conant collection, C. V. Starr East Asian Library, Columbia University (hereafter TCC).

52. Lee Young-il and Choe Young-chol, *History of Korean Cinema*, 263, 286; Minutes of the Meeting of the Board of Directors of the KMPCA, January 31, 1962, box P-280, file Media-Audio-Visual-Films-Korean Motion Picture Cultural Association KMPCA II-Reports-Korea-Program, TAF; Kim Mee hyun, ed., *Korean Cinema* (Seoul: Communications Books/KOFIC, 2007), 179.

53. Miller, "Korean Motion Picture Industry" (1955); Miller, Preface to "Paper on the Korean Motion Picture Industry" (1956).

54. "Kisses, Communism Taboo in ROK Films," *Stars and Stripes* (Pacific Edition), January 16, 1955, 9; Jinsoo An, *Parameters of Disavowal* (Oakland: University of California Press, 2018), 35–40; "Fun Facts About Korean Cinema," Korean Film Archive, https://eng.koreafilm.or.kr/kmdb/trivia/funfacts/BC_0000005076?page =, accessed May 13, 2019; Miller, "Paper on the Korean Motion Picture Industry" (1956).

55. "P'allinŭn yŏnghwa & anp'allinŭn yŏnghwa" [Films that sell and films that don't], *Han'guk ilbo*, April 7, 1957, 6, in *KFN, 1945–57*.

56. Yi Hyo-in and Park Ji-Yeon, *A History of Korean Cinema from Liberation through the 1960s* (Seoul: Korean Film Archive, 2005), 56; Miller, "Paper on the Korean Motion Picture Industry" (1956); Letter, Oh Young-jin to Charles Tanner, March 22, 1954, box P-148, file Oh Young-jin-Korea-Individual, TAF; Korean Film Archive, *Traces of Korean Cinema*, 188, 212.

57. Miller, "Paper on the Korean Motion Picture Industry" (1956); Kim, "South Korean Golden-Age Comedy," 42. In 1955 Rhee established an annual import quota of fifty foreign films, but it was not enforced; in 1957, for example, 145 films were imported. "Private Export and Import Program for the First Half of Fiscal Year 55/56," *Monthly Statistical Review* 79 (June 1955): 62; Yi Hyo-in and Park Ji-Yeon, *A History of Korean Cinema*, 61, 114; *Han'guk yŏnghwa charyo p'yŏllam (ch'och'anggi-1976-yŏn)* [A guide to sources on South Korean film: beginnings to 1976], comp. Kim Kang-yun et al. (Seoul: Yŏnghwa chinhŭng kongsa, 1977), Table 7I, 82–108.

58. *Madame Freedom* in 1957, *The Pure Love* in 1958, *Because I Love You* in 1959, *A Female Boss* in 1960: "5 kae chakp'umŭl sŏnjŏng" [5 excellent domestic films selected for preferential treatment], *Kyŏnghyang sinmun*, October 15, 1957, 2, in *KFN, 1945–57*; "Usu kuksan yŏnghwa 19-il sisang" [Outstanding Korean films awarded on the 19th], *Seoul sinmun*,

July 21, 1958, 3; "*Chonggak* tŭng 5 p'yŏn sŏnjŏng" [Five films selected including *The Bell Tower*], *Han'guk ilbo*, July 4, 1959, 3; "Usu yŏnghwa 5 p'yŏn sŏnjŏng" [Five outstanding films selected], *Tonga ilbo*, September 7, 1960, 3, in *Sinmun kisa ro pon Han'guk yŏnghwa, 1958–1961* [Korean Films in Newspapers, 1958–1961], ed. Han'guk Yŏngsang Charyowŏn (Seoul: Konggan kwa Saramdŭl, 2005).

59. A reliable system for tallying admissions did not exist during this period. "Madame Freedom," KMDb, www.kmdb.or.kr/eng/db/kor/detail/movie/K/00297, accessed May 13, 2019; "Kwan'gaeng tongwŏn suesŏ pon kungnaeoe yŏnghwa pesŭt'ŭt'en" [Top 10 Korean and foreign movies in terms of audience], *Seoul sinmun*, December 29, 1957, in *KFN, 1945–57*.

60. No In-taek oral history, in *TSKC 1950s*, 102; Kim Kee-duk oral history, 2:106; Lee Young-il and Choe Young-chol, *History of Korean Cinema*, 295.

61. Miller, "Paper on the Korean Motion Picture Industry" (1956).

62. Yu Hyun-mok, "1957-nyŏn ŭi pansŏng" [Reflecting back on 1957], *Tonga ilbo*, December 15, 1957, 4; No In-taek oral history, in *TSKC 1950s*, 104; No In-taek oral history, in *KFS 1950s*, 3:99–100.

63. "Sŭt'adio t'ambang: Samsŏng Sŭt'adio p'yŏn" [Visiting the studio: Samsung studio], *Han'guk ilbo*, November 3, 1957, 5, in *KFN, 1945–57*.

64. Lee Young-il and Choe Young-chol, *History of Korean Cinema*, 305; Kim Mee hyun, ed., *Korean Cinema*, 153–54; Miller, "Paper on the Korean Motion Picture Industry" (1956); I Kyŏng-sun, *Soriŭi ch'angjo* [The creation of sound] (Seoul: Hanjinch'ulp'ansa, 1996), 133.

65. Charles K. Armstrong, "The Cultural Cold War in Korea, 1945–1950," *Journal of Asian Studies* 62, no. 1 (February 2003): 71–99; Han Sang Kim. "Uneven Screens, Contested Identities" (PhD diss., Seoul National University, 2013), 46–47; Lee Young-il and Choe Young-chol, *History of Korean Cinema*, 96; Korean Film Archive, *Traces of Korean Cinema, 1945–1959*, 143.

66. Korean Film Archive, *Traces of Korean Cinema, 1945–1959*, 155; Han Sang Kim, "Cold War and the Contested Identity Formation of Korean Filmmakers," *Inter-Asia Cultural Studies* 14, no. 4 (2013): 551–63.

67. Lee Hyung-pyo worked closely with UNKRA filmmaker Theodore Conant before moving into the commercial film industry as a cinematographer, producer, and director; see TCC.

68. Lee Young-il and Choe Young-chol, *History of Korean Cinema*, 101; Korean Film Archive, *Traces of Korean Cinema, 1945–1959*, 204; Han Hyung-mo, "Yŏnghwa kwŏn ŭl changbi wa kyohwan han nal," 57–62, 109.

69. Memorandum for R&D's Record, April 18, 1957, box P-60, file Media-Audio-Visual-Films-John Miller-Korea-Program, TAF; AP-8599, Exchange for Korean Motion Picture Cultural Association, March 1959, box P-280, file Media-Audio-Visual-Films-Korean Motion Picture Cultural Association KMPCA II-Reports-Korea-Program, TAF; "New Movie Studio Dedicated," United Nations archive, www.flickr.com/photos/70217867@ N07/7889480720/in/album-72157631309490876/, accessed June 27, 2019; "Modern Film Processing Center Inaugurated in Seoul Ceremony," *Korean Republic*, January 16, 1959, TCC; "Audio-Visual: Reaching Millions through Sight and Sound," *Progress 1959*, 67–68, TCC; Miller, "Paper on the Korean Motion Picture Industry" (1956).

70. "Motion Pictures in Korea," *Voice of Korea* 13, no. 219, 10 August 1956, 1–2, box P-60, file Media: Audio-Visual-Films-John Miller-Korea-Program, TAF; Miller, "Paper on the Korean Motion Picture Industry" (1956).

71. Ma Yong-cheon oral history, in *TSKC 1950s*, 138. UNKRA filmmaker Theodore Conant, for instance, gave Shin Sang-ok sound recording equipment and helped him access theaters on US military bases so that he could check the quality of his films on a big screen; personal anecdote by Conant at "The Korean War and Its Aftermath: Cinematic Memories from the Theodore Conant Collection," Columbia University, March 39, 2012.

72. Miller, "Paper on the Korean Motion Picture Industry" (1956); Robert A. Haines, "Military Theater Equipment Modernization," *Journal of the SMPTE* 65 (April 1956): 222–26; Jeon Jo-myeong oral history, in *Han'guk yŏnghwa rŭl mal handa: Han'guk yŏnghwa ŭi rŭnesangsŭ 1* [To speak on Korean cinema: The renaissance of Korean cinema 1] (Seoul: Han'guk Yŏngsang Charyowŏn [Korean Film Archive], 2005), 364.

73. Personnel in Tokyo Office, February 26, 1953, box P-20, file Budget (Allocations and Aps)-1952/53-Japan-Administration, TAF; Staff Biography: John Miller, July 8, 1952, box P-39, file Miller, John (Films)-US and Int.-Individual, TAF; Miller, "Oegugini pon han'guk yŏnghwa," 31.

74. Stewart had a background in propaganda/information. He worked in the OWI during World War II as the chief of psychological warfare for the China theater, and in Korea from 1947 to 1950, first as director of public information for the USAMGIK during the occupation period and subsequently as public affairs officer for the US embassy and director of USIS. In 1951 he joined the Asia Foundation, where he became director of operations. Charles Burress, "James L. Stewart—Longtime Liaison to Asia," *SFGate*, January 29, 2006, www.sfgate.com/bayarea/article/James-L-Stewart-longtime-liaison-to-Asia-2523343.php.

75. Tanner worked with Stewart at the USIS in Seoul as a film editor, then served as motion picture officer with the USIS in Manila (1950–52) and Tokyo (1952–53). He joined the Asia Foundation's San Francisco office in 1953 and served as liaison to the Hollywood community until 1955. CovenantPlayers.org, http://covenantplayers.org/about-us/, accessed June 19, 2018.

76. "Noel Busch, Author and Correspondent for Life Magazine," *New York Times*, September 11, 1985, D27.

77. "Biographical/Historical Note," Rockefeller Foundation archives, http://dimes.rockarch.org/FA668/biohist, accessed June 19, 2018.

78. Tina Mai Chen, "International Film Circuits and Global Imaginaries in the People's Republic of China, 1949–57," *Journal of Chinese Cinemas* 3, no. 2 (2009): 149–61; Lanjun Xu, "The Southern Film Corporation, Opera Films, and the PRC's Cultural Diplomacy in Cold War Asia, 1950s and 1960s," *Modern Chinese Literature and Culture* 29, no.1 (Spring 2017): 239–81; Gregg A. Brazinsky, *Winning the Third World* (Chapel Hill: University of North Carolina Press, 2017), 132–65.

79. Stephen Teo, *Hong Kong Cinema* (London: British Film Institute, 1997), 14–23; Jing Jing Chang, *Screening Communities* (Hong Kong University Press, 2019), 49.

80. John Miller, "Recommendation for a CFA-Japan Motion Picture Program," September 11, 1953, box P-9, file Tokyo-TV-Movies-1953, TAF. See also Christopher Howard, "Re-Orienting Japanese Cinema," *Historical Journal of Film, Radio, and Television* 36, no. 4 (2016): 529–47.

81. John Miller, "Recommendations for a CFA-Japan Motion Picture Program," TAF; Keiko McDonald, *Reading a Japanese Film* (Honolulu: University of Hawai'i Press, 2006), 8.

82. Miller, "Paper on the Korean Motion Picture Industry" (1956); Jay Dresser, "Final Report on Motion Picture Research on Southeast Asia," July 14, 1953, box P-9, file Cascade Pictures-General Correspondence, TAF.

83. Charles Leary, "The Most Careful Arrangements for a Careful Fiction," *Inter-Asia Cultural Studies* 13, no. 4 (2012): 554; Testimony of Eugene W. Castle before the Subcommittee on Appropriations, United States Senate, 84th Congress, 1205, box P-9, file Rivers, TAF; Cable, July 1, 1953, box P-9, file Tokyo-TV-Movies-1953, TAF.

84. Memorandum from Hong Kong representative, July 11, 1959, box P-171, file Media-Audio Visual-Movies-Asia Pictures, 1958–59-Hong Kong-Program, TAF; Sangjoon Lee, "Creating an Anti-Communist Motion Picture Producers' Network in Asia." *Historical Journal of Film, Radio and Television* 37, no. 3 (2016): 517–38; Memorandum, Motion Picture Project, July 28, 1953, box P-58, file Media-Audio-Visual-Movies-Asia Pictures Correspondence-Hong Kong-Program, TAF; Memorandum from John F. Sullivan, February 3, 1959, box P-171, file Media-Audio Visual-Movies-Asia Pictures, 1958–59-Hong Kong-Program 1959, TAF.

85. Memorandum from John Miller, June 3, 1953, box P-9, file Tokyo-TV-Movies-1953, TAF; Memorandum from Noel F. Busch, May 5, 1954, box P-9, file Writer Project (Japan), TAF.

86. The festival launched as the Southeast Asian Film Festival in 1954 and was renamed the Asian Film Festival in 1957 and the Asia-Pacific Film Festival in 1982. Sangjoon Lee, "The Emergence of the Asian Film Festival," in *The Oxford Handbook of Japanese Cinema*, ed. Daisuke Miyao (Oxford: Oxford University Press, 2014), 226–44; The Southeast Asian Film Festival, box P-18, file Film Festival-FMPPSEA-3rd-Hong Kong-1956-Korea-802-Conferences, TAF; John Miller, "Recommendations for a CFA-Japan Motion Picture Program," TAF; "Film Men's Messages to First South East Asian Movie Festival," *Rengo Tsushin (Rengo News)*, March 29, 1954, box P-14, file Film Festival-FMPPSEA-1st Japan, 1954-US & Int.-Conferences, TAF; Michael Baskett, "Japan's Film Festival Diplomacy in Cold War Asia," *The Velvet Light Trap* 73, no. 1 (2014): 4–18.

87. John Miller, "Report and Evaluation of Recent Meetings with the Motion Picture Producers of Japan," June 3, 1953, box P-9, file Tokyo-TV-Movies-1953, TAF; Letter, John Miller to Irving Maas, April 9, 1954, box P-14, file Film Festival-FMPPSEA-1st Japan-1954-US & Int.-Conferences, TAF; Charles Tanner, "Motion Picture Program for Korea," October 20, 1953, box P-60, File Media-Audio-Visual-Motion Pictures-General-1956-Korea-Program, TAF; C. M. Tanner, "Visit of Oh Yong Jin, President of North Korean Cultural Association," December 3, 1953, box P-148, file Oh Young-jin-Korea-Individual, TAF; Philip G. Rowe, "Miller Mission to Korea," December 19, 1954, box P-60, file Media-Audio-Visual-Motion Pictures-General-1956-Korea-Program, TAF; "Minutes of Meeting with Government Officials and a Top Member of National Federation of Cultural Organizations," TAF. For an overview of the KMPCA project, see Lee, "Creating an Anti-Communist Motion Picture Producer's Network."

88. Miller, "Paper on the Korean Motion Picture Industry" (1956).

89. "Assistance to the Korean Motion Picture Industry," n.d., box P-59, file Budget-AP's & Allocations, etc. 1955/56-Korea-Administrative, TAF; Summary Report on KMPCA,

March 15, 1966, box P-280, file Media-Audio-Visual-Films-Korean Motion Picture Cultural Association KMPCA II-Reports-Korea-Program, TAF; Miller, "Paper on the Korean Motion Picture Industry" (1956); Miller, "Korean Motion Picture Industry" (1955).

90. Robert Blum, "Notes on Visit to Korea, October 29–November 2, 1956," box P-61, file General-1956-Korea-Program, TAF; John Miller, "Report on the Development of the Korean Motion Picture Cultural Association, Inc.," August 7, 1956, box P-60, file Media-Audio-Visual-Films-John Miller-Korea-Program, TAF; John Miller, "Articles of Incorporation and Membership of the Korean Motion Picture Cultural Association," July 11, 1956, box P-60, file Media-Audio-Visual-Films-John Miller-Korea-Program, TAF. Members of the Board included: chairman, Chang Ki-young, president of Han'guk Ilbo Publishing Co.; managing director, Lee Jae-myung, film producer; auditor, Lee Tai-hi, professor of Law at Ewha; members: Kim Kwan-soo, film producer; Lee Byong-il, film director; Lee Yong-min, cameraman-director; Lee Chol-hyok, film producer; Oh Yong-jin, critic and screenwriter; Min Byong-do, banker.

91. Miller, "Paper on the Korean Motion Picture Industry" (1956); KMPCA Monthly Activity Report, November 5, 1956, box P-60, file Media-Audio-Visual-KMPCA-Reports 1956 & 1957-Korea 803 Program, TAF; Cho Tong-jae, Korea Motion Picture Cultural Association, March 15, 1966, box P-280, file Media-Audio-Visual-Films-Korean Motion Picture Cultural Association KMPCA II-Reports-Korea-Program, TAF; KMPCA Monthly Activity Report, September 9, 1957, box P-60, File Media-Audio-Visual-KMPCA-Reports 1956 & 1957-Korea 803 Program, TAF; KMPCA Field Report, June 1957, box P-280, file Media-Audio-Visual-Films-Korean Motion Picture Cultural Association KMPCA I-Korea-Program, TAF; Cho Tong-jae, "General Convention of KMPCA Members," May 9, 1958, box P-280, file Media-Audio-Visual-Films-Korean Motion Picture Cultural Association KMPCA-Reports-Korea-Program, TAF.

92. Jack E. James, "Award from Korean Motion Picture Producers Association," October 26, 1959, box P-280, file Media-Audio-Visual-Films-Korean Motion Picture Cultural Association KMPCA II-Reports-Korea-Program, TAF.

93. Memorandum, KMPCA, March 7, 1957, box P-280, file Media-Audio-Visual-Films-Korean Motion Picture Cultural Association KMPCA I-Korea Program, TAF; "Approved Project No. 611," May 31, 1957, box P-59, file Korea Budget 1957/58, AFR. (4261); "Letter of Agreement," April 10, 1958, file O Young-jin-Korea-Individual, TAF; Letter from Masaichi Nagata, May 8, 1956, box P-18, file Film Festival FMPPSEA-3rd Hong Kong 1956-Korea 802 (Conferences), TAF.

94. 1957: *The Wedding Day* (1956), *Idiot Adada* (1956). 1958: *Hyperbolae of Youth* (1956), *Forever with You* (1958). 1959: *Because I Love You* (1958), *The Love Marriage* (1958), *The Seizure of Life* (1958). 1960: *Romance Papa* (1960).

95. Lee Young-il and Choe Young-chol, *History of Korean Cinema*, 140; "Domestic Movie Industry Enjoys Unprecedented Boom," *Korean Republic*, August [n.d.], 1959, TCC.

96. Han Hyung-mo, "Yŏnghwa chejak ŭi chase" [Attitude towards film production], *Chosŏn ilbo*, July 9, 1956, 4, in *KFN, 1945–57*.

97. Letter, Jack E. James to Chang Key Young, May 17, 1962, and Letter of Agreement, May 25, 1962, box P-280, file Media-Audio-Visual-Films-Korean Motion Picture Cultural Association KMPCA II-Reports-Korea-Program, TAF; Cho Tong-jae, "Summary Report on KMPCA," March 15, 1966, box P-280, file Media-Audio-Visual-Films-Korean

Motion Picture Cultural Association KMPCA II-Reports-Korea-Program, TAF. It is difficult to find hard data documenting the extent of KMPCA's impact on the industry. Extant records show that thirty-five separate companies rented equipment, studio space, and the laboratory during fourteen months in 1957–58. Monthly Activity Reports, box P-60, file Media-Audio-Visual-KMPCA-Reports 1956 & 1957-Korea 803 Program, and file Media-Audio-Visual-Films-Korean Motion Picture Cultural Association KMPCA-Reports-Korea-Program, TAF. This represents 70 percent of the total number of film companies estimated to be in operation in 1958. Chung, *Split Screen Korea*, 37.

98. Meredith Sumpter, ed., *Partner for Change: 50 Years of the Asia Foundation in Korea, 1954-2004* (Seoul: Asia Foundation, 2004), 22. Not all members of Korea's film community, it appears, were quite so sanguine about TAF's interventions in Korea's public culture. The foundation makes a rather unflattering appearance in Gwon Yeong-sun's film *Drifting Island* (1960), about a café hostess accused of murdering a man. At her trial she testifies about the incident, which begins when the victim, a suave hustler, tells a friend in the publishing business that he knows "a foreigner in the AS Foundation" who can get him access to paper supplies and thus make him "the king of publishers." When the foreigner, Mr. Smith (played by a balding actor who resembled both Robert Blum and John Miller), shows up at the café the next day, the hustler makes a deal to trade sexual access to the café hostess, whom he passes off as his girlfriend, for "the newsprint that comes through the AS Foundation Association." Mr. Smith, eyeing the hostess, agrees to the exchange. When the hostess realizes what is happening, she throws a heavy vase at the hustler and kills him instantly. Convicted at trial and sent to prison, she shares a cell with an illegal trader in US dollars and a woman who boasts bitterly of having been sexually pursued by "big-nosed American soldiers." Director Gwon, unlike the KMPCA board members, seems to have regarded the Asia Foundation not as the benefactor of Korean cinema but as one more group of Americans ready to exploit vulnerable Koreans for their own self-interest.

99. Chung Chong-hwa, "Director Introduction," *Madame Freedom* DVD booklet; KMPCA Activity Report, August 1957, box P-60, file Media-Audio-Visual-KMPCA-Reports 1956 & 1957-Korea 803 Program, TAF.

100. Cho Junhyoung, "The Front Line of Korean Popular Movies in the 1950s," in *Han Hyung-mo: The Alchemist of Popular Genres*, 34–35.

101. No In-taek oral history, in *TSKC 1950s*, 109–11; Cho Junhyoung, "Front Line of Korean Popular Movies," 34.

102. Lee Hyung-pyo oral history, in *KFS 1950s*, 1:296–97; "Capturing an Era with a New Audacity"; Kim Kee-duk oral history, 2:101, 140–41, 148; "Han Hyung-mo," in DVD booklet, *Hyperbolae of Youth*, 31.

103. Oh Young-sook, "Realistic but Popular," 48.

104. Oh Young-sook, 57–58; John Lie, *Han Unbound* (Stanford, CA: Stanford University Press, 1998), 36; Cho Junhyoung, "Front Line of Korean Popular Movies," 39.

4. THE APRÈS GIRL: CHARACTER AND PLOT

1. On the changing attitudes towards family organization and arranged marriage in this period, see: "Students Conduct Survey on Changing Family System," *Korea Journal* 2, no. 10 (October 1962): 37; Kim Doo-hun, "Historical Review of Korean Family Life," and Choe

Jae-sok, "Process of Change in Korean Family Life," *Korea Journal* 3, no. 10 (October 1963): 4–15, 32.

2. Mica Nava, *Visceral Cosmopolitanism* (Oxford: Berg, 2007); Mica Nava, "Cosmopolitan Modernity," *Theory, Culture, and Society* 19, no. 1–2 (2002): 82.

3. Steven Chung, *Split Screen Korea* (Minneapolis: University of Minnesota Press, 2014): 54; Kim Sunah, "The Dilemma of Modern Times," in *Han Hyung-Mo: The Alchemist of Popular Genres* (Seoul: Korean Film Archive, 2008), 70.

4. A *gye* is an informal, household-based savings club / loan association that is often run by married women; unique to Korea, *gyes* were common during the economically insecure postwar years, with about 38 percent of Seoul's household participating in one. Bank of Korea, "Estimation and Analysis of National Savings in Korea, Part II," *Monthly Statistical Review* 15, no. 9 (September 1961): 41.

5. Charles R. Kim, *Youth for Nation* (Honolulu: University of Hawai'i Press, 2018), 50–53.

6. Nava, "Cosmopolitan Modernity," 86, 83, 90, 93.

7. Charles R. Kim, "The April 19th Generation and the Start of Postcolonial History in South Korea," *Review of Korean Studies* 12, no. 3 (September 2009): 74; Charles R. Kim, *Youth for Nation*, 49; Letter from Y. H. Chu of International Feature Service, December 14, 1954, box P-61, file Media-Publishers-General-(reports)-Korea-Program, The Asia Foundation Records, Hoover Institution Archives.

8. Yu Jiyŏng, *Chŏnhu mellodŭrama yŏnghwae chaehyŏndoen "ap'ŭregŏl"* ["Après girls" represented in post–Korean War melodrama films] (PhD diss., Yonsei University, 2008); Choe Mijin, "1950nyŏndae shinmunsosŏre nat'anan ap'ŭre kŏl" [Après-girls in newspaper novels of the 1950s], *Taejungsŏsayŏn'gu* 13, no. 2 (2007): 119–53; Chungmoo Choi, "Nationalism and Construction of Gender in Korea," in *Dangerous Women*, ed. Elaine H. Kim and Chungmoo Choi (New York: Routledge, 1998), 25.

9. Peter Brooks, *The Melodramatic Imagination* (New Haven, CT: Yale University Press, 1995), 20, 17.

10. Chung, *Split Screen Korea*, 43–44.

11. Byun Jai-ran, "The Problematic Perception of Women Wavering Between 'Madame' and 'Freedom,'" DVD booklet, *Women on Screen* (Seoul: Korean Film Archive, 2012), 59, 54, 61, 62; Barbara Molony, Janet Theiss, and Hyaewoeol Choi, *Gender in Modern East Asia* (Boulder, CO: Westview Press, 2016), 430. Not all scholars have read *Madame Freedom* as a conservative critique of the après girl: see, for instance, Soyoung Kim, "Questions of Woman's Films," in *South Korean Golden Age Melodrama*, ed. Kathleen McHugh and Nancy Abelmann (Detroit: Wayne State University Press, 2005), 194; Travis Workman, "Other Scenes," *Journal of Japanese and Korean Cinema* 7, no. 1 (2015): 31–32.

12. Thomas Elsaesser, "Tales of Sound and Fury," in *Home Is Where the Heart Is*, ed. Christine Gledhill (London: British Film Institute, 1987), 43–69; Workman, "Other Scenes," 31–32.

13. Miriam Hansen, "Fallen Women, Rising Stars, New Horizons" *Film Quarterly* 54, no. 1 (2000): 15, 20; Miriam Hansen, "The Mass Production of the Senses," *Modernism/Modernity* 6, no. 2 (1999): 71.

14. Byun, "Problematic Perception," 51; Kim, *Youth for Nation*, 22.

15. Jeong Bi-seok, "The Original Work and the Film," *Han'guk ilbo*, June 14, 1956, reprinted in DVD booklet, *Women on Screen*, 70.

16. Quoted in Sook Suh, "Dance and Democracy," *Asian Journal of Women's Studies* 6, no. 3 (2000): 18.

17. Jeong Bi-seok, *Chayu buin* [Madame Freedom], ed. Ch'u Sŏnchin (Seoul: Chishikŭlmandŭnŭnjishik, 2013), 569, 671, 694.

18. Chŏng Chonghyŏn, "Chayuwa minju, shingminji yulligamgagŭi chaemaengnak'wa" [Re-contextualizing freedom, democracy, and colonial morals], in Kwŏn Podŭrae, *Ap'ŭre Gŏl Sasanggye rŭl ikta* [The après girl reads Sasanggye], ed. Munhwa Haksul Ch'ongsŏ (Seoul: Tongguk Taehakkyo Ch'ulp'anbu, 2009).

19. Kathleen McHugh, "South Korean Film Melodrama," in *South Korean Golden Age Melodrama*, 35–36.

20. Jeong Bi-seok, *Chayu buin*, 671–72, 664, 676, 674.

21. On the role of *hangul* in the film, see Theodore H. Hughes, *Literature and Film in Cold War South Korea* (New York: Columbia University Press, 2012), 119–26.

22. Jeong Bi-seok, *Chayu buin*, 694, 701.

23. Jeong Bi-seok, "The Original Work and the Film," 71.

24. Scott Bukatman, "Spectacle, Attractions, and Visual Pleasure," in *The Cinema of Attractions Reloaded*, ed. Wanda Strauven (Amsterdam: Amsterdam University Press, 2006), 75. See also: Lea Jacobs, *The Wages of Sin* (Berkeley: University of California Press, 1995).

25. Janey Place, "Women in Film Noir," in *Women in Film Noir*, ed. E. Ann Kaplan (London: British Film Institute, 1978), 36, 54.

26. Kim, "Questions of Woman's Films," 194.

27. "Kiss Scene Controversy," *Tonga ilbo*, June 10, 1956, reprinted in DVD booklet, *Women on Screen*, 68, 66; Jeong Bi-seok, "The Original Work and the Film," 71.

28. Eunsun Cho, "Transnational Modernity, National Identity, and South Korean Melodrama (1945–1960s)" (PhD diss., University of Southern California, 2006), 92.

29. Oh Young-sook, "Realistic but Popular," 52.

30. Kim Kee-duk oral history, in *1950nyŏndae han'guk yŏnghwa sŭt'ail* [Korean film style in the 1950s] (Seoul: Han'guk Yŏngsang Charyowŏn [Korean Film Archive], 2009), 2:131.

31. Kim Sunah, "Dilemma of Modern Times," 77.

32. Quoted in Ki-young Shin, "The Politics of the Family Law Reform Movement in Contemporary Korea," *Journal of Korean Studies* 11, no. 1 (2006): 100; Kim Hwallan, *Kŭ pit sok ŭi chagŭn saengmyŏng* [A small life within that light], 2nd ed. (Seoul: Ihwa Yŏja Taehak-kyo Ch'ulp'anbu, 1999), 149.

33. David E. James, "Im Kwon-taek," in *Im Kwon-taek*, ed. David E. James and Kyung Hyun Kim (Detroit: Wayne State University Press, 2002), 56.

34. For comparison, see the female characters in Lee Byung-il's *The Love Marriage* (1958), Shin Sang-ok's *It's Not Her Sin* (1959) and *Seong Chunhyang* (1961), Kim Ki-young's *The Housemaid* (1960), Gwon Yeong-sun's *A Drifting Story* (1960), and Lee Yong-min's *Holiday in Seoul* (1956).

35. On *han*, see: James, "Im Kwon-taek," 55; Chung-moo Choi, "The Politics of Gender, Aestheticism, and Cultural Nationalism in *Sopyonje* and *The Genealogy*," 110; Eunsun Cho, "The Female Body and Enunciation in *Adada* and *Surrogate Mother*," 86–96, all in James and Kim, eds., *Im Kwon-taek*.

36. Joshua D. Pilzer, "The 'Comfort Women' and the Voices of East Asian Modernity," in *Vamping the Stage*, ed. Andrew N. Weintraub and Bart Barendregt (Honolulu: University of Hawai'i Press, 2017), 107–8.

37. On *shinpa*, see Cho, "Transnational Modernity," 22–30; Hye Seung Chung and David Scott Diffrient, *Movie Migrations* (New Brunswick, NJ: Rutgers University Press, 2015), 22–23.

38. Oh Young-sook, "Realistic but Popular," 58–59.

39. Quoted in Chung, *Split Screen Korea*, 79.

40. Matt Treyvaud, "Coo-Coo the *Après Girl*," *No-Sword* blog, March 29, 2010, http://no-sword.jp/blog/2010/03/coo-coo_the_apres_girl.html.

41. Jan Bardsley, *Women and Democracy in Cold War Japan* (London: Bloomsbury Academic, 2014), 75, 76, 81; Mark J. McLelland, *Love, Sex, and Democracy in Japan during the American Occupation* (New York: Palgrave Macmillan, 2012), 11.

42. Poshek Fu, "Modernity, Diasporic Capital, and 1950's Hong Kong Mandarin Cinema," *Jump Cut*, no. 49 (2007), http://www.ejumpcut.org/archive/jc49.2007/Poshek/text.html; Jean Ma, *Sounding the Modern Woman* (Durham, NC: Duke University Press, 2015); Brian Hu, "Star Discourse and the Cosmopolitan Chinese," *Journal of Chinese Cinemas* 4, no. 3 (2010): 183–209.

5. FILM CULTURE, SOUND CULTURE: SETTING, CINEMATOGRAPHY, AND SOUND

1. Michel de Certeau, *The Practice of Everyday Life* (Berkeley: University of California Press, 1984), 169.

2. Henry Jenkins, *Textual Poachers* (New York: Routledge, 1992).

3. Homi Bhabha, "Of Mimicry and Man," in *The Location of Culture* (London: Routledge, 2004), 123.

4. Jonathan Letham, "The Ecstasy of Influence," *Harper's Magazine*, February 2007, 59+.

5. Miriam Hansen, "Fallen Women, Rising Stars," *Film Quarterly* 54, no. 1 (2000): 10, 12.

6. Kathleen McHugh and Nancy Abelmann, eds., *South Korean Golden Age Melodrama* (Detroit: Wayne State University Press, 2005), 25 and contributors; Hye Seung Chung and David Scott Diffrient, *Movie Migrations* (New Brunswick, NJ: Rutgers University Press, 2015), 9; Andre Schmid, *Korea between Empires, 1895–1919* (New York: Columbia University Press, 2002).

7. Andrew Higson,"The Concept of National Cinema," in *Film and Nationalism*, ed. Alan Williams (New Brunswick: Rutgers University Press), 63–65.

8. Kang Beom-gu oral history, in *1950nyŏndae han'guk yŏnghwa sŭt'ail* [Korean film style in the 1950s] (Seoul: Han'guk Yŏngsang Charyowŏn [Korean Film Archive], 2009) (hereafter *KFS 1950s*), 1:105–6, 90–92.

9. Brian Yecies and Ae-Gyung Shim, *Korea's Occupied Cinemas, 1893–1948* (New York: Routledge, 2011), 150–52; Korean Film Archive, *Traces of Korean Cinema, 1945–1959* (Seoul: Munhak Sasangsa, 2003), 80, 83.

10. "Fun Facts About Korean Cinema: What is the first Korean movie banned for violating the National Security Law?," KMDb, https://eng.koreafilm.or.kr/kmdb/trivia/funfacts/BC_0000005076?page, accessed July 30, 2018.

11. Andrei Lankov, "Ban on Japanese Pop Culture," *Korea Times*, December 29, 2011.

12. Jinsoo An, *Parameters of Disavowal* (Oakland: University of California Press, 2018), 35–51.

13. Han Sang Kim, "Uneven Screens, Contested Identities" (PhD diss., Seoul National University, 2013); Sueyoung Park-Primiano, "South Korean Cinema between the Wars" (PhD diss., New York University, 2015); Wolsan Liem, "Telling the Truth to Koreans" (PhD diss., New York University, 2010).

14. Kim Kang-yun et al., comps., *Han'guk yŏnghwa charyo p'yŏllam (ch'och'anggi-1976-yŏn)* [A guide to sources on South Korean film] (Seoul: Yŏnghwa chinhŭng kongsa, 1977), Table 7I, 82–108.

15. Korean Film Archive, *Traces of Korean Cinema, 1945–1959*, 114–16, 197.

16. Park-Primiano, "South Korean Cinema between the Wars," 131–34; Kwang Woo Noh, "Transformations of Korean Film Industry during the US Military Occupation Era (1945–1948), *Asian Cinema* 14, no. 2(2003): 95; "Hwalbal haejinŭn sichŏnggak kyoyukkye" [Audiovisual education perking up], *Han'guk ilbo*, March 29, 1958, 4, in *Sinmun kisa ro pon Han'guk yŏnghwa, 1958–1961* [Korean films in newspapers, 1958–1961] (Seoul: Han'guk Yŏngsang Charyowŏn [Korean Film Archive]/Konggan kwa Saramdŭl, 2005) (hereafter *KFN 1958–61*).

17. Alastair Phillips, "Pictures of the Past in the Present," *Screen* 44, no. 2 (2003): 154–66.

18. Phillips, 166.

19. An, *Parameters of Disavowal*, 45

20. Yecies and Shim, *Korea's Occupied Cinemas*.

21. Lee Hyung-pyo oral history, in *KFS 1950s*, 1:360.

22. Ham Wanseob oral history, 3:298–99; Kang Beom-gu oral history, 1:18–19, 31–32, 47–48; Kim Kee-duk oral history, 2:35, 75, all in *KFS 1950s*; Brian Yecies and Aegyung Shim, *The Changing Face of Korean Cinema* (London: Routledge, 2015), 91.

23. Kim Ji-heon oral history, in *Han'guk yŏnghwa rŭl mal handa: 1950nyŏndae han'guk yŏnghwa* [To speak on Korean cinema: Korean cinema in the 1950s] (Seoul: Han'guk Yŏngsang Charyowŏn [Korean Film Archive]/Ichae, 2004 (hereafter *TSKC 1950s*), 78–79.

24. The script was published in *Kinema Junpo* 39, June 1, 1952.

25. No In-taek interview, DVD video extra, *Hand of Fate* (Seoul: Korean Film Archive, 2005); No In-taek oral history, in *KFS 1950s*, 3:96.

26. Oh Young-jin, "1958 nyŏn munhwagye kyŏlsan" [Wrap-up of cultural news in cinema] *Tonga ilbo*, December 29, 1958, 4, in *KFN 1958–61*, 139–40; An, *Parameters of Disavowal*, 45, 151n36; Yecies and Shim, *Changing Face of Korean Cinema*, 90–98; Lee Hyung-pyo oral history, in *KFS 1950s*, 1:360; "Maenbarŭi chŏngch'unesŏ chŏpsokkkaji" [From *Barefoot Youth* to *The Contact*], episode of program "Nonp'iksyŏn 11" [Non-Fiction 11], aired on MBC March 4, 1999; Im Won-sik oral history, in *Shin p'illŭm 2* [Shin Film 2] (Seoul: Han'guk Yŏngsang Charyowŏn [Korean Film Archive], 2008), 54–57.

27. David Scott Diffrient notes that "According to most sources, *Barefoot Youth* is nearly a shot-for-shot recasting (or unsanctioned remake) of Ko Nakahira's 1963 youth film *Purity Stuck in the Mud*." Diffrient, "*Over That Hill*," *Journal of Japanese and Korean Cinema* 1, no. 2 (2009): 106. Chung Chonghwa argues that Kim did not copy the visual style of Ko's original; he also notes that producers sometimes purchased the rights to the novels upon which the plagiarized Japanese screenplays were based and argues that the localization of these

screenplays entailed a degree of adaptation. Chung Chonghwa, "Topography of 1960s Korean Youth Film," *Journal of Japanese and Korean Cinema* 8, no. 1 (2016): 11–24, and Chung Chonghwa, "Mode of Cinematic Plagiarism and Adaptation," *Korea Journal* 57, no. 3 (Autumn 2017): 56–82. A side-by-side comparison of select scenes from the two films, however, does show significant visual similarities, as can be seen in "Maenbarŭi chŏngch'unesŏ chŏpsokkkaji."

28. Lee Hyung-pyo oral history, in *KFS 1950s*, 1:360.

29. Andrei Lankov, *The Dawn of Modern Korea* (Seoul: EunHaeng NaMu, 2007), 330; Mire Koikari, *Pedagogy of Democracy* (Temple University Press, 2008).

30. Kang Beom-gu oral history, 1:18–19, and Kim Kee-duk oral history, 2:30–35, 92, in *KFS 1950s*.

31. There were, of course, exceptions. *Spring in the Korean Peninsula* (1941, Lee Byung-il) opens with a dramatic camera movement that pulls back from a medium to a long shot, revealing a scene being shot for a film-within-the-film. *Street Angels* (1941, Choi In-gyu) had a comparatively fast pace and dynamic editing patterns, a result perhaps of Choi's early experience as a projectionist in a theater that showed mostly Hollywood films.

32. Kim Kee-duk oral history, 2:30–35, 121, and No In-taek oral history, 3:28–29, in *KFS 1950s*.

33. Lee Min and No In-taek interviews, DVD video extra, *Madame Freedom* (Seoul: Korean Film Archive, 2005); Chung Chong-hwa, "The Technical Advancement of Cinematic Style in Korean Cinema," in *Han Hyung-mo: The Alchemist of Popular Genres* (Seoul: Korean Film Archive, 2008), 93; No In-taek oral history, in *TSKC 1950s*, 104; No In-taek oral history, in *KFS 1950s*, 3:93–95.

34. Quoted in Oh Young-sook, "Realistic but Popular," in *Han Hyung-mo: The Alchemist of Popular Genres*, 56–57.

35. Lee Min interview, *Madame Freedom*, DVD video extras; *Yŏwŏn*, October 1956.

36. No In-taek oral history, in *KFS 1950s*, 3:76–78.

37. No In-taek oral history, in *TSKC 1950s*, 104; No In-taek oral history, in *KFS 1950s*, 3:76–78, 98–99.

38. No In-taek oral history, in *KFS 1950s*, 3:88–91.

39. No In-taek oral history, in *KFS 1950s*, 3:88–91.

40. No In-taek interview, DVD video extra, *Madame Freedom*.

41. Kim Kee-duk oral history, in *KFS 1950s*, 2:178.

42. Yecies and Shim, *Korea's Occupied Cinemas*, 80, 81, 94; Michael Baskett, *The Attractive Empire* (Honolulu: University of Hawai'i Press, 2008), 72–105.

43. Yecies and Shim, *Korea's Occupied Cinemas*, 149–52.

44. Yecies and Shim, 141–61; Hiroshi Kitamura, *Screening Enlightenment* (Ithaca, NY: Cornell University Press, 2010); Quotations from Motion Picture Association of America, in Park-Primiano, "South Korean Cinema between the Wars," 110, 106.

45. Park-Primiano, "South Korean Cinema between the Wars," 168–71, 278, 293–96; Kim Kang-yun et al., comps., *Han'guk yŏnghwa charyo p'yŏllam*, 78.

46. Park-Primiano, "South Korean Cinema between the Wars," 145, 115.

47. Kim Kang-yun et al., comps., *Han'guk yŏnghwa charyo p'yŏllam*, 82–108.

48. No In-taek oral history, 3:40; Ma Yong-cheon oral history, 3:166–68; Kim Kee-duk oral history, 2:89, 93; Lee Hyung-pyo oral history, 1:319–20, 295–97; Kang Beom-gu oral history, 1:90–92, 232, 238, all in *KFS 1950s*.

49. Quoted in Cho Junhyoung, "The Front Line of Korean Popular Moves in 1950's," in *Han Hyung-mo: The Alchemist of Popular Genres*, 34.

50. Darcy Paquet, "A History of the Korean Musical to 1980," www.koreanfilm.org/feff.html#goldenage, accessed June 6, 2016; "I Am Alone," in *Han Hyung-mo: The Alchemist of Popular Genres*, 142; Yi Chunhŭi, *Norae ro tŭnnŭn yŏnghwa, yŏnghwa ro ponŭn norae* [Movies heard through songs, songs seen through movies] (Seoul: Han'guk Yŏngsang Charyowŏn), 2012, 82–89.

51. An, *Parameters of Disavowal*, 40–41.

52. Choi Hyeon-rye oral history, in *TSKC 1950s*, 1:325–28, 322–23.

53. John Lie, *K-Pop* (Oakland: University of California Press, 2014), 38.

54. Shim Wooseob oral history, 2:328–29, and Kim Kee-duk oral history, 2:148, in *KFS 1950s*; "Popular Song and the Recording Industry," *Korea Journal* 2, no. 9 (September 1962): 30. There were some exceptions: original music was composed for Han's *The Hand of Destiny* (1954) by Park Shi-chun and for Kim Ki-young's *Boxes of Death* (1955) by Han Sang-gi. Yi Chunhŭi, *Norae ro tŭnnŭn yŏnghwa*, 118–24.

55. Kim Kee-duk oral history, in *KFS 1950s*, 2:148.

56. Spencer Leigh, "Roger Williams," *Independent*, October 14, 2011, www.independent.co.uk/news/obituaries/roger-williams-pianist-whoseautumn-leaves-topped-the-charts-2370312.html.

57. E. Taylor Atkins, "Toward a Global History of Jazz," in *Jazz Planet*, ed. E. Taylor Atkins (Jackson: University Press of Mississippi, 2003), xiv.

58. Christina Klein, *Cold War Orientalism* (Berkeley: University of California Press, 2003).

59. Yi Hyo-in, *Shin Sang-ok*, trans. Colin A. Mouat, Korean Film Directors series (Seoul: Seoul Selection, 2008), 19.

60. Yongwoo Lee, "Embedded Voices in between Empires" (PhD diss., McGill University, 2010), 58.

61. Roald Maliangkay, "Supporting Our Boys," in *Korean Pop Music*, ed. Keith Howard (Kent, England: Global Oriental, 2006), 21–33; Pil Ho Kim and Hyunjoon Shin, "The Birth of 'Rok,'" *Positions* 18, no. 1 (2010): 199–230.

62. "LP chaesaeng changch'i" [LP Record Player], *Tonga ilbo*, October 4, 1956; "Ch'oego sŏngnŭng ŭi ŭmhyang changch'i" [Top performing acoustic system], *Tonga ilbo*, October 3, 1957, 4; "Tosiin ŭi ŭmak kamsang" [Urbanites listen to music], *Tonga ilbo*, May 4, 1959, 4.

63. Kim Kee-duk oral history, in *KFS 1950s*, 2:158–60.

64. Hyunjoon Shin, "The Stage Show and the Dance Floor," in *Made in Korea*, ed. Hyunjoon Shin and Sung-Ah Lee (New York: Routledge, 2017), 17.

65. Hwang Yeongmin, "Enuriga ŏpta 'nŭn p'yŏngŭl p'yŏngham'" [Criticizing the review 'without such a discount'], *Han'guk ilbo*, June 15, 1956.

66. Travis Workman, "Other Scenes," *Journal of Japanese and Korean Cinema* 7, no. 1 (2015): 33.

6. CONSUMER CULTURE AND THE BLACK MARKET: MISE-EN-SCÈNE

1. Thomas Elsaesser, "Tales of Sound and Fury," in *Home Is Where the Heart Is*, ed. Christine Gledhill (London: British Film Institute, 1987), 52, 68.

2. Laura C. Nelson, *Measured Excess* (New York: Columbia University Press, 2000), 24; Grant David McCracken, *Culture and Consumption* (Bloomington: Indiana University Press, 1988), xi.

3. Robert Oppenheim, "Crafting the Consumability of Place," in *Consuming Korean Tradition in Early and Late Modernity*, ed. Laurel Kendall (Honolulu: University of Hawai'i Press, 2011), 106.

4. Daniel Miller, quoted in Kendall, introduction to *Consuming Korean Tradition*, 1.

5. Introduction to *The Social Life of Things*, ed. Arjun Appadurai (Cambridge: Cambridge University Press, 1986), 5.

6. Karal Ann Marling, *As Seen on TV* (Cambridge, MA: Harvard University Press, 1994), 242–83.

7. Paul Swann, "The Little State Department," *American Studies International* 29, no. 1 (April 1991): 2–19.

8. Anthony Giddens, *Modernity and Self-Identity* (Stanford, CA: Stanford University Press, 1991), 81.

9. Noh In-taek oral history, in *Han'guk yŏnghwa rŭl mal handa: 1950nyŏndae han'guk yŏnghwa* [To speak on Korean Cinema: Korean cinema in the 1950s] (Seoul: Han'guk Yŏngsang Charyowŏn/Ichae [Korean Film Archive]/Ichae, 2004) (hereafter *TSKC 1950s*), 109; Kim Chong-wŏn et al., *Han'guk yŏnghwa kamdok sajŏn* [Dictionary of Korean film directors] (Seoul: Kukhak Charyowŏn, 2004), 654.

10. "Interview with Kim Kee-duk," in *Han Hyung-mo: The Alchemist of Popular Genres* (Seoul: Korean Film Archive), 129; Kim Kee-duk oral history, in *1950nyŏndae han'guk yŏnghwa sŭt'ail* [Korean film style in the 1950s] (Seoul: Han'guk Yŏngsang Charyowŏn [Korean Film Archive], 2009) (hereafter *KFS 1950s*), 2:97.

11. Kim Kee-duk oral history, in *KFS 1950s*, 2:125.

12. Kim Chong-wŏn et al., *Han'guk yŏnghwa kamdok sajŏn*, 654.

13. Noh In-taek oral history, in *TSKC 1950s*, 102–4; Noh In-taek oral history, in *KFS 1950s*, 3:116–17.

14. Lise Sanders, *Consuming Fantasies* (Columbus: Ohio State University Press, 2006), 1; Erika Diane Rappaport, *Shopping for Pleasure* (Princeton, NJ: Princeton University Press, 2000), 192–202.

15. Im Hyang-su, Shin Hye-su, Kim Sŏn-su, Kim Bu-ong, "Urijikchanghop'ŭ" [The hope of our workplace], *Yŏwŏn*, April 1956, 77–80; Shin Suk-gyung, "P'igonŭl p'ul kyŏrŭlto ŏmnŭn saenghwal" [A life without even a moment to rest], *Yŏwŏn*, February 1958, 67; Elise K. Tipton, "Moving Up and Out," in *Modern Girls on the Go*, ed. Alisa Freedman, Laura Miller, and Christine R. Yano (Stanford, CA: Stanford University Press, 2013), 21–39.

16. Grant David McCracken, *Culture and Consumption II* (Bloomington: Indiana University Press, 2005), 4; McCracken, *Culture and Consumption*, 88, xii.

17. Daniel Miller, "Consumption as the Vanguard of History," in *Acknowledging Consumption*, ed. Daniel Miller (New York: Routledge, 2005), 27.

18. Timothy Burke, *Lifebuoy Men, Lux Women* (Durham, NC: Duke University Press, 1996); Kathy Peiss, "Making Up, Making Over," in *The Sex of Things*, ed. Victoria De Grazia (Berkeley: University of California Press, 1996), 311–36.

19. Laurel Kendall, introduction to *Consuming Korean Tradition*, 8.

20. McCracken, *Culture and Consumption*, 29.

21. Kristin Hoganson, *Consumer's Imperium* (Chapel Hill: University of North Carolina Press, 2007), 13–56.

22. Cho Haejoang, "Living with Conflicting Subjectivities," in *Under Construction,* ed. Laurel Kendall (Honolulu: University of Hawai'i Press, 2002), 171.

23. Noh In-taek oral history, in *KFS 1950s,* 3:50–53.

24. Kim Kee-duk oral history, in *KFS 1950s,* 2:125–28.

25. Nelson, *Measured Excess,* 143.

26. Korean Film Archive, *Traces of Korean Cinema, 1945–1959* (Seoul: Munhak Sasangsa, 2003), 114–16; Uchang Kim, "The Agony of Cultural Construction," in *State and Society in Contemporary Korea,* ed. Hagen Koo (Ithaca, NY: Cornell University Press, 1993), 174–76.

27. Pak Chisa, "Chiyang twaeya hal yŏnghwa bip'yŏng" [Film criticism that should be avoided], *Chosŏn ilbo,* May 31, 1958, 4, in *Sinmun kisa ro pon Han'guk yŏnghwa, 1945–1957* [Korean Films in Newspapers, 1945–1957], ed. Han'guk Yŏngsang Charyowŏn [Korean Film Archive] (Seoul: Konggan kwa Saramdŭl, 2004), 55–56.

28. Nelson, *Measured Excess,* 107.

29. Laurel Kendall, introduction to *Under Construction,* 17.

30. John Lie, *Han Unbound* (Stanford, CA: Stanford University Press, 1998), 40–41.

31. Katarzyna J. Cwiertka, "Dining Out in the Land of Desire," in *Consuming Korean Tradition,* 21–38.

32. Carter J. Eckert, *Offspring of Empire* (Seattle: University of Washington Press, 1991), 46.

33. Bank of Korea, "1956 Balance of International Payment and Foreign Trade," *Monthly Statistical Review* 11, no. 7 (July 1957): xxxviii.

34. Stephen Haggard, Richard N. Cooper, and Chung-in Moon, "Policy Reform in Korea," in *Political and Economic Interactions in Economic Policy Reform,* ed. Robert H. Bates and Anne O. Krueger (Cambridge: Blackwell, 1993), 301; Stephan Haggard, Byung-Kook Kim, and Chung-in Moon, "The Transition to Export-Led Growth in South Korea," *Journal of Asian Studies* 50, no. 4 (November 1991): 852; Gregg A. Brazinsky, *Nation Building in South Korea* (Chapel Hill: University of North Carolina Press, 2007), 35.

35. Memorandum from Henry Costanzo, August 16, 1956, RG 469, box 46, file Trade—Import/Exports, National Archives and Records Administration (hereafter NARA); Letter from Korean Tire Association, 1959, RG 469, box 104, file Committees-Black Market, NARA.

36. J. Tom Graham, "Colorful Black Market Faces Bleak Future," *Stars and Stripes* (Pacific Edition), February 2, 1968, 23.

37. Ministry of Commerce and Industry, Republic of Korea, *Trade Statistics by Commodity* 3 (1959): 80, 92, 350–51, 349, 464–65, 450, 427; "Imports by Commodity," Bank of Korea, *Monthly Statistical Review* 14, no. 11 (November 1960): 61.

38. Memorandum from Henry Costanzo, August 16, 1956; "Economic Trends in the Republic of Korea, July 1957," Bank of Korea, *Monthly Statistical Review* 11, no.7 (July 1957): xxix–xxx.

39. Agnes Davis Kim, *I Married a Korean* (New York: John Day, 1953); "Richest Korean in Jail," *New York Times,* February 19, 1946, 12; Irma Tennant Materi, *Irma and the Hermit* (New York: W. W. Norton, 1949), 188–200; "Memo from Korea," *US News & World Report,* March 12, 1954, 46; *Black Market and South Korean Trade Practices,* Hearing before the

Subcommittee on Oversight of Government Management, One Hundred First Congress, first session, October 19, 1989 (Washington: US Government Printing Office, 1990).

40. Letter from William E. Warne, January 27, 1959, RG 469, box 105, file Committees-CEB (1959), NARA.

41. Total legal imports in 1960 were $343 million: Edward Mason, *The Economic and Social Modernization of the Republic of Korea* (Cambridge, MA: Harvard University Press, 1980), 140. The exchange rate in 1959 was 500 hwan to the dollar. Steven Hugh Lee, "Development without Democracy," in *Transformations in Twentieth Century Korea*, ed. Steven Hugh Lee and Yun-shik Chang (New York: Routledge, 2006), 167.

42. Charles Grutzner, "Army Goods Sold Openly in Seoul," *New York Times*, October 31, 1950, 3; "Pusan Fire Wrecks the Black Market," *New York Times*, January 31, 1953, 3.

43. "Memo from Korea," *US News & World Report*, March 12, 1954, 46; Minutes of Joint Black Market Committee, January 16, 1959, RG 469, box 104, file Committees-Black Market, NARA.

44. Memorandum from Lester Levey, September 17, 1958, RG 469, box 104, file Committees-Black Market, NARA.

45. Graham, "Colorful Black Market Faces Bleak Future."

46. "PX Scrip Sparks Trade at Seoul," *New York Times*, March 26, 1961, 9; United States General Accounting Office, *Internal Controls,* Report to the Chairman, Subcommittee on Oversight of Government Management, Committee on Governmental Affairs, U.S. Senate (1990), 3; "Three Tons of Coffee Reach Korean Markets Daily," *Korean News Round Up*, September 1, 1960, RG 388, box 1499, file Newspaper files (1960) (Sept.–Oct.) World—Korean News Round Up, NARA.

47. Anonymous, photograph of street vender stall, 1959: www.flickr.com/photos/58451159@N00/25397862022/in/pool-666616@N21/.

48. "Minutes of Joint Black Market Control Committee," February 20, 1959, RG 469, box 104, file Committees-Black Market, NARA.

49. Memorandum from Lester Levey, September 17, 1958; Appendices, Case Related to the Measure to Prevent Smuggling (No. 67), Bill No. 129, deliberated in the National Assembly on July 25, 1958, Assembly Records of the National Affairs in National Archives of Korea, http://theme.archives.go.kr/next/pages/viewer/archiveViewer.jsp?archiveEventId = 0028648831&singleData = Y (special viewing software required); Yi Chŏlho, "Milsu" [Smuggling], *Sin Tonga*, April 1965, 230–45; Donald Stone Macdonald, *US-Korean Relations from Liberation to Self-Reliance* (Boulder: Westview Press, 1991), 248.

50. John Lie, *Zainichi (Koreans in Japan)* (Berkeley: University of California Press, 2008); Richard H. Mitchell, *The Korean Minority in Japan* (Berkeley: University of California Press, 1967); John W. Dower, *Embracing Defeat* (New York: W. W. Norton, 1999), 143, 580n39.

51. "Fundamental Counter-measures for Preventing Smuggling Activities," RG 469, box 105, file Committees-CEB Sub-Committee for Smuggling Surveillance, NARA; Norman Sklarewitz, "Black Marketeers Face Unbeatable Odds," *Stars and Stripes* (Pacific Edition), September 30, 1956, 1; AP, "AF Convicts Airman of Korea Smuggling," *Stars and Stripes* (Pacific Edition), January 13, 1953, 7.

52. UPI, "ROK Calls for More Aid to Spur 5-Year Program," *Stars and Stripes* (Pacific Edition), September 16, 1962; Materi, *Irma and the Hermit*, 192–93; "Artful Youths Loot

U.N. Troops' Valuables as Authorities Warn against Seoul Gangs," *Stars and Stripes* (Pacific Edition), April 25, 1954; "Memo from Korea," *US News & World Report*, March 12, 1954, 46; William Armour Murdoch, *Republic of South Korea, 1957–1959* (Bloomington: Author House, 2007), 74.

53. ROK officials largely saw black marketing as a violation of Korean import laws and thus a problem for Americans to solve.

54. Whitney Taejin Hwang, "Borderland Intimacies" (PhD diss., University of California Berkeley, 2010), 71–73; *Korean News Round Up*, RG 388, box 1499, files Newspapers Files (1960), NARA; "South Korea: Slicky Boy," *Time*, March 10, 1958.

55. Incident list of thefts; Memorandum, Safeguarding of Fans, July 11, 1958; Memorandum, Theft of U.S. Gov't Property, March 3, 1958, RG 469, box 64, file Crimes-Theft, NARA; Minutes of Joint Black Market Control Committee, April 24, 1959, RG 469, box 104, file Committees—Black Market, NARA; AP, "ROK Gas Rationed, 9,000 Cars Idle," *Stars and Stripes* (Pacific Edition), December 2, 1957; Minutes of Joint Black Market Control Committee, February 20, 1959, RG 469, box 104, file Committees-Black Market, NARA.

56. "Memo from Korea," *US News & World Report*, March 12, 1954, 46; Murdoch, *Republic of South Korea, 1957–1959*, 67, 151–52, 147–50; Minutes of Joint Black Market Control Committee, June 26, 1959, RG 469, box 104, file Committees-Black Market, NARA.

57. "Official Warns against Misuse of PX," *Stars and Stripes* (Pacific Edition), June 12, 1958, 27; James Wade, *One Man's Korea* (Seoul: Hollym Corporation, 1967), 19; Minutes, Black Market Committee, August 28, 1959, RG 469, box 104, file Black Market Committees, NARA; Minutes of Joint Black Market Committee, January 16, 1959, RG 469, box 104, file Committees—Black Market, NARA.

58. Park, Wan-so, *The Naked Tree*, trans. Yu Young-nan (Ithaca, NY: Cornell University Press, 1995), 15.

59. "Official Warns against Misuse of PX," *Stars and Stripes* (Pacific Edition), June 12, 1958, 27.

60. United States General Accounting Office, *Internal Controls*, 17–18; "South Korea: The PX Affair," *Time*, November 9, 1959; Minutes of Joint Black Market Committee, November 7, 1958; Minutes of Joint Black Market Committee, June 26, 1959; Memorandum, Black Market Control Actions, March 26, 1959; Minutes of the Joint Black Market Committee, May 29, 1959; "The Black Market Trap," RG 469, box 104, file Committees—Black Market, NARA.

61. Theodore and Ellen Conant, interviews with author, May 2013, Dartmouth College, Hanover, NH.

62. "Black Market Trap."

63. Pat Frank, *The Long Way Around* (Philadelphia: J. B. Lippincott Co., 1953), 96.

64. Minutes of Joint Black Market Control Committee, August 28, 1959, RG 469, box 104, file Committees-Black Market; Theodore and Ellen Conant interviews; *Korean Report* 6 (1958): 133.

65. "Fundamental Counter-measures for Preventing Smuggling Activities," RG 469, box 105, file Committees—CEB Sub-Committee for Smuggling Surveillance, NARA.

66. AP, "New Korean President Is Austerity-Minded," *Stars and Stripes* (Pacific Edition), August 15, 1960; "Seoul Students Seize Legislators' Jeeps," *Stars and Stripes* (Pacific Edition), September 23, 1960, 8.

67. On labor protests by civilian employees of the US military, see *Korean News Round Up*, January 15, 1960, January 23, 1960, RG 388, box 1499, file 265/58-Newspapers Files (1960) (Jan.–Feb.), NARA; Minutes of Joint Black Market Committee, November 7, 1958, RG 469, box 104, file Committees—Black Market, NARA; Murdoch, *Republic of South Korea*, 168, 67; Frank, *The Long Way Around*, 96; Theodore and Ellen Conant interviews.

68. McCracken, *Culture and Consumption*, 109, 110.

69. Quoted in Nelson, *Measured Excess*, 76.

70. Shunya Yoshimi, "'America' as Desire and Violence," *Inter-Asia Cultural Studies* 4, no. 3 (2003): 432–50.

71. Korean Film Archive, *Traces of Korean Cinema*, 125.

72. "Official Warns Against Misuses of PX," *Stars and Stripes* (Pacific Edition), June 12, 1958, 27; "Busan Storage Center," www.globalsecurity.org/military/facility/pusan-sf.htm; "Camp Market," www.globalsecurity.org/military/facility/camp-market.htm; "Camp Market," Wikipedia, https://en.wikipedia.org/wiki/Camp_Market, accessed October 23, 2018.

73. Kang Beom-gu oral history, in *KFS 1950s*, 1:121–22, 124–26.

74. Noh In-taek oral history, 3:54–55, and Shim Wooseob oral history, 2:284–85, in *KFS 1950s*.

75. Noh In-taek oral history, in *KFS 1950s*, 3:33, 26–27; Lee Hyung-pyo oral history, in *Shin p'illŭm 2* [Shin Film 2] (Seoul: Han'guk Yŏngsang Charyowŏn [Korean Film Archive], 2008), 184–98; Kim Hee-su oral history, in *TSKC 1950s*, 90–92.

76. Noh In-taek oral history, 3:28–32, 93–96; Ma Yong-cheon oral history, 3:188–89; Kim Kee-duk oral history, 2:146–48, all in *KFS 1950s*.

77. Noh In-taek oral history, in *KFS 1950s*, 3:50–60, 84; Noh In-taek oral history, in *TSKC 1950s*, 108–9; Philip Shabecoff, "South Korea's Economy Booming with Cheap Labor," *New York Times*, May 12, 1970, 57.

78. Noh In-taek oral history, in *KFS 1950s*, 3:50–59, 76–78.

7. A COMMITMENT TO SHOWMANSHIP: SPECTACLE

1. Cho Junhyoung, "The Front Line of Korean Popular Movies in 1950s," in *Han Hyung-mo: The Alchemist of Popular Genres* (Seoul: Korean Film Archive), 36; Tom Gunning, "The Whole Town's Gawking," *Yale Journal of Criticism* 7, no. 2 (1994): 190; Laura Mulvey, "Visual Pleasure and Narrative Cinema," *Screen* 16, no. 3 (1975): 6–18.

2. Kim Kee-duk oral history, in *1950nyŏndae han'guk yŏnghwa sŭt'ail* [Korean film style in the 1950s] (Seoul: Han'guk Yŏngsang Charyowŏn [Korean Film Archive], 2009) (hereafter *KFS 1950s*), 2:111–12.

3. Cho, "Front Line of Korean Popular Movies," 29. On the persistence of the enlightenment impulse in Korean filmmaking, see Steven Chung, *Split Screen Korea* (Minneapolis: University of Minnesota Press, 2014).

4. Charles R. Kim, *Youth for Nation* (Honolulu: University of Hawai'i Press, 2017), 45–48.

5. Kristin Thompson, "The Concept of Cinematic Excess," in *Film Theory and Criticism*, 6th ed., ed. Leo Braudy and Marshall Cohen (New York: Oxford University Press, 2004), 523–24; Thomas Elsaesser, "Vincent Minnelli," and Richard Dyer, "Entertainment and Utopia," in *Genre: The Musical*, ed. Rick Altman (London: Routledge & Kegan Paul, 1981), 8–27, 175–89.

6. Pak Chŏngjun, "Yudo sajŏl p'agu ŭi ŭiŭi" [The significance of the judo delegation to Europe], *Kyŏnghyang sinmun*, June 18, 1955, 4; "Han'guk ŭn yudo ŭi palsangji" [Korea is the birthplace of judo], *Kyŏnghyang sinmun*, August 20, 1960, 4.

7. Carter J. Eckert, *Park Chung Hee and Modern Korea* (Cambridge, MA: Harvard University Press, 2016), 265; Udo Moenig and Kim Minho, "The Invention of Taekwondo Tradition, 1945–1972," *Acta Koreana* 19, no. 2 (December 2016): 131–64; Inoue Shun, "The Invention of Martial Arts," in *Mirror of Modernity*, ed. Stephen Vlastos (Berkeley: University of California Press, 1998), 163–73; Shohei Sato, "The Sportification of Judo," *Journal of Global History* 8 (2013): 299–317; "History of Judo in Korea," Judo Union of Asia, www.onlinejua.org/country_member.php?cid = 19&zid = 3, accessed November 1, 2018; Korea Judo Association website: http://judo.sports.or.kr/, accessed November 1, 2018; "History," Agape Black Belt Center, http://agapebbc.com/about/history-behind-abbc/, accessed November 1, 2018.

8. Hye Seung Chung and David Scott Diffrient, *Movie Migrations* (New Brunswick, NJ: Rutgers University Press, 2015), 75, 83; Kelly Jeong, "The Quasi Patriarch," in *The Korean Popular Culture Reader*, ed. Kyung Hyun Kim and Youngmin Choe (Durham, NC: Duke University Press, 2014), 141.

9. "Sŭp'idŭ innŭn hyŏndae higŭk" [A speedy modern comedy], *Chosŏn ilbo*, October 29, 1961, 4.

10. "Mun yang kwa yudo" [Mun and judo], *Kyŏnghyang sinmun*, June 25, 1961.

11. Gustavo Perez Firmat, *Life on the Hyphen* (Austin: University of Texas Press, 2012), 73, 76, 82, 72, 83.

12. David. F. García, *Arsenio Rodrigues and the Transnational Flows of Latin Popular Music* (Philadelphia: Temple University Press, 2006), 75.

13. Al Ricketts, "On the Town," *Stars and Stripes* (Pacific Edition), September 19, 1956.

14. Robert Farris Thompson. "Teaching the People to Triumph over Time," in *Caribbean Dance from Abajua to Zouk*, ed. Susanna Sloat (Gainesville: University of Florida Press, 2002), 339, 338, 343.

15. Manuel Quezon III, "Magsaysay Didn't Boogie but Boy, Could He Mambo," *Spot*, September 1, 2017, www.spot.ph/newsfeatures/the-latest-news-features/71287/magsaysay-didnt-boogie-but-boy-could-he-mambo-a1507-20170901-lfrm2; "Mambo tŭng ŭro kwangt'ae, Chunggong edo ttaensŭ yŏl" [Mambo madness in communist China as well], *Tonga ilbo*, April 9, 1957; "Chŏsok'an mambo ch'um, il chŏngnyŏnch'ŭng e sŏnghaeng" [Indecent mambo dance rampant among Japanese youth], *Tonga ilbo*, September 11, 1955, 3; "Ban 'Cha-cha-cha' Song," *Stars and Stripes* (Pacific Edition), June 3, 1961, 6; "Hei! Mambo" [Hey! Mambo], *Kyŏnghyang sinmun*, September 6, 1957; David F García, "Going Primitive to the Movements and Sounds of Mambo," *Musical Quarterly* 89, no. 4 (2006): 505–23.

16. Jean Ma, *Sounding the Modern Woman* (Durham, NC: Duke University Press, 2015), 139, 146, 179–80; Brian Hu, "Star Discourse and the Cosmopolitan Chinese," *Journal of Chinese Cinemas* 4, no. 3 (2010): 183–209; "Princess Suga Marks 100th Deejay Show," *Stars and Stripes* (Pacific Edition), August 28, 1960, 2.

17. Andrew F. Jones, "Circuit Listening," in *Audible Empire*, ed. Ronald Radano and Tejumola Olaniyan (Durham, NC: Duke University Press, 2016), 66–92; Kathleen McHugh, "South Korean Film Melodrama," in *South Korean Golden Age Melodrama*, ed. Kathleen McHugh and Nancy Abelmann (Detroit: Wayne State University Press, 2005), 17–42.

18. Penny M. Von Eschen, *Satchmo Blows Up the World* (Cambridge, MA: Harvard University Press, 2004), 43.

19. "Skokiaan" is a fine example of the transnational flows of music in the postwar period. Rhodesian songwriter August Musarurwa wrote the song in 1947, and his 1954 recording became a hit in South Africa. It reached the charts in the United States after a commercial airline pilot delivered a record to a trend-setting DJ in Cleveland, and within a year over nineteen cover versions had been recorded by musicians around the world, including Pérez Prado's mambo version. "Skokiaan," https://en.wikipedia.org/wiki/Skokiaan, accessed June 17, 2019.

20. "Cugat's Latins Stage Colorful One-Night Stand," *Stars and Stripes* (Pacific Edition), November 2, 1953, 7; "Xavier Cugat, Other Works," IMDB, www.imdb.com/name/nm0191265/otherworks, accessed June 17, 2019; "Prado Unit to Play in Korea," *Stars and Stripes* (Pacific Edition), September 10, 1956, 14; "King Perez Mambos for Troops," *Stars and Stripes* (Pacific Edition), September 15, 1956, 14; "Prado Gives Seoul Treat with Long Mambo Fete" and "Mambo King Performs at Front Line," *Stars and Stripes* (Pacific Edition), September 19, 1956, 14.

21. "Koreans Give U.N. Servicemen Song, Dance 'Christmas Gift,'" *Stars and Stripes* (Pacific Edition), December 24, 1956, 11.

22. E. Taylor Atkins, *Blue Nippon* (Durham, NC: Duke University Press, 2001); Christine R. Yano, "Diva Misora Hibari as Spectacle of Postwar Japan's Modernity," in *Vamping the Stage*, ed. Andrew N. Weintraub and Bart Barendregt (Honolulu: University of Hawai'i Press, 2017), 133–34; Albert D. Ricketts, "On the Town," *Stars and Stripes* (Pacific Edition), October 14, 1955, 15.

23. "Japan Tops with U.S. Stars—and Vice Versa," *Stars and Stripes* (Pacific Edition), January 3, 1957, 7; Japanese TV listings, *Stars and Stripes* (Pacific Edition), September 23, 1956; "On the Town," *Stars and Stripes* (Pacific Edition), September 13, 1956; "Chŏsok'an mambo ch'um, il chŏngnyŏnch'ŭng e sŏnghaeng."

24. E. Taylor Atkins, "Toward a Global History of Jazz," in *Jazz Planet*, ed. E. Taylor Atkins (Jackson: University Press of Mississippi, 2003), xvii.

25. Perez Firmat, *Life on the Hyphen*, 85; Thompson, "Teaching the People to Triumph over Time," 337; García, "Going Primitive."

26. "Hyŏndaein" [Modern people], *Tonga ilbo*, August 10, 1959, 4; "Sŏul ŭi ch'uksop'an, Myŏngdong ŭi haru" [A day in Myeongdong, miniature of Seoul], *Tonga ilbo*, November 25, 1957, 3; "Mambo paji nŭn wae imna" [Why wear mambo pants?], *Kyŏnghyang sinmun*, November 24, 1957, 3.

27. Advertisement, *Kyŏnghyang sinmun*, October 12, 1960; Ch'oe Sejin, "Chunggunk Sanghae esŏ chaejŭ rŭl molgo toraon sanai" [The guy who brought jazz from Shanghai, China], February 20, 2004, https://cafe.naver.com/rudyjazz/71; February 25, 2004, https://cafe.naver.com/rudyjazz/81; March 6, 2004, https://cafe.naver.com/rudyjazz/103; March 10, 2004, https://cafe.naver.com/rudyjazz/113; April 5, 2004, https://cafe.naver.com/rudyjazz/173.

28. For a brief history of twentieth-century Korean music, see John Lie, *K-Pop* (Oakland: University of California Press, 2015), 7–65.

29. Han's penultimate film, *Let's Meet at Walkerhill* (1966), featured cameos by the Okhooyeon Modern Dancing Team, the Park Chun-seok Orchestra, Hyeon Mi, Lee Geumhee, and Lee Mi-ha; *Han Hyung-mo: The Alchemist of Popular Genres*, 15.

30. Pil Ho Kim and Hyunjoon Shin, "The Birth of 'Rok,'" *Positions* 18, no. 1 (2010): 199–230; Roald Maliangkay, "Koreans Performing for Foreign Troops," *East Asian History* 37 (2011): 59–72; Roald Maliangkay, "Supporting Our Boys," in *Korean Pop Music*, ed. Keith Howard (Kent, England: Global Oriental, 2006), 21–33.

31. Roald Maliangkay, "Koreans Got Talent," *Situations* 11, no. 1 (2019): 64; Report, Special Services Section, October 1954, RG 338L, box 572, file 353.8, August–December, National Archives and Records Administration (hereafter NARA).

32. Shin Hyunjoon and Ho Tung-hung, "Translation of 'America' during the Early Cold War Period," *Inter-Asia Cultural Studies* 10, no. 1. (2009): 93; "Men Earning Foreign Currencies," *Korean News Round Up*, October 29, 1960, RG 388, box 1499, file Newspaper files (1960) (Sept.–Oct.) World-Korean News Round Up, NARA; "Sale of Domestic Supplies to Armed Forces," *Korean Report* 6 (1958): 134.

33. *Korean News Round Up*, October 29, 1960, RG 388, box 1499, file Newspaper files (1960) (Sept.–Oct.) World-Korean News Round Up, NARA; "Kiťarisǔťǔ Kim Hǔigap kwaǔi intŏbyu" [Interview with Kim Hee-gap, guitarist], http://blog.naver.com/delos1, accessed April 10, 2014.

34. Maliangkay, "Koreans Got Talent," 67–68; Maliangkay, "Supporting Our Boys"; Benjamin Han, "Transpacific Talent," *Pacific Historical Review* 87, no. 3 (2018): 473; Sue Kim, interview with author, January 7, 2013; Myoung-ja Lee Kwon, "An Interview with Sook-ja Kim," Las Vegas Women in Gaming and Entertainment Oral History Project, University of Nevada, Las Vegas.

35. David Scott Diffrient, "*Over That Hill*," *Journal of Japanese and Korean Cinema* 1, no. 2 (2009): 105–27.

36. Kim and Shin, "The Birth of 'Rok,'" 2–3.

37. Poshek Fu, "Modernity, Diasporic Capital, and 1950's Hong Kong Mandarin Cinema," *Jump Cut*, no. 49 (2007); Christine R. Yano, "Jet-Age Nationhood," in *Japan since 1945*, ed. Christopher Gerteis and Timothy S. George (London: Blooomsbury, 2013), 208–22.

38. "Chikjang yŏsŏng ech'ik'el" [Working woman etiquette], *Yŏwŏn*, November 1955, 77–80.

39. Chung, *Split Screen Korea*, 62.

40. Ted Polhemus and Lynn Procter, *Fashion and Anti-Fashion* (London: Thames and Hudson, 1978); Elizabeth Wilson, *Adorned in Dreams* (Berkeley: University of California Press, 1987); Malcolm Barnard, *Fashion Theory* (New York: Routledge, 2014), 37; Grant David McCracken, *Culture and Consumption* (Bloomington: Indiana University Press, 1988), 61; Anthony Giddens, *Modernity and Self-Identity* (Stanford, CA: Stanford University Press, 1991).

41. Kim Kee-duk oral history, in *KFS, 1950s*, 2:146, 115, 139.

42. Michael E. Robinson, *Korea's Twentieth-Century Odyssey* (Honolulu: University of Hawai'i Press, 2007), 79; Todd A. Henry, *Assimilating Seoul* (Berkeley: University of California Press, 2014), 92–129; Youngna Kim, "Urban Space and Visual Culture," in *A Companion to Asian Art and Architecture*, ed. Rebecca Brown and Deborah Hutton (Hoboken, NJ: Wiley-Blackwell, 2011), 153–77.

43. E. Taylor Atkins, *Primitive Selves* (Berkeley: University of California Press, 2010), 56–57, 83; Robinson, *Korea's Twentieth-Century Odyssey*, 92.

44. Hyung Il Pai, *Heritage Management in Korea and Japan* (Seattle: University of Washington Press, 2013), 144, 153, 159.

45. Sunae Park, Patricia Campbell Warner, and Thomas K. Fitzgerald, "The Process of Westernization," *Clothing and Textile Research Journal* 11, no. 3 (1993): 39–47; Joo Seong-hee, "An Overview of Modern Fashion in Korea," *Koreana* 15, no. 1 (2001); Kungnip Minsok Pangmulgwan, *Han'guk poksik munhwa 2000-nyŏn chŏn* [2000 Years of Korean Fashion and Culture] (Seoul: National Folk Museum of Korea, 2001).

46. Park et al., "Process of Westernization," 45.

47. Helen Kim, *Grace Sufficient* (Nashville: The Upper Room, 1964), 142.

48. William Armour Murdoch, *Republic of South Korea, 1957–1959* (Bloomington, IN: Author House, 2007), 72, 124–25.

49. Park et al., "Process of Westernization," 45.

50. Gore, "Yangjae yangjang yongŏhaesŏl" [Explanation of Western tailoring and clothing terminology], *Yŏwŏn*, November 1958, 276–77, December 1958, 276–77.

51. Ok Hye-myung, "Purajya pattŭ mandŭlgi" [How to make a brassiere band], *Yŏwŏn*, February 1958, 244–45; Yu Han-chul, "Chŏnghyŏngsusurŭn ŏdikkaji shinyonghalsuinnŭn'ga" [To what point can one trust plastic surgery?"], *Yŏwŏn*, January 1958, 226.

52. Nora Noh, *Nora Noh, yŏlchŏngŭl tijainhada* [Nora Noh designs passion] (Seoul: Hwanggŭmnach'imban), 2007; *Nora Noh* (dir. Sung-hee Kim, 2013).

53. *Nora Noh*.

54. *Nora Noh*.

55. Nora Noh, *Nora Noh, yŏlchŏngŭl tijainhada*, 133.

56. Kim Yoo-kyung, "Nora Noh: A Living Legend," *Koreana* 28, no. 1 (2014): 69.

57. Park Shin Mi, "20segi chung·huban han'gukp'aesyŏn koch'al" [An observation on mid- to late-twentieth-century Korean fashion], *Pokshik* [Journal of the Korean Society of Costume] 64, no. 4 (2014): 52–75; Choi Sun-ho, "P'aesyŏnsyo" [Fashion shows], *Chosŏn ilbo*, September 4, 2003; *Yŏwŏn*, August 1957. *Yŏwŏn* also covered her May 1958 show at the Bando hotel (*Yŏwŏn*, July 1958) and the 1958 Miss Universe beauty pageant in California (*Yŏwŏn*, October 1958). Andrei Lankov, *Dawn of Modern Korea* (Seoul: EunHaeng NaMu, 2007), 263; Nora Noh, *Nora Noh, yŏlchŏngŭl tijainhada*, 193–202.

58. *Nora Noh*.

59. Nora Noh, *Nora Noh, yŏlchŏngŭl tijainhada*, 201, back cover.

60. Park Shin Mi, "Maech'ebunsŏkŭl t'onghae pon norano p'aesyŏn'gwa han'gung p'aesyŏn koch'al (1)" [A Study on Nora Noh fashion and Korean modern fashion through the analysis of the media (1)], *Han'gukp'aesyŏndijainhak'oeji* [Journal of the Korean Society of Fashion Design] 16, no. 4 (2016): 89–107.

61. *Nora Noh*; Chung, *Split Screen Korea*, 59.

62. *Nora Noh*.

63. Kim Kang-yun et al., comp., *Han'guk yŏnghwa charyo p'yŏllam (ch'och'anggi-1976-yŏn)* [A guide to sources on South Korean film: Beginnings to 1976] (Seoul: Yŏnghwa chinhŭng kongsa, 1977), 84.

64. Bosley Crowther, "The Screen in Review," *New York Times*, May 28, 1954.

65. Lee Byung-il's *The Wedding Day* (1956) was the first Korean film to win a prize at an international film festival when it won the best comedy award at the fourth Asian Film

Festival held in Tokyo in 1957; "The Truth of Korean Movies," Korean Film Archive, http://recruit.koreafilm.or.kr/feature/ans_21.asp, accessed March 22, 2017; "Yŏnghwa Chayubuin tŭng tae Hyanghang such'ul ŭl ch'ujin" [*Madame Freedom* and *Holiday in Seoul* are to be exported to Hong Kong], *Chosŏn ilbo*, February 10, 1957, 2, in *Sinmun kisa ro pon Han'guk yŏnghwa, 1945-1957* [Korean Films in Newspapers, 1945–1957], ed. Han'guk Yŏngsang Charyowŏn [Korean Film Archive] (Seoul: Konggan kwa Saramdŭl, 2004).

66. Donna Ong discovered a Chinese-language version of the script in the Hong Kong Film Archive. Park Seong-ho, *Because I Love You / Love for You*, Hong Kong Film Archive, call number HB534X. All subsequent quotations from the script are from this source.

67. *Love for You* press book, Hong Kong Film Archive, call number HB534X.

68. Jiang Ming, "A Tragedy with Insufficient Reasoning—About *Love for You*," *Ta kung pao*, November 9, 1959, 7.

69. Hollywood films in the 1950s and 1960s were also inserting touristic spectacles to render noncommunist Asia visible to American audiences. See, for example, *Macao* (1952), *Love Is a Many Splendored Thing* (1955), and *The World of Suzy Wong* (1960).

70. There is some confusion in the historical record over which prize the film won, although the prize for choreography seems most likely. Korean newspapers reported that it won the folk culture award. Sources from multiple other countries, however, identify the prize as the choreography award. These include: the Tokyo-based *Far East Film News*, June 1959, which covered the festival closely for years; advertisements in Hong Kong newspapers; and the handbill of the Chinese-language version of the film. Numerous sources also identify the Malayan film *Mahsuri* as the winner of the folk culture award, including the Singapore *Straits Times*, May 9, 1959, and the National Film Development Corporation Malaysia.

71. "Hop'yŏng padŭn uri yŏn'gi" [Our acting receives good reviews], *Seoul sinmun*, May 16, 1959, 4.

72. *Because I Love You*, KMDb, www.kmdb.or.kr/db/kor/detail/movie/K/00418, accessed June 19, 2019.

73. P'yŏnjip parhaeng Taehan Min'guk Oemubu [Department of Foreign Affairs, Republic of Korea] *Han'guk oegyo 30-yŏn: 1948-1978* [Thirty years of Korean foreign relations: 1948–1978] (Seoul: Oemubu, 1979), 250–53.

74. Yongwoo Lee, "Embedded Voices in between Empires" (PhD diss., McGill University, 2010).

75. Materials from the Asian Peoples' Anti-Communist League Conference, Manila, March 9, 1955, History and Public Policy Program Digital Archive, B-392–001, Documents Related to the Asian Anti-Communist League Conference, Papers Related to Treaty-Making and International Conferences, Syngman Rhee Institute, Yonsei University. http://digitalarchive.wilsoncenter.org/document/118346 (hereafter APACL-SRI).

76. Letter, Young Kee Kim to Chung Whan Cho, December 19, 1955, http://digitalarchive.wilsoncenter.org/document/123301; Letter, Young Kee Kim to Chung Whan Cho, January 18, 1956, http://digitalarchive.wilsoncenter.org/document/123296; Letter, Young Kee Kim to Chung Whan Cho, November 19, 1956, http://digitalarchive.wilsoncenter.org/document/123167; Weekly Report from Pyung Sik Son to the President (Syngman Rhee), February 15, 1957, http://digitalarchive.wilsoncenter.org/document/120924, all Reports from

the Korean Mission to the United Nations and Republic of Korea Embassies and Legations, Syngman Rhee Institute (hereafter RKM-SRI).

77. Weekly Report from Pyung Sik Son to the President (Syngman Rhee), May 3, 1957, http://digitalarchive.wilsoncenter.org/document/120909, RKM-SRI.

78. CDS Report No. 59 from Choi Duk Shin to the President (Syngman Rhee), October 18, 1957, http://digitalarchive.wilsoncenter.org/document/121055, RKM-SRI.

79. Han Sang Kim, "Uneven Screens, Contested Identities" (PhD diss., Seoul National University, 2013), 191–95; Joon Young Park, "Korea's Return to Asia" (PhD diss., Columbia University, 1981), 34; P'yŏnjip parhaeng Taehan Min'guk Oemubu, *Han'guk oegyo 30-yŏn*, 250–52.

80. *Taehan News*, May 13 and May 20, 1957, February 25, March 25, April 1, April 8, April 22, www.ehistory.go.kr/page/koreanews/korea_news.jsp; "Han'guk yesul sajoldan tongnama pangum" [Korean cultural goodwill mission to Southeast Asia] (Liberty News, USIS-Korea, film, 1958), http://kfilm.khistory.org/?mod = 25&MOVIE_SEQ = 7267&KIND_CLSS = 24.

81. Alan C. Heyman, "Kim Paik-bong," in *International Encyclopedia of Dance*, ed. Selma Jeanne Cohen (Oxford: Oxford University Press, 1998), 4:12–13.

82. "Pangk'ok-eso ch'um ch'unun Kim Paek-pong" [Kim Paik-bong dancing in Bangkok] (Liberty News, USIS-Korea/USIS-Thailand, film, 1958), RG 306, 306.6354, NARA.

83. Kim, "Uneven Screens, Contested Identities," 194.

84. Kim Paik-bong, "Hangukyesul-ui dongnamasunrye" [A Southeast Asian tour of Korean art], *Yŏwŏn*, July 1958, 71–74.

85. Sangjoon Lee, "The Transnational Asian Studio System" (PhD diss., New York University, 2011), 298.

86. *Because I Love You*, KMDb.

87. Huang Zhuohan, *Dianying rensheng: Huang Zhuohan huiyilu* [A life in film: Memoir of Wong Cheuk-hon] (Taipei: Wangxiang Tushu, 1994), 102–3; Park Seong-ho, "Saenggak nanŭn taero: Hyanghang e wasŏ ch'waryŏng ŭl hamyŏ" [Whatever comes to my mind: Filming in Hong Kong], *Kukche yŏnghwa*, November 1958, 48–49. While much of the story is set in Singapore and the production planned to shoot in Kuala Lumpur, Malaya, there is uncertainty as to whether the crew was actually able to shoot there. According to Sangjoon Lee, shooting was moved to Hong Kong due to an epidemic in Malaya. Lee, "Transnational Asian Studio System," 298. Most Korean newspapers reported that the film had been shot in Malaya, although one quoted the Korean judge at the Asian Film Festival as saying that the Malayan scenes were shot in Hong Kong.

88. Huang Zhuohan, *Dianying rensheng*, 102–3; "Kuksan yŏnghwa ch'oech'o ro haeoe such'ul" [First domestic film to be exported overseas], *Han'guk ilbo*, April 26, 1959, 5.

89. Chung-kang Kim, "South Korean Golden-Age Comedy" (PhD diss., University of Illinois at Urbana-Champaign, 2010), 61; Im Hwa-su, "Hapchak yŏnghwa ŭi ŭiŭi" [The significance of coproduction films], *Chosŏn ilbo*, May 28, 1957, Im Hwa-su, Hapchak yŏnghwa ŭi kanŭngsŏng [The potential of coproduction films], *Chosŏn ilbo*, February 20, 1958, 4.

90. "Oeguk e such'ul t'orok / Yi taet'ongnyŏng kuksan yŏnghwa rŭl ch'ingch'an" [Hope to export overseas, President Rhee praises Korean films], *Han'guk ilbo*, January 3, 1959, 4, and "Yi Sŭngman taet'ongnyŏng kuksan yŏnghwa chejak kyŏngnyŏ" [President Rhee Syngman

encourages Korean film production], *Chosŏn ilbo*, January 3, 1959, 7, in *Sinmun kisa ro pon Han'guk yŏnghwa, 1958-1961* [Korean Films in Newspapers, 1958–1961], ed. Han'guk Yŏngsang Charyowŏn [Korean Film Archive] (Seoul: Konggan kwa Saramdŭl, 2005) (hereafter *KFN, 1958–61*), 142.

91. Kim, "South Korean Golden Age Comedy," 82n179.

92. Park Seong-ho, "Saenggak nanŭn taero," 48–49.

93. "Sino-Korean Film Cooperation Miscalculates Box Office Earnings," *United Daily News* (Taiwan), October 20, 1958, 6; Law Kar and Frank Bren, *Hong Kong Cinema* (Lanham, MD: Scarecrow, 2004), 201–17; Brian Hu, "Star Discourse and the Cosmopolitan Chinese," *Journal of Chinese Cinemas* 4, no. 3, 183–209; Mary Wong, "Women Who Cross Borders," in *The Cathay Story*, ed. Wong Ain-ling (Hong Kong: Hong Kong Film Archive, 2002), 162–75; Huang, *Dianying rensheng*, 102–3. Wang Yuanlong, who played the director of the Malayan dance organization, was founder and president of the Hong Kong and Kowloon Filmmakers Free General Association, Ltd. From Donna Ong, personal communication to author.

94. Pak Chisa, "Chiyang twaeya hal yŏnghwa bip'yŏng" [Film criticism that should be avoided], in *KFN, 1958–61*; Park Seong-ho, "Saenggak nanŭn taero," 48–49.

95. Letter from Jack E. James to Kim Sungmin, August 11, 1958, box P-150, file Media-Audio-Visual-Films-General-Korea-Program, The Asia Foundation Records, Hoover Institution Archives (hereafter TAF).

96. Korea Program Budget 1958/59, box P-59, file Korea Budget 1957/58, TAF.

97. Memorandum, Attached Motion Picture Project, January 21, 1953, box P-9, file Tokyo-TV-Movies-1953; Memorandum, Recommendations for a CFA, Japan Motion Picture Program, September 18, 1953, box P-9, file Tokyo-TV-Movies-1953; Memorandum, Trip to Hollywood, December 31, 1953, box P-9, file Writer Project (Japan), all TAF.

98. Southeast Asian Film Festival, box P-18, file Film Festival FMPPSEA-3rd Hong Kong 1956-Korea; "Report on the 4th Asian Film Festival," June 25, 1957, box P-88, file Fourth Asian Film Festival-1957-US & Int.-Conferences; Memorandum, "Proposed Itinerary for Remainder of Film Advisory and Research Assignment," February 11, 1957, box P-39, file Miller, John (Films)-US and Int.-Individual; Memorandum, "Fifth Asian Film Festival," Manila, March 20, 1958, box P-90, file Fifth Asian Film Festival-Manila, 1958-US & Int.-Conferences; Cho Tong-jae, "My Personal Impressions of the 6th Asian Film Festival in Kuala Lumpur," May 19, 1959, box P-93, file Film Festival-6th Asian-Kuala Lumpur-1959, all TAF.

99. *Love for You* script, SCR2492.4, Hong Kong Film Archive.

100. "*Love for You*'s 7 Major Achievements," *Kung Sheung* [Hong Kong] *Evening News*, November 7, 1959, 6; "Best Choreography Award Winning Film *Love for You* about to be released," *Kung Sheung Daily News*, November 28, 1959, 11. The film was known by other names as well. Liberty Films translated the Mandarin title into English as *Twinkling Stars*, while the Hong Kong Movie Database today lists the film under the title *As Glamourous as the Galaxy*. The film appears in the Asia Foundation documentation as *For Love's Sake*.

101. Based on newspaper articles, advertisements, and reviews.

102. "*Love for You*'s 7 Major Achievements"; "Han-Mare hapchak yŏnghwa *Sarang hanŭn kkadak e*" [Korea-Malaysia coproduction film *Because I Love You*], *Chosŏn ilbo*,

December 7, 1958, 4; "Sin yŏnghwa pyŏng" [Reviews of new films], *Kukche yŏnghwa*, January 1959, 100; "Sin yŏnghwa" [New film], *Sŏul sinmun*, December 12, 1958, 4.

CONCLUSION

1. Charles Kim, *Youth for Nation* (Honolulu: University of Hawai'i Press, 2017), 183.

2. *Time,* June 1961, quoted in "A Country Boy Running Korea," on blog *Gusts of Popular Feeling,* May 17, 2007, http://populargusts.blogspot.com/2007/05/country-boy-running-korea.html.

3. A. M. Rosenthal, "Again Korea Is Being Tested," *New York Times,* November 12, 1961, SM72, SM79.

4. "T'ŭkchŏng wŏeraep'um p'anmae gŭmji bŏp" [Law for the Prohibition of Sale of Specific Foreign Products], May 10, 1961, www.law.go.kr.

5. *Time,* March 1962, quoted in, "A Country Boy Running Korea," on blog *Gusts of Popular Feeling,* May 17, 2007, http://populargusts.blogspot.com/2007/05/country-boy-running-korea.html.

6. AP, "Smuggled Products Burned," *Stars and Stripes* (Pacific Edition), March 3, 1962; "'Austerity' in Tea Rooms Bans U.S. Coffee Sale," *Stars and Stripes* (Pacific Edition), May 31, 1961.

7. Kim, *Youth for Nation,* 194.

8. Charles R. Smith, "Junta's Long-Range Policy Called Murky," *Stars and Stripes* (Pacific Edition), June 17, 1961.

9. Kyung-Koo Han, "The Kimchi Wars in Globalizing East Asia," in *Consuming Korean Tradition in Early and Late Modernity,* ed. Laurel Kendall (Honolulu: University of Hawai'i Press, 2010), 154; Laura C. Nelson, *Measured Excess* (New York: Columbia University Press, 2000), 113.

10. Bruce Cumings, *Korea's Place in the Sun,* 2nd ed. (New York: W. W. Norton, 2005), 319–21.

11. John Lie, *Han Unbound* (Stanford, CA: Stanford University Press, 1998), 103–4; Kim, *Youth for Nation,* 187.

12. Seungsook Moon, "Begetting the Nation," in *Dangerous Women,* ed. Elaine H. Kim and Chungmoo Choi (New York: Routledge, 1998), 37.

13. Michael E. Robinson, "Contemporary Cultural Production in South Korea," *New Korean Cinema,* ed. Chi-Yun Shin and Julian Stringer (New York: New York University Press, 2005), 22–23.

14. Codruta Sintionean, "Heritage Practices during the Park Chung Hee Era," in *Key Papers on Korea,* ed. Andrew Davis Jackson (Leiden: Brill, 2013), 262.

15. Youngna Kim, "Urban Space and Visual Culture," in *A Companion to Asian Art and Architecture,* ed. Rebecca Brown and Deborah Hutton (Hoboken, NJ: Wiley-Blackwell, 2011), 167.

16. Kim, *Youth for Nation,* 202–3.

17. Mun Gwan-gyu, *Lee Man-hee,* trans. Colin A. Mouat, Korean Film Directors series (Seoul: Seoul Selection, 2009).

18. Lee Young-il and Choe Young-chol, *The History of Korean Cinema,* trans. Richard Lynn Greever (Seoul: Jimoondang, 1998), 143–48; Kim Mee hyun, ed., *Korean Cinema* (Seoul: Communications Books/KOFIC, 2007), 177–83.

19. "Conversation with Park Chan-wook," event at Harvard University, March 5, 2019; Bong Joon-ho, interview with author, Harvard University, March 2010. Bong has identified *The Housemaid* as an inspiration for his most recent film, *Parasite* (2019).

20. Christina Klein, "The AFKN Nexus," *Transnational Chinese Cinemas* 3, no. 1 (2012): 19–39.

FILMS DIRECTED BY HAN HYUNG-MO

Information about each of Han's films, including plot summary, credits, and still images, can be found on the Korean Movie Database website (www.kmdb.or.kr/eng/db/per/00002080) which is run by the Korean Film Archive.

Breaking the Wall (1949, lost)

An Assault on Justice, Part 1 (1951)

An Assault on Justice, Part 2 (1952)

The Hand of Destiny (1954)
KOFA YouTube: www.youtube.com/watch?v=OANGhypaYCg&t=338s

Madame Freedom (1956)
KOFA YouTube: www.youtube.com/watch?v=FkAbVQhfpmw&t=3537s&has_verified=1

Hyperbolae of Youth (1956)
KOFA YouTube: www.youtube.com/watch?v=cVxQGfWDBR8&t=4123s&has_verified=1

The Pure Love (1957)
Available via VOD at the Korean Film Archive website

The Devil (1957, lost)

Because I Love You (1958, lost)

I Am Alone (1958, lost)

A Female Boss (1959)
KOFA YouTube: www.youtube.com/watch?v=T5vT42pCwfI&t=5513s

Men vs. Women (1959)
Available via VOD at the Korean Film Archive website

Poor Lovers (1959, lost)

A Jealousy (1960, lost)

A Dream of Fortune (1961)
KOFA YouTube: www.youtube.com/watch?v=5lSqCzt7foQ&has_verified=1

My Sister Is a Hussy (1961)
KOFA YouTube: www.youtube.com/watch?v=maAQNkLhPrQ&t=4220s

Prince Hodong (1962)
Available via VOD at the Korean Film Archive website

The Heaven and the Hell (1963, lost)

Let's Meet at Walkerhill (1966)
Available via VOD at the Korean Film Archive website

The Queen of Elegy (1967)
Available via VOD at the Korean Film Archive website

BIBLIOGRAPHY

ARCHIVES

CIA, Freedom of Information Act Electronic Reading Room (CIA)
C. V. Starr East Asian Library, Columbia University, Theodore Richard Conant Collection (TCC)
Hong Kong Film Archive
Hoover Institution Library and Archives, Stanford University, The Asia Foundation Records (TAF)
Korean Film Archive
National Archives and Records Administration (NARA)
Smith College Libraries, Special Collections, Sophia Smith Collection (SSC)
Syngman Rhee Institute, Yonsei University, Wilson Center Digital Archive (SRI)
Yale University Library, Manuscripts and Archives, Robert Blum papers (RBP)

PERIODICALS

Far East Film News
Korea Journal
Korean Reports: Reports from the Cabinet Ministries of the Republic of Korea
Monthly Statistical Review
New York Times
Stars and Stripes (Pacific Edition)
Time
U.S. News & World Report
Yŏwŏn
Hong Kong newspapers via Old Hong Kong Newspapers Collection, Hong Kong Public Library

Korean newspapers via Naver News Library
Taiwan newspapers via Taiwan News Smart Web
Singapore newspapers via NewspapersSG

SELECT BIBLIOGRAPHY

1950nyŏndae han'guk yŏnghwa sŭt'ail [Korean film style in the 1950s]. 3 vols. Seoul: Han'guk Yŏngsang Charyowŏn [Korean Film Archive], 2009.

Altman, Rick, ed. *Genre, the Musical: A Reader*. British Film Institute Readers in Film Studies. London: Routledge & Kegan Paul, 1981.

An, Jinsoo. *Parameters of Disavowal: Colonial Representation in South Korean Cinema*. Oakland: University of California Press, 2018.

Anderson, George L, ed. *Issues and Conflicts: Studies in Twentieth Century American Diplomacy*. Lawrence: University of Kansas Press, 1959.

Anderson, Gerald H. *Biographical Dictionary of Christian Missions*. New York: Macmillan Reference USA, 1998.

Appadurai, Arjun. *Modernity at Large: Cultural Dimensions of Globalization*. Minneapolis: University of Minnesota Press, 1996.

———, ed. *The Social Life of Things: Commodities in Cultural Perspective*. Cambridge: Cambridge University Press, 1986.

Appadurai, Arjun, and Carol Breckenridge. "Public Modernity in India." In *Consuming Modernity: Public Culture in a South Asian World*, edited by Carol Breckenridge, 1–20. Minneapolis: University of Minnesota Press, 1995.

Armstrong, Charles K. "The Cultural Cold War in Korea, 1945–1950." *Journal of Asian Studies* 62, no. 1 (2003): 71–99.

———. *Korean Society: Civil Society, Democracy and the State*. 2nd ed. New York: Routledge, 2006.

Atkins, E. Taylor. *Blue Nippon: Authenticating Jazz in Japan*. Durham, NC: Duke University Press, 2001.

———. *Primitive Selves: Koreana in the Japanese Colonial Gaze, 1910–1945*. Berkeley: University of California Press, 2010.

———. "Toward a Global History of Jazz." In *Jazz Planet*, edited by E. Taylor Atkins, xi–xxvii. Jackson: University Press of Mississippi, 2003.

———, ed. *Jazz Planet*. Jackson: University Press of Mississippi, 2003.

Bae, AhRan Ellie. "Helen Kim as New Woman and Collaborator: A Comprehensive Assessment of Korean Collaboration under Japanese Colonial Rule." *International Journal of Korean History* 22, no. 1 (2017): 107–37.

Bardsley, Jan. *Women and Democracy in Cold War Japan*. London: Bloomsbury Academic, 2014.

Barnard, Malcolm. *Fashion Theory: An Introduction*. London: Routledge, 2014.

Baskett, Michael. *The Attractive Empire: Transnational Film Culture in Imperial Japan*. Honolulu: University of Hawai'i Press, 2008.

———. "Japan's Film Festival Diplomacy in Cold War Asia." *Velvet Light Trap* 73, no. 1 (2014): 4–18.

Bates, Robert H., and Anne O. Krueger, eds. *Political and Economic Interactions in Economic Policy Reform: Evidence from Eight Countries*. Oxford: Blackwell, 1993.

Belmonte, Laura A. *Selling the American Way: U.S. Propaganda and the Cold War*. Philadelphia: University of Pennsylvania Press, 2008.

Berry, Chris. "Scream and Scream Again: Korean Modernity as a House of Horrors in the Films of Kim Ki-young." In *Seoul Searching*, edited by Frances Gateward, 99–114. Albany: State University of New York Press, 2007.

Bhabha, Homi. "Of Mimicry and Man: The Ambivalence of Colonial Discourse." In *The Location of Culture*, 152–60. Berkeley: University of California Press, 1997.

Blum, Robert. "The Work of the Asia Foundation." *Pacific Affairs* 29, no. 1 (1956): 46–55.

Brandt, Kim. "Japan the Beautiful: 1950s Cosmetic Surgery and the Expressive Asian Body." In *The Affect of Difference: Representations of Race and in East Asian Empire*, ed. Christopher P. Hanscom and Dennis Washburn, 261–85. Honolulu: University of Hawai'i Press, 2016.

Brazinsky, Gregg A. *Nation Building in South Korea: Koreans, Americans, and the Making of a Democracy*. Chapel Hill: University of North Carolina Press, 2007.

———. *Winning the Third World: Sino-American Rivalry during the Cold War*. Chapel Hill: University of North Carolina Press, 2017.

Breckenridge, Carol, ed. *Consuming Modernity: Public Culture in a South Asian World*. Minneapolis: University of Minnesota Press, 1995.

Breckenridge, Carol, Homi K. Bhabha, Sheldon Pollock, and Dipesh Chakrabarty, eds. *Cosmopolitanism*. Durham, NC: Duke University Press, 2002.

Brooks, Peter. *The Melodramatic Imagination: Balzac, Henry James, Melodrama, and the Mode of Excess*. New Haven, CT: Yale University Press, 1995.

Brown, Rebecca M., and Deborah S. Hutton, eds. *A Companion to Asian Art and Architecture*. Hoboken, NJ: Wiley-Blackwell, 2011.

Bukatman, Scott. "Spectacle, Attractions and Visual Pleasure." In *The Cinema of Attractions Reloaded*, edited by Wanda Strauven, 71–82. Amsterdam: Amsterdam University Press, 2006.

Burton, Antoinette M. *The Postcolonial Careers of Santha Rama Rau*. Durham, NC: Duke University Press, 2007.

Byun, Jai-ran, "The Problematic Perception of Women Wavering between 'Madame' and 'Freedom.'" DVD booklet, *Women on Screen*. Seoul: Korean Film Archive, 2012.

Cha, Victor D. *Powerplay: The Origins of the American Alliance System in Asia*. Princeton, NJ: Princeton University Press, 2016.

Chang, Jing Jing. *Screening Communities*. Hong Kong: Hong Kong University Press, 2019.

Chang, Yun-Shik. "Conclusion: South Korea; In Pursuit of Modernity." In *Transformations in Twentieth Century Korea*, edited by Yun-Shik Chang and Steven Hugh Lee, 345–73. New York: Routledge, 2006.

Chang, Yun-Shik and Steven Hugh Lee, eds. *Transformations in Twentieth Century Korea*. New York: Routledge, 2006.

Chatterjee, Partha. *The Nation and Its Fragments: Colonial and Postcolonial Histories*. Princeton, NJ: Princeton University Press, 1993.

Chen, Tina Mai. "International Film Circuits and Global Imaginaries in the People's Republic of China, 1949–57." *Journal of Chinese Cinemas* 3, no. 2 (2009): 149–61.

Chi, James Sang. "Teaching Korea: Modernization, Model Minorities, and American Internationalism in the Cold War Era." PhD diss., University of California, Berkeley, 2008.

Cho, Eunsun. "The Female Body and Enunciation in *Adada* and *Surrogate Mother*." In *Im Kwon-Taek*, edited by David E. James and Kyung Hyun Kim, 84–106. Detroit: Wayne State University Press, 2002.

———. "Transnational Modernity, National Identity, and South Korean Melodrama (1945–1960s)." PhD diss., University of Southern California, 2006.

———. "*The Stray Bullet* and the Crisis of Korean Masculinity." In *South Korean Golden Age Melodrama*, edited by Kathleen McHugh and Nancy Abelmann, 99–116. Detroit: Wayne State University Press, 2005.

Cho, Grace M. *Haunting the Korean Diaspora: Shame, Secrecy, and the Forgotten War.* Minneapolis: University of Minnesota Press, 2008.

Cho, Haejoang. "Living with Conflicting Subjectivities: Mother, Motherly Wife, and Sexy Woman in the Transition from Colonial-Modern to Postmodern Korea." In *Under Construction*, edited by Kendall Laurel, 165–96. Honolulu: University of Hawai'i Press, 2002.

Cho, Hye-jung. "Film Technology in Disarray." In *Korean Cinema*, ed. Kim Mee hyun, 113–14. Seoul: Communications Books/KOFIC, 2007.

Cho Junhyoung. "The Front Line of Korean Popular Movies in the 1950s." In *Han Hyung-mo: The Alchemist of Popular Genres*, ed. Lee Sang-yong and Yang Ayoung, 11–42. Seoul: Korean Film Archive, 2008.

Choe Mijin. *1950nyŏndae shinmunsosŏre nat'anan ap'ŭre kŏl* [Après-girls in newspaper novels of the 1950s]. *Taejungsŏsayŏn'gu* [Popular narrative studies] 13, no. 2 (2007): 119–53.

Choi, Chungmoo. "Nationalism and Construction of Gender in Korea." In *Dangerous Women: Gender and Korean Nationalism*, edited by Elaine H. Kim and Chungmoo Choi, 17–40. New York: Routledge, 1998.

———. "The Politics of Gender, Aestheticism, and Cultural Nationalism in *Sopyonje* and *The Genealogy*." In *Im Kwon-Taek*, edited by David E. James and Kyung Hyun Kim, 107–33. Detroit: Wayne State University Press, 2002.

Choi, Hyaeweol. "Debating the Korean New Woman: Imagining Henrik Ibsen's "Nora" in Colonial Era Korea." *Asian Studies Review* 36, no. 1 (2012): 59–77

———. *Gender and Mission Encounters in Korea: New Women, Old Ways.* Berkeley: University of California Press, 2009.

———. "Wise Mother, Good Wife: A Transcultural Discursive Construct in Modern Korea." *Journal of Korean Studies* 14, no. 1 (2009): 1–34.

———, ed. *New Women in Colonial Korea: A Sourcebook.* New York: Routledge, 2013.

Chung Chonghwa. "Mode of Cinematic Plagiarism and Adaptation." *Korea Journal* 57, no. 3 (2017): 56–82.

———. "The Technical Advancement of Cinematic Style in Korean Cinema." In *Han Hyung-mo: The Alchemist of Popular Genres*, ed. Lee Sang-yong and Yang Ayoung. Seoul: Korean Film Archive, 2008.

———. "The Topography of 1960s Korean Youth Film: Between Plagiarism and Adaptation." *Journal of Japanese and Korean Cinema* 8, no. 1 (2016): 1–14.

Chung, Hye Seung, and David Scott Diffrient. *Movie Migrations: Transnational Genre Flows and South Korean Cinema.* New Brunswick, NJ: Rutgers University Press, 2015.

Chung, Steven. *Split Screen Korea: Shin Sang-ok and Postwar Cinema*. Minneapolis: University of Minnesota Press, 2014.

Chung, Yeon Shim. "The Modern Girl (*Modeon Geol*) as a Contested Symbol in Colonial Korea." In *Visualizing Beauty: Gender and Ideology in Modern East Asia*, edited by Aida Yuen Wong, 79–90. Hong Kong: Hong Kong University Press, 2012.

Cohen, Selma Jeanne, ed. *International Encyclopedia of Dance*. Oxford: Oxford University Press, 1998.

Cole, David C., and Princeton N. Lyman. *Korean Development: The Interplay of Politics and Economics*. Cambridge, MA: Harvard University Press, 1971.

Cull, Nicholas John. *The Cold War and the United States Information Agency: American Propaganda and Public Diplomacy, 1945–1989*. Cambridge: Cambridge University Press, 2008.

Cumings, Bruce. *Korea's Place in the Sun: A Modern History*. 2nd ed. New York: W. W. Norton, 2005.

———. *The Origins of the Korean War*, vol. 2: *The Roaring of the Cataract 1947–1950*. Princeton, NJ: Princeton University Press, 1990.

Cwiertka, Katarzyna J. *Cuisine, Colonialism and Cold War: Food in Twentieth-Century Korea*. London: Reaktion Books, 2012.

———. "Dining Out in the Land of Desire: Colonial Seoul and the Korean Culture of Consumption." In *Consuming Korean Tradition in Early and Late Modernity*, edited by Laurel Kendall, 21–38. Honolulu: University of Hawai'i Press, 2010.

de Certeau, Michel. *The Practice of Everyday Life*. Translated by Steven Rendall. Berkeley: University of California Press, 1984.

Deuchler, Martina. *The Confucian Transformation of Korea: A Study of Society and Ideology*. Cambridge, MA: Harvard University Press, 1992.

Diffrient, David Scott. "*Over That Hill*: Cinematic Adaptations and Cross-Cultural Remakes, from Depression-Era America to Post-War Korea." *Journal of Japanese and Korean Cinema* 1, no. 2 (2009): 105–27.

Dower, John W. *Embracing Defeat: Japan in the Wake of World War II*. New York: W. W. Norton, 1999.

Duncan, John. "The Problematic Modernity of Confucianism: The Question of 'Civil Society' in Chosŏn Dynasty Korea." In *Korean Society*, edited by Charles K. Armstrong, 33–52. New York: Routledge, 2006.

Dyer, Richard. "Entertainment and Utopia." In *Genre, the Musical*, edited by Rick Altman. London: Routledge & Kegan Paul, 1981.

Eckert, Carter J. *Offspring of Empire: The Koch'ang Kims and the Colonial Origins of Korean Capitalism, 1876–1945*. Seattle: University of Washington Press, 2014.

———. *Park Chung Hee and Modern Korea: The Roots of Militarism, 1866–1945*. Cambridge, MA: Harvard University Press, 2016.

Elsaesser, Thomas. "Tales of Sound and Fury." In *Home Is Where the Heart Is: Studies in Melodrama and the Woman's Film*, ed. Christine Gledhill, 43–69. London: British Film Institute, 1987.

———. "Vincent Minnelli." In *Genre, the Musical*, edited by Rick Altman, 8–27. London: Routledge & Kegan Paul, 1981.

Faderman, Lillian. *Surpassing the Love of Men: Romantic Friendship and Love between Women from the Renaissance to the Present*. New York: Morrow, 1981.

Frank, Pat. *The Long Way Around*. Philadelphia: J. B. Lippincott, 1953.

Freedman, Alisa, Laura Miller, and Christine Reiko Yano, eds. *Modern Girls on the Go: Gender, Mobility, and Labor in Japan*. Stanford, CA: Stanford University Press, 2013.

Fu, Poshek. "Modernity, Diasporic Capital, and 1950's Hong Kong Mandarin Cinema." *Jump Cut: A Review of Contemporary Media* 49 (2007). www.ejumpcut.org/archive/jc49.2007/Poshek/text.html.

García, David F. *Arsenio Rodríguez and the Transnational Flows of Latin Popular Music*. Philadelphia: Temple University Press, 2006.

———. "Going Primitive to the Movements and Sounds of Mambo." *Musical Quarterly* 89, no. 4 (2006): 505–23.

Gateward, Frances, ed. *Seoul Searching: Culture and Identity in Contemporary Korean Cinema*. Albany: State University of New York Press, 2007.

Gerteis, Christopher, and Timothy S. George. *Japan since 1945: From Postwar to Post-Bubble*. London: Bloomsbury, 2013.

Giddens, Anthony. *Modernity and Self-Identity: Self and Society in the Late Modern Age*. Stanford, CA: Stanford University Press, 1991.

Gilman, Nils. *Mandarins of the Future: Modernization Theory in Cold War America*. Baltimore: Johns Hopkins University Press, 2003.

Gledhill, Christine, ed. *Home Is Where the Heart Is: Studies in Melodrama and the Woman's Film*. London: British Film Institute, 1987.

Gunning, Tom. "The Whole Town's Gawking: Early Cinema and the Visual Experience of Modernity." *Yale Journal of Criticism* 7, no. 2 (1994): 189–201.

Haggard, Stephan, Byung-kook Kim, and Chung-in Moon. "The Transition to Export-led Growth in South Korea: 1954–1966." *Journal of Asian Studies* 50, no. 4 (1991): 850–73.

Haggard, Stephan, Richard Cooper, and Chung-in Moon. "Policy Reform in Korea." In *Political and Economic Interactions in Economic Policy Reform*, edited by Robert H. Bates and Anne O. Krueger. 294–332. Oxford: Blackwell, 1993.

Han, Benjamin. "Transpacific Talent: The Kim Sisters in Cold War America." *Pacific Historical Review* 87, no. 3 (2018): 473–98.

Han, Kyung-Koo. "The Kimchi Wars in Globalizing East Asia." In *Consuming Korean Tradition in Early and Late Modernity*, edited by Laurel Kendall, 149–66. Honolulu: University of Hawai'i Press, 2010.

Han Namhee. "Desiring from a Distance: Cinematic Theatricality and South Korea's Cold War Gaze in Madame Freedom (1956)." *Acta Koreana* 20, no. 2 (2017): 349–76.

Han, Sujin. "Gender at Work: Working Women in Postwar South Korea, 1953–1960." MA thesis, Harvard University, 2018.

Han'guk Yŏsŏng Munhak Hakhoe, "Yŏwŏn" Yeongu Moim. *"Yŏwŏn" yŏn'gu: Yŏsŏng, gyoyang, maeje* [Research on "Yowon": Women, culture, media]. Seoul: Kukhak Charyowŏn, 2008.

Han'guk yŏnghwa rŭl mal handa: 1950nyŏndae han'guk yŏnghwa [To Speak on Korean Cinema: Korean Cinema in the 1950s]. Seoul: Han'guk Yŏngsang Charyowŏn/Ichae, 2004.

Han'guk yŏnghwa rŭl mal handa: Han'guk yŏnghwa ŭi rŭnesangsŭ 1 [To Speak on Korean Cinema: The Renaissance of Korean Cinema 1]. Seoul: Han'guk Yŏngsang Charyowŏn/Ichae, 2005.

Han'guk Yŏngsang Charyowŏn [Korean Film Archive], ed. *Sinmun kisa ro pon Han'guk yŏnghwa, 1945–1957* [Korean films in newspapers, 1945–1957], ed. Han'guk Yŏngsang Charyowŏn [Korean Film Archive]. Seoul: Konggan kwa Saramdŭl, 2004.

———, ed. *Sinmun kisa ro pon Han'guk yŏnghwa, 1958–1961* [Korean films in newspapers, 1958–1961]. Seoul: Konggan Kwa Saramdŭl, 2005.

Hansen, Miriam. "Fallen Women, Rising Stars, New Horizons: Shanghai Silent Film as Vernacular Modernism." *Film Quarterly* 54, no. 1 (2000): 10–22.

———. "The Mass Production of the Senses: Classical Cinema as Vernacular Modernism." *Modernism/Modernity* 6, no. 2 (1999): 59–77.

Henderson, Gregory. *Korea, the Politics of the Vortex*. Cambridge, MA: Harvard University Press, 1968.

Henry, Todd A. *Assimilating Seoul: Japanese Rule and the Politics of Public Space in Colonial Korea, 1910–1945*. Berkeley: University of California Press, 2014.

Heyman, Alan C. "Kim Paik-bong." In *International Encyclopedia of Dance*, edited by Selma Jeanne Cohen. Oxford: Oxford University Press, 1998.

Higson, Andrew. "The Concept of National Cinema." In *Film and Nationalism*, edited by Alan Larson Williams, 36–47. New Brunswick: Rutgers University Press, 2002.

Hoganson, Kristin L. *Consumers' Imperium: The Global Production of American Domesticity, 1865–1920*. Chapel Hill: University of North Carolina Press, 2007.

Hohn, Maria, and Seungsook Moon, eds. *Over There: Living with the U.S. Military Empire from World War Two to the Present*. Durham, NC: Duke University Press, 2010.

Hŏ To-san. *Han'guk ŭi ŏmŏni Yi T'ae-yŏng* [The mother of Korea Lee Tai-young]. rev. ed. Seoul: Chayu Chisŏngsa, 1999.

Howard, Christopher. "Re-Orientating Japanese Cinema: Cold War Criticism of 'Anti-American' Films." *Historical Journal of Film, Radio and Television* 36, no. 4 (2016): 529–47.

Howard, Keith, ed. *Korean Pop Music: Riding the Wave*. Folkestone: Global Oriental, 2006.

Hsu, Victor. "Pacific Destinies: The Asian People's Anti-Communist League (1953–1962) and the Anti-Communist Struggle in Asia Pacific." MA thesis, Columbia University, 2016. www.academia.edu/31528465.

Hu, Brian. "Star Discourse and the Cosmopolitan Chinese: Linda Lin Dai Takes On the World." *Journal of Chinese Cinemas* 4, no. 3 (2010): 183–209.

Hughes, Theodore H. *Literature and Film in Cold War South Korea: Freedom's Frontier*. New York: Columbia University Press, 2012.

Huang Zhuohan. *Dianying rensheng: Huang Zhuohan huiyilu* [A life in film: memoir of Wong Cheuk-hon]. Taipei: Wangxiang Tushu, 1994.

Hwang, Whitney Taejin. "Borderland Intimacies: GIs, Koreans, and American Military Landscapes in Cold War Korea." PhD diss., University of California, Berkeley, 2010.

Iber, Patrick J. "Anti-Communist Entrepreneurs and the Origins of the Cultural Cold War in Latin America." In *De-Centering Cold War History*, edited by Jadwiga E. Pieper Mooney and Fabio Lanza. New York: Routledge, 2012.

Ibsen, Henrik. *The Doll's House: A Play*. Translated by Henrietta Frances Lord. New York: D. Appleton, 1901.

Inoue, Shun. "The Invention of Martial Arts: Kanō Jigorō and Kōdōkan Judo." In *Mirror of Modernity*, edited by Stephen Vlastos, 163–73. Berkeley: University of California Press, 1998.

Jackson, Stevi, Jieyu Liu, and Juhyun Woo, eds. *East Asian Sexualities: Modernity, Gender and New Sexual Cultures*. London: Zed Books, 2008.

James, David. E. "Im Kwon-Taek: Korean National Cinema and Buddhism." In *Im Kwon-Taek: The Making of a Korean National Cinema*, edited by David E. James and Kyung Hyun Kim, 47–83. Detroit: Wayne State University Press, 2002.

James, David E., and Kyung Hyun Kim, eds. *Im Kwon-Taek: The Making of a Korean National Cinema*. Detroit: Wayne State University Press, 2002.

Jenkins, Henry. *Textual Poachers: Television Fans & Participatory Culture*. New York: Routledge, 1992.

Jeong Bi-seok, *Chayu buin* [Madame Freedom]. Edited by Ch'u Sŏnchin. Seoul: Chishikŭlmandŭnŭnjishik, 2013.

Jeong, Kelly Y. *Crisis of Gender and the Nation in Korean Literature and Cinema: Modernity Arrives Again*. Lanham, MD: Lexington Books, 2011.

———. "The Quasi-Patriarch." In *The Korean Popular Culture Reader*, edited by Kyung Hyun Kim and Youngmin Choe, 126–44. Durham, NC: Duke University Press, 2014.

———. "The Spectacle of Affect: Postwar South Korean Melodrama Films," in *East Asian Transwar Popular Culture: Literature and Film from Taiwan and Korea*. edited by Pei-yin Lee and Su Yun Kin, 235–60. Singapore: Palgrave Macmillan US, 2019.

Jeong Min, Hyun. "New Women and Modern Girls: Consuming Foreign Goods in Colonial Seoul." *Journal of Historical Research in Marketing* 5, no. 4 (2013): 494–520.

Joo Seong-hee. "An Overview of Modern Fashion in Korea." *Koreana* 15, no. 1 (2001).

Kendall, Laurel, ed. *Consuming Korean Tradition in Early and Late Modernity: Commodification, Tourism, and Performance*. Honolulu: University of Hawai'i Press, 2010.

Kendall, Laurel, ed. *Under Construction: The Gendering of Modernity, Class, and Consumption in the Republic of Korea*. Honolulu: University of Hawai'i Press, 2002.

Kim, Agnes Davis. *I Married a Korean*. New York: J. Day Company, 1953.

Kim, Charles R. "The April 19th Generation and the Start of Postcolonial History in South Korea." *Review of Korean Studies* 12, no. 3 (2009): 71–99.

———. "Unlikely Revolutionaries: South Korea's First Generation and the Student Protests of 1960." PhD diss., Columbia University, 2007.

———. *Youth for Nation: Culture and Protest in Cold War South Korea*. Honolulu: University of Hawai'i Press, 2017.

Kim, Chung-kang. "South Korean Golden-Age Comedy Film: Industry, Genre, and Popular Culture (1953–1970)." PhD diss., University of Illinois at Urbana-Champaign, 2010.

Kim, Elaine H., and Chungmoo Choi, eds. *Dangerous Women: Gender and Korean Nationalism*. New York: Routledge, 1998.

Kim, Haesook. "Lee Tai-Young (1914–1998): The Pioneer Woman Lawyer of South Korea." In *Women in the World's Legal Professions*, edited by Ulrike Schultz and Gisela Shaw, 451–64. Oxford: Hart Publishing, 2003.

Kim, Han Sang. "Cold War and the Contested Identity Formation of Korean Filmmakers: On *Boxes of Death* and Kim Ki-yŏng's USIS Films." *Inter-Asia Cultural Studies* 14, no. 4 (2013): 551–63.

———. "Uneven Screens, Contested Identities: USIS, Cultural Films, and the National Imaginary in South Korea, 1945–1972." PhD diss., Seoul National University, 2013.

Kim Hwallan. *Grace Sufficient: The Story of Helen Kim*. Nashville: Upper Room, 1964.

Kim, Hyun Sun. "Life and Work of Korean War Widows during the 1950s." *The Review of Korean Studies* 12, no. 4 (2009): 87–109.

Kim Keong-Il. "Modernity and Tradition in Everyday Life of the 1950s." *Seoul Journal of Korean Studies* 14 (2001): 263–97.

Kim Kang-yun et al., *Han'guk yŏnghwa charyo p'yŏllam (ch'och'anggi-1976-yŏn)* [A guide to sources on South Korean film: Beginnings to 1976]. Seoul: Yŏnghwa chinhŭng kongsa, 1977.

Kim, Kyung Hyun, and Youngmin Choe, eds. *The Korean Popular Culture Reader*. Durham, NC: Duke University Press, 2014.

Kim, Mee hyun, ed. *Korean Cinema: From Origins to Renaissance*. Seoul: Communication Books, 2007.

Kim, Pil Ho, and Shin, Hyunjoon. "The Birth of 'Rok': Cultural Imperialism, Nationalism, and the Globalization of Rock Music in South Korea, 1964–1975." *Positions: East Asia Cultures Critique* 18, no. 1 (2010): 199–230.

Kim, Soyoung. "Questions of Woman's Film: *The Maid, Madame Freedom* and Women." In *South Korean Golden Age Melodrama*, edited by Kathleen McHugh and Nancy Abelmann, 185–200. Detroit: Wayne State University Press, 2005.

Kim Sunah. "The Dilemma of Modern Times." In *Han Hyung-mo: The Alchemist of Popular Genres*, 67–87. Seoul: Korean Film Archive, 2008.

Kim, Uchang. "The Agony of Cultural Construction." In *State and Society in Contemporary Korea*, edited by Hagen Koo, 174–76. Ithaca, NY: Cornell University Press, 1993.

———. "Confucianism, Democracy, and the Individual in Korean Modernization." In *Transformations in Twentieth Century Korea*, edited by Steven Hugh Lee and Yunshik Chang, 221–44. New York: Routledge, 2006.

Kim, Yoo-kyung. "Nora Noh: A Living Legend." *Koreana* 28, no. 1 (Spring 2014).

Kim, Youngna. *20th Century Korean Art*. London: Laurence King, 2005.

———. "Urban Space and Visual Culture: The Transformation of Seoul in the Twentieth Century." In *A Companion to Asian Art and Architecture*, edited by Rebecca M. Brown and Deborah S. Hutton. Hoboken, NJ: Wiley-Blackwell, 2011.

Kim, Yung-hee. "In Quest of Modern Womanhood: *Sinyŏja*, a Feminist Journal in Colonial Korea." *Korean Studies* (2013): 44–78.

Kitamura, Hiroshi. *Screening Enlightenment: Hollywood and the Cultural Reconstruction of Defeated Japan*. Ithaca, NY: Cornell University Press, 2010.

Klein, Christina. "Cold War Cosmopolitanism: The Asia Foundation and 1950s Korean Cinema." *Journal of Korean Studies* 22, no. 2 (2017): 281–316.

———. *Cold War Orientalism: Asia in the Middlebrow Imagination, 1945–1961*. Berkeley: University of California Press, 2003.

Koikari, Mire. *Cold War Encounters in US-Occupied Okinawa: Women, Militarized Domesticity, and Transnationalism in East Asia*. Cambridge: Cambridge University Press, 2015.

———. *Pedagogy of Democracy: Feminism and the Cold War in the U.S. Occupation of Japan*. Philadelphia: Temple University Press, 2008.

Koo, Hagen, ed. *State and Society in Contemporary Korea.* Ithaca, NY: Cornell University Press, 1993.

Korean Film Archive, *Traces of Korean Cinema, 1945–1959.* Seoul: Munhak Sasangsa, 2003.

Kraus, Charles. "'The Danger Is Two-Fold': Decolonisation and Cold War in Anti-Communist Asia, 1955–7." *International History Review* 39, no. 2 (2017): 256–73.

Kwak, Kwang Sub. "US-ROK Alliance, 1953–2004: Alliance Institutionalization." PhD diss., Southern Illinois University, Carbondale, 2006.

Kwon, Insook. "Feminists Navigating the Shoals of Nationalism and Collaboration: The Post-Colonial Korean Debate over How to Remember Kim Hwallan." *Frontiers: A Journal of Women Studies* 27, no. 1 (2006): 39–66.

Kwŏn Podŭrae, ed. *Ap'ŭre Gŏl Sasanggye rŭl ikta: 1950-yŏndae munhwa ŭi chayu wa t'ongje* [The après girl reads *Sasanggye*: freedom and control in 1950s culture]. Edited by Munhwa Haksul Ch'ongsŏ. Seoul: Tongguk Taehakkyo Ch'ulp'anbu, 2009.

Lankov, Andrei N. *The Dawn of Modern Korea: The Transformation in Life and Cityscape.* Seoul: EunHaeng NaMu, 2007.

Laville, Helen. "The Committee of Correspondence: CIA Funding of Women's Groups, 1952–1967." *Intelligence and National Security* 12, no. 1 (1997): 104–21.

Leary, Charles. "The Most Careful Arrangements for a Careful Fiction: A Short History of Asia Pictures." *Inter-Asia Cultural Studies* 13, no. 4 (2012): 548–58.

Lee, Bae-yong. *Women in Korean History.* Seoul: Ewha Womans University Press, 2008.

Lee Im Ha. "The Korean War and the Role of Women." *Review of Korean Studies* 9, no. 2 (2006): 89–110.

Lee, Jid. *To Kill a Tiger: A Memoir of Korea.* New York: Overlook Press, 2010.

Lee, Sang-Dawn. *Big Brother, Little Brother: The American Influence on Korean Culture in the Lyndon B. Johnson Years.* Lanham, MD: Lexington Books, 2002.

Lee, Sangjoon. "Creating an Anti-Communist Motion Picture Producers' Network in Asia: The Asia Foundation, Asia Pictures, and the Korean Motion Picture Cultural Association." *Historical Journal of Film, Radio and Television* 37, no. 3 (2017): 517–38.

———. "The Emergence of the Asian Film Festival: Cold War Asia and Japan's Reentrance to the Regional Film Industry in the 1950s." In *The Oxford Handbook of Japanese Cinema,* edited by Daisuke Miyao, 226–44. Oxford: Oxford University Press, 2014.

———. "On John Miller's 'The Korean Film Industry': The Asia Foundation, KMPCA, and Korean Cinema, 1956." *Journal of Japanese and Korean Cinema* 7, no. 2 (2015): 95–112.

———. "The Transnational Asian Studio System: Cinema, Nation-State, and Globalization in Cold War Asia." PhD diss., New York University, 2011.

Lee Sang-yong. Forward to *Han Hyung-mo: The Alchemist of Popular Genres.* Seoul: Korean Film Archive, 2008.

Lee Sang-yong and Yang Ayoung, eds. *Han Hyung-mo: The Alchemist of Popular Genres.* Seoul: Korean Film Archive, 2008.

Lee, Steven Hugh. "Development without Democracy: The Political Economy of US–South Korea Relations, 1958–1961." In *Transformations in Twentieth Century Korea,* edited by Yun-Shik Chang and Steven Hugh Lee, 169–99. New York: Routledge, 2006.

Lee, Tai-young, "Elevation of Korean Women's Rights," *Korea Journal* 4, no. 2 (February 1, 1964): 5, 8.

Lee, Yongwoo. "Embedded Voices in between Empires: The Cultural Formation of Korean Popular Music in Modern Times." PhD diss., McGill University, 2010.

Lee Young-il, and Choe Young-Chol. *The History of Korean Cinema*. Translated by Richard Lynn Greever. Seoul: Jimoondang, 1998.

Lie, John. *Han Unbound: The Political Economy of South Korea*. Stanford, CA: Stanford University Press, 1998.

———. *K-Pop: Popular Music, Cultural Amnesia, and Economic Innovation in South Korea*. Oakland: University of California Press, 2015.

———. *Zainichi (Koreans in Japan): Diasporic Nationalism and Postcolonial Identity*. Berkeley: University of California Press, 2008.

Liem, Wolsan. "Telling the 'Truth' to Koreans: US Cultural Policy in South Korea during the Early Cold War, 1947–1967." PhD diss., New York University, 2010.

Ma, Jean. *Sounding the Modern Woman: The Songstress in Chinese Cinema*. Durham, NC: Duke University Press, 2015.

Macdonald, Donald Stone. *U.S.-Korean Relations from Liberation to Self-Reliance: The Twenty-Year Record*. Boulder: Westview Press, 1991.

Maliangkay, Roald. "Koreans Got Talent: Auditioning for US Army Gigs in Korea." *Situations* 11 (2018): 59–79.

———. "Koreans Performing for Foreign Troops: The Occidentalism of the C.M.C. and K.P.K.," *East Asian History* 37 (2011) 59–72.

———. "Supporting Our Boys: American Military Entertainment and Korean Pop Music in the 1950s and Early-1960s." In *Korean Pop Music*, edited by Keith Howard. Folkestone: Global Oriental, 2006.

Mason, Edward S. *The Economic and Social Modernization of the Republic of Korea*. Cambridge, MA: Harvard University Press, 1980.

Materi, Irma Tennani. *Irma and the Hermit: My Life in Korea*. New York: W. W. Norton, 1949.

McCracken, Grant David. *Culture and Consumption: New Approaches to the Symbolic Character of Consumer Goods and Activities*. Bloomington: Indiana University Press, 1988.

———. *Culture and Consumption II: Markets, Meaning, and Brand Management*. Bloomington: Indiana University Press, 2005.

McDonald, Keiko I. *Reading a Japanese Film: Cinema in Context*. Honolulu: University of Hawai'i Press, 2006.

McHugh, Kathleen. "South Korean Film Melodrama: State, Nation, Woman, and the Transnational Familiar." In *South Korean Golden Age Melodrama*, edited by Kathleen McHugh and Nancy Abelmann, 17–42. Detroit: Wayne State University Press, 2005.

McHugh, Kathleen, and Nancy Abelmann, eds. *South Korean Golden Age Melodrama: Gender, Genre, and National Cinema*. Detroit: Wayne State University Press, 2005.

McLelland, Mark. *Love, Sex, and Democracy in Japan during the American Occupation*. New York: Palgrave Macmillan, 2012.

Miller, Daniel. "Consumption as the Vanguard of History: A Polemic by Way of an Introduction." In *Acknowledging Consumption*, edited by Daniel Miller, 1–52. New York: Routledge, 2005.

———, ed. *Acknowledging Consumption: A Review of New Studies*. New York: Routledge, 2005.

Mitchell, Richard H. *The Korean Minority in Japan*. Berkeley: University of California Press, 1967.

Miyao, Daisuke, ed. *The Oxford Handbook of Japanese Cinema*. Oxford: Oxford University Press, 2014.

Moenig, Udo, and Minho Kim. "The Invention of Taekwondo Tradition, 1945–1972: When Mythology Becomes 'History.'" *Acta Koreana* 19, no. 2 (2016): 131–64.

Molony, Barbara, Janet M. Theiss, and Hyaeweol Choi. *Gender in Modern East Asia: An Integrated History*. Boulder: Westview Press, 2016.

Molony, Barbara, and Kathleen Uno, eds. *Gendering Modern Japanese History*. Cambridge, MA: Harvard University Press, 2005.

Moon, Katharine H. S. *Sex among Allies: Military Prostitution in U.S.-Korea Relations*. New York: Columbia University Press, 1997.

Moon, Seungsook. "Begetting the Nation." In *Dangerous Women: Gender and Korean Nationalism*, edited by Elaine H. Kim and Chungmoo Choi, 33–66. New York: Routledge, 1998.

———. "Regulating Desire, Managing Empire: U.S. Military Prostitution in South Korea, 1945–1970." In *Over There: Living with the U.S. Military Empire from World War Two to the Present*, ed. Maria Hohn and Seungsook Moon, 39–77. Durham, NC: Duke University Press, 2010.

Mooney, Jadwiga E. Pieper, and Fabio Lanza, eds. *De-Centering Cold War History: Local and Global Change*. New York: Routledge, 2012.

Mulvey, Laura. "Visual Pleasure and Narrative Cinema." *Screen* 16, no. 3 (1975): 6–18.

Murdoch, William Armour. *Republic of South Korea, 1957–1959*. Bloomington: Author House, 2007.

Nam, Sanghui. "The Women's Movement and the Transformation of the Family Law in South Korea: Interactions between Local, National and Global Structures." *European Journal of East Asian Studies* 9, no. 1 (2010): 67–86.

Nava, Mica. "Cosmopolitan Modernity: Everyday Imaginaries and the Register of Difference." *Theory Culture Society* 19, no. 1–2 (2002): 81–99.

———. *Visceral Cosmopolitanism: Gender, Culture and the Normalisation of Difference*. Oxford: Berg, 2007.

Nelson, Laura C. *Measured Excess: Status, Gender, and Consumer Nationalism in South Korea*. New York: Columbia University Press, 2000.

Noh, Kwang Woo. "Transformation of Korean Film Industry during the US Military Occupation Era (1945–1948)." *Asian Cinema* 14, no. 2 (2003): 91–101.

Noh, Nora. *Nora Noh, yŏlchŏngŭl tijainhada* [Nora Noh designs passion]. Seoul: Hwanggŭmnach'imban, 2007.

Oh Yeong-suk. "Realistic but Popular." In *Han Hyung-mo: The Alchemist of Popular Genres*, 45–64. Seoul: Korean Film Archive, 2008.

Oppenheim, Robert. "Crafting the Consumability of Place: *Tapsa* and *Paenang Yŏhaeng* as Travel Goods." In *Consuming Korean Tradition in Early and Late Modernity*, edited by Laurel Kendall, 105–26. Honolulu: University of Hawai'i Press, 2010.

Osgood, Kenneth Alan. *Total Cold War: Eisenhower's Secret Propaganda Battle at Home and Abroad*. Lawrence: University of Kansas, 2006.

Pai, Hyung Il. *Heritage Management in Korea and Japan.* Seattle: University of Washington Press, 2013.

Pak Ch'a Min-jŏng. *Chosŏn ŭi k'wiŏ: kŭndae ŭi t'ŭmsae e sumŭn pyŏnt'aedŭl ŭi ch'osang* [Chosŏn's queers: a portrait of the perverts hidden in the cracks of modernity]. Seoul: Hyŏnsil Munhwa Yŏn'gu, 2018.

Park, Joon Young. "Korea's Return to Asia: An Analysis of Korea's New Moves in Diplomacy in the 1960s and 1970s." PhD diss., Columbia University, 1981.

Park, Junghyun. "Frustrated Alignment: The Pacific Pact Proposals from 1949 to 1954 and South Korea–Taiwan Relations." *International Journal of Asian Studies* 12, no. 2 (2015): 217–37.

Park, Sunae, Patricia Campbell Warner, and Thomas K Fitzgerald. "The Process of Westernization: Adoption of Western-Style Dress by Korean Women, 1945–1962." *Clothing and Textiles Research Journal* 11, no. 3 (1993): 39–47.

Park, Wan-so, *The Naked Tree.* Translated by Yu Young-nan. Ithaca, NY: Cornell University Press, 1995.

Park-Primiano, Sueyoung. "South Korean Cinema between the Wars: Screening Resistance and Containment under US Intervention and Influence, 1945–60." PhD diss., New York University, 2015.

Pérez Firmat, Gustavo. *Life on the Hyphen: The Cuban-American Way.* Austin: University of Texas Press, 2012.

Pflugfelder, Gregory M. "'S' is for Sister: Schoolgirl Intimacy and 'Same-Sex Love' in Early Twentieth-Century Japan." In *Gendering Modern Japanese History,* edited by Barbara Molony and Kathleen Uno, 133–90. Cambridge, MA: Harvard University Press, 2005.

Pharr, Susan J. "The Politics of Women's Rights." In *Democratizing Japan: The Allied Occupation,* edited by Robert E. Ward and Sakamoto Yoshikazu, 221–52. Honolulu: University of Hawai'i Press, 1987.

Phillips, Alastair. "Pictures of the Past in the Present: Modernity, Femininity and Stardom in the Postwar Films of Ozu Yasujiro." *Screen* 44, no. 2 (2003): 154–66.

Pilzer, Joshua D. "The 'Comfort Women' and the Voices of East Asian Modernity." In *Vamping the Stage,* edited by Andrew N. Weintraub and Bart Barendregt, 107–24. Honolulu: University of Hawai'i Press, 2017.

Pini, In Kyung Kim. "A New God, a New Education, and a New Generation of Women: Three Educational Biographies of Korean Women (Helen Kim, Induk Pahk, Tai Young Lee)." PhD diss., Columbia University, 2002.

Place, Janey. "Women in Film Noir." In *Women in Film Noir,* edited by E. Ann Kaplan, 35–67. London: British Film Institute, 1978.

Polhemus, Ted, and Lynn Procter. *Fashion and Anti-fashion: Anthropology of Clothing and Adornment.* London: Thames & Hudson, 1978.

Pollock, Sheldon, Homi K. Bhabha, Carol Breckenridge, and Dipesh Chakrabarty. "Cosmopolitanisms." In *Cosmopolitanism,* edited by Carol Breckenridge, Homi K. Bhabha, Sheldon Pollock, and Dipesh Chakrabarty. Durham, NC: Duke University Press, 2002.

Prown, Jules David. *Art as Evidence: Writings on Art and Material Culture.* New Haven, CT: Yale University Press, 2001.

Radano, Ronald, and Tejumola Olaniyan, eds. *Audible Empire: Music, Global Politics, Critique*. Durham, NC: Duke University Press, 2016.

Rayns, Tony. "Poet of Time." *Sight and Sound* 5, no. 9 (September 1995): 12–14.

Robinson, Michael. "Contemporary Cultural Production in South Korea." In *New Korean Cinema*, edited by Chi-Yun Shin and Julian Stringer, 15–31. New York: New York University Press, 2005.

———. *Korea's Twentieth-Century Odyssey: A Short History*. Honolulu: University of Hawai'i Press, 2007.

———. "Perceptions of Confucianism in Twentieth-Century Korea." In *The East Asian Region*, edited by Gilbert Rozman, 204–25. Princeton, NJ: Princeton University Press, 1991.

Rotella, Carlo. *Good with Their Hands: Boxers, Bluesmen, and Other Characters from the Rust Belt*. Berkeley: University of California Press, 2002.

Rozman, Gilbert. *The East Asian Region: Confucian Heritage and Its Modern Adaptation*. Princeton, NJ: Princeton University Press, 1991.

Sanders, Lise. *Consuming Fantasies: Labor, Leisure, and the London Shopgirl, 1880–1920*. Columbus: Ohio State University Press, 2006.

Sato, Shohei. "The Sportification of Judo: Global Convergence and Evolution." *Journal of Global History* 8, no. 2 (2013): 299–317.

Schultz, Ulrike, and Gisela Shaw, eds. *Women in the World's Legal Professions*. Oxford: Hart Publishing, 2003.

Shenin, Sergei Y. *America's Helping Hand: Paving the Way to Globalization (Eisenhower's Foreign Aid Policy and Politics)*. New York: Nova Science Publishers, 2005.

Shin, Gi-wook, and Michael Robinson. *Colonial Modernity in Korea*. Cambridge: Harvard University Press, 1999.

Shin, Hyunjoon. "The Stage Show and the Dance Floor." In *Made in Korea: Studies in Popular Music*, edited by Hyunjoon Shin and Seung-Ah Lee, 15–22. New York: Routledge, 2017.

Shin, Hyunjoon, and Ho Tung-Hung. "Translation of 'America' during the Early Cold War Period: A Comparative Study on the History of Popular Music in South Korea and Taiwan." *Inter-Asia Cultural Studies* 10, no. 1 (2009): 83–102.

Shin, Hyunjoon, and Seung-Ah Lee, eds. *Made in Korea: Studies in Popular Music*. New York: Routledge, 2017.

Shin, Ki-young. "The Politics of the Family Law Reform Movement in Contemporary Korea: A Contentious Space for Gender and the Nation." *Journal of Korean Studies* 1, no. 1 (2006): 93–125.

Sintionean, Codruta. "Heritage Practices during the Park Chung Hee Era." In *Key Papers on Korea*, edited by Andrew Davis Jackson, 253–74. Leiden: Brill, 2013.

Sloat, Susanna, ed. *Caribbean Dance from Abakuá to Zouk: How Movement Shapes Identity*. Gainesville: University Press of Florida, 2002.

Strauven, Wanda, ed. *Cinema of Attractions Reloaded*. Amsterdam: Amsterdam University Press, 2006.

Strawn, Sonia Reid. *Where There Is No Path: Lee Tai-Young, Her Story*. Seoul: Korean Legal Aid Center for Family Relations, 1988.

Suh, Sook. "Dance and Democracy." *Asian Journal of Women's Studies* 6, no. 3 (2000): 11–35.

Sumpter, Meredith, ed. *Partner for Change: 50 Years of the Asia Foundation in Korea, 1954–2004*. Seoul: Asia Foundation, 2004.

Sumpter, Meredith, and John Rieger, eds. *A Partner for Change: Six Decades of the Asia Foundation in Korea, 1954–2017*. Seoul: The Asia Foundation, 2017.

Swann, Paul. "The Little State Department: Hollywood and the State Department in the Postwar World." *American Studies International* 29, no. 1 (1991): 2–19.

Teo, Stephen. *Hong Kong Cinema: The Extra Dimensions*. London: British Film Institute, 1997.

Thompson, Kristin. "The Concept of Cinematic Excess." In *Film Theory and Criticism: Introductory Readings*, edited by Leo Braudy and Marshall Cohen. Oxford: Oxford University Press, 2004.

Thompson, Robert Farris. "Teaching the People to Triumph over Time." In *Caribbean Dance from Abakuá to Zouk*, edited by Susanna Sloat. Gainesville: University Press of Florida, 2002.

Tipton, Elise K. "Moving Up and Out." In *Modern Girls on the Go*, edited by Alisa Freedman, Laura Miller and Christine R. Yano, 21–39. Stanford, CA: Stanford University Press, 2013.

Vlastos, Stephen, ed. *Mirror of Modernity: Invented Traditions of Modern Japan*. Berkeley: University of California Press, 1998.

von Eschen, Penny M. *Satchmo Blows Up the World: Jazz Ambassadors Play the Cold War*. Cambridge, MA: Harvard University Press, 2004.

Walker, Richard L. "The Developing Role of Cultural Diplomacy in Asia." In *Issues and Conflicts: Studies in Twentieth Century American Diplomacy*, edited by George L. Anderson, 43–62. Lawrence: University of Kansas Press, 1959.

Ward, Robert E., and Sakamoto Yoshikazu, eds. *Democratizing Japan: The Allied Occupation*. Honolulu: University of Hawai'i Press, 1987.

Weinbaum, Alys Eve, Lynn M. Thomas, Priti Ramamurthy, Uta G. Poiger, Madeleine Yue Dong, and Tani E. Barlow, eds. *The Modern Girl around the World: Consumption, Modernity, and Globalization*. Durham, NC: Duke University Press, 2008.

Westad, Odd Arne. *The Global Cold War: Third World Interventions and the Making of Our Times*. Cambridge: Cambridge University Press, 2007.

Wilford, Hugh. *The Mighty Wurlitzer: How the CIA Played America*. Cambridge, MA: Harvard University Press, 2008.

Williams, Alan Larson, ed. *Film and Nationalism*. New Brunswick: Rutgers University Press, 2002.

Wilson, Elizabeth. *Adorned in Dreams: Fashion and Modernity*. Berkeley: University of California Press, 1987.

Wong, Aida Yuen, ed. *Visualizing Beauty: Gender and Ideology in Modern East Asia*. Hong Kong: Hong Kong University Press, 2012.

Wong, Ain-ling, ed. *The Cathay Story*. Hong Kong: Hong Kong Film Archive, 2002.

Wong, Mary. "Women Who Cross Borders: MP&GI's Modernity Programme." In *The Cathay Story*, edited by Wong Ain-ling. Hong Kong: Hong Kong Film Archive, 2002.

Workman, Travis. "Other Scenes: Space and Counterpoint in Cold War Korean Melodrama." *Journal of Japanese and Korean Cinema* 7, no. 1 (2015): 28–40.

Xu, Lanjun. "The Southern Film Corporation, Opera Films, and the PRC's Cultural Diplomacy in Cold War Asia, 1950s and 1960s." *Modern Chinese Literature and Culture* 29, no.1 (2017): 239–81.

Yano, Christine R. "Diva Misora Hibari as Spectacle of Postwar Japan's Modernity." In *Vamping the Stage*, edited by Andrew N. Weintraub and Bart Barendregt, 127–43. Honolulu: University of Hawai'i Press, 2017.

———. "Jet-Age Nationhood: Pan-American World Airways in Postwar Japan." In *Japan since 1945: From Postwar to Post-Bubble*, edited by Christopher Gerteis and Timothy S. George. London: Bloomsbury, 2013.

Yecies, Brian, and Ae-Gyung Shim . *The Changing Face of Korean Cinema, 1960 to 2015*. New York: Routledge, 2016.

———. *Korea's Occupied Cinemas, 1893–1948*. New York: Routledge, 2011.

Yi Hyo-in. *Shin Sang-ok*. Korean Film Directors series. Translated by Colin A. Mouat. Seoul: Seoul Selection, 2008.

Yi Hyo-in and Park Ji-Yeon, *A History of Korean Cinema from Liberation through the 1960s*. Seoul: Korean Film Archive, 2005.

Yoo, Theodore Jun. *The Politics of Gender in Colonial Korea: Education, Labor, and Health, 1910–1945*. Berkeley: University of California Press, 2008.

Yoshimi, Shunya, and David Buist. "'America' as Desire and Violence: Americanization in Postwar Japan and Asia during the Cold War." *Inter-Asia Cultural Studies* 4, no. 3 (2003): 433–50.

Yuh, Ji-Yeon. *Beyond the Shadow of Camptown: Korean Military Brides in America*. New York: New York University Press, 2002.

AFKN radio and TV (US military network), 142,
191, 229
Aimless Bullet (Yu, 1961), 81, 160, 226
Americanization, 5, 16, 22. *See also*
Westernization
anticommunism, 7, 26, 45, 55, 59, 60, 70, 101, 220;
anticommunist film genre, 81, 136; of CFA,
28; Cold War bloc building and, 213, 217;
mass media as tool for dissemination of, 57;
of Rhee's government, 16, 25, 67; TAF film
program and, 75
Anyang Studio, 71–72, 77
"après girl" (*apure kol*), 87–91, 94, 95, 102, 105,
132, 155, 181, 193, 214; as conservative foil, 92;
as Han Hyung-mo's alter ego, 177; in Hong
Kong, 107; in Japan, 106–7; Kim Jeong-rim
as, 142; liberated from logic of suffering, 105;
urban space inhabited freely by, 103; Western
consumer goods and, 147, 149; Western-style
fashion and, 193, 196–97, 201
"Arirang" (Korean folk song), 191, 215
Asia Foundation, the (TAF), 6, 7, 44–45, 195;
as CIA front organization, 28, 29–30;
cosmopolitan consciousness and, 56; film
industry and, 68, 73–79, 250n98; Free World
international travel and, 197, 198; Han Hyung-
mo and, 72; international coproductions
supported by, 220–21; "Plan for Korea" (1955),
58–59; as "port of entry" for resources, 8–9;
role in cultural rebirth of South Korea, 57–60;

Social Science Research Library, 45; Tokyo
office, 60; women in training programs of,
39; *Yŏwŏn* magazine and, 61, 62. *See also*
Committee for a Free Asia
Asian Film Festival (AFF), 6, 119, 161, 220,
248n86; in Kuala Lumpur (1959), 78, 212,
213, 216, 220–22; cosmopolitan mode of
production and, 219; TAF and, 75–76, 77, 78;
transnational networks of, 9, 176
Asian People's Anti-Communist League
(APACL), 6, 26–27, 45, 217, 218
Asia Pictures, Ltd., 75, 77
Assault on Justice, An, Part 1 (Han, 1951), 67
Assault on Justice, An, Part 2 (Han, 1952), 67

Baek Seol-hui, 136, 194
Bandung conference (1955), 27
Bang Dae-hun, 94, 123
Barefoot Youth (Kim, 1964), 120, 254n27
Because I Love You (Han, 1958), 3, 79, 135, 244n36;
alternate titles of, 222, 268n100; at Asian
Film Festival (AFF), 78, 212, 216, 266n70; as
coproduction with Hong Kong, 219–20, 221;
exported to Southeast Asia, 244n37; traditional
dance as spectacle in, 182, 212–23, *216*
Beyond the Forest (Vidor, 1949), 1
Bicycle Thieves (De Sica, 1948), 113
Black Hair (Lee, 1964), 227
black market, 9, 60, 119, 161, 171–73, 209, 219;
American cash and goods in, 18; APO

110; industrial economy absent in 1950s, 23; integration into Free Asia and Free World, 15, 23–27, *25, 26,* 30, 31, 55, 111, 134, 197, 214; legal and illegal imports into, 9, 162–73; mambo craze in, 190–194; military coup (1961), 3, 4, 224–25; modernization of, 4, 15, 57; postwar poverty of, 17–18; unequal relationship with United States, 20–22, 37, 56

Korea Legal Aid Center for Family Relations, 46–47, 48

Korea Times, The (English-language newspaper), 44

Korean Entertainment Company, 220

Korean language, 2, 16, 90, 179; *hangul* alphabet, 58, 95, 98; popular music in, 195, 196

Koreanness, 34, 91, 154; debate on nature of, 49; suppressed under Japanese colonial rule, 16, 23, 50

Korean War, 2, 3, 17, 20, 24, 28, 67, 111, 142; après girl" (*apure kol*) and, 88–89; armistice (1953), 27; emergence of black market and, 164, 165, 166–67; film industry and, 67–68; population losses and other tolls of, 18; women's mass entrance into workforce during, 48; Yongsan bombing campaign, 13, *14*

Korea Times, The (English-language newspaper), 44

Kyeongseong Broadcasting Station, 201–2

Latin America, 5, 39, 44, 141, 189

Lee Bong-rae, 205

Lee Bong-seon, 149, 153, 156, 162

Lee Byung-il, 78, 79, 266n65

Lee Gyu-hwan, 71, 104

Lee Hyang, 155

Lee Hyung-po, 73, 80, 120, 133

Lee Jong Ai, 43–44, 52

Lee Kang-cheon, 101, 102, 136

Lee Man-hee, 227

Lee Mi-ja, 135, 228

Lee Rae-won, 123

Lee Sang-man, 136

Lee Su-ryeon, 207

Lee Tai-young, 41, 45–50, *46,* 102, 241n58, 204; adultery law (1953) supported by, 48, 96; efforts to revise Family Law, 49, 51, 204; Ibsen's Nora as inspiration for, 47; pink- and blue-trimmed aprons of, 48; refusal of "slave" role for women, 47, 185; as woman-in-public, 41, 65

Lee Yong-min, 102, 249

lesbianism, 32–34, *33,* 50, 80, 104, 237n4

Let's Meet at Walkerhill (Han, 1966), 135, 263n29

Lie, John, 4, 5, 136, 162

Lin Dai, Linda, 107, 190

Literature and the Arts magazine, 60

Love in the Afternoon (Wilder, 1957), 133

Love Is a Many Splendored Thing (King, 1955), 266n69

Love Marriage, The (Park, 1958), 205

Love with an Alien (Im, 1957), 219

Macao (Von Sternberg, 1952), 159, 266n69

Madame Freedom (Han, 1956), 1–2, 69, 87, *138;* "après girl" (*apure kol*) figure in, 87–91, *90,* 103; automobile and female mobility in, 115, 118, 197, 214; box office success of, 71, 80; *budae jjigae* cinema and, 134; camera crane used for, 79, 122–23, 126–27; cinematography in, 121, 123–30, *124, 125, 128,* 139, 181; comparison with source novel, 8, 94–98; dance hall set in, 13–14, *15;* "feminine '50s" and, 101–2; *The Flavor of Green Tea Over Rice* (Ozu, 1952) compared to, 114–18, 121; interpreted against the grain of conservative conclusion, 91–101, *93;* made with material poached from US Army, 175; as melodrama, 81, 91–92; mise-en-scène of, 1, 144–45, *145,* 149–50, 152–53, 163; opening scene of unhappy marriage, 85–86, *86;* patriarchy restored in ending scene, 92, *93,* 98, 104; plot summary, 1; poaching and, 108, *109,* 110–11; smuggling subplot, 2, 156; as women's picture, 1

Madame Freedom, music in, 1, 135–41, *143;* "Autumn Leaves" (Kosma), 137–38, 140–41; "Bésame Mucho" bolero, 140; "Cherry Pink and Apple Blossom White" mambo, 140, 141, 188; "La Cumparsita" tango, 140; "Gypsy Airs" (Sarasate), 140, 141; Latin mambo dance in, 140, 181–82, 187–96; "Melody of Love," 141; "The Merry Widow Waltz" (Lehar), 138, 139; "Que Rico el Mambo," 140, 188, 189; "Saint Louis Blues" (Handy), 138, 141; "Someone to Watch over Me" (Gershwin), 140, 141; "That's the Chance You Take" (Lippman), 137, 141

Madame Freedom (Jeong novel, 1954), 97–98, 106, 114, 121

magazine publishing, 66; Asia Foundation support for, 57, 61, 62; cultural Cold War and, 38, 60; in *A Female Boss,* 3, *82,* 207, 210; New Women and, 36, 43;

Malaya, 3, 212, 214–16, 219, 222, 267n87

Founded in 1893,
UNIVERSITY OF CALIFORNIA PRESS
publishes bold, progressive books and journals
on topics in the arts, humanities, social sciences,
and natural sciences—with a focus on social
justice issues—that inspire thought and action
among readers worldwide.

The UC PRESS FOUNDATION
raises funds to uphold the press's vital role
as an independent, nonprofit publisher, and
receives philanthropic support from a wide
range of individuals and institutions—and from
committed readers like you. To learn more, visit
ucpress.edu/supportus.